Place-Branding Experiences

*In grateful memory of a brilliant teacher and mentor,
The Honourable Roger Thomas Hughes, KC.*

Place-Branding Experiences

Perspectives from Intellectual Property Owners, Users and Lawyers

Edited by

Catherine W. Ng

School of Law, University of Aberdeen, UK

Titilayo Adebola

School of Law, University of Aberdeen, UK

Abbe E. L. Brown

School of Law, University of Aberdeen, UK

Cheltenham, UK • Northampton, MA, USA

© The Editors and contributing authors severally 2024

The editors and contributors have asserted their moral rights.

All rights reserved. No part of this publication may be reproduced, stored in a retrieval system or transmitted in any form or by any means, electronic, mechanical or photocopying, recording, or otherwise without the prior permission of the publisher.

Published by
Edward Elgar Publishing Limited
The Lypiatts
15 Lansdown Road
Cheltenham
Glos GL50 2JA
UK

Edward Elgar Publishing, Inc.
William Pratt House
9 Dewey Court
Northampton
Massachusetts 01060
USA

A catalogue record for this book
is available from the British Library

Library of Congress Control Number: 2024946479

This book is available electronically in the **Elgar**online
Law subject collection
https://doi.org/10.4337/9781035311071

Printed on elemental chlorine free (ECF)
recycled paper containing 30% Post-Consumer Waste

ISBN 978 1 0353 1106 4 (cased)
ISBN 978 1 0353 1107 1 (eBook)

Printed and bound in the USA

Contents

List of figures	viii
List of contributors	ix
Foreword	xv
Acknowledgments	xix

PART I   INTRODUCTION

1   Place-Branding and the Law 　　　　　　　　　　　　　　　2
    Catherine W. Ng, Titilayo Adebola and Abbe E. L. Brown

PART II   HOW PLACE-BRANDING STARTED

2   History of the Napa Valley Brand and AVA –
    A Multigenerational Insider's Perspective   　　　　　　　14
    Ian Swanson and Michael Mondavi

3   Napa Valley: Small Place, Big Reputation   　　　　　　　21
    Rex Stults

4   Place-Branding in the Coffee Culture of Colonial Kenya:
    Tracing the Provenance of a Reputation for Quality   　　32
    Philip Magowan

5   Scotch Whisky: Provenance, Authenticity, and Ownership   41
    Julie Bower and David M. Higgins

PART III   THE IMPACT OF PLACE-BRANDING

6   Defending the Scottishness of Scotch Whisky   　　　　　57
    Atsuko Ichijo

7   Building Brand Napa   　　　　　　　　　　　　　　　　75
    Ian Malcolm Taplin

8   The Commercial Power of Place-Branding   　　　　　　　92
    Henry Farr, Rosie Mallory and Penny Erricker

9	Authentic Place-Branding of Kenya's Coffee Through Certification Mark: Practice and Prospects *Tom Kabau*	110

PART IV   INTELLECTUAL PROPERTY LAW IN PRACTICE

10	The Legal Protection of Geographical Indications in the United States: Following the Footsteps of Napa Valley *J. Scott Gerien*	135
11	Protection of Place Brands in Germany: Opportunities, Challenges and Strategies from a Practitioner's Perspective *Katharina Hendrike Reuer and Wiebke Baars*	150
12	Protection and Enforcement of 'Place Brands' in the United Kingdom *Gareth Jenkins, Kirsten Gilbert, Claire Keating, Elise Cant and Ann Lee*	164
13	IP Law in Practice: the Case of Kenya *Chebet Koros and Melissa Omino*	179

PART V   INTELLECTUAL PROPERTY LAW IN POLICY ANALYSIS

14	The International Legal Landscape for Geographical Indications *Titilayo Adebola*	196
15	Legal Protection of Scotch Whisky, Napa Valley AVA and Coffee Kenya by Distinctive Signs in the Digital Market *Pilar Montero*	225
16	Extended Passing Off – Protecting Goodwill in Place Brands and Other Tales *Catherine W. Ng*	251

PART VI   THE PRODUCERS' EXPERIENCES OF PLACE-BRANDING

17	Place-Branding – Scotch Whisky *Graham G. Stewart and Anne Anstruther*	277
18	Scotch Whisky – A Perspective From Islay *Anthony Wills*	284

19	The Large Producers' Experiences of Place-Branding *Ian Swanson*	289
20	What's in a Name? Thoughts on 50 Years of Winemaking in the Napa Valley *Dawnine Dyer*	293
21	Place Brand and Coffee: Perspectives from the Gichangi Coffee Estate *Owen Gichangi*	299
22	Perspective From a Kenyan Coffee Grower: Selling to Market Through a Co-operative *James Ireri John*	303

PART VII CONCLUSIONS

| 23 | Place-Branding Experiences – Perspectives From Three Case Studies
Catherine W. Ng, Titilayo Adebola and Abbe E. L. Brown | 309 |

| *Index* | 320 |

Figures

1A.1	Map of whisky-producing areas in Scotland	11
1B.1	Map of coffee-producing regions of Kenya	12
3.1	Map of Napa Valley American Viticultural Area and Nested AVAs	25
18.1	Photograph of Kilchoman	286

Contributors

Titilayo Adebola is the Theme Coordinator for International Intellectual Property and Information Law and Director of the Centre for Commercial Law at the University of Aberdeen. Her research interests include international economic law, intellectual property ('IP') law, and food law. She is the President of the African International Economic Law Network and Senior Advisor to the United Nations Special Rapporteur on the Right to Food. Dr Adebola serves, inter alia, on the Editorial Board of the Journal of International Economic Law.

Anne Anstruther (BSc, BEng) has long-standing expertise in the history and evolution of whisky and beer worldwide. She worked at the International Centre for Brewing and Distilling at Heriot-Watt University and is now with GGS Associates. She co-edited *Handbook of Brewing* (3rd edn, Boca Raton, 2018).

Wiebke Baars (LLM, UCL, London) is a partner with Taylor Wessing in Hamburg, Germany. She has award-winning expertise in all aspects of intellectual property, including trade mark litigation, brand portfolio management and commercial agreements. She holds a doctorate in broadcasting law.

Julie Bower is a Senior Lecturer in the Graduate School of Management, Birmingham City University. Her research focuses on the structure and operation of the alcoholic beverages industry.

Abbe E. L. Brown is Professor in IP Law at the University of Aberdeen. She has a particular interest in how IP law intersects, and does not intersect, with other legal fields. Before returning to academia, Abbe practised as an intellectual property litigator in London, Melbourne, and Edinburgh. Her publications include *Contemporary Intellectual Property: Law and Policy* (with colleagues, OUP 2023) and *Intellectual Property, Climate Change and Technology* (Edward Elgar 2019).

Elise Cant is a Trainee Trade Mark Attorney at Marks & Clerk, based in the London office. She graduated from Queen Mary University of London in 2019 with a distinction in Management of Intellectual Property. Amongst other clients, Elise represents an innovative Fife-based distillery.

Graham Dutfield is Professor of International Governance at the University of Leeds. He has research interests in governance of technology, knowledge and property in the context of such major global challenges as public health, food security, biodiversity conservation, ecosystems management, and climate change. His latest books are *Dutfield and Suthersanen on Global Intellectual Property Law* (2nd edn, Edward Elgar Publishing 2020) and *That High Design of Purest Gold: A Critical History of the Pharmaceutical Industry, 1880-2020* (World Scientific 2020).

Dawnine Dyer has been active in winemaking in California's Napa Valley for five decades. From harvest enologist at the Robert Mondavi Winery, to VP, Winemaker at Domaine Chandon, and finally, with husband Bill Dyer, to starting their own brand in the Diamond Mountain District. Dawnine has worked on defining and protecting the integrity of the Napa name both in the US and globally.

Penny Erricker is a Senior Communications Executive at Brand Finance. During her time at Brand Finance, Penny has worked to communicate the value and strength of brands to an external audience, helping to support their brand strategy. Penny has further experience in Investor Relations within the financial services industry. Penny holds an MA in Language, Culture & Communications, and a BA in English Language & Linguistics from the University of Birmingham.

Henry Farr is an Associate Director at Brand Finance, the world's leading independent brand valuation consultancy. There, he is responsible for all valuations across the food and drink sectors. He has conducted valuations across these sectors, and works with brands to grow brand equity and brand value. Henry also lectures in Brand Valuation at UK universities and societies. He is a Chartered Accountant with ICAEW and holds a degree in Economics & Management from Keble College, Oxford University.

J. Scott Gerien is a Partner at Dickenson, Peatman & Fogarty in Napa, California and heads the firm's Intellectual Property Department. Scott practises before the US Patent and Trademark Office, and counsels on the protection, licensing, and acquisition of intellectual property, and enforcement and litigation in state and federal courts. He has special expertise in the area of geographical indications and represents the Napa Valley Vintners and is US counsel for Cognac, Basmati rice and Aceto Balsamico di Modena.

Owen Gichangi grew up amidst the aroma of freshly brewed coffee. Born and raised in the heart of Gichangi Coffee Estate in Kirinyaga County, Kenya, his early years were steeped in the rich traditions of coffee farming. He joined college to pursue a diploma in Automotive Engineering, fuelling his passion for machinery innovation. However, his love and passion for coffee informed his pivot from pistons to coffee beans and his enrolment in the Roast and Barista College.

Kirsten Gilbert is a Partner and Head of Brand Exploitation, Protection and TM Litigation UK at Marks & Clerk. Whilst Kirsten has been recognized for her sound approach to pre-litigation strategies, trade mark litigation and brand portfolio management, she also has significant experience in advising clients on registration strategies, and licensing of all types of IP rights. Kirsten has significant experience of working with clients in the food and drink sector, particularly in relation to alcoholic beverages.

David M. Higgins is a Professor in the Accounting and Finance Division, Newcastle University Business School in the UK. He has published extensively on merchandise and trade marks.

Atsuko Ichijo is Associate Professor in Sociology at Kingston University, UK. Her main research interest lies in the study of nationalism. She is the author of *Food, National Identity and Nationalism* (with Ronald Ranta, 2nd edn, Palgrave 2022), 'Food and nationalism: Gastronationalism revisited' (2020) 48(2) *Nationalities Papers* 215–23 and 'What has the Brexit process done to Scotch Whisky?' (2019) 90(4) *Political Quarterly* 637–44.

Gareth Jenkins has been practising in the field of trade marks for over 22 years. He acts for a variety of clients from individuals to multinationals, and has particular experience in the management of global trade mark portfolios, counterfeiting issues, the assignment of intellectual property rights and trade mark strategies. Gareth spearheads the firm's Food and Drink practice and has many clients in this sector, in particular the wine and spirits sector.

James Ireri John is a qualified environmentalist. He is currently pursuing a postgraduate degree in Development Studies at Mount Kenya University. James is a committed and passionate coffee farmer (he grows two varieties of coffee: Batian and Ruiru II). His coffee farming has been on an upward trend since 2014. However in 2024, his coffee farming has been affected by the vagaries of climate change. He delivers his harvested coffee beans to New Kirimiri Coffee Factory.

Tom Kabau is a Senior Lecturer at the School of Law, Jomo Kenyatta University of Agriculture and Technology, and a legal consultant and practitioner. He holds a PhD in Public International Law from the University of Hong Kong, and LLM and LLB degrees from the University of Nairobi. His research interests are in Public International Law, Law and Development, Property Law, and Dispute Resolution.

Claire Keating is a Principal Associate at Marks & Clerk, leading the Trade Marks Practice for the firm's Cambridge office. With almost twenty years' experience in the field of trade mark law, her practice covers a wide spread of sectors, including food and drink, with particular focus on craft breweries, cider distilleries and confectioners.

Chebet Koros, a skilled IP lawyer, holds a Master's in IP law from Queen Mary University, London. Leading studies at the Centre for IP & Information Technology Law, she focuses on the intersection of IP law and innovation. Her ongoing research explores the evolution of IP law in the emerging technology landscape. Driven by a passion for IP awareness, she authors manuals on copyright protection in Kenya and conducts training sessions to efficiently disseminate IP management knowledge.

Ann Lee is a Trainee Trade Mark Attorney at Marks & Clerk, based in the Birmingham office. Ann graduated from the University of Nottingham with a first class degree in Law in July 2021 and has been called to the Bar of England and Wales. Her clients include a historic Birmingham brewery and a Wales-based drinks manufacturer.

Philip Magowan is the Founder of *Exemplar Coffee*, a quarterly coffee roasting and magazine project dedicated to shedding light on coffee-industry trends through the collaborative insights of academics and industry professionals. In 2022 Philip completed an MPhil in Economic and Social History at the University of Cambridge. His research focuses on the construction of quality-oriented commodity value chains, with an emphasis on coffee in colonial East Africa.

Rosie Mallory is a Senior Communications Executive. At Brand Finance, Rosie uses her in-house brand experience to create bespoke multimedia campaigns for clients. Rosie holds a BA in English and French from the University of Nottingham in 2022. She moved to London soon after to begin her career after graduating.

Michael Mondavi's family name has been intertwined with California's Napa Valley for four generations. Raised at the Charles Krug winery in St Helena, Michael's career began in 1966 when he and his father Robert co-founded the Robert Mondavi Winery in Oakville, Napa Valley. Following the company's public offering in 1994, Michael was appointed President and CEO. In 1999, Michael and his family members purchased land in Napa Valley for crafting wines under the Michael Mondavi Family label.

Pilar Montero is Commercial Law Professor of the University of Alicante, expert on IP. Director of the Magister Lvcentinvs, Master on IP and Digital Innovation, and Professor of the 'Plant breeding and Distinctive Quality Signs

Specialist Diploma'. Author of books and articles namely on trade marks, geographical indications, and digitalization, with a book on geographical indications. She is IP expert in several European and international institutions, legal advisor to producer groups, private and public institutions.

Catherine W. Ng is a Senior IP Law Lecturer at the University of Aberdeen. She first read Marketing (BComm, University of British Columbia) and then Law. She gained her DPhil in IP Law at Oxford University after a period of corporate commercial practice in Canada. Her chapter 'Extended Passing Off – Protecting Goodwill in Place Brands and Other Tales' builds on her book *Goodwill in Passing Off – a Common Law Perspective* (Edward Elgar Press 2021).

Melissa Omino is an IP expert with a research focus on the development and negotiation of IP provisions in international trade agreements by and with Global South countries. A cum laude graduate with practical legal experience both in academia and practice, Dr Omino holds a Doctorate in Law (focusing on IP and Trade Law). Her range of expertise also includes the legal frameworks within the sphere of artificial intelligence and data governance policy and regulations.

Katharina Hendrike Reuer (M.Jur., Madrid) is a Partner with Taylor Wessing in Hamburg, Germany. She has award-winning expertise in all aspects of IP law especially including litigation regarding trademark and unfair competition, advertising campaigns and brand portfolio management. Katharina has extensive experience in the field of GI protection and enforcement, especially with respect to the spirit drinks sector. Driven by a passion for the comprehensive protection of intellectual property, she is also heading the „Fachinstitut Gewerblicher Rechtsschutz beim Deutschen Anwaltsinstitut e.V." ("Specialist Institute for Intellectual Property at the German Lawyers' Institute").

Graham G. Stewart is Emeritus Professor in Brewing and Distilling at Heriot-Watt University, Visiting Professor at Nottingham University and provides consultancy services at GGS Associates. He was Professor and Director of the International Centre for Brewing and Distilling at Heriot-Watt (1994–2007). He is a Liveryman of the Worshipful Company of Brewers and has over 300 publications (including patents and I Russell, GG Stewart and J Kellershohn (eds), *Whisky and Other Spirits: Technology, Production and Marketing* (3rd edn, Academic Press 2021)).

Rex Stults is Vice President of Industry Relations for the Napa Valley Vintners. He oversees the association's work on wine industry issues, from protecting the Napa Valley name worldwide to furthering the region's commitment to preserving agriculture. Rex was CEO of the St Helena Chamber of Commerce before joining the NVV in 2006. His community work includes serving on the City of Napa Parks and Recreation Commission and the boards of Free the Grapes! and Friends of the Napa River.

Ian Swanson is a graduate of the University of Aberdeen and a Chartered Accountant. His career covers almost four decades of experience in global finance and operations across several Fortune 500 companies, including almost 25 years within the spirits and wine industries, most recently as CFO with Delicato Family Wines based in Napa, California and the fourth largest winery in the US. There, Ian gained unique insights into Napa Valley's role within the wine industry and family and corporate-owned wineries.

Ian Malcolm Taplin is Professor of Sociology, Management and International Studies at Wake Forest University and Visiting Professor at Kedge Business School, Bordeaux where he has taught Business Strategy in the wine MBA program. At Wake Forest he teaches courses on Business and Society, Global Capitalism and Technology, Culture and Change. His research interests are widespread and include books on the history of the North Carolina wine industry, the growth of luxury goods and iconic wines in Napa Valley.

Anthony Wills has been involved in the drinks trade for over 45 years, the last 30 in the Scotch Whisky industry. Anthony and his family moved to Scotland in 1995 and started an independent single malt bottling company. In 2005 he founded Kilchoman Distillery on the west coast of Islay. Every aspect of production is carried out on site from growing the barley, malting, distilling, maturing and bottling. Kilchoman now exports to over 60 countries worldwide.

Foreword

GEOGRAPHICAL INDICATIONS: WHAT ARE THEY GOOD FOR?

This book provides a hugely valuable service in terms of identifying the positives of place-branding, and optimising the benefits of doing so, whilst being mindful that this is not always easy to achieve or to replicate, and that pitfalls do exist. Whilst far from being the only means of acquiring and deploying place-branding market power, geographical indications (GIs) can have an essential role to play. In this short piece, I would like to offer a personal and even-handed perspective on what is in some senses a rather peculiar intellectual property (IP) right.

Geographical indications are a curious item amongst that disparate bundle of legal exclusionary rights known as intellectual property. Not only do they have nothing to do with innovation, originality, or for that matter with anything at all that is shiny and new; on the contrary, they *counter* innovation by carving out a space in the marketplace for venerable old products made – in large part – in old ways. These might otherwise have been squeezed out of the commercial world by hordes of higher-volume upstarts whose producers are mostly indifferent towards the wisdom of past generations. GIs do this in the form of exclusivities in the use of place-signifying or evoking names that supposedly say more about the products so indicated than any other signage possibly could. All IP rights oppose unfettered competition in certain ways and, in some cases, for limited periods. But GIs do so on the basis of a rationale that several countries in the world today have little sympathy for. This is especially the case with the European GI system which seeks to ensure competitive advantage in international trade, and to contribute to living cultural and gastronomic heritage, and to rural development including less favoured areas and mountain and remote regions of Europe.[1] Why should Europe monopolise place names, many of which were adopted in non-European countries where Europeans

---

[1] Regulation (EU) No 1151/2012 of the European Parliament and of the Council of 21 November 2012 on quality schemes for agricultural products and foodstuffs [2012] OJ L343/1. Recital 4 does not elaborate on the meaning of

settled and whose descendants became the majority population? And does the world really owe European farmers and producers a living?

These are not unfair questions. Cynicism about Europe's devotion towards GIs is amply justified. Nonetheless, GIs have their uses, and the rather vague and unsubstantial language of the relevant articles of TRIPS is quite helpful. In contrast to patents, copyright and trade marks, their legal forms are very loosely prescribed under international law, the primary instrument being the World Trade Organization's TRIPS Agreement. This means that their design is largely a choice for national governments unconstrained by having to adhere to regulatory specificity. Consequently, much flexibility is possible that does not exist for the ways other standard IP rights may be provided. This is of course a big opportunity if we accept the view, as we ought, that countries, especially the low and middle income ones, should have broad freedoms to design their laws to make them compatible with their economic, social and cultural priorities and circumstances, and their competitive advantages. And who is against the pursuit of rural development and promotion of heritage? Both are important to a large number of low and middle income countries. But how to ensure GIs can optimally serve as a tool to achieve these ends is hardly straightforward. Besides, some developing countries are net exporters of agricultural produce and may have their own concerns about market-distorting policies to support small-scale farmers and producers. Thus the Cairns Group of Fair Trade Nations, which is devoted to liberalising agriculture trade comprises not just Australia and Canada but also Argentina, Colombia, the Philippines, South Africa and Vietnam. GIs are hardly a manifestation of trade liberalisation in legal/regulatory form. But perhaps this is a false dichotomy. GI protection of Scotch Whisky doesn't prevent a thriving global trade in the water of life (the meaning of the Scottish Gaelic *uisce beatha*). There is plenty of space in the world's supermarket or on liquor store shelves for Argentinian Malbec and South African Sauvignon Blanc. Some might say that this is not really the point: why can't sparkling wine producers in California and South Australia call their products Champagne where there is no deception as to true origin? And at what point does over-zealous protection of the integrity of a GI become anti-competitive?

Let us suppose we accept that GIs should be protected and we are clear about the goals we want such protection to achieve. Does this make it an easy matter to – to borrow the words of geographer Warren Moran – turn rural

---

'less favoured areas', but one can reasonably assume that these are relatively low-income rural districts that may also be to some degree isolated.

space into IP?[2] Not necessarily. Pinpointing the primary source of a living resource and knowledge associated with it may be impossible to objectively establish. Origin may be a subject of modern mythology in such forms as invented tradition or false attribution of place or people. Of course, GIs are *not about* who came up with the product first or where these original producers happened to be. We cannot say that the wine producers in Champagne were the first to come up with sparkling wine of decent quality. Accordingly, one might suppose that none of this is relevant. It is surely purely academic who was first to distil beer to make whiskey, drink fermented grape juice for conviviality, or make a stimulating drink out of roasted coffee beans, or where exactly they did it. And yet, getting origins right does still matter.

Search for Pisco or Tequila on Google Maps and you will be sent to the city of Pisco halfway between Lima and Nazca (home of the famous Lines), and to the small town of Tequila to the northwest of Guadalajara in Mexico in the state of Jalisco. And yet neither beverage bearing these names is made exclusively in either place, and for Pisco not even in the same country. Stilton cheese is not, and never has, been made in the village of Stilton in Cambridgeshire, England. And must Parma Ham really only be sliced in the region of the Italian city of Parma for the sake of the GI's integrity?[3] Where is the art in slicing meat and putting it in a plastic pack? Talking of slicing, Feta is not a place name;[4] and nor is it a Greek word but merely Italian for 'slice'. Curiously, prepared for the famous Greek salad it is not cut in slices but served in one large piece. Australia, a country where GIs go to die, so to speak, correctly spells the word with two 't's on its alternative product as well as its imports of the counterpart damp white stuff imported from Denmark. But shops there also sell cheese labelled as Persian fetta, and as also Australia made 'Traditional' fetta, presumably by Australians of Greek origin of which there are a substantial number. If in need, one can purchase prosecco made in Italy or in Australia, and in the same store. For Manuka honey you are free to choose New Zealand Manuka or, to the consternation of many Kiwis, Manuka made in Australia, which in my experience is cheaper and inferior in quality. Australians have little *legal* deference for old products.[5] But are they wrong?

---

[2] Warren Moran, 'Rural Space as Intellectual Property (1993) 12(3) Political Geography 263.

[3] Case C-108/01 *Consorzio del Prosciutto di Parma and Salumificio S. Rita SpA v Asda Stores Ltd & Hygrade Foods Ltd* [2003] ECR I-05121.

[4] Joined Cases C-465/02 and C-466/02 *Federal Republic of Germany and Kingdom of Denmark v Commission of the European Communities* [2005] ECR I-09115.

[5] By virtue of the Wine Australia Act 2013, GI registration is available for wines. But no other type of product can be legally registered. Otherwise, Australian law provides for certification marks.

After all the 'real' thing is available there too and consumers are free to choose it, or the various alternatives. They would not be so prominently on sale if people were not buying them.

For the law, and if long-term rural prosperity is its aim, *where* these supposedly unique products, their ingredients, and the human-environmental interactions that make them possible, do *and do not* come from, matters a lot more than many people think. These are meant to be small-scale short value-chain local products whose production is under local control. Expanding the area purely to meet high demand, as with Tequila for example, undermines the integrity of the indication, and is unlikely to favour local income capture or important cultural landscapes. Otherwise trade marks can be used.

Of course, boundary and turf disputes are hardly specific to GIs. All property rights must draw lines between what's yours and what's somebody else's, or nobody's. For the purpose of vesting a legal right, we identify an inventor on the basis of their written description, an author in relation to the original artistic or literary work in their name, or a business entity for its visually-perceptible sign. Complex disputes can and do frequently arise regarding the boundaries of such property rights. However, many countries have a rich body of jurisprudence enabling their resolution, and other countries with less experience are free to draw on such experience or else to devise their own legal approaches. But national and regional pride can arguably make GI disputes especially emotive and contentious.

To conclude, the sustainable and human development benefits of GIs – broadly construed – would appear to depend on the following acts and aims:

1. effectively identifying a bounded, authentic and preferably uncontentious *terroir,*
2. guaranteeing the integrity of the product without compromising biodiversity and genetic resource sustainability, *especially if the product becomes successful and supply struggles to meet demand,*
3. ensuring that the users are the 'right' ones (that is, those producers who do most to maintain the quality of, and goodwill in, the product), and
4. retaining as much of the benefits from commercialisation as possible in the hands of the local small-scale producer communities.

Graham Dutfield

Acknowledgments

Our first thanks must go to all our contributors who have so very generously shared their own voices, experiences, insights, and expertise in this volume, and done so while balancing their other commitments, notably during the harvest seasons for grapes in Napa Valley and coffee beans in Kenya. Most of them have not only worked on their own pieces but have also reviewed and provided constructive comments on pieces by other contributors in the volume. We are therefore most grateful indeed for all their work, their generosity of spirit, and their patience in working with us.

Additionally, we have a long list of colleagues and others who have assisted and supported us throughout this project. First and foremost is our editor Stephanie Tytherleigh at Edward Elgar Publishing who suggested approaching the issue through a diverse lens. We took on board her suggestion and developed the three case studies presented here. She has also been tirelessly and helpfully guiding us throughout this project.

The University of Aberdeen Development Trust was most resourceful in putting us in touch with the vast array of supportive alumni who have contributed directly and indirectly to this project. Among the indirect supporters and alumni is Blair Bowman. We are very much indebted to him and to Meena Murrin for their infectious passion for knowledge about the Scotch Whisky industry. We are also thankful to our colleague Jackson Armstrong, who from his work with a team that uncovered in the Aberdeen Burgh Records the earliest reference (in 1505) to a still for distilling Scotch Whisky as a drink, helped connect us with the work of the Development Trust.

Likewise, our discussions with Joseph Kieyah about Coffee Kenya in the early stages of that case study were inspiring and encouraged us in pursuing it further.

Our old friends and colleagues Dev Gangjee, Tshimanga Kongolo, and John Noble have been most supportive in guiding us toward various contacts for the project. Dev and also Claudio Lombardi have additionally reviewed and provided comments on chapters in the volume. Alan Park and David Vaver have also provided comments at various points of the project. All errors in the volume remain those of the editors.

Jamie Bowie of the Cartography Team at the University of Aberdeen provided significant expertise and assistance regarding maps of Scotland and Kenya, for which we are most grateful. The Library Services at the University of Aberdeen has also been tremendously helpful throughout the project, and we must thank Liam Moorhouse for his expertise and support in the final process.

To all the direct and indirect contributors to the project, we hope you will accept our utmost gratitude for all your help in bringing together this diverse set of voices and perspectives.

To you our readers, we very much hope that, like us, you too will find the journey that this project will take you on to be both enjoyable and informative.

Catherine W. Ng,
Titilayo Adebola,
Abbe E. L. Brown,
University of Aberdeen
2024

PART I

Introduction

1. Place-Branding and the Law

Catherine W. Ng, Titilayo Adebola and Abbe E. L. Brown

INTRODUCTION

This volume explores the impact of place brands in the marketplace in view of the extended protection increasingly accorded to them under intellectual property (IP) laws. It is a collection of perspectives about place-branding from traders who use place brands, lawyers who protect them, marketers who promote them, consumers who buy goods by relying on them, as well as academics who study them. For reasons explained further on, it offers three place brands as case studies: Scotch Whisky, the Napa Valley AVA, and the Coffee Kenya figurative mark.[1]

Place brands such as these serve as additional branding on the labels of corporate brands such as JOHNNIE WALKER[2] or the Striding Man figurative mark[3] for a brand of Scotch Whisky. Typically, place-branded goods would be presented collectively as a category in the digital as well as physical marketplace and other social contexts, as distinguished from other types of equivalent or similar goods (for example, whiskies or Irish whiskies in particular) in those contexts. Some consumers may attribute the taste of Scotch Whisky or other place-branded goods to *terroir*: the soil, climate, topographical conditions as well as the local expertise in producing the goods. In turn, the eponymous

---

[1] See figurative mark by accessing the World Intellectual Property Organization, Global Brand Database at <https:// www .wipo .int/ reference/ en/ branddb/> accessed 17 April 2024, typing WO500000001250302 under 'Number', and entering 'Search'.

[2] 'Trade mark number: UK00000308458' (Intellectual Property Office) <https:// trademarks .ipo .gov .uk/ ipo -tmcase/ page/ Results/ 1/ UK00000308458> accessed 17 April 2024.

[3] 'Trade mark number: UK00003099444' (Intellectual Property Office) <https:// trademarks .ipo .gov .uk/ ipo -tmcase/ page/ Results/ 1/ UK00003099444> accessed 17 April 2024.

place (for example Scotland in the case of Scotch Whisky) may enrobe the place-branded goods with its own identity. This identity may then be adopted as part of the identity of the consumers, especially the connoisseurs and afficionados among them.

Place brands are also different from the traders' perspective. Unlike corporate brands or trade marks that are registered and thus 'owned' by a single corporate entity, 'Scotch Whisky'-type place brands which do signify a place connection with the goods in the consumers' mind (unlike, for example, PHILADELPHIA for cream cheese[4]) are 'shared' by traders who sell goods that meet certain specifications, some of which are typically connected in some way with the geographical origin of these goods. The geographical proximity among traders who share a place brand can allow them to be organized and defined as a collective vis-à-vis traders of other brands of equivalent or similar goods. This proximity also means that the success of these traders can have enormous impact on the socio-economic development in the eponymous place. For individual traders, the shared branding brings a visibility to consumers by the sheer mass presence of the place brand used alongside diverse corporate brands in the marketplace and social environments. This shared branding marks out a category of goods from other equivalent or similar goods which do not bear the branding and thus limits competition in the consumers' mind. When cloaked with a collective identity that evokes the eponymous place of the branding in the consumers' mind, individual traders share the prestige and the increased pricing potential often associated with the identity. They can also leverage this advantage to secure a better position when negotiating the sale of their goods, whether or not place-branded, within the chain of commerce.

For the broader communities, politicians who are also geographically organized can deploy geographical indications (GIs) as tools to achieve aims such as rural development, economic, social, and environmental sustainability for their constituents.[5]

---

[4] 'Philadelphia Original: Our Story' (Mondelēz International) <https://www.philadelphia.co.uk/our-story/> accessed 9 October 2024.

[5] Riccardo Crescenzi, Fabrizio De Filippis, Mara Giua and Cristina Vaquero-Piñeiro, 'Geographical Indications and Local Development: the strength of territorial embeddedness' (2022) 56(3) Regional Studies 381; see preamble, Council Regulation (EEC) No 2081/92 of 14 July 1992 on the Protection of Geographical Indications and Designations of Origin for Agricultural Products and Foodstuffs [1992] OJ L208/1 (no longer in force), more recently, Regulation (EU) 2024/1143 of the European Parliament and of the Council of 11 April 2024 on geographical indications for wine, spirit drinks and agricultural products, as well as traditional specialities guaranteed and optional quality terms for agricultural products, amending Regulations (EU) No 1308/2013, (EU) 2019/787 and (EU)

IP laws have been extending protection to that type of place brand and its underlying goodwill, beyond that granted to brands for individual corporate entities. Trade marks for corporate brands that denote the geographical origins of the underlying goods are excluded from registration unless they have 'acquired a distinctive character' through use in the marketplace.[6] Similarly, the classic version of the law of passing off affords little or no protection to the goodwill associated with brand names that are descriptive of the origin of the underlying goods unless those names have acquired a 'secondary meaning' in the consumers'[7] mind to refer unequivocally to the trader of those branded goods (as opposed to the primary meaning to refer broadly to traders of the goods as described by the name). This exclusion from protection keeps place names available for use by all traders of similar or equivalent goods from the same geographical origins to enable free and fair competition among traders.

Trade mark legislation in jurisdictions such as the United Kingdom (UK) also includes collective and certification marks within the definition of 'trade marks'.[8] Collective and certification marks can protect the marks of an association of traders[9] or a certifier in respect of the origin of goods.[10] Further, the law of passing off, which classically protects the goodwill associated with a brand name of a single trader as it relates to that trader, has, in recent decades, been extended to protect the goodwill shared among traders from using a common brand identity to refer to a specific class of goods.[11] In addition there are specific laws governing GIs and these extend beyond the more individual trade mark premise of protecting consumers from being confused into purchasing, for example, other types of whisky when they intend to purchase Scotch Whisky, of protecting traders from having their well-reputed shared brands and the distinctive character in them impaired or taken unfair advantage of without due cause by third-party use.[12] As explained below and within the volume, the range of GI protection has expanded particularly in the sui generis GI system operated within the European Union (EU). The new GI Regulations[13] adopted on 28 February 2024 affirm these broader aims and secure further protection for GIs used in ingredient branding and in digital

---

2019/1753 and repealing Regulation (EU) No 1151/2012 [2024] OJ L1143, Recital 10, art. 32(2)(d).

[6] Trade Marks Act 1994, s. 3(1)(c).
[7] *Reddaway v Banham* [1896] AC 199 (HL).
[8] Trade Marks Act 1994, s. 1(2).
[9] Ibid., s. 49(1A).
[10] Ibid., s. 50(2).
[11] Ng Ch. 16.
[12] See Trade Marks Act 1994, s. 10(1)–(3).
[13] Regulation (EU) 2024/1143.

contexts.[14] The views contained in this volume were collected as of the end of August 2023, although in some cases we have included developments after that date.

This volume uses Scotch Whisky,[15] the Napa Valley AVA,[16] and the Coffee Kenya figurative mark,[17] as case studies to expose the diverse ways that traders can protect their place brands. Each of them offers a different perspective because of its own legislative history and the time at which the place-branding for their goods received legal recognition. We are not considering how these case studies fit within the 'Old World - New World' or 'Global North – Global South' debates[18] in this volume.

This volume takes an interdisciplinary approach to engage with producers, marketers, sociologists, legal academics, as well as practitioners in the three industry sectors, allowing them to share their perspectives on the workings of place brands. By including voices from farmers and traders, and empirical evidence from consumers, this work seeks to illuminate how IP laws and the place brands they protect impact on consumers, traders, and regional development more broadly.

THE PROJECT AS A JOURNEY (FROM A READERS' PERSPECTIVE)

This volume begins with a provocative Foreword by Dutfield asking 'Geographical Indications: What are They Good for?' The volume explores this theme in five substantive parts: 'How Place-Branding Started', 'The Impact of Place-Branding', 'IP Law in Practice', 'IP Law in Policy Analysis, and 'The Producers' Experiences of Place-Branding'. In each of these parts, it is clear that the stakeholders do not take a uniform view on the role of IP law within their arena of place-branding. At times, their differences lie on policy grounds; at other times, on practical grounds.

The first substantive part begins with 'How Place-Branding Started' which presents three very different perspectives from the three case studies. The

---

[14] Ibid., Recitals 18, 20, 25, 35a, 36, arts 27(1), 28, 34, 43.
[15] See Appendix A for 'Map of whisky-producing areas in Scotland'.
[16] See Stults (Ch. 3), Figure 3.1 'Map of Napa Valley American Viticultural Area and Nested AVAs'.
[17] See Appendix B for 'Map of coffee producing regions of Kenya'.
[18] Enrico Bonadio, Magali Contardi and Nicola Lucchi, 'Geographical Indications Between the Old World and the New World, and the Impact of Migration' (2024) 73(1) GRUR International 3, 5–7; Irene Calboli and Wee Loon Ng-Loy, *Geographical Indications at the Crossroads of Trade, Development and Culture: Focus on Asia-Pacific* (Cambridge University Press 2017).

piece by Swanson and Mondavi (Chapter 2) is a historical account of how Napa Valley began as a wine-growing region and gained prominence through the work of individuals such as Robert Mondavi who helped transform Napa Valley wine from being a mass-produced commodity to drinks coveted by connoisseurs. This community knowledge-building, making the most of climatic, soil, and topographical conditions, and collective marketing catapulted the Napa Valley brand onto the world stage. Stults' work (Chapter 3) then tells of the journey that led to the establishment of the American Viticultural Area (AVA) to protect the Napa Valley brand, with a nested system to further protect regional brands within Napa Valley. Stults explores how the Napa Valley Vintners (NVV), as the guardian of the collective reputation in Napa Valley, has instigated legal protection for 'Napa Valley' as used in association with wines. While the Napa Valley wine industry remains 'the ultimate product of place',[19] the Napa Valley brand has impact well beyond the wine industry in the region.[20]

Magowan's work (Chapter 4) tracing the association of 'Kenya' with coffees of distinctive flavour profiles in the development of the sector, however, raises questions regarding the degree to which, in the future, these flavours are traceable to the soil, climatic, and topographical conditions of the region, and indeed necessarily the human resources there. Similarly in 'Scotch Whisky: Provenance, Authenticity, and Ownership', Higgins and Bower (Chapter 5) trace the origin of 'Scotch Whisky' in definitional, corporate ownership and ingredient terms and raise the question of Scottishness and its diverse meanings and the role of *terroir* in the making of Scotch Whiskies. They note: 'What is remarkable ... is how Scotch Whisky has retained a reputation for heritage and authenticity given its [largely non-Scottish-based] ownership structure, the broad geographical indication of the category, and the scale and scope of the production process.'[21]

'The Impact of Place-Branding' part analyzes the issue of place-branding from the perspectives of sociologists and marketers. The first piece here by Ichijo (Chapter 6) finds the Scottishness in Scotch Whisky to lie in the carefully curated imageries of Scotland that are used to market the product, however incongruous they are to the realities of Scotland as a whole. The chapter explores views of the work of the representative trade body, the Scotch Whisky Association (SWA), and the power and influence it can be considered to have on broad political issues that may affect the Scotch Whisky industry. Taplin's piece (Chapter 7) then observes, from a sociologist's perspective,

---

[19] Stults (Ch. 3) (n. 16).
[20] Taplin (Ch. 7).
[21] Higgins and Bower (Ch. 5), abstract.

the journey upon which Napa Valley has travelled both in wine cultivation terms and in marketing terms to garner its current reputation worldwide by creating and selling wines that are perceived to be distinctive of Napa Valley as compared with other Californian wines. It exposes how Napa Valley wine has moved in the consumers' eyes from being a drink, then a quality drink, to a status marker, and how the winemaking industry has thereby transformed the region and the imageries that Napa Valley projects as a region. Farr, Erricker and Mallory (Chapter 8) take a marketer's perspective to analyze how place brands may be effectively deployed to position the branded goods in consumers' minds. While this positioning often works to the benefit of the branding traders, the piece also highlights some of the potential pitfalls. Crucially, this piece brings to the volume the consumers' perspective through extant empirical research on how place brands affect consumers' purchase decisions. Finally, Kabau's work (Chapter 9) analyzes the challenges the Kenyan Government faces in institutionalizing Coffee Kenya as a place brand for coffees grown in Kenya to instil consumer trust in the authenticity of 'Kenya'-branded coffees as distinctive unblended coffees grown in Kenya. Kabau also demonstrates the shortcomings in consumer appeal in using certification marks alone to protect a place brand.

In the next part on IP Law in Practice, law practitioners share their insights on protecting place brands primarily in their own jurisdictions. The section begins with Gerien's account (Chapter 10) of the journey the NVV took to gain protection not only in the United States (US) but also internationally, and critically explores the GI protection landscape in the US. The US has opted to devise its own specific protected appellation of US and foreign viticultural areas. For example, 'Napa Valley'-branded wines must consist of at least 85% grapes grown within the AVA and finished within California.[22] The US (like the UK) also uses certification and collective marks[23] to protect GIs, in addition to the conventional protection available to corporate trade marks which have become distinctive of the corporate registrants' goods in commerce[24] and unregistered mark protection available through common law. GIs however must be registered to be protected in the US. Reuer and Baars (Chapter 11) draw from cases and legislation to illustrate the broader protection accorded to place brands in Germany and the EU with the EU's own sui generis GI protection system in addition to certification marks and conventional corporate trade mark protection. Within the sui generis system, certain GIs are protected against not only practices liable to mislead consumers as to the true origin of

---

[22] Gerien (Ch. 10).
[23] 15 U.S.C. § 1054.
[24] 15 U.S.C. § 1052 (f).

the goods, but also 'misuse, imitation or evocation' or if the protected name is translated or accompanied by expressions such as 'style' or 'type', even if the true origin is indicated[25] (for example, 'Scotch Whisky-style spirit distilled in the USA').

Jenkins, Gilbert, Keating, Cant and Lee (Chapter 12) explain firstly that while the UK left the EU as of 1 February 2020, much of the new post-Brexit UK GI-specific protection is derived from EU law and thus far continues to run substantively as it was pre-Brexit apart from the change in jurisdictional scope[26] (while the EU regime continues to apply in Northern Ireland). Beyond the expansive EU-initiated sui generis protection for place brands, this chapter also considers GI protection as certification and by collective mark in the UK; and also that each of England and Wales, Scotland, and Northern Ireland also protects the goodwill or consumer brand recognition under the judge-made law of passing off. The part ends with Omino and Koros (Chapter 13) illustrating through case law how the Kenyan regime deploys a combination of certification, collective, and conventional corporate trade marks as well as the judge-made law of passing off to protect place brands. As in other jurisdictions, corporate marks are only protected where they do not hinder others from using the same geographical name for similar goods. The chapter goes on to assess the extent to which EU-style place brand specific protection would be desirable for Kenya where attempts to create GI-specific protection have been proposed but remain inconclusive.

---

[25] Regulation (EU) 2019/787 of the European Parliament and of the Council of 17 April 2019 on the definition, description, presentation and labelling of spirit drinks, the use of the names of spirit drinks in the presentation and labelling of other foodstuffs, the protection of geographical indications for spirit drinks, the use of ethyl alcohol and distillates of agricultural origin in alcoholic beverages, and repealing Regulation (EC) No 110/2008 [2019] OJ L130/1, art. 21(2).

[26] For wines: Regulation (EU) No 1308/2013 of the European Parliament and of the Council of 17 December 2013 establishing a common organisation of the markets in agricultural products and repealing Council Regulations (EEC) No 922/72, (EEC) No 234/79, (EC) No 1037/2001 and (EC) No 1234/2007 [2013] OJ L347/671, arts 92 et seq.; for aromatised wine products: Regulation (EU) No 251/2014 of the European Parliament and of the Council of 26 February 2014 on the definition, description, presentation, labelling and the protection of geographical indications of aromatised wine products and repealing Council Regulation (EEC) No 1601/91 [2014] OJ L84/14, arts 10 et seq.; for spirit drinks: Regulation (EU) 2019/787; for agricultural products and foodstuffs which do not fall under the scope of one of the other three more specific regulations: Regulation (EU) No 1151/2012 of the European Parliament and of the Council of 21 November 2012 on quality schemes for agricultural products and foodstuffs [2012] OJ L343/1.

These tools for place brand protection come under further analysis from a broader policy perspective in 'The IP Law in Policy Analysis' part. Adebola (Chapter 14) maps the international legal landscape for GIs and discusses the complexities in GI law-making by unpacking the GI provisions in the Agreement on Trade Related Aspects of Intellectual Property Rights and World Intellectual Property Organization treaties alongside selected regional and national developments. She notes how 'GI consensus setting has predominantly shifted from the multilateral to bilateral level'[27] in recent decades and the impact this shift has had on the development of domestic protection regimes in countries such as Kenya. Montero (Chapter 15) addresses the difficult but underexplored issues of the protection afforded to place brands when used in digital marketing such as in domain names, on various digital platforms, on virtual goods in the metaverse and by influencers on social media. Ng (Chapter 16) takes the angle of the judge-made law of passing off that can offer protection without any prior formal requirements such as registration. She explores how this law has been extended to protect the goodwill that is shared among traders of particular classes of goods through the use of place brands, inter alia, and rationalizes this development with the classic version of the law of passing off which offers little or no protection to the goodwill that is associated with descriptive or generic brands unless the brands have acquired secondary meanings to refer unequivocally to specific traders.

'The Producers' Experiences of Place-Branding' part exposes the producers' first-hand experiences with place-branding, from the perspectives of well-established and larger sector participants as well as newer, smaller ones, for each of the three case studies. Stewart and Anstruther (Chapter 17) start by highlighting the challenges and rewards of building up Scotch Whisky as an industry with the necessary consumer brand recognition, and the ripple effect that this recognition has brought not only in related tourism industries, but also more broadly as a cultural icon and an indirect economic force for Scotland. Wills (Chapter 18) shares how he and his family began their unique Kilchoman distillery in Islay, Scotland and staked out a stance for their whiskies with flagship annual releases that featured ingredients and processing from or within proximity of the farm distillery. For Napa Valley wines, Swanson (Chapter 19) reflects on how the larger wineries often gain strategic advantages within the chain of commerce by investing in and having Napa Valley branded wines represented within their portfolio. Dyer (Chapter 20) remarks on how the use of the Napa Valley AVA and the sub-AVA of Diamond Mountain District within Napa Valley has helped bring smaller regionally branded wines such as those of the Dyer Vineyard to the attention of broader retail consumers, and how

---

[27] Adebola (Ch. 14).

the AVA and sub-AVA have transformed the region. In respect of the Coffee Kenya brand, Gichangi (Chapter 21) writing from the perspective of his family estate, sees opportunities for using the brand for his direct sale of coffee to domestic as well as international markets. As a small scale coffee grower, John (Chapter 22) shares his experiences of selling coffee and of working with his co-operative in doing so. He also shares his thoughts on the potential benefits and drawbacks of the Coffee Kenya brand.

The volume then concludes with a joint chapter by the editors reflecting upon these three case studies and highlighting some of the lessons learned from them to respond to some of the questions raised in Dutfield's thought-provoking Foreword in which he asks what are GIs good for?

THE PROJECT AS A JOURNEY (FROM THE EDITORS' PERSPECTIVE)

As instigators of the project and editors of the volume, we have set out to investigate how three drinks can become place-branded and endowed with IP rights to protect their traders and consumers and to advance regional development.

We are very excited to have contributors from academia as well as producers, industry experts, representative bodies, and law practitioners on the supply side and consumer research on the demand side to provide a diverse range of perspectives. This collection sets out the experiences and insights of our authors drawn from their individual contexts of a wider environment. We recognize that this can involve confidentiality and matters of trade and policy sensitivity. The collection does not tell a complete story and could never do so: there is a diversity of views across contributors and also readers.

This volume aims to provide a new richness in depth and breadth by introducing the three case studies in an interdisciplinary manner. It also aims to open spaces for discussions at a more intimate level for the stakeholders in place-branding than is usually available within trade, legal and academic discourse.

We hope that readers will now enjoy this journey with us.

APPENDIX 1.A

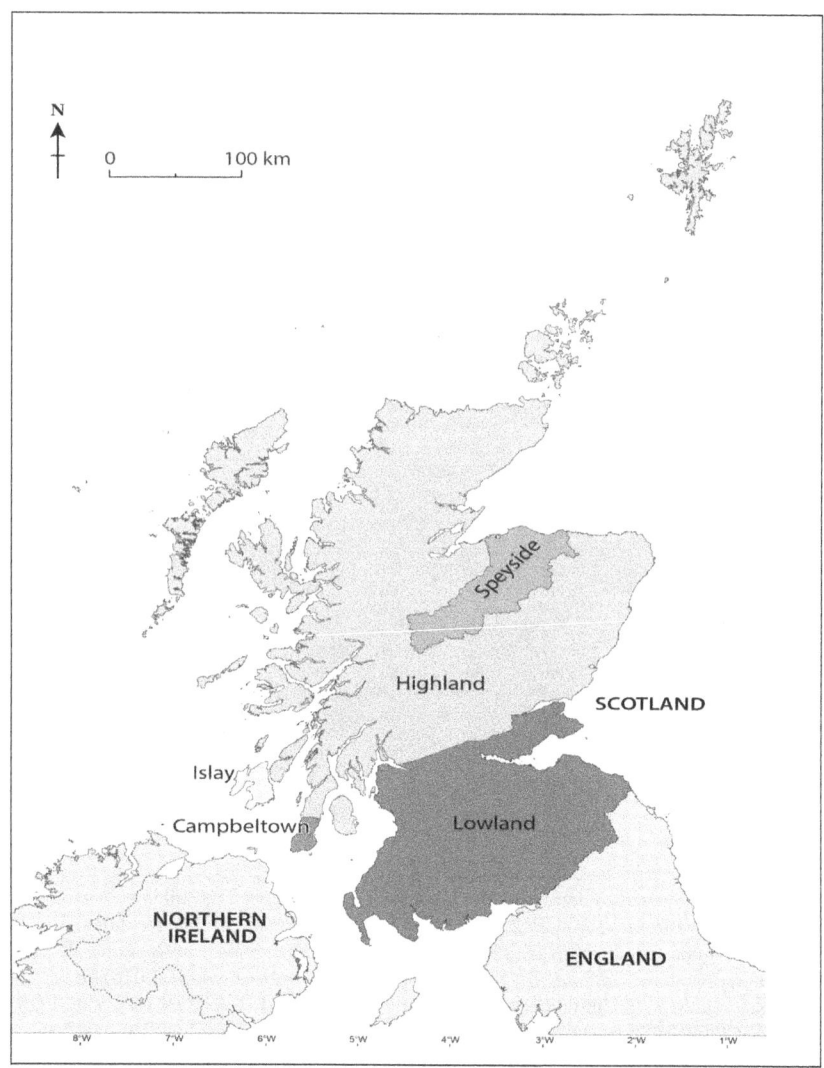

Source: Map prepared by Jamie Bowie, University of Aberdeen. This builds on a map of Scotland from Edina Digimap © Crown copyright and database rights 2024 Ordnance Survey (AC0000851941) pursuant to End User Licence Agreement educational use

Figure 1A.1   Map of whisky-producing areas in Scotland

APPENDIX 1.B

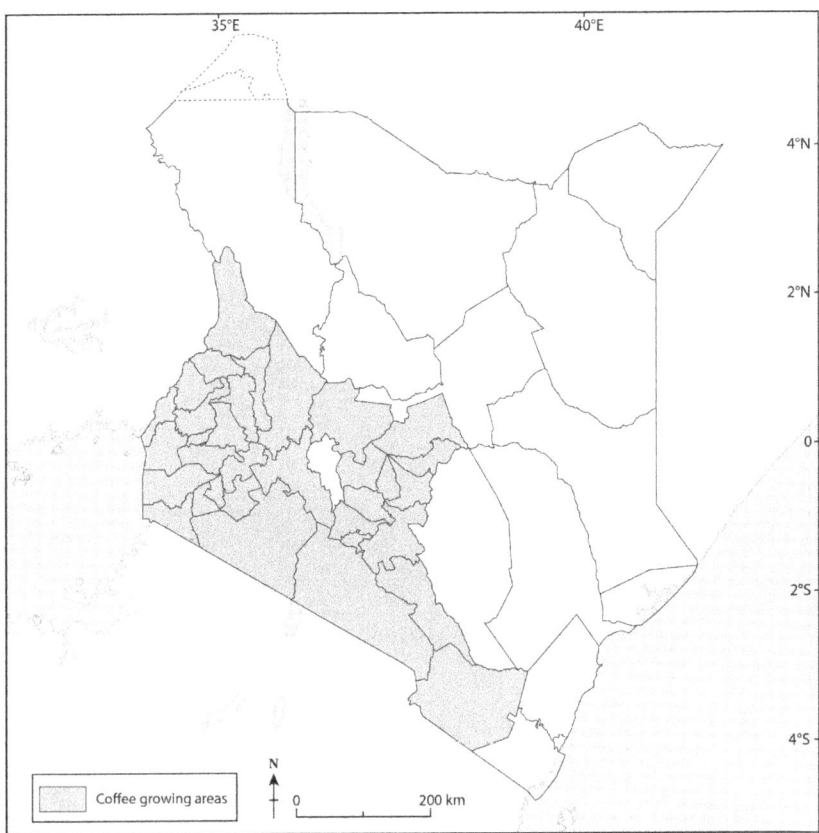

Source: Map prepared by Jamie Bowie, University of Aberdeen. The builds on a map of Kenya from OpenStreetMap licensed under CC BY-SA 2.0 licence: https://creativecommons.org/licenses/by-sa/2.0/ and draws from information in Republic of Kenya, *Report of the National Task Force on Coffee Sub-Sector Reforms* (2016) https://ushirika.go.ke/wp-content/uploads/2022/05/REPORT-OF-THE-NATIONAL-TASK-FORCE-ON-COFFEE-SUB-SECTOR-REFORMS-FINAL.pdf p. 65, Heading; 'Annex 2 – Coffee Growing Zones'; and Coffee Directorate *Coffee Book Year 2017-18* Reports (www.agricultureauthority.go.ke) p. 1 Figure 1: MAP OF COFFEE GROWING COUNTIES IN KENYA

Figure 1B.1   Map of coffee-producing regions of Kenya

PART II

How Place-Branding Started

2. History of the Napa Valley Brand and AVA – A Multigenerational Insider's Perspective

Ian Swanson and Michael Mondavi

Situated in California, an hour north of San Francisco, Napa Valley is a renowned destination for wine enthusiasts. Although just 30 miles long, the valley contains many microclimates from the valley floor to the surrounding hills. But it wasn't always known for its wines. This region has undertaken a captivating journey from its Indigenous inhabitants to its transformation into the world-class wine-producing area it is today. Some of the success came from farmers seeing opportunity, taking risks, and putting in the hard work, and some simply from luck and unintended consequences.

Napa Valley was home to the Wappo people,[1] who thrived on its fertile lands fed by the Napa River and its flood plains, which provided a plentiful source of nuts, greens, and root vegetables along with wild foods such as game and fish. Their presence in the region can be traced back thousands of years. However, the arrival of Spanish explorers in the 18th century brought significant changes to the area. In 1821, a Spanish military expedition led by Lieutenant Luis Arguello,[2] the first governor of California, explored the region and adopted the name Napa, likely derived from the language of the Wappo people.[3]

---

[1] 'Wappo Indian Tribe Facts' (*Native American Indian Facts*) <https://native-american-indian-facts.com/ California-American-Indian-Facts/ Wappo-Indian-Tribe-Facts.shtml> accessed 20 October 2024.

[2] Luis Antonio Argüello, Vivian C Fisher and Arthur Quinn, *The Diary of Captain Luis Antonio Argüello 1821: The Last Spanish Expedition in California* (Berkeley: The Friends of Bancroft Library, University of California 1992).

[3] Alexandria Brown, 'Napa or Nappa?' (Napa County Historical Society 28 May 2014) <https:// napahistory .org/ napa-or-nappa/ #: ~: text = Yet %20still %20others %20have %20claimed ,corruption %20of %20a %20Wappo %20word> accessed 20 October 2024.

Among the first European settlers, Nathan Coombs, considered the founder of Napa,[4] and Salvador Vallejo,[5] arrived in the mid-19th century. Coombs was the first European settler to recognize the agricultural potential of Napa Valley and envisioned it as a prosperous farming community. His efforts were instrumental in attracting more settlers to the region. Agriculture, particularly wheat farming, flourished in Napa during this time.

In the late 1850s, the arrival of Charles Krug, a Prussian immigrant and sea captain, established the first commercial winery.[6] Krug's winery laid the foundation for the viticultural industry that would eventually define the region.

The arrival of Gustave Niebaum, a Finnish sea captain turned winemaker, proved to be the first turning point in Napa's history. In 1879, Niebaum purchased the Inglenook Winery (now known as the Niebaum-Coppola Estate Winery) from William C. Watson,[7] who had planted the vineyard in 1873. Niebaum introduced advanced winemaking techniques, and his success attracted more attention to Napa Valley as a premier wine region. Thousands of acres of vineyards were planted between 1850 and 1900. Then came two events that threatened the existence of the wine industry in the valley.

First, at the turn of the century, the valley saw the arrival of phylloxera, a root louse that devastated the vines. Approximately 80% of the valley's vineyards were destroyed.[8] Then in 1920, Prohibition was enacted,[9] just as Napa Valley began to recover from the phylloxera. The Prohibition era (1920–33) presented a significant challenge for the wine industry. Many vineyards were uprooted, and wineries had to find alternative means of survival. Some winemakers, such as Berringer and Christian Brothers, resorted to producing

---

[4] 'Nathan Coombs, Napa's Founder' (*Napa Valley Roots* 27 March 2021) <https://napavalleyroots.org/nathan-coombs-napas-founder/> accessed 20 October 2024.

[5] Nancy Brennan, 'Remembering Salvador Vallejo' (Napa County Historical Society 28 July 2015) <https://napahistory.org/remembering-salvador-vallejo/> accessed 20 October 2024.

[6] 'History of Wine in the Napa Valley' (Napa Valley Vintners) <https://napavintners.com/napa_valley/history.asp#:~:text=Charles%20Krug%20is%20credited%20with,)%20and%20Inglenook%20(1879)> accessed 20 October 2024.

[7] 'Inglenook History' (Inglenook Winery) <https://inglenook.com/our-story/> accessed 20 October 2024.

[8] Winecountry Collective, 'The History of Notorious Napa Valley' (*Napavalley.com* 23 May 2016) <https://www.napavalley.com/blog/napa-valley-history/> accessed 20 October 2024.

[9] 'Prohibition' (*History.com* 24 April 2023) <https://www.history.com/topics/roaring-twenties/prohibition> accessed 20 October 2024.

sacramental and medicinal wines or converting their operations to grape juice production. But many wineries went under.

It has been said that nothing did more to increase the consumption of alcohol in the United States (US) than Prohibition, and indeed, for spirits, that was true. But, for Napa, it was more challenging. In the years following Prohibition, the few surviving wineries and vineyards resumed legal operations and began the slow recovery process. Vineyards were replanted, winemaking equipment was updated, and production steadily increased. It took time to rebuild the industry, but the region's favorable climate and fertile soil supported the resurgence.

At first, in the years following the end of Prohibition, the thinking was that the future of the wine industry, including that in Napa Valley, was in growing and shipping bulk wine to the major cities. Wineries shipped railcars containing 15,000 gallons each to wholesalers in the major cities, where they were blended and bottled under local labels in gallon and half-gallon jugs. And this was how Cesare Mondavi entered the wine industry.

In 1921, Cesare had moved to Lodi from Minnesota, where, after a brief spell working in the iron mines, he worked in a cafe and saloon. The owner of the cafe and saloon asked him to go to California to purchase grapes and winemaking supplies because it was legal to produce 200 gallons of wine per household. After settling in Lodi, Cesare developed an independent business. buying and shipping fresh grapes back to his customers, who were Italian immigrant winemakers. Following the end of Prohibition, he began producing wine in the San Joaquin Valley near Lodi, California, where he lived. Beginning in 1937, his son Robert joined him in the Napa Valley. Robert began making and shipping wine for his father at the Sunny St. Helena Winery, which they leased (in partnership with Jack Riorda) in the late 1930s. There was already a recognition of the flavors of wines from Napa, and they commanded a higher price than other wines. The Napa wines were blended into the final wines bottled to improve their overall flavor and quality.

A sequence of events then transpired, resulting in the shift from shipping railcars full of bulk wine around the country to wineries bottling their wines as consumer products. That triggering event was the imposition of wage and price controls in 1942.[10] As part of the war effort to control prices, bulk wine, as a commodity, could only be sold at 12½ cents per gallon. With Napa wines costing more than this to produce, the Mondavis realized that the only way to stay in business was to bottle the wine as a consumer product and not a commodity, sell it as a branded bottle of wine and therefore avoid the price controls. The owners of the Sunny St. Helena Winery were convinced that the

---

[10] US Congress, United States Code: Emergency Price Control Act of 1940, 50a USC §§ 901-946 (Suppl II 1940).

model of shipping bulk wine to the bottlers across the US was the preferred model and would not put a bottling line into the winery. Robert Mondavi had, however, identified the Charles Krug winery as a good location to produce and bottle wines. It had suffered during Prohibition and had not produced in some time, but it had the potential for a bottling line and vineyards. Cesare and his family purchased the winery in 1943 and began bottling and selling premium Napa Valley bottled wines under the Charles Krug label.[11] Robert believed you could sell Napa Valley Cabernet Sauvignon under the Charles Krug label, a brand with a long history and reputation for quality, for 25 cents a bottle which equaled $1.25 per gallon, far better than 12-1/2 cents per gallon. The CK Mondavi label sold in gallon and half gallon jugs also included Napa wine for quality but was blended with wines from the San Joaquin Valley.

Napa Valley winemakers worked to improve their wine quality in the years that followed. They experimented with different grape varietals, adopted modern winemaking techniques, and implemented rigorous quality control measures. These efforts helped elevate the reputation of Napa Valley wines, but winemaking was still relatively small. Through the 1940s and 1950s, the vineyards would still only have a few rows of grapes, with the rest being prune trees as farmers were making more money on prunes than grapes or wine. Memories were that the schools started late so the high schoolers could help harvest the prunes.

Up until the 1960s, few people knew about Napa Valley wines and the quality they represented. Then, a series of events occurred destined to permanently reshape Napa Valley and its wine industry. Firstly, in 1966, Robert Mondavi, with his son Michael, co-founded the Robert Mondavi Winery.[12] The winemakers who joined the winery in those early years included Warren Winiarski (later the founder of Stag's Leap Wine Cellars)[13] and Mike Grgich (later the winemaker of Chateau Montelena).[14] Then, in 1972, a group known

---

[11] 'Legacy' (Charles Krug Winery) <https://www.charleskrug.com/legacy> accessed 20 October 2024.

[12] 'Our Family' (Michael Mondavi Family Estate) <https://www.michaelmondavifamilyestate.com/About-Us/Family-History#:~:text=In%201966%2C%20Michael%20and%20his,but%20all%20Napa%20Valley%20wine> accessed 20 October 2024.

[13] Laura Ness, 'Wine's Most Inspiring People 2023: Warren Winiarski – Viticulturist, Preservationist, Philanthropist' (Advisor Wine Industry Network 20 January 2023) <https://wineindustryadvisor.com/2023/01/20/wines-most-inspiring-people-2023-warren-winiarski-viticulturist-preservationist-philanthropist> accessed 20 October 2024.

[14] 'Immigrant Winemaker' (The National Museum of American History) <https://americanhistory.si.edu/explore/exhibitions/food/online/wine-table/judgement-paris/immigrant-winemaker> accessed 20 October 2024.

as the 'Class of 1972' entered the industry – a group of winemakers and new wineries that would soon become some of the most famous names in the industry: Silver Oak, Caymus, Chateau Montelena, Cakebread, Clos du Val, Stag's Leap Wine Cellars, Diamond Creek, and others. Although launched independently of one another, a collaborative relationship was established to grow the awareness of Napa Valley wines. Knowledge and techniques were freely shared as they sought to further develop Napa.

Secondly, from this loose federation, in addition to collaborating on winemaking, they realized they still needed to tell the world about the wines they were making in Napa Valley. Several influential winery owners and winemakers from this group, including Michael Mondavi, Jack Cakebread (from Cakebread Cellars), Jack Davies (from Schramsberg Vineyards), and others, embarked on promotional tours across the US. They hosted tastings, conducted educational seminars across the country, including Boston, New York, and Dallas, and engaged with wine professionals, distributors, consumers, and anyone who would listen to introduce and showcase the quality and diversity of Napa Valley wines. As a group, they could get the attention of the wine trade and restauranteurs at events, whereas individually, only some would show up. Their efforts aimed to dispel the notion that only French wines could produce world-class quality. By demonstrating the exceptional wines crafted in Napa Valley, the group played a crucial role in reshaping the perception of American wines and elevating the status of Napa Valley wines globally.

Third, and perhaps most importantly, building on the work of the preceding ten years, there was the Judgment of Paris. The Judgment of Paris,[15] a historic wine-tasting event in 1976, had a profound and transformative impact on Napa Valley. This blind tasting, organized by British wine merchant Steven Spurrier, pitted a selection of California wines against some of the most prestigious French wines in a competition expected to favor the French. However, the unexpected outcome forever altered the perception of Napa Valley wines and elevated the region to global prominence.

In the tasting, a panel of French judges, consisting of renowned sommeliers and wine experts, blind-tasted a collection of red and white wines from California and France. To the astonishment of the French judges and the wine world, California wines emerged victorious in both categories. Stag's Leap Wine Cellars' 1973 Cabernet Sauvignon triumphed over renowned Bordeaux wines, and Chateau Montelena's 1973 Chardonnay surpassed prestigious white Burgundies.

---

[15] 'The Judgement of Paris 1976' (Christopher Stewart Wines & Spirits 20 March 2024) <https:// www .christopherstewart .com/ Articles/ history/ the -judgement-of-paris-1976/> accessed 20 October 2024.

Overall, the Judgment of Paris transformed Napa Valley from a relatively unknown wine region into a globally recognized powerhouse. It opened doors for Napa Valley winemakers, who became pioneers in their pursuit of excellence and continued to raise the bar for quality wine production. The event catalyzed the region's growth, and its impact can still be felt today, making the Judgment of Paris a pivotal moment in the history of Napa Valley.

Immediately, the success at the Judgment of Paris led to a tremendous boost in Napa Valley's reputation. The victory put Napa Valley firmly on the global wine map. It shattered the perception that only French wines could excel and set a new benchmark for quality wine production. The region's wines gained credibility and prestige, attracting worldwide attention from wine enthusiasts, collectors, and investors. There was a significant increase in investment in Napa Valley over the years that followed. A great example of this was the collaboration between Robert Mondavi and Baron Philippe de Rothschild to merge old-world and new-world wine styles into one grand opus – a Bordeaux-style wine based on Napa Valley Cabernet Sauvignon.

The joint venture between Mondavi and Baron Rothschild was announced in 1980, though plans for the winery had been developing between the two men since they had met in Hawaii in the early 1970s. In 1980, Robert Mondavi sold 35 acres from his To Kalon Vineyard in the Oakville American Viticultural Area (AVA) to the joint venture. This vineyard would serve as the backbone for the blend, and soon after, the estate built the Opus One winery in Oakville, which has become an icon of the Napa Valley. The collaboration in winemaking techniques produced one of the most highly sought-after wines ever produced in Napa Valley. The first vintage was released in 1984, and for a while, it was the most expensive Californian wine sold. To date, it still ranks among the most expensive red wines produced in Napa Valley.

Over the 14 years following the Judgment of Paris, wineries grew from about 69 in 1976 to over 400 in 1990, vineyards were planted with premium grape varietals, increasing in acreage from approximately 10,000 acres to over 40,000, and innovative winemaking techniques were adopted.

All this was reflected in price as well, with the average bottle price increasing from $5 to $50 over the period, no doubt helped by wines such as Opus One. The region experienced a surge in the number of wineries and the quality of wines produced. It also influenced winemaking practices and highlighted the importance of terroir, showcasing the region's unique microclimate and soil composition, sparking a focus on producing wines that express the distinct characteristics of Napa Valley, leading to a greater emphasis on vineyard management, grape quality, and sustainable practices.

The Judgment of Paris also marked the beginning of wine tourism and its economic growth. Wine enthusiasts and tourists flocked to the region to taste and experience the wines that had triumphed in the historic event. This influx of visitors stimulated the local economy, supporting various industries, such as hospitality, restaurants, and retail. This was the beginning of the Napa Valley that we know today.

Coincidentally, the AVA system was established around the same time as the Judgment of Paris. There was recognition that the *terroir*, that is, the air, soil, and water quality, played an essential part in the quality and style of the wine. Therefore, the Federal Alcohol and Tobacco Tax and Trade Bureau designated AVAs covering specific winemaking areas, beginning in 1978, with Napa Valley being among the first in 1981.[16] Under an AVA, strict rules provide a regulatory framework for wine production and labeling, requiring that for the region (in this case, Napa Valley) to be placed on the label, at least 85% of the grapes are required to come from the AVA. By establishing the AVAs, enforcement of the specific regulations and standards within a designated area was possible, including rules related to grape varieties, viticultural practices, labeling requirements, and geographic indications. AVAs help protect the integrity of wine appellations and prevent misleading or deceptive labeling practices, further adding to the value of the Napa Valley label – and coincidentally probably drive the wine, grape, and land prices up for the most sought-after wines.

Today, Napa Valley is a testament to the perseverance and passion of its early settlers and winemakers. Its rich history, coupled with its exceptional wines, has made it one of the most celebrated wine regions in the world. In this place, tradition, innovation, and the love of wine converge in a truly captivating way.

---

[16] 'Napa Valley Nested AVAs' (Napa Valley Vintners) <https://napavintners.com/ napa _ valley/ appellations .asp #: ~: text = The %20Napa %20Valley %20is %20itself,second%20in%20the%20United%20States> accessed 20 October 2024.

3. Napa Valley: Small Place, Big Reputation

Rex Stults

Wine is an agricultural product of place, reflective of the terroir, or complete natural environment, where it was grown and produced. Winegrowers have known this for centuries.

Portugal is credited with establishing the wine world's first legal demarcated boundaries which were created by then-Portuguese Prime Minister Marquis da Pombol to protect the authenticity of Port wine in 1756.[1] Other European countries with notable wine producing areas, such as France, Spain and Italy, have followed suit over the years, enacting strict regulations that govern key grape-growing, winemaking and labeling practices, among other aspects of the trade. France has the world's most comprehensive system of tying wine to place in its *Appellation d'Origine Controlée* (AOC). Created in 1935, the AOC system is founded on the principle that distinct geographical locations (rather than solely grape varieties) are responsible for the unique character of wines.[2] The AOC system regulates production areas, grape varieties, yields, viticultural and winemaking practices, as well as labeling.

It wasn't until 1980 that the United States (US) created the American Viticultural Area (AVA) system, with the purpose of it being to allow vintners to describe more accurately the origin of their wine to consumers, as well as to help consumers identify wines they may purchase. Administered by the US Department of Treasury's Alcohol and Tobacco Tax and Trade Bureau (TTB), the AVA system does provide for more grape-growing and winemaking flexibility compared to European wine regulatory systems, which may have rules that apply to nearly every aspect of wine production, including grape varieties that may be utilized, minimum alcohol levels and aging requirements, among other things, but nevertheless it does stipulate that American wines featuring AVAs, such as Napa Valley, on labels include at least 85% fruit from the

---

[1] Karen MacNeil, *The Wine Bible* (2nd edn, Workman Publishing Company 2015) 925.
[2] DK Publishing, *Wines of the World* (DK Publishing 2006) 52.

region featured on the label. The TTB does permit AVAs within AVAs, or nested AVAs. The criteria for establishing a nested AVA are no different from the original AVA in which it is situated. The petitioner must demonstrate how the terroir merits further distinction from the larger AVA it is set within. Napa Valley is California's first AVA and the second in the country. The Napa Valley AVA was created in 1981, trailing the Augusta AVA in Missouri by slightly less than a year. There are currently 16 nested AVAs within the Napa Valley. While the AVA system is comparatively new, the understanding that wine is tied to place is not. And, with wine being inextricably tied to place, place-branding in wine may be nearly as old as wine itself.

In the late 1930s and early 1940s, winemakers in the Napa Valley were facing challenges including price controls and labor and supply shortages. A group of vintners that regularly got together over food and wine determined that they could better take on industry issues – and elevate the status of Napa Valley wines – by working together. The Napa Valley Vintners Association (NVV) was hence established in 1944 when a formal agreement was drafted and signed by seven vintners: Georges de Latour of Beaulieu Vineyard, Elmer Salmina of Larkmead, Charles Fornia of the Napa Valley Co-op, Robert Mondavi of CK Mondavi and Sons, John Daniel, Jr. of Inglenook, Louis M. Martini and Louis Stralla.[3] Now representing nearly 550 Napa Valley wineries, the NVV has focused on advocating for the best interests of Napa Valley, including fighting to protect the integrity of the Napa Valley name, driving awareness and demand for Napa Valley wines and giving back to the community ever since.

NVV founding member Robert Mondavi is frequently credited with charting the course for both elevating wine quality and brand awareness of Napa Valley wines. He encouraged vintners to collaborate on oenological best practices to improve overall wine quality while promoting marketing efforts of Napa Valley as a whole, in addition to their own individual brands, in marketing efforts. In 2013, the NVV held a reception in the courtyard of the association's home in the Napa Valley town of St. Helena, where a heritage olive tree was dedicated to celebrate the memory and collective spirit of Robert Mondavi. At the ceremony, NVV President and CEO Linda Reiff remarked, "The spirit in which Mr. Mondavi lived his life is the same spirit that has always guided the Napa Valley Vintners. He often said, 'A rising tide lifts all boats,' – a philosophy still shared by our more than 450 winery members and

---

[3] 'History of the Napa Valley Vintners' (Napa Valley Vintners) <https://napavintners.com/about/history.asp> accessed 9 October 2024.

the NVV's leadership."[4] Whether bringing key members of the wine trade, media and other influencers to the Napa Valley, or taking groups of vintners to targeted domestic and international markets, NVV continues to focus its marketing strategies on Napa Valley itself as a premier winegrowing region. Furthermore, the spirit of camaraderie among vintners in the Napa Valley, originally inspired by Robert Mondavi, remains as strong as ever.

Looking back, the 1976 Judgment of Paris is frequently cited as the moment when wines from the Napa Valley ascended to being recognized among the world's best. Steven Spurrier, a then-34-year-old Englishman who owned and operated a wine shop and wine school in Paris, organized a blind tasting of top wines from Napa Valley against the same varieties from France. The wines were judged by an experienced panel of qualified French wine trade and media members. Coming out on top was a 1972 Cabernet Sauvignon from Napa Valley's Stag's Leap Wine Cellars, ahead of its counterparts from Bordeaux. The top white wine in the competition also came from Napa Valley – a 1973 Chardonnay from Chateau Montelena. Afterwards, Chateau Montelena owner Jim Barrett said, "Not bad for kids from the sticks."[5]

In 1981 – the same year that Napa Valley became California's first AVA – the NVV created the Napa Valley Wine Auction, which eventually was rebranded as Auction Napa Valley. Members of the NVV created auction lots centered around donated wine; wine lovers from around the world were invited to come to Napa Valley for several days of wine, food and Napa Valley hospitality, culminating in a wine auction. The first auction raised $140,000 which the NVV passed on to local hospitals. It did not take long before wine media worldwide turned their attention to Napa Valley during the first weekend of June, when the event was held, shining a bright spotlight on Napa Valley for a very good reason: leveraging Napa Valley's famed wine quality to generate much needed funds for charitable non-profit organizations in the Napa community. The NVV issued grants to local non-profit partners in identified areas of need, which expanded beyond local hospitals to general community health, youth and education, affordable housing and targeted special initiatives. In the 40-year history of Auction Napa Valley, the NVV was able to donate more than $225 million to those causes.[6]

---

[4] 'Napa Valley Vintners Dedicate Heritage Olive Tree in Honor of Robert Mondavi' (Napa Valley Vintners) <https://napavintners.com/press/press_release_detail.asp?ID_News=400023> accessed 9 October 2024.

[5] 'Modern Living: Judgment of Paris' *Time* (7 June 1976) <https://time.com/archive/6880821/modern-living-judgment-of-paris/> accessed 9 October 2024.

[6] 'The First 40 Years of Community Investment: Napa Valley Vintners Retrospective Impact Report' (Napa Valley Vintners January 2024).

In 2020, during the height of the COVID-19 pandemic, the NVV Board of Directors voted to retire Auction Napa Valley. What was innovative in 1981 was now often replicated, both around the country and even within the Napa Valley, where many of the non-profits supported by the NVV from Auction Napa Valley-generated funding hosted their own wine auctions as well. Vintner leaders spent countless hours debating on what, if anything, should replace Auction Napa Valley. In 2022 the NVV launched Collective Napa Valley, which features smaller, more intimate, seasonal events with a refined focus on authentic Napa Valley and a narrowed focus on where the money raised would be distributed. In just over a year since its inception, the NVV has raised nearly $6 million via Collective Napa Valley and the money has gone to two identified areas of need in the community: improving access to resources for youth mental health and helping to minimize the risk of future devastating wildfires, while responsibly replanting areas burned in the 2017 and two 2020 wildfires that devasted the county to the tune of more than $2 billion in 2020 alone, as estimated by bw166, a local business specializing in research and data collection in the alcohol beverage space.

The positive attention the Napa Valley has earned from global wine media due to the success of Auction Napa Valley and Collective Napa Valley has been helpful in assuring Napa's place on the global wine stage. The NVV has long considered cultivating the reputation of Napa Valley wines in the international marketplace as an important part of building the Napa Valley brand, and the auctions have been helpful in that regard. But in addition to bringing international wine media, trade, and consumers to Napa, the NVV has been taking vintners from Napa Valley on trade missions for more than 30 years. The association's first international trade mission was to the United Kingdom (UK) in 1991. In 1998, NVV held its first trade mission to Asia. The NVV ensures Napa Valley's presence at notable global wine trade fairs such as ProWein and VinExpo while working to expand Napa Valley's visibility in targeted markets throughout Asia, Europe, and North America.

In 1997, NVV sought to boost its operating revenue while providing opportunities for exposure and brand building to vintner members – all while attracting more attention to the Napa Valley – by creating Premiere Napa Valley. "Premiere", as it is referred to, features one-of-a-kind wines made by vintners in the Napa Valley specifically for this event. The wines are donated to the event where they are auctioned off to members of the wine trade, who come from all over the world to purchase these exclusive wines. Premiere is often referred to as Napa Valley's homecoming week, where resellers of wine get to spend quality time visiting with old vintner friends and establishing new relationships in the Napa wine community. For the NVV it has become an important revenue stream to support the association's work to promote, protect and enhance the Napa Valley.

ABOUT NAPA VALLEY

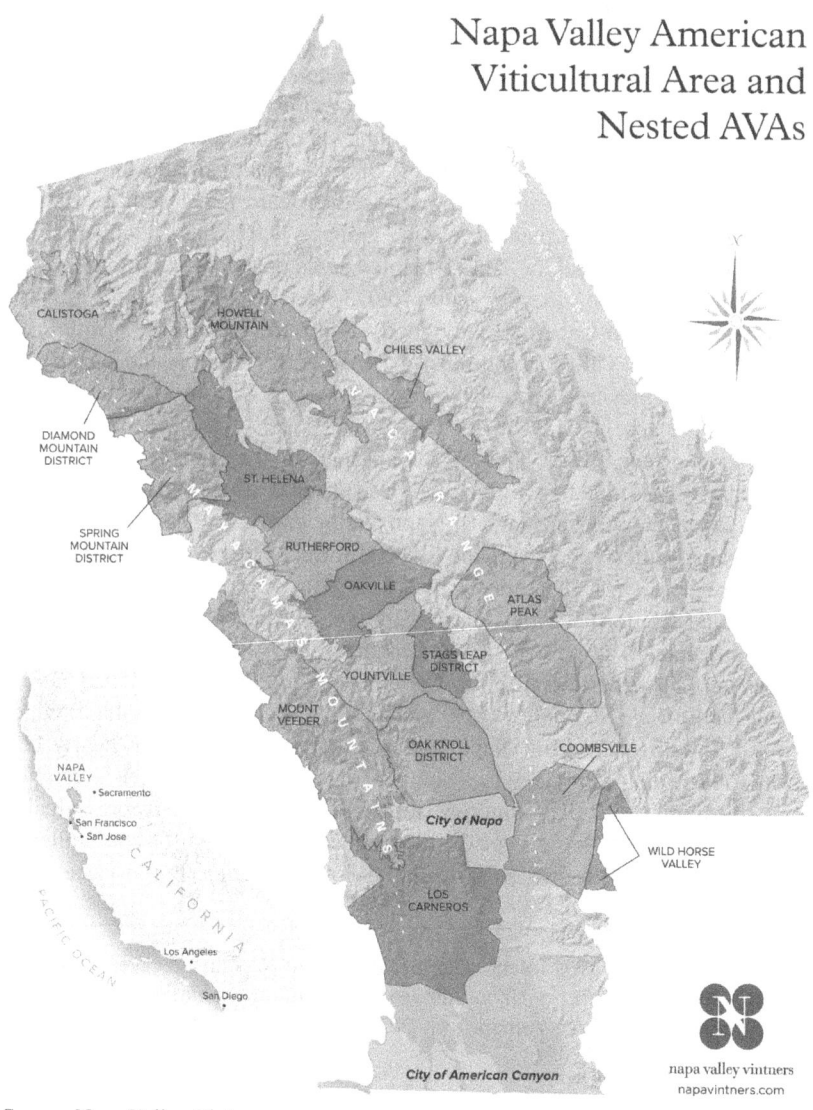

Napa Valley American Viticultural Area and Nested AVAs

Source: Napa Valley Vintners

Figure 3.1   Map of Napa Valley American Viticultural Area and Nested AVAs

While Napa Valley's reputation is big, the place itself is rather small, both in terms of planted hectares and total wine production. From the City of Napa in the southern end of the valley to the town of Calistoga in the north, the Napa Valley is approximately 30 miles (48 kilometers) long and ranges between 1–5 miles wide (1.6 and 8 kilometers) with a slight bend to the west at the northern end. Each side of the valley is framed by a mountain range: the Mayacamas Mountains on the west and the Vaca Mountains on the east. Within this area there are 19,073 hectares (47,131 acres) of vineyards planted. Many people, even residents of Napa Valley, are surprised to learn that less than 10% of the land in the county is planted to wine grapes (19,073 hectares planted out of 196,300 hectares total, or 47,131 planted acres out of 485,000 total acres). More than half of the vineyard land (10,023 hectares/24,767 acres) in Napa Valley is planted to Cabernet Sauvignon.[7] Vineyard land in the prime locations of the Napa Valley is the most expensive agricultural land in the US. As of 2021, a vineyard in the Napa Valley may cost $1.2 million per hectare ($500,000 per acre).[8] Only 4% of California's total wine production comes from grapes grown in the Napa Valley, but that small amount accounts for an astounding 30% of the total value of all California wines produced.[9]

Not only is the vineyard land in Napa Valley expensive, but the wines can be too. Napa Valley wines were the first California wines to cross the $100 per bottle threshold (1987 Diamond Creek Lake Vineyard Cabernet Sauvignon) and the first California wines to cross the $1,000 per bottle threshold (2014 Screaming Eagle). Cabernet Sauvignons from the Napa Valley are far more expensive than generic California Cabernets. According to the *2023 Direct to Consumer Wine Shipping Report* prepared by Sovos ShipCompliant, wines shipped to consumers from Napa Valley wineries accounted for nearly half of the total value of all US wines shipped. The value of Cabernet Sauvignon shipped from Napa Valley wineries was more than three times more valuable on a cost per bottle basis than California wines in general (Napa Valley = $82.39 average bottle price; California = $25.11 average bottle price).[10] A

---

[7] Napa County Department of Agriculture and Weights & Measurements, *Napa County Agricultural Crop Report* (Agricultural Commissioner's Office 2023) <http://www.countyofnapa.org/258/Crop-Reports> accessed 9 October 2024.

[8] MacNeil (n. 1) 505.

[9] Stonebridge Research Group, *The Economic Impact of Napa County's Wine and Grapes, 2016* (Napa Valley Vintners 2017) <https://napavintners.com/community/docs/Economic_Impact_Report_2017.pdf> accessed 9 October 2024.

[10] *2023 Direct to Consumer Wine Shipping Report* (Sovos ShipCompliant 2023) <https://sovos.com/shipcompliant/wp-content/uploads/sites/9/2023/01/2023-Direct-to-Consumer-Wine-Shipping-Report.pdf> accessed 9 October 2024.

2010 paper published by the Organization for an International Geographical Indications Network (oriGIn) pointed out that wines from Napa Valley are 61% more expensive than similar wines with a California appellation.[11]

Be it the value of the land, the grapes or the wine, Napa Valley leads the way in the US wine market. However, being recognized for top quality presented a new challenge to Napa Valley and the NVV: attempts by some to capitalize on the renown of the Napa Valley name in the wine world, without meeting the US federal grape sourcing requirements to legally do so.

PROTECTING BRAND NAPA VALLEY

The NVV has long been concerned with protecting the integrity of the Napa Valley name. The first clear evidence of that occurred in 1990 when, due to the establishment of nested AVAs within the Napa Valley, and concern that, in the competition for distinctiveness, the Napa Valley may lose status, the NVV sponsored a bill in the California Legislature which states:[12]

> (a) Any wine labeled with a viticultural area appellation of origin established pursuant to Part 9 (commencing with Section 9.1) of Title 27 of the Code of Federal Regulations, other than the viticultural area 'Napa Valley,' and which is located entirely within a county of the 29th class, shall bear the designation 'Napa Valley' on the label in direct conjunction therewith in a type size not smaller than 1mm less than that of the viticultural area designation, provided neither designation is smaller than 2mm on containers of more than 187ml or smaller than 1mm on containers of 187ml or less. This requirement shall apply to all wines bottled on or after January 1, 1990.
> (b) The department may suspend or revoke the license of any person who violates this section.

This law, known as the Napa Valley Conjunctive Labeling Law, has since been replicated by other California winegrowing regions.

A second California law sponsored by the NVV was passed by the state legislature in 2000, in response to a specific and significant threat to the integrity of the Napa Valley name. Bronco Wine Company, a large-scale wine producer in California's Central Valley, was making a large volume of wine under its

---

[11] Elizabeth Barham (ed), 'American Origin Products (AOPs): Protecting a Legacy' (oriGin 2010).

[12] California Legislative Information: Business and Professions Code – BPC – Division 9. Alcoholic Beverages [23000 – 25762] Chapter 13. Labels and Containers [25170 – 25248] Article 3. Wine [25235 – 25248] State of California, <https://leginfo.legislature.ca.gov/faces/codes_displayText.xhtml?lawCode=BPC&division=9.&title=&part=&chapter=13.&article=3> accessed 24 August 2023.

Napa Ridge brand. The problem with this, however, was that the grapes in Napa Ridge did not come from Napa; they came from Lodi, another growing region located more than 60 miles east of Napa Valley, in the much warmer Central Valley. In response to this, and to prevent future consumer confusion and erosion of the Napa Valley brand, the NVV sponsored the "Napa Name Law" (California Business & Professions Code 25241):[13]

> (a) (1) The Legislature finds and declares that for more than a century, Napa Valley and Napa County have been widely recognized for producing grapes and wine of the highest quality. Both consumers and the wine industry understand the name Napa County and the viticultural area appellations of origin contained within Napa County (collectively 'Napa appellations') as denoting that the wine was created with the distinctive grapes grown in Napa County.
> (2) The Legislature finds, however, that certain producers are using Napa appellations on labels, on packaging materials, and in advertising for wines that are not made from grapes grown in Napa County, and that consumers are confused and deceived by these practices.
> (3) The Legislature further finds that legislation is necessary to eliminate these misleading practices. It is the intent of the Legislature to assure consumers that the wines produced or sold in the state with brand names, packaging materials, or advertising referring to Napa appellations in fact qualify for the Napa County appellation of origin.
> (b) No wine produced, bottled, labeled, offered for sale or sold in California shall use, in a brand name or otherwise, on any label, packaging material, or advertising, any of the names of viticultural significance listed in subdivision (c), unless that wine qualifies under Section 4.25a of Title 27 of the Code of Federal Regulations for the appellation of origin Napa County and includes on the label, packaging material, and advertising that appellation or a viticultural area appellation of origin that is located entirely within Napa County, subject to compliance with Section 25240.

With the upmost intent of the legislative solution being to uphold truth in labeling, the bottom line of the Napa Name Law is: if it says "Napa" on the label, it must be Napa in the bottle. The Napa Name Law was challenged in court by Bronco Wine Company,[14] but, after more than five years in the California and US court system, the law was ultimately upheld.

As the Napa Name Law was tangled up in the courts, the publicity surrounding it attracted the attention of winemakers, as well as wine trade associations, elsewhere in the world who were also frustrated with lack of protections for their own winegrowing place names. This led to the Joint Declaration to Protect Wine Place & Origin, signed in 2005 in Napa by the leaders of European regions Champagne, Porto, Jerez and US wine regions including Oregon and Willamette Valley, Washington State, Walla Walla Valley and Napa Valley.

---

[13] California Legislative Information: Business and Professions Code (n 12).
[14] *Bronco v. Jolly*, 33 943, (Calif SC 2004) and 129 988, (Cal App 4th 2004).

The Declaration is a set of principles aimed at educating consumers and policymakers about the importance of location to winemaking. Subsequently renamed the Wine Origins Alliance,[15] the group has grown from its eight founding members to 33 wine regions spanning six continents and continues to focus its efforts on the protection of all winegrowing place names, as well as eliminating tariffs on wine so that these global competitors can compete on an even playing field. The Wine Origins Alliance has also commissioned studies on US wine consumers' perspectives on truth in labeling. The most recent study, done by GBA Strategies in 2018, showed that an overwhelming 94% of American wine drinkers would support laws that protect consumers from misleading labels, underscoring the importance that place plays in wine.[16]

Fans of American football know that football coaches often say it is important to execute in all three phases of the game to win: offense, defense and special teams. The NVV employs all three strategies to protect the integrity of the Napa Valley name, with the leadership and involvement in Wine Origins Alliance being the "special teams".

The NVV's outside counsel of Dickenson, Peatman & Fogarty monitors trademark applications worldwide. If "Napa", "Napa Valley", or any of its nested AVAs improperly appears in trademark applications for alcohol beverage products, the firm will take action as directed by the NVV.

Additionally, in 2015, the NVV obtained a Certification Mark for Napa Valley from the US Patent and Trademark Office (USPTO), making Napa Valley the first wine region in the US to gain this level of protection for its name. It was not an easy achievement for the association to get the Certification Mark, as vintner volunteers from the board-appointed Napa Name Protection Committee, NVV staff and counsel had to reach out to every existing trademark owner in the US with "Napa" or "Napa Valley" included in the mark for alcohol beverage products and get their consent in writing to NVV's objective to obtain the Certification Mark. The outreach effort took more than a year, but what the association learned was that when the existing trademark owner understood this effort was to further protect the integrity of the Napa name, which in turn also further protected their own Napa mark, they quickly consented. Now, when a business or individual applies for a US trade-

---

[15] 'When it Comes to Wine, Location Matters' (Wine Origins Alliance) <http://www.origins.wine>.

[16] 'New Poll Shows Broad Support for Laws to Protect Against Misleading Wine Labels' (Wine Origins Alliance 5 March 2018) <http://www.origins.wine/post/new-poll-shows-broad-support-for-laws-to-protect-against-misleading-wine-labels> accessed 9 October 2024.

mark for alcohol beverage that includes "Napa" or "Napa Valley", the USPTO directs them to the NVV to get a consent agreement in advance.

Other proactive measures to protect the Napa name undertaken by the NVV have centered around international efforts to secure geographic indication or certification mark protections from foreign governments. In 2007 NVV obtained geographic indication protection for Napa Valley wines in the European Union (EU), making Napa the first wine region outside of the EU to receive that level of protection. In 2012, after years of work and multiple trips to Beijing, including a hearing before a technical panel, NVV was awarded geographic indication status in China, ahead of every other wine region in the world. Since 2007, the NVV has successfully obtained protection for the Napa name, via geographic indication or certification mark, in 17 countries plus the EU. Among the countries that now protect the Napa name are Brazil, Russia, India, and China.

WHY IT MATTERS

Napa Valley is small, both geographically and in terms of total wine production, yet it has a significant economic impact in Napa County ($9.4 billion per year), the State of California ($17.3 billion per year) and in the US ($33.5 billion per year).[17] Notwithstanding those powerful economic figures, it remains an agricultural product of its place – Napa Valley. Ultimately it comes down to farming. The grapevines are grown in the valley's diverse soil types and in its Mediterranean climate, tended to by hand by hard-working farmworkers. The grapes are harvested at just the right time and cellar crews turn those grapes into wine – vinted, bottled and sold in the marketplace, year in and year out, since George Yount planted the first wine grapes in Napa Valley in 1839.

In 1944 a group of Napa Valley vintners were brought together by a common belief that, by working together, they could move the local wine industry forward. That common belief rings louder and truer today. Today the 540 members of the NVV, 95% of which are family-owned businesses and 80% of which are small – producing less than 10,000 cases of wine per year – focus on preserving Napa Valley as a viticultural and oenological treasure; producing the highest quality wines; and marketing them in the national and international marketplace, while advocating on issues of interest, especially the integrity of the Napa Valley name. With wine being the ultimate product of place, winegrowing place names are critically important to regional producers, as those names carry with them reputations associated with quality.

---

[17] Stonebridge (n. 9).

Winegrowing place names become sort of a collective brand or intellectual property of the region, and the integrity of that brand must be protected from misuse. If the winegrowing place name is not protected, it allows for brand erosion and consumer confusion.

4. Place-Branding in the Coffee Culture of Colonial Kenya: Tracing the Provenance of a Reputation for Quality

Philip Magowan

INTRODUCTION

For many coffee-producing regions place-branding has historically proven a potent and economically deterministic tool. While certain producing countries have been affiliated with high-quantity, low-quality production – *both intentionally and inadvertently* – such as Brazil or Vietnam, other coffee origins are synonymous with a high-quality cup: Ethiopia, Colombia, and Kenya.[1] And while it was only in 2015 that Kenya's Coffee Directorate unveiled the new 'Coffee Kenya' mark of origin – complete with the sensual *'so rich, so Kenyan'* tagline – Kenya's global reputation for distinctive, premium quality coffee traces back to its inaugural coffee harvests which took place under British settlers in the late-nineteenth century. In these circumstances, how did the global market come to hold Kenyan coffee in such high regard?

This chapter demonstrates how, during the colonial period (c. 1893–1963), Kenyan coffee was marketed as being of high quality both because of its inherent physical – or *material* – qualities, and also because of its *symbolic* value as a British Imperial product produced by British settlers. This chapter explores how these ideas constituted a form of 'place-branding' – emphasizing the human role in terroir – and moreover raises questions about current efforts in place-branding by the Kenyan Government.

---

[1] For other studies on the potency of place-branding in coffee, see: Julia Smith, 'Coffee Landscapes: Specialty Coffee, Terroir, and Traceability in Costa Rica' (2018) 40(1) Culture, Agriculture, Food and Environment 36; Milda Rosenberg, 'Transforming Burundian "taste of place": From shunned in commercial blends to specialty coffee' (2023) 77(4) Norwegian Journal of Geography 255.

SETTING THE STAGE FOR QUALITY

The early construction of quality in Kenya's coffee industry was multifaceted and complex. Under British colonial rule (1895–1963) several stars aligned to propagate the inception of the quality-driven coffee industry that flourishes today, namely: environmental and agricultural factors impacting the material quality of the product (often summarized under 'terroir'), access to the British Empire's marketing machine, the existence of a quality-discerning market who *perceived* Kenyan coffee to be of the premium value that it was marketed as, and finally, a collective of producers who saw opportunity in quality-driven production. Here, we examine the constellation of factors that nurtured Kenya's embryonic, quality-oriented coffee culture.

Before producers and other commodity-chain actors can reap the marketing benefits of quality products, the product must possess *material*, high-quality attributes to be marketed as such. As Topik notes, 'no mechanical tests of coffee's essence could be conducted as with sugar (sweetness), metals (assay), or cotton (fiber strength)'.[2] Instead of objective, mechanized grading – coffee is instead subject to classification using human sensory facilities to assess aroma (olfactory), taste and appearance. It is through these procedures that Kenya's wet-processed arabica coffees have consistently ranked among the most valued on the global market.[3]

The distinct and iconic flavors that we prize Kenyan coffee for today quickly secured a place in quality-discerning markets.[4] The Coffee Board of colonial Kenya promoted the 'blackcurrant flavours of upper Kiambu' long before we would describe the same sensorial experiences in street-corner, hipster cafes.[5] These flavors are somewhat owed to the growing conditions in Kenya's coffee regions – volcanic soils, high altitudes, sufficient rainfall and an equatorial climate – which proved auspicious for arabica cultivation and wet processing.[6] However, without appropriate marketing mechanisms

---

[2] Steven Topik, 'The Integration of the World Coffee Market', in William Gervase Clarence-Smith and Steven Topik (eds), *The Global Coffee Economy in Africa, Asia and Latin America, 1500-1989* (CUP 2003) 24.

[3] Today, wet and dry processes are referred to as 'washed' and 'natural' respectively.

[4] On unique, location-derived flavours creating value, see: Edward F Fischer, *Making Better Coffee: How Maya Farmers and Third Wave Tastemakers Create Value* (University of California Press 2022).

[5] *Monthly Bulletin* (Coffee Board of Kenya May 1947) 57.

[6] During the colonial period there were a few, short-lived robusta-growing experiments in Kenya (1927, 1932–33, and in Meru and Kavirondo in 1936 and 1934 respectively), see: Mervin F Hill, *Planters' Progress: The Story of Coffee*

– or symbolic-value creation – to support such an endeavor by finding niche, quality-discerning markets, then the above exists without any material gains or market functionality. Now, we will observe how Kenyan coffee debuted on the British consumer market.

BRITISH EMPIRE AND KENYA COFFEE

Although Kenya borders Ethiopia – the historical origin of arabica coffee cultivation – in 1893, European missionaries were the first to plant coffee in Kenyan soil.[7] Concurrently, throughout the 1890s, British political aspirations led to the government's commission of the Ugandan railway. The railway was completed by 1902, traversing Kenya from the coastline at Mombasa to Lake Victoria in Uganda. However, initial surveys did not find the region to be mineral rich, and vexed British politicians aroused popular frustration about how the £11 million 'lunatic railway' would be made to pay.[8]

From 1903, Kenya's inchoate administration encouraged European settlement, hoping that trials with potential commodity exports would present solutions to repaying the railway. Initial prospects with coffee cultivation seemed promising, and much to the British Government's relief, a rapidly increasing number of coffee-filled hessian sacks became the anxiously anticipated cargo of freight carriages travelling along the railway for export. Booming prices – rising from £27.76 per ton in 1909 to £73.79 per ton in 1920 – solidified coffee cultivation as an attractive enterprise to incoming settlers.[9]

To entice quality-discerning buyers, settlers marketed their coffee comparably to the 'single origin' coffee of today. Each producer stencilled their coffee sacks with 'estate marks' denoting producer, farm, and region.[10] These marks ensured buyers of a 'consistent standard' and specific, nuanced tastes resulting from a particular farm's climate and cultivation methods. This contrasted with the practice of quantity-oriented producers in 'bulking' coffee from larger

---

in Kenya (Coffee Board of Kenya 1956) 74. And Anne Thurston, *Smallholder Agriculture in Colonial Kenya: The Official Mind and the Swynnerton Plan* (Cambridge African Monographs 1987) 12. And, on Meru and South Kavirondo: Irvine D Talbott, 'Agricultural innovation and policy changes in Kenya in the 1930s' (PhD Thesis, West Virginia University, 1976) 237–40.

[7] John A Kieran, 'The Origin of Commercial Arabica Coffee Production in East Africa'(1969) 2(1) African Historical Studies 51–67.

[8] Maurice Peter Keith Sorrenson, *Origins of European Settlement in Kenya* (Oxford University Press 1968) 27–8.

[9] Data extracted from: Hill (n. 6) 203.

[10] F H Sprott, *Practical Coffee Planting* (The Caxton (BEA) Printing & Publishing 1922) 84.

regions. Haarer noted 'bulking coffee... tends to lower quality as a whole. It is uneven in characteristics... and destroys the initiative of those who strive to obtain a name for a special mark.'[11]

Kenya's distinctive and consistent standard of coffee quality also helped it to establish a reputation in more discriminating markets, where premiums were paid for favored growths. In global terms, Kenya was a small producer, though securing niche markets through unique, qualitative traits meant that consumer demand was maintained despite global trade variations.[12]

For Britain, obtaining a new colony able to produce *'Colombian Mild'* coffee was a relief. In the 1890s, the collapse of Sri Lanka's (formerly 'Ceylon') coffee industry – which had previously supplied over a quarter of Britain's coffee – ripped open a supply void in British consumption. Stuart McCook has recently shown that Britain did not reduce its coffee consumption but instead adapted by diversifying where it purchased coffee.[13] Much of the market was initially claimed by Costa Rica, another quality-oriented producer which 'in spite of the heavier duty it carries [as a non-British territory]... had obtained foremost positions on the London market on account of its pure liqouring qualities.'[14] The British Government were therefore adamant on sourcing a new coffee supplier from within its own Imperial borders.

Kenya's Senior Coffee Officer, Le Poer Trench, reported on Costa Rica's cultivation techniques in 1936, stating, 'it is of paramount importance for the coffee planter to produce marketable coffee...such coffee must have "quality" to compete with mild coffees from other countries.'[15] Similarly, the Coffee Board of Kenya, emphasized the need to 'displace competing coffees which have no publicity agreements'.[16] The Board's marketing memorandum proudly demonstrated how Britain's consumption of Kenyan coffee increased from 104,113 cwts. in 1935 to 122,211 cwts. in 1939, while Costa Rican coffee decreased from 121,874 cwts. to 114,167 cwts.[17]

---

[11] Today, 'bulking' is referred to as blending. See: Alec Ernest Haarer, *Modern Coffee Production* (3rd edn, Leonard Hill 1958) 267.

[12] For instance, see: Isac F Moreithi, 'The Kenyan Coffee Industry and its International Background' (Masters Thesis, McGill University 1963) 66.

[13] Stuart McCook, *Coffee is Not Forever* (Ohio University Press 2019) 36–65.

[14] K S Watt,'African Coffee'(1937) 36(143) Journal of the Royal African Society 196–8.

[15] A D Le Poer Trench, 'Notes on Conditions Influencing Quality in Coffee' (1936) 1 East African Agricultural Journal 281.

[16] The National Archives, CO 852/193/5: R Wollen, 'The Coffee Board of Kenya: Memorandum No. 475: A Request to Government for Financial Assistance Towards the Publicity Work of the Coffee Board of Kenya' (9 June 1939) 14.

[17] Ibid.

Therefore, the British market not only recognized value in the quality of Kenyan coffee, but moreover in the opportunities to kickstart settler industry in Kenya, repay the railway, and consolidate the colony's economic self-sufficiency. Further, Kenyan coffee's quality advanced domestic Imperial buying strategies by addressing the market void left by the decimation of Ceylon's coffee culture. On the back of these Imperial ambitions, the quality brand for Kenyan coffee was constructed.

IF 'THE EMPIRE IS YOUR GARDEN', THEN KENYA IS YOUR COFFEE TREE

Upon observing the first-harvest benefits of Kenya's blossoming coffee culture, the British Government hastily embedded the industry within the robust Empire marketing machine which campaigned to promote the importance of purchasing Imperial goods. The Coffee Board of Kenya and the Empire Marketing Board took up the task of advertising Kenyan coffee to the British public. Similar to the advertising poise of the specialty coffee industry of today, the Board focused on assuring prospective consumers that the price was not exorbitant but was rather a reflection of quality.[18]

Public knowledge of Kenyan coffee was bolstered through the 'Snowball' scheme, which sought to charm and educate consumers with a 'personal touch'. Planters provided a list of their British contacts, each of whom were then sent a sample of coffee and a booklet: 'Kenya coffee and how to brew it'.[19] The Coffee Board then asked these recipients to provide lists of their own contacts, and hoped that they would in turn supply further contacts. Less than one year after scheme's implementation, the list carried 11,000 names.[20] This system provided an immense means for information dissemination. Bull, the Board's London representative, wrote that, 'The scheme... creates a "peaceful penetration" of the name of Kenya Coffee into the minds of thousands of consumers.'[21]

The global, nebulous nature of the British Empire facilitated unprecedented platforms for marketing, dissemination of knowledge and advertising. British governmental agencies also readily promoted the colonies and their produce. Empire exhibitions featured East-African pavilions where the central features

---

[18] *Monthly Bulletin* (The Coffee Board of Kenya July 1936) 134.
[19] H C H Bull, 'Sales Propaganda in the United Kingdom', in *Monthly Bulletin* (The Coffee Board of Kenya April 1936) 60.
[20] Ibid., 66.
[21] Ibid., 67.

of cafes distributed cups of Kenyan coffee to spectators.[22] At the center of these campaigns were the British settlers, who were motific in the Empire's marketing strategies. Their unique, estate marks were championed by the Board, which confiscated a great deal of settlers' profits to ensure consistent buyers in the British market.[23]

QUALITY AND EXCLUSION: PAST AND PRESENT

While we have explored how Kenya's quality brand financially benefited producers and the British Empire from a marketing perspective, we should also consider how particular constructions of quality can manipulate supply chains in favor of certain actors. With coffee, it has often been the case that those who decide the formation of quality are those who benefit from the most material gains of that very formation.[24]

Until 1935, European settlers' estates were the sole venues of Kenya's coffee agriculture, and before 1950 the colonial administration greatly restricted the number of African cultivators to trial environments. Elsewhere, I have demonstrated how throughout the colonial period settlers harnessed coffee quality as a political tool to exclude African producers from coffee production, thereby sustaining a monopoly over coffee production.[25]

Originally, this monopoly had existed unchallenged, but eventually in the 1920s, post-war humanitarian discontent with European settlers' power rippled across Britain's Empire.[26] Kenya's coffee production was a conspicuous target for such concerns, and British parliamentarians fervently debated the 'Native Coffee Growing Question.' While the Kenyan administration could not promote the preservation of settlers' labor supplies as reason to restrict African coffee growing, the *preservation of the quality of Kenya's*

---

[22] For example, the Summer 1936 Edinburgh Exhibition, see: *Monthly Bulletin* (The Coffee Board of Kenya April 1936) 60. And, Jonathan Woodham, 'Images of Africa and Design at the British Empire Exhibitions between the Wars' (1989) 2(1) Journal of Design History 15.

[23] Masao Yoshida, *Agricultural Marketing Intervention in East Africa: A Study in the Colonial Origins of Marketing Policies, 1900-1965* (Sole agent Maruzen Co 1984) 54–75.

[24] Fischer (n. 4).

[25] Philip Magowan, 'African Exclusion in the Quality-Oriented Coffee Industry of Colonial Kenya (c. 1893-1950)' (MPhil Dissertation, University of Cambridge, 2021).

[26] Sana Aiyar, 'Empire, Race and the Indians in Colonial Kenya's Contested Public Political Sphere, 1919-1923' (2011) 81(1) Africa: Journal of the International African Institute 132.

primary agricultural export was instead the rhetoric employed to stifle the diffusion of coffee production to Africans. Indeed, at the 1932 Coffee Planters' Conference in Nairobi, attendees including 200 coffee growers unanimously passed a resolution on 'Coffee Growing by the Natives' urging the 'indefinite postponement of a step so utterly unwise'.[27] Their grounds for postponement of the step so utterly unwise? Preserving *quality*.

Settlers contested that the high-value arabica plant was fragile, 'susceptible to diseases and pests, and for this and other reasons… it is unsuitable for native cultivation unless under skilled European supervision'.[28] Upon being asked why it was 'illegal' for Africans to grow coffee, Ormsby-Gore responded, 'It is illegal…except under special conditions, because in Ceylon this particular coffee grown in Kenya was wiped out by disease in one year'.[29] Settlers and their sympathizers took advantage of the prevailing popular understanding of the severity of coffee diseases affected by the collapse of Ceylon's industry. In actuality, Coffee Leaf Rust's effects in Kenya had been minimal, and further, the Department of Agriculture was encouraging settlers to continue cultivating without any remedy; with coffee officer Le Poer Trench stating elsewhere that '[CLR], would never be a serious menace to the coffee of East Africa'.[30]

Moreover, while settlers sold their large, estate coffee crops in small consignments, which were graded by liquorers (tasters) and sold with the name of the estate stamped on each bag.[31] The settlers expressed concern that the 'marketing of native coffee' cultivated 'haphazardly' on much smaller acreages risked 'injuring the good reputation possessed by Kenyan coffee'.[32]

In a recent article scrutinizing European agriculture in African colonies, the author concluded that 'the long-term success of settler agriculture required *sustained* political support'.[33] In Kenya, the settlers' rhetoric of quality played a pivotal role in maintaining administrative support for the settler coffee industry. Through manipulating the popular understanding of *what constitutes*

---

[27] Department of Agriculture, *Coffee Conference 1932* (Nairobi, 1932) 26.

[28] Department of Agriculture, *Coffee Conference 1927* (Nairobi, June 1927) 28.

[29] Palestine And East Africa Loans (Guarantee) Bill HC (1926-7) [200] Col 2043.

[30] Hill (n. 6) 32–3.

[31] The National Archives Kew CO 852/67/6 'Liquoring Service' in *The Coffee Board of Kenya: Annual Report 1936-37* (The Coffee Board of Kenya 1937) 22.

[32] Department of Agriculture, *Coffee Conference 1932* (Nairobi, June–July 1932) 28.

[33] Ewout Frankema, Erik Green and Ellen Hillbom, 'Endogenous Processes of Colonial Settlement. The Success and Failure of European Settler Farming in Sub-Saharan Africa' (2016) 34(2) Revista de Historia Económica 237, 260–1.

quality and *where quality is created*, settlers were able to skew the value chain, and in turn generate political support for their industry. The British settlers claimed expertise was therefore used as a place-branding tool to market Kenyan coffee's quality. The settlers and their supporters on the Marketing Boards and in government harnessed these claims to fund and preserve settler-monopolized coffee culture.[34]

How concepts of quality were employed by British settlers as a means of fabricating exclusionary measures for African producers bears some striking similarities to the specialty coffee landscape of today. While place-branding offers producers from specific regions the opportunity to market distinctive, geographic advantages. On the contrary, recent trends in specialty coffee attribute less value to location-derived traits, and instead place more value on new flavors achieved through emerging processing and fermentation techniques.[35] Novel processing techniques typically manipulate flavor to produce coffee taste profiles that are much less a result of unique environmental and agricultural conditions (terroir), and instead could be used by producers in different geographical settings to achieve *homogenized* flavor profiles.[36] That is to say, often these processing methods could be applied to coffee beans *from any location* to achieve very similar results.[37]

With these emerging processing methods in mind, it is important to flag two threats to place-branding when considering the future landscape of the quality-oriented coffee industry. First, these processing methods have the potential to render terroir and geographical indicators obsolete (at least in terms of *material* value creation). And second, they often tip the scales in favor of production methods that are often accessible to only the wealthiest of producers possessing the capital to invest in new laboratories, bioreactors, and whatever equipment the latest processing methods demand.[38] Ironically and unfortunately, these steps to achieve quality can often defeat the very purpose with which specialty coffee set out in the first place. That is, instead of paying the historically exploited coffee producer a 'fairer' price, we instead end up

---

[34] Magowan (n. 25).

[35] Processing denotes the method by which the coffee seed is removed from its surrounding fruit.

[36] For a glossary of emerging processing methods, see: Christopher Feran, 'A sort of glossary of coffee processes' (*Christopher Feran Blog*, 22 August 2022) <https://christopherferan.com/2022/08/19/a-sort-of-glossary-of-coffee-processes/> accessed 13 October 2024.

[37] Lucia Solis, 'Tasting Authenticity - When Different Countries Have Similar Flavor Profiles' (*Making Coffee With Lucia Solis*, 28 July 2020) <https://www.buzzsprout.com/604165/episodes/4732664> accessed 9 October 2024.

[38] Ibid.

paying the wealthiest while the former are faced with an insurmountable barrier to market entry.[39]

The market demand for new processing methods is a stark reminder that even with efforts to protect and control coffee quality tied to location such as place-branding, it is the consumer and those supply-chain actors closest to the consumer who decide which products equate to quality. The 'blackcurrants of Kiambu' and the traditional Kenya coffee profile are only rewarded by the market for as long as the market considers these to be the most prized flavor profile. In this sense, place-branding can only offer limited protection to coffee producers exposed to the vagaries of the fluctuating and unpredictable quality discerning market.

In many ways, the notion of quality is a concept untethered to the moral concepts of exclusion or equality. If what we taste in the cup is scored objectively, then why should we care which producer gets paid? With that said, it is important that we recognize the power and influences behind quality-driven marketing and branding. Concepts such as place-branding and the new buzzword terms for the latest processing methods (anaerobic, carbonic maceration, and so on) can easily shape consumers' understanding of quality with total disregard for other supply-chain actors impacted by such a shift. Therefore, when promoting these concepts, we should ascertain some awareness of the symbolic value creation that takes, and moreover aim to understand *whom* and *what* exactly we are rewarding.

---

[39] Exemplar Quarterly, 'Processing: the weird, the wild, the wonderful' (2023) 1(2) *Exemplar Coffee* (Belfast, Autumn/Winter 2023).

5. Scotch Whisky: Provenance, Authenticity, and Ownership[1]

Julie Bower and David M. Higgins

INTRODUCTION

The aim of this chapter is to explain how the Scotch Whisky industry and its major brands have retained the integrity of the marque, with its inherent place-based heritage, through the transition from cottage to industrial-scale production and distribution. The significance of 'place' and 'image' is important to many industries for which authenticity is a key part of the marketing image and identity.[2] The alcoholic beverages industry is characterized by such attributes, and Scotch Whisky is a significant international category within this industry.

To contextualize our analysis, we anchor our study in theories of resource partitioning and legitimacy emanating from organization and strategic management scholarship. Resource partitioning seeks to explain how new categories emerge at the periphery of a consolidated and commoditized category to

---

[1] Throughout this chapter, Scotch Whisky is spelled without an 'e'. This practice follows official convention, such as The Scotch Whisky Order 1990 (SI 1990/998); The Scotch Whisky Regulations 2009 (SI 2009/2890), and Regulation (EC) No 110/2008 of the European Parliament and of the Council of 15 January 2008 on the definition, description, presentation, labelling and the protection of geographical indications of spirit drinks and repealing Council Regulation (EEC) No 1576/89 [2008] OJ L39/16. The exceptions are when 'whiskey' appears in quotations, and when official reports are cited.

[2] The literature on this topic is extensive. See, for example, Bertil Sylvander, Dominique Barjolle, and Filippo Arfini (eds), *The Socioeconomics of Origin-Labelled Products in Agri-Food Supply Chains: Spatial, Institutional and Co-ordination Aspects* (vols 1 and 2, European Association of Agricultural Economists 2000); David M. Higgins, *Brands, Geographical Origin, and the Global Economy* (Cambridge University Press 2018).

establish authenticity, or as a process of revival of traditional arrangements.[3] As applied to Scotch Whisky, prior research has sought to illuminate if, and to what extent, substantial foreign ownership of this industry has impacted consumer perceptions of what is authentic Scotch Whisky.[4]

Our chapter offers a historical narrative centered on the evolution of the leading brand portfolios owned by Diageo, Pernod Ricard, and their major privately-owned competitors such as Edrington, and William Grant. The source material is a rich archive spanning the extensive proceedings leading to the findings of the 1909 Royal Commission, debates reported in *Hansard*, reports of the Monopolies and Mergers Commission, and additional firm-specific information that is available in the public domain or from the authors on request. It is important to note that access to the records of both Distillers Company Limited (DCL) and the Scotch Whisky Association (SWA) are now embargoed, therefore, where necessary, we refer to the prior analysis of other scholars. While not overtly 'legal' in the sense of relying on litigation and/or European Union (EU) regulations, these sources are outlined where appropriate.

This chapter proceeds as follows. In the next section we provide a historical perspective on the failure to establish a rigorous and comprehensive definition of Scotch Whisky, and why, therefore, there was uncertainty about the extent to which this appellation could be used legitimately to signal authenticity. We then provide a brief overview of the legal difficulties that confronted the SWA as it sought to legitimize Scotch Whisky. Drawing on the insights provided by resource partitioning theory, we then discuss how the bifurcated structure of the Scotch Whisky industry exacerbated the problem of conveying authenticity. In the penultimate section, we explain how the prospect of foreign ownership of a substantial part of the industry revitalized the political campaign to protect 'Scotch' whisky, which culminated in the Scotch Whisky Act 1988. We then present our conclusions.

---

[3] Glenn Carroll, 'Concentration and Specialization: Dynamics of Niche Width in Populations of Organizations' (1985) 90(6) American Journal of Sociology 1262; Glenn Carroll and Anand Swaminathan, 'Why the Microbrewery Movement? Organizational Dynamics of Resource Partitioning in the American Brewing Industry After Prohibition' (2000) 106(3) American Journal of Sociology 715; Jochem J Kroezen and Pursey P M A R Heugens, 'What is Dead May Never Die: Institutional Regeneration Through Logic Reemergence in Dutch Beer Brewing' (2019) 64(4) Administrative Science Quarterly 976.

[4] David G McKendrick and Michael T Hannan, 'Oppositional Identities and Resource Partitioning: Distillery Ownership in Scotch Whisky, 1826-2009' (2014) 25(4) Organization Science 1272.

HISTORICAL CONTEXT

As research on wine appellation history has shown, attempting to define an authentic product in an authoritative manner involves the need to generate consensus around the product specifications (and often evidence of its opposite), the streamlining of multiple overlapping practices to conform to a single specification, the occasional invention of traditions, the editing out of certain producer groupings and their interests – and in the case of certification trade marks – tensions between the sign as conceived by the registered proprietor and its actual use by the trade or semantic reception by the consuming public.[5] Does the appellation have any specific meaning and what message does it convey over time? There is also the constant market pressure for innovation and change to satisfy fluctuations in demand, which has to be reconciled with the need to conform to registered specifications. Finally, while a paradigm appellation product such as wine has relatively stronger and empirically verifiable geographical links to a defined region of production, what is the algorithm for determining the nature of the linkages and geographical region of production for Scotch Whisky?

One issue that needs to be addressed at the outset is that it is not easy to delineate the attributes of 'Scottishness' and 'heritage'. As one scholar noted, 'invented' traditions are, 'largely factitious'.[6] As far as Scotland is concerned, it has been suggested that, 'the whole concept of a distinct Highland culture and tradition is a retrospective invention'.[7] Moreover, the 'romanticized' imagery associated with Scotland – glens, lochs and stunning mountain ranges – contrasts with the reality of urban deprivation, slums, and the harsh living conditions in pit villages and steel towns.[8] A further issue is that consumer perceptions of Scotch Whisky could be communicated without using the

---

[5] See, especially, Dev Gangjee, *Relocating the Law of Geographical Indications* (Cambridge University Press 2012); Kolleen M Guy, *When Champagne Became French: Wine and the Making of a National Identity* (Johns Hopkins University Press 2003); Alessandro Stanziani, 'Wine Reputation and Quality Controls: The Origin of the AOCs in 19th Century France' (2004) 18 European Journal of Law and Economics 149.

[6] Eric Hobsbawm, 'The Invention of Tradition' in Eric Hobsbawm and Terence Ranger (eds), *The Invention of Tradition* (Cambridge University Press 1983) 2.

[7] Hugh Trevor Roper, 'The Invention of Tradition: The Highland Tradition of Scotland' in Eric Hobsbawm, and Terence Ranger (eds), *The Invention of Tradition* (Cambridge University Press 1983), 15.

[8] Andrew Blaikie, 'Imagining the Face of a Nation: Scotland, Modernity and the Places of Memory' (2011) 4(4) Memory Studies 416, 427.

term, 'Scotch', for example, saltires, tartan, and thistles. Use of such indicia on non-genuine Scotch Whisky simultaneously debased these images of Scottishness and made them unreliable indicators of provenance when applied to products that were genuinely Scottish.[9]

The earliest official investigation concerned solely with determining the precise meanings of whisky and Scotch Whisky was a Royal Commission established in 1908.[10] The catalyst for this Commission were the 'Islington cases' of 1905, in which one of the defendants was charged under the Sale of Food and Drugs Act 1875, for selling an alcoholic beverage which was, 'not of the nature, substance, or quality' of Scotch Whisky. In finding for the applicants, the magistrate held that, by itself, patent still spirit (that is, grain whisky) was not whisky. Consequently, it could not be 'Scotch Whisky' even though it was made in Scotland, and that 'Scotch Whisky' was a spirit which was made entirely from malt.[11]

This decision provoked consternation in the whisky industry and representatives of the major grain distillers, malt distillers, and blenders' associations, met in Glasgow to petition that a Royal Commission be established to determine whether application of the term 'whiskey' should be restricted solely to spirit made in pot stills; was it permissible to apply the term 'whiskey' to spirit made entirely in patent stills, or when mixed with pot still spirit, and what restrictions should be imposed on the constituents of whisky. Scotch Whisky and Irish Whiskey are often distinguished in spelling. According to the SWA, American whiskey is usually spelt with an 'e', while English, Welsh, Japanese and most other world whiskies are not. Historically, however, Scotch Whisky has been spelt in official documents with an 'e', including in the Royal Commission 1909, as discussed below, although more recently this is not the case.

Nonetheless, there remained a lack of consensus about the precise definition of 'whisk(e)y' and 'Scotch Whisky'. The senior partner of Robert Brown &

---

[9] *Lang Brothers Ltd v Goldwell Ltd* 1980 SC 237.

[10] Royal Commission on Whiskey and other Potable Spirits, *Final Report of Royal Commission on Whiskey and other Potable Spirits* (BPP XLIX 451 1909) (*Royal Commission*). See also: 'Royal Commission on Whiskey and other Potable Spirits' (1909) 2(2537) The British Medical Journal 399. Select Committees were appointed in 1890 and 1891 to determine, inter alia, whether, on grounds of public health, specific categories of British and foreign spirits should be blended, and kept in bond for a definite period before being consumed. *Report from the Select Committee on British and Foreign Spirits*, (BPP 316 X849 1890), *Report from the Select Committee on British and Foreign Spirits* (BPP 210 XI351 1891).

[11] 'Whisky. The Islington Cases: Appeal to Sessions' [1906] British Food Journal 116.

Co stated that Scotch Whisky was any whisky manufactured in Scotland from cereals, irrespective of whether it was made using the pot or patent still method, or was a blend of both spirits. Alexander Cowie, proprietor of the Mortlach distillery, opined that Scotch Whisky was a spirit made in Scotland, containing a mixture of grain and malt in such proportions that the whisky would have the characteristics of pot still malt whisky. The North of Scotland Malt Distillers' Association, which Cowie represented, believed that 50% pot still and 50% patent still conformed to its definition of Scotch Whisky. Alexander Walker, the Managing Director of John Walker & Sons, was in agreement with Cowie because it was necessary to, 'protect the reputation of Scotch pot still whiskey, the prestige value of Scotch whiskey in foreign countries being an enormous asset of Scotland'.[12] Conversely, witnesses representing John Gillon & Co, Wright & Greig Co, and Ben Nevis Distilleries, stated that Scotch Whisky was *any* whisky manufactured in Scotland.[13] In view of these competing claims, the Commission concluded that Scotch Whisky was a spirit obtained from the distillation of cereals, saccharified by diastase of malt, and distilled in Scotland.[14]

This definition anchored the process of distillation to Scotland, and *only* in this sense was a clear relationship between product and place established. However, this definition was not legally binding. The failure to enact this recommendation until 1988 meant that during the intervening period:

> The practical difficulty in dealing with this (restrictions on labelling) matter is while there are cases of suspected mis-description, such cases can seldom be proved, owing to the absence at present of authoritative definitions of the different kinds of whiskey ... For instance, not only is there no legal definition of "Irish Whiskey" or "Scotch Whiskey," but hitherto expert opinion has been widely divided as to what the definition should be, and consequently the Revenue Authorities have no sanction of law or custom by reference to which they could prohibit the use of these descriptions on labels.[15]

Two themes are pertinent to the question: what is Scotch Whisky? The first is authenticity, which is crucial to the meanings that consumers attach to a brand. As applied to alcoholic beverages, claims to authenticity involve a connection to time and place which is important for consumers because it affirms

---

[12] *Index and Digests of Evidence Taken by the Royal Commission on Whiskey and Other Potable Spirits* (BPP XLIX785 1909), 23, 27, 65–66.
[13] Ibid 29, 35, 43.
[14] *Royal Commission* (n 10), 23.
[15] *Royal Commission* (n 10), 45.

tradition.[16] The second is legitimacy – the extent to which an organization conforms with established norms. For example, one study argued that the ascendancy of the Ontarian fine-wine industry could be attributed to the ways in which firms in this industry aligned their production methods, and quality certification schemes, with globally recognized protocols.[17]

What is intriguing about the Scotch Whisky industry – in contrast to the brands owned by its member companies – is that it was difficult to communicate authenticity because there was no legally-binding definition of 'Scotch' whisky. Similarly, the efforts of the SWA to legitimize this term in national and global markets were hindered by the absence of globally recognized criteria for this spirit.[18] This latter observation meant the legitimacy of the terms 'whisky' and 'Scotch Whisky' were contested, particularly in certain export markets. Manufacturers of inauthentic products could use advertising and branding to project an aura of authenticity for their products.[19] Such practices were a constant matter for litigation by the Scotch Whisky industry, as evident in high-profile litigation in Uruguay and Ecuador, where labels for inauthentic products contained Scottish names and were embellished with images of tartan, and tartan imagery, such as the tam o'shanter.[20]

Litigation would have been facilitated if the SWA had registered Scotch Whisky as a certification mark. Such marks were incorporated in the Trade Marks Acts of 1905 and 1938.[21] In 1955, the SWA considered that this option might assist in restricting the export of immature Scotch Whisky which was damaging the reputation of the matured variety and, by implication, 'traditional' Scotch Whisky. However, it decided not to exercise this option, partly because it was concerned that if it became the registered owner of 'Scotch'

---

[16] Michael B Beverland, 'Crafting Brand Authenticity: The Case of Luxury Wines' (2005) 42(5) Journal of Management Studies 1003, 1007.

[17] Maxim Voronov, Dirk De Clercq, and CR Hinings, 'Conformity and Distinctiveness in a Global Institutional Framework: The Legitimation of Ontario Fine Wine' (2013) 50(4) Journal of Management Studies 607.

[18] Julie Bower and David M Higgins, 'Litigation and Lobbying in Support of the Marque: The Scotch Whisky Association, c. 1945 – c. 1990' (2023) 24(1) Enterprise & Society 286.

[19] Jonatan Södergren, 'Brand Authenticity: 25 Years of Research' (2021) 45 International Journal of Consumer Studies 645, 648.

[20] *John Walker & Sons Ltd and Others v Henry Ost and Co Ltd and Another* [1970] RPC 489; *White Horse Distillers Ltd and Others v Gregson Associated Ltd and Others* [1984] RPC 61. Actions involving similar misleading statements include: *Schutzverbrand der Spirituosen-Industrie eV v Egon Schöppe* [1969] Decision of the West German Supreme Court 402.

[21] Trade Marks Act 1905 s 62; Trade Marks Act 1938 s 37.

whisky, it would be in the invidious position of determining which companies could use this mark. Other concerns were that it would take many years, and considerable expense, to secure registration even in countries which permitted registration of certification marks.[22]

Consequently, in the United Kingdom (UK) the SWA had to rely on passing off actions, which are generally less certain in outcome and more expensive, compared to an action for trade mark infringement. Litigation in foreign countries relied on the doctrine of unfair competition.

AUTHENTICITY AND OWNERSHIP

Resource partitioning theory seeks to explain the rise of late-stage specialist segments within an established industry following the consolidation of large generalist organizations competing for market share in the mass market.[23] The appeal of these specialist organizations emanates from their identity and/or location, for example, in the case of specialty 'estate' wines as a partition in the context of the mass market 'jug' or standard wines.[24] The theory supports the hypothesis that two apparently opposing trends of consolidation and new business formation can sometimes occur simultaneously within the same industry. While generalist organizations choose markets composed of large heterogeneous segments, specialist organizations choose narrow homogenous areas. When resources are sufficient to sustain a specialist segment, the market is 'partitioned' in that superficially generalist and specialist organizations do not compete; the shared understanding of the peripheral firms' offerings is such that the offerings of the dominant firms cannot substitute for those of the peripheral firms.[25]

Resource partitioning theory has been extended to situations where there is an evident return to heritage, authenticity and traditional scale and production methods. This reflects a realignment of core identity, image, and reputation

---

[22] The National Archives (TNA) MAF 84/897, 'Export of Scotch Whisky: General Correspondence, The Distillers Company Limited to Board of Trade 12 April 1957'. Sometimes, registrable collective trade marks in foreign countries can operate as certification trade marks. Norma Dawson, *Certification Trade Marks* (Intellectual Property Publishing 1988), 84.

[23] Carroll and Swaminathan (n 3).

[24] Anand Swaminathan, 'Resource Partitioning and the Evolution of Specialist Organizations: The Role of Location and Identity in the U.S. Wine Industry' (2001) 44(6) Academy of Management Journal 1169.

[25] McKendrick and Hannan (n 4).

with changing societal values and entrepreneurial opportunities.[26] Academic research which has applied the resource partitioning model to the Scotch Whisky industry reported the resurgence of interest in 'traditional' and 'authentic' single malt whiskies.[27] However, somewhat counterintuitively to the theory, consumers were not deterred by the fact that many of the leading single malts are owned by the mass market producers of blended Scotch Whisky. Unlike micro-brewing, and wine,[28] consumers of single malts do not appear to equate authenticity with distillery ownership, at least in the timeframe studied. This was partly attributable to an inability to seed a cluster in home distilling (expense, technical and legal criteria) in the manner observed in micro-brewing, where additionally there is no requirement for lengthy maturation.[29] The foreign acquisition of famous whisky companies many years ago (Table 5.1) has meant that the industry has become little more than, 'a network of interlocking financial and industrial interests, with Canadian, American, French, and Japanese firms involved'.[30]

Whatever real or imagined characteristics *are* associated with Scottishness, they are insufficient to explain how the Scotch Whisky industry established a global presence that has been sustained when other Scottish heritage industries did not. For example, traditional small-scale Scottish knitwear manufacturers based within the tightly defined Borders region experienced more than 100 years of success only to fail abruptly due to the inability to adapt to technological change and the challenges posed by new foreign rivals.[31] Conversely, the focus on small-scale, traditional production methods in a geographically delimited area was central to the enduring success of HARRIS TWEED. Unlike the SWA, the Harris Tweed Association secured registration and the higher legal protection of the Orb trade mark, and HARRIS TWEED. The regulations governing this standardization trade mark stated: HARRIS

---

[26] William M. Foster, Roy Suddaby, Alison Minkus and Elden Wiebe, 'History as Social Memory Assets: the Example of Tim Hortons' (2011) 6(1) Management & Organizational History 101. Andrew Popp and Robin Holt, 'The Presence of Entrepreneurial Opportunity' (2013) 55(1) Business History 9.

[27] McKendrick and Hannan (n 4).

[28] Carroll and Swaminathan (n 3); Swaminathan (n 24); Giacomo Negro, Michael T Hannan and Hayagreeva Rao, 'Category Reinterpretation and Defection: Modernism and Tradition in Italian Winemaking' (2011) 22(6) Organization Science 1449; Kroezen and Heugens (n 3).

[29] McKendrick and Hannan (n 4), 1283.

[30] David Daiches, *Scotch Whisky: Its Past and Present* (Fontana 2002), 93.

[31] Joseph F Porac, Howard Thomas and Charles Baden-Fuller, 'Competitive Groups as Cognitive Communities: The Case of Scottish Knitwear Manufacturers Revisited' (2011) 48(3) Journal of Management Studies 646.

Table 5.1 Defining acquisitions of Scotch Whisky assets

Year	Acquiror	Target	Key Brands
1925	DCL	'The Big Amalgamation' of Buchanan-Dewar, and John Walker & Sons	Dewar's, Buchanan, Johnnie Walker
1972	Grand Metropolitan	Watney Mann/ International Distillers & Vintners (IDV)	J&B Rare Single malts Auchroisk, Knockando, Strathmill and Glen Spey
1974	Pernod Ricard	S Campbell & Son	Clan Campbell Single malt Aberlour
1985	Guinness	Arthur Bell & Sons	Bell's Single malt Blair Athol
1986	Guinness	DCL	Johnnie Walker, Dewar's Smaller brands including White Horse, Haig, VAT 69 Single malts Cardhu, and Classic Malt range (Lagavulin, Dalwhinnie, Glenkinchie, Cragganmore, Oban and Talisker)
1986	Allied-Lyons	Hiram Walker	Ballantine's Single malts Scapa, Balblair and Ardbeg
1990	Allied-Lyons	Whitbread (divestment)	Long John Single malt Laphroaig
1996	Highland Distillers	Macallan-Glenlivet	The Macallan
1997	Grand Metropolitan	Guinness (merger, forming Diageo)	Johnnie Walker, Dewar's, Bell's, J&B Rare
1998	Bacardi-Martini	Diageo (divestment)	Dewar's
1999	Edrington (R&B)/ William Grant	Highland Distillers	The Famous Grouse Single malts The Macallan and Highland Park
2001	Diageo/Pernod Ricard	Seagram (split of portfolio)	Chivas Regal, Glen Grant and single malt, The Glenlivet (to Pernod Ricard)

Year	Acquiror	Target	Key Brands
2004	LVMH	Glenmorangie	Glenmorangie and Ardbeg
2005	Pernod Ricard/ Fortune Brands	Allied Domecq (split of portfolio)	Ballantine's (to Pernod Ricard) Laphroaig (to Fortune Brands)

Source: compiled by the authors.

TWEED means a Tweed made from pure virgin wool produced in Scotland, spun, dyed, and finished in the Outer Hebrides and handwoven by the Islanders at their own homes in the islands ... all known as the Outer Hebrides.'[32]

'Traditional' single malt whiskies are inextricably linked via the blending process to the major mass market brands owned by the international alcoholic beverage conglomerates.[33] The large well-known brands are blends of many different whiskies (up to 40 in the case of JOHNNIE WALKER Black Label) many of which were sourced historically from third-party independent malt distillers.[34] This relationship was crucial to the rapid growth of the industry from the late nineteenth century.[35] Consequently, in considering category boundaries in the context of resource partitioning theory the same set of producers operate within both the center and periphery of a single organization form.

The major acquisitions that pertain to the leading Scotch Whisky brands are shown in Table 5.1. During 1979, Canadian firm Hiram Walker launched a hostile bid for Highland Distilleries, owner of The Famous Grouse brand, which was blocked by the Monopolies and Mergers Commission (MMC) At that point ownership of Scotch Whisky assets was such that, of Scotland's 117 malt distilleries, DCL owned 45, followed by Canadian family firm Seagram with nine, and Hiram Walker with eight.[36] Following various mergers in the 1980s, 1990s, and 2000s, Diageo currently owns 29 of the 135 fully operating malt distilleries, with French multinational Pernod Ricard owning 12. Both firms own one of the seven large grain distilleries, with Diageo having a joint venture interest with Edrington, owner of The Famous Grouse, in an additional

---

[32] Dawson (n 22), 76.

[33] Julie Bower, 'Scotch Whisky: History, Heritage and the Stock Cycle' (2016) 2(2) Beverages 11.

[34] Monopolies and Mergers Commission [1979-80] HC 743 (5 August 1980), 7.

[35] See, for example, evidence of John Blanche and William Ross, *Index and Digests of Evidence Taken...* (n 12), 20; 53.

[36] Monopolies and Mergers Commission (n 34), 9.

grain distillery.[37] Aside from French firm La Martiniquaise's grain distillery which opened in 2010, new entry has tended to be via acquiring and re-opening mothballed malt distilleries previously owned by other firms. The increased demand for single malt whisky has been met by existing brands extending capacity; the largest two, The Glenlivet and Glenfiddich, operate at 21 million liters pure alcohol (mlpa) capacity.[38] Table 5.2 shows the estimated market shares of the leading Scotch Whisky firms based on their share of Scotch Whisky sales.

Table 5.2   Sales and market shares by volume[39]

Firm	Ownership	Grain Distilleries	Malt Distilleries	Sales (m cases)	Market Share
Diageo	Public (UK)	2 (one is jv with Edringon)	29	37.5	41.1%
Pernod Ricard	Public (France)	1	12	20.2	22.2%
William Grant & Sons	Private (UK)	1	4	7.3	8.0%
La Martiniquaise	Private (France)	1	1	5.3	5.8%
Bacardi	Private (Bermuda)	-	5	5.0	5.1%

---

[37] There are seven grain distilleries, five of which are in the Lowlands region. Cameronbridge (Diageo) and Girvan (Wm Grant) are both 110 mlpa capacity. North British (joint venture between Diageo and Edrington) is 72 mlpa. Strathclyde (Pernod Ricard), Invergordon (Whyte & Mackay) and Starlaw (La Martiniquaise) are 39 mlpa, 36 mlpa and 25 mlpa respectively. Loch Lomond is 21 mlpa of which 18 mlpa is dedicated to grain production. See <www.whiskyinvestdirect.com/about-whisky/grain-whisky-distilleries-in-scotland>.

[38] There are 135 malt distilleries, around half of which are in the Speyside region. The Glenlivet (Pernod Ricard) and Glenfiddich (Wm Grant) are both 21 mlpa capacity, followed by The Macallan (Edrington) at 15 mlpa. The majority of malt distilleries are less than 3 mlpa, with only 18 of the total above 5 mlpa. See 'Grain Whisky Distilleries in Scotland' (*Whisky Invest Direct*) <www.whiskyinvestdirect.com/ about -whisky/ grain -whisky -distilleries -in -scotland> accessed 3 May 2024.

Firm	Ownership	Grain Distilleries	Malt Distilleries	Sales (m cases)	Market Share
Edrington Group	Private (UK)	1 (JV with Diageo)	3	4.6	5.0%
Whyte & Mackay	Public (Philippines)	1	4	3.8	4.2%
Beam Suntory	Private (Japan)	-	5	1.4	1.6%
Loch Lomond	Private (UK/Asia)	1	2	1.0	1.0%
Ian Macleod Distillers	Private (UK)	-	2	1.0	1.0%

Source: Grain whisky distilleries in Scotland | WhiskyInvestDirect; Malt whisky distilleries in Scotland | WhiskyInvestDirect, and Top 10 Scotch Whisky companies | WhiskyInvestDirect (accessed 7 October 2024).

Even though the Hiram Walker/Highland Distilleries bid was blocked, it did little to deter subsequent merger and acquisition activity, which ignited a series of heated debates in Parliament with each bid that emerged. Scottish MPs became increasingly fraught as parts of Scotland's heritage were redomiciled either to London, or further afield.

Between 1985 and 1987, Anglo-Irish brewer Guinness attained leadership of the Scotch Whisky industry, firstly through the acquisition of Arthur Bell, followed by the controversial and notorious acquisition of DCL.[40] In the first of several high-profile interventions, Conservative MP Bill Walker, pointed to other motives for Guinness's acquisition of Arthur Bell:

> Guinness cannot get its overseas profits into this country ... Guinness is writing off advance corporation tax and it does not have enough United Kingdom earnings to pay its dividend. Guinness is in trouble and Bell's is not ... Everyone in Bell's is treated alike and everyone works hard. The Scottish institutions, ... have remained with Bell's and I am thankful to them for that. They recognise that if Scotland has no home-based, profitable firms, the very reason for the existence of the Scottish financial centre will vanish. If we lose Bell's, which company will be next?... Perhaps Mr. Saunders will have his eye on Distillers which, again, is in my constituency.[41]

Within a year, DCL was the subject of rival bids from Scotland-based conglomerate, Argyll Group, and Guinness. The initiating Argyll bid was hostile

---

[40] The Takeover Panel, 'Takeover Panel Requires Guinness to Make Payments to Former Distillers Shareholders' (14 July 1989/13).
[41] HC Deb 25 July 1985, vol 83, cols 391–9.

but was not referred to the MMC. In contrast, because Guinness owned Bell's, there was the prospect of a referral, notwithstanding its role as the White Knight bidder. The ensuing debate was essentially the preserve of Scottish MPs, united across the political spectrum. The relative merits of the competing bids focused on more than the potential concentration in the industry (between 35 and 50% of whisky production, depending on how spare capacity and mothballed distilleries were accounted for). The benefits to Scotland, and support for traditional industries and job prospects, received particular attention. The Liberal Democrat Malcolm Bruce MP said:

> Argyll launched its bid with an attractive statement—attractive to me as a Scottish Member—which claims that the company will bring Scotch whisky back home. It would establish a new company in Scotland. Its management team would be based in Scotland and the industry would be run from there. Argyll claim that its management team has a marketing background which can revitalise the industry, and it feels that its actions are a logical development of its own business. Guinness countered that by claiming that it had greater international marketing expertise which would be much healthier and better for the industry. It also claimed that it would establish headquarters in Scotland ... I think we can learn something from the way the producers of Armagnac and Cognac have established the imprimatur on their quality product in a way which Scotch Whisky could benefit from if it is to establish itself as top of the heap ... Distillers had a distillery in my constituency but closed it many years ago.[42]

In an Adjournment debate, vocal Scottish Conservative MP, Bill Walker, raised the matter of what became known as the 'Guinness affair', recounting the acquisition of Arthur Bell and the firm pledges given by Guinness in the offer document for that company:

> The first pledge says: Bells will continue to be managed from Perth as an autonomous company, subject only to overall strategic direction and normal disciplines of financial reporting ... Bell's is no longer an autonomous company. The overseas sales department has been moved to Hammersmith in London. The United States sales operation has been closed down, and the promised advertising in the United States has not been implemented. Export staff have been told that they are being moved from Bell's to Dewars ... Bell's premium brand is being sold at a discount and is now just one of the many brands in the Guinness stable ... Brand name and reputation are everything in the Scotch Whisky industry. Unlike beer, whisky cannot be offered at a discount to vendors and the public without destroying the reputation and the up-market image of the brand.[43]

---

[42] HC Deb 3 February 1986, vol 91, cols 20–6.
[43] HC Deb 3 March 1987, vol 111, cols 845–52.

54   *Place-branding experiences*

Mr Walker continued his campaign for the heritage and traditional status of Scotch Whisky through aggressive lobbying of his fellow Conservative Government ministers. Ultimately this led to the passing of the Scotch Whisky Bill.[44] Subsequently, the Scotch Whisky Act 1988 prohibited the production in Scotland of whisky other than Scotch Whisky, and the Scotch Whisky Order 1990 provided a statutory definition of Scotch Whisky.[45] This domestic legislation became enshrined in EU law.[46]

CONCLUSIONS

In this chapter we have used the insights provided by resource partitioning theory to explain why the bifurcated industrial structure of the Scotch Whisky industry has blurred consumer perceptions of 'authentic' Scotch Whisky. We have also argued that the failure of the SWA to secure statutory protection of 'Scotch' Whisky until the late twentieth century, exacerbated the problems that confronted this Association as it sought to legitimize 'Scotch' whisky.

Scotch Whisky does not fit the standard appellation paradigm, with its traditional emphasis on small-scale, highly localized production. The Scotch Whisky industry is dominated by multinational companies. Most of the leading champagne brands, including Krug, Moët & Chandon, and Veuve Clicquot, are owned by the multinational LVMH (Moët Hennessy Louis Vuitton). However, champagne can only be produced from grapes grown in the tightly defined region centered on the city of Reims and the town of Épernay. In contrast, there are no restrictions on the geographical origin of inputs (cereals) used in the production of Scotch Whisky, although in practice a large proportion of the barley used in the manufacture of malt whisky is grown in Scotland. In fact, only two requirements tie this spirit to Scotland: the whisky must be distilled, and matured, in Scotland.

Viewed from this perspective, terroir appears unimportant.[47] Terroir, which refers to environmental conditions, especially climate, soil, and topography, was fundamental to early European efforts to control the use of wine appellations. Distillation and maturation are traditional processes that have been used

---

44 HC Deb 11 December 1987, vol 124, cols 681–735.
45 Scotch Whisky Act 1988; The Scotch Whisky Order 1990 (SI1990/998).
46 Council Regulation (EEC) No 1576/89 of 29 May 1989 laying down general rules on the definition, description and presentation of spirit drinks [1989] OJ L160/; Regulation (EC) No 110/2008 of the European Parliament and of the Council of 15 January 2008 on the definition, description, presentation, labelling and the protection of geographical indications of spirit drinks [2008] OJ L39/16.
47 The industry would argue that there is a terroir effect from the type of peat used, and the climatic conditions where maturation takes place.

in the production of Scotch Whisky for over 200 years. Moreover, despite the absence of a legally binding definition of this term for most of this period, historically, Scotch Whisky has been associated with Scotland. This reputational alignment between product and place underpins global regulations governing geographical indications (GIs).[48] It is debatable that Scotch Whisky secured recognition as a GI only on the basis of this reputational link. Certainly, it cannot be argued that the processes of distillation and maturation were unique to Scotch Whisky.

A final conclusion relates to the possible conflict between heritage, which is socially constructed and inter-temporal, versus 'fixity' of place. A substantial literature in the field of geography indicates that, 'place is, and always has been, fundamentally unreliable. Although we are wooed by the nostalgic fancy that places never change, this is a fiction that is all too readily exposed'.[49] This observation is consonant with the varying connotations of Scottishness discussed earlier, and it raises the beguiling question: how 'Scottish' will Scotch Whisky be if (when) the industry is entirely owned by companies many of which are multinational firms domiciled outside the UK?

---

[48] Agreement on Trade-Related Aspects of Intellectual Property Rights (TRIPS) (adopted 15 April 1994) 1869 UNTS 299 article 22.1.

[49] Bronwyn Parry, 'Geographical Indications: Not All "Champagne and Roses"' in Lionel Bently, Jennifer C Davies and Jane C Ginsburg (eds), *Trade Marks and Brands: An Interdisciplinary Critique* (Cambridge University Press 2008), 366.

PART III

The Impact of Place-Branding

6. Defending the Scottishness of Scotch Whisky
Atsuko Ichijo

INTRODUCTION

Scotch Whisky is one of the best known, global brands. Its status as 'Scotland's national drink' is undisputed and it is widely recognized as Scotland's 'biggest export'.[1] Scotch Whisky's recognition is second to none: it is even claimed that throughout the world, 'the word "whisky" is "Scotch" and "Scotch" is "whisky"'.[2] Scotch Whisky, in other words, is now elevated to a well-understood shorthand referring to whisky in general, most likely to the frustration of the producers of other whiskies. And what makes this iconic product Scotch Whisky is the place, Scotland. Consequently, in marketing terminology, Scotch Whisky is a place brand, in particular, a type of 'strong territorial brand'.[3] Befitting for one of the best known place brands, Scotch Whisky has been registered as a Geographical Indication (GI) with the European Union (EU).[4] A GI is a legal instrument to protect the brand's identity with respect

---

[1] 'Scotch Whisky' (VisitScotland) <https://www.visitscotland.com/things-to-do/food-drink/whisky> accessed 9 October 2024.

[2] Alistair Durie, Ian Yeoman and Una McMahorn-Beattie, 'How the History of Scotland Creates a Sense of Place' (2006) 2(1) Place Branding 43, 46.

[3] Michael Moss and John Hume, *The Making of Scotch Whisky: A History of the Scotch Whisky Distilling Industry* (Canongate Books 2000); S R H Jones 'Brand Building and Structural Changes in the Scotch Whisky Industry Since 1975' (2003) 45(3) Business History 72; Andy Smith, 'Territory and the Regulation of Industry: Examples from Scotland and Aquitaine' (2008) 18(1) Regional and Federal Studies 37; Andy Smith, 'Industries as Spaces for the Politics of Territory: The Case of Scotch Whisky' (2010) 20(3) Regional and Federal Studies 389; and Steve Charters and Nathali Spielmann, 'Characteristics of Strong Territorial Brands: The Case of Champagne' (2014) 67(7) Journal of Business Research 1461.

[4] Scotch Whisky was recognized as a Geographical Indication in the EU in 2008. See: Regulation (EC) No 110/2008 of the European Parliament and of the Council of 15 January 2008 on the definition, description, presentation, label-

to its geographical origin. Where the regulation of GIs does not apply, the Scotch Whisky Association (SWA),[5] the powerful trade body for Scotch Whisky, seeks to secure trade mark and other forms of registration to protect Scotch Whisky's integrity and reputation. In short, the SWA strives to protect the identity of Scotch Whisky through the system of intellectual property (IP) protection.

While under legal protection afforded to all manners of IPs, the brand of Scotch Whisky as a place brand is qualitatively different from some other IPs such as a certification mark that a place brand is fundamentally tied to a place, not to a set of quantified description. A place certainly refers to a physical location which can be described with geographic coordinates. However, what distinguishes a place from a space is that the former is imbued with symbols, emotions and meaning, something that evades quantitative capture.[6] In other words, a place brand is linked to images of the place it is tied to, and this is where the social relationship surrounding GIs can be observed. In the case of Scotch Whisky, it is existentially tied to Scotland, or more precisely, certain images of Scotland. It follows that, in practice, GIs are means to protect and prevent misuse of these images. There are, however, a multitude of images of Scotland and, while some of them are conducive to the promotion of Scotch Whisky the brand, some of them may not be appropriate or relevant. In other words, there has to be a process through which some images are adopted and promoted while some are rejected by the industry in its endeavor to protect the brand of Scotch Whisky. The chapter provides a broadly sociological exploration of this dynamic rather than legal arguments of IP. It looks into questions including what image(s) of Scotland is/are associated with Scotch Whisky, how the Scottishness of Scotch Whisky has been established by various actors, including the SWA, how the SWA has defended the brand and the ways in which the images the SWA have chosen to defend Scotch Whisky related to those in other attempts to brand Scotland.

---

ling and the protection of geographical indications of spirit drinks and repealing Council Regulation (EEC) No 1576/89 [2008] OJ L39/16. With the UK's withdrawal from the EU (commonly known as Brexit), it was also registered as a GI in the UK GI scheme on 31 December 2020 <www.gov.uk/protected-food-drink-names/scotch-whisky> accessed 4 October 2024.

[5] See <https://www.scotch-whisky.org.uk/> accessed 21 October 2024.

[6] George Ritzer and J Michael Ryan (eds), *The Concise Encyclopedia of Sociology* (Blackwell Publishing Ltd 2011), 443-4.

THE SCOTTISHNESS OF SCOTCH WHISKY

Scotch Whisky is a type of whisky, which is a type of spirit, an alcoholic beverage distilled from fermented grain mash. As a type of distilled alcoholic beverage, its history could go back a long way, but the earliest record of what could be directly attributed to today's Scotch Whisky was from the fifteenth century and it is found in the tax record of the day.[7] As the production of distilled spirit increased, it attracted the Scottish Government's attention as a source of taxation and the first tax on Scotch Whisky was levied in 1644; since then, the story of Scotch Whisky is dominated by the cat and mouse game between the government, first the Scottish and then the United Kingdom (UK) Government, wanting to tax the drink and producers trying their utmost to avoid taxation.[8] The taxation system has become more sophisticated, and tax has largely ceased to be the focus of governmental attention on Scotch Whisky. With the expansion of trade and commerce, Scotch Whisky has grown into a major industry in Scotland as well as the UK. The SWA cites the following to describe its industry as of 2022:

- in 2022, Scotch Whisky exports were worth £6.2 billion;
- in 2022, Scotch Whisky accounted for 77% of Scottish food and drink exports and 25% of all UK food and drink exports;
- in 2022, Scotch Whisky accounted for 26% of all Scotland's international goods exports and 1.5% of all UK goods exports;
- the Scotch Whisky industry provides £5.5 billion in gross value added (GVA) to the UK economy (2018);
- more than 11,000 people are directly employed in the Scotch Whisky industry in Scotland and over 42,000 jobs across the UK are supported by the industry;
- 7,000 of these jobs are in rural areas of Scotland providing vital employment and investment to communities across the Highlands and Islands.[9]

As shown above, the Scotch Whisky industry is indeed large and carries non-negligible economic weight for both Scotland and the UK. This is, unsurprisingly, one of the reasons why the protection of the brand of Scotch Whisky is important for both the industry as well as various authorities. This in turn implies that Scotch Whisky the brand in fact constitutes a space in which

---

[7] 'Story of Scotch' (Scotch Whisky Association) <https://www.scotch-whisky.org.uk/discover-scotch/story-of-scotch/> accessed 9 October 2024.
[8] Ibid.
[9] 'Facts and Figures' (Scotch Whisky Association) <https:// www .scotch -whisky.org.uk/industry-insights/facts-figures/> accessed 9 October 2024.

actors with varied interest in it engage with negotiation, if not outright power struggles *, to maintain influence on what Scotch Whisky is and means.

Naturally, the awareness of Scotch Whisky the brand emerged as it slowly became a global commodity chiefly on the back of the expanding British Empire. The first attempt to legally define Scotch Whisky was made in 1933 in the form of the Finance Act 1933.[10] Later in the century, the UK Parliament enacted the Scotch Whisky Act 1988, a piece of legislation dedicated to Scotch Whisky. This suggests the UK Government's acknowledgement of the importance of Scotch Whisky in the UK economy. The Act has now been superseded by the Scotch Whisky Regulations 2009 which cover every aspect of its making, bottling, labelling and promotion. The SWA summarizes the Regulations as follows:

> Scotch Whisky is whisky wholly produced and matured in Scotland. With the exception of Single Malt Scotch Whisky, it may be bottled overseas by verified companies but the only permitted additions are water and, if necessary, plain caramel colouring to adjust the final colour of the spirit. The use of any other additive, such as sugar, flavouring or other alcohol is illegal and means that the product cannot be sold as Scotch Whisky.[11]

The Regulations are the tool by which Scotch Whisky the brand is legally protected in the UK. While they define protected localities and regions in reference to Scotch Whisky (Regulation 10), they only give location information and do not provide any description of geographical or environmental features that are supposed to make Scotch Whisky Scottish. In other words, what the Regulations convey is more technical than symbolic, a feature that distinguishes the Regulations from the GIs.

In contrast, the GIs, given that they are a formalized/legalized expression of the idea of *terroir*, the essential link between the location of production

---

[10] Finance Act 1933 s 24 Amendment as to permits and certificates accompanying spirits:
> For the purpose of subsection (9) of section one hundred and five of the Spirits Act, 1880 (which relates to the accuracy of the description of spirits in a permit or certificate), spirits described as Scotch whisky shall not be deemed to correspond to that description unless they have been obtained by distillation in Scotland from a mash of cereal grains saccharified by the diastase of malt and have been matured in a bonded warehouse in casks for a period of at least three years.

[11] 'Help Protect Scotch Whisky' (Scotch Whisky Association 2021) <www.scotch-whisky.org.uk/media/1895/help-us-protect-scotch-whisky_july2021.pdf> accessed 9 October 2024.

and specific quality attributes[12] or a socio-cultural construct produced through communicative action among a wide range of stakeholders,[13] are more explicit in signalling certain images of the place.[14] According to the EU, its GIs system 'protects the names of products that originate from specific regions and have specific qualities or enjoy a reputation linked to the production territory'.[15]

Accordingly, the role of geography in making Scotch Whisky Scotch whisky is detailed in the *Technical File for Scotch Whisky*,[16] one of the provisions to maintain Scotch Whisky's GI.[17] The *Technical File* consists of several sections and following a few business-like sections such as 'Description of Scotch Whisky', 'Geographical areas concerned' (accompanied by a coloured map of Scotland) and 'Method of production for Scotch Whisky', which are filled with technical details such as the physical property of Scotch Whisky, geographical coordinates, description of the terrain, equipment to be used to produce Scotch Whisky and physical conditions under which it should be produced, comes a section entitled 'The links with geographical origin and environment'. Here, the geography, geology as well as climate of Scotland, water, peat, factors influencing fermentation and influence of climate on maturation are listed as 'natural factors in the geographical area' that distinguish Scotch Whisky from other whiskies. The section then describes how the reputation of Scotch Whisky is linked to 'the geographical area', that is, Scotland. The first point is history:

1. **Historical origins** – Scotch Whisky has been produced in Scotland for more than 500 years and has been exported from Scotland for around 200 years. The term "whisky" derives originally from the words in the Gaelic language

---

[12] Martijin Huysmans and Johan Swinnen, 'No Terroir in the Cold?: A Note on the Geography of Geographical Indications' (2019) 70(2) Journal of Agricultural Economics 550.

[13] Eric Casteló, 'The Will for Terroir: A Communicative Approach' (2021) 86 Journal of Rural Studies 386.

[14] Ordinarily, this signalling is carried out through words as we shall see below.

[15] The European Commission, 'Geographical Indications and Quality Schemes Explained' (European Commission) <https:// agriculture .ec .europa .eu/ farming/ geographical -indications -and -quality -schemes/ geographical -indications -and -quality-schemes-explained_en> accessed 9 October 2024.

[16] Department of Environment, Food and Rural Affairs, *Technical File for Scotch Whisky* (Department for Environment, Food & Rural Affairs 2019) <www .gov.uk/protected-food-drink-names/scotch-whisky> accessed 4 October 2024.

[17] The other instrument is the Verification Scheme operated by the HMRC. See 'Protecting Scotch Whisky outside the UK' (Scotch Whisky Association) <https://www.scotch-whisky.org.uk/industry-insights/protecting-scotch-whisky/> accessed 9 October 2024.

"Uisge Beatha" or "Usquebaugh". Gaelic is the traditional language spoken in the Highlands of Scotland and Ireland. The Gaelic description first evolved into "Uiskie" and then "Whisky". A Royal Commission was set up in 1908 in the United Kingdom to decide what restrictions should apply as to how Scotch Whisky was made. It issued its report in 1909. The Immature Spirits (Restriction) Act 1915 required ageing of Scotch Whisky in barrels for at least 2 years, which was extended to 3 years in 1916. Subsequently, Scotch Whisky was defined by statute in UK law in 1933, and it has been defined in UK legislation since that date.[18]

The fact that a 'technical' document to make the case of the connection between a product and a geographical area contains a description of history clearly shows that a place is inevitably imbued with meaning. Scotland is not just a geographical location with a particular climate pattern where pure and authentic ingredients are obtained but where the spirit has been continuously produced and enjoyed by generations; Scotch Whisky is therefore intricately intertwined with experiences and memories of people who have lived in Scotland and beyond. This makes a place brand yet another arena where actors involved in the project constantly negotiate what the brand should symbolize.

The Technical File then goes back to the description of the impact of geography and geology by identifying 'Specific characteristics of the spirit drink attributable to the geographical area' and provides a detailed description of how natural ingredients such as water, peat and the endogenous barley enzymes and climatic features of Scotland make Scotch Whisky distinctive.

The image of Scotland, where Scotch Whisky is produced, that emerges from the *Technical File* is that of a land of pristine nature with a cool and wet climate. The emphasis on the unspoilt environment in a description of Scotch Whisky's GI is not surprising as the document's aim is to make the case for unrivalled quality of the product which is anchored to the natural environment where it is produced. In other words, the emphasis on the pristine nature of Scotland is not in itself particularly ideological. Given the necessary link to the natural environment, it is not too difficult for the description of Scotch Whisky's GI to be aligned with some form of environmentalism, but this has not been particularly prominent.[19]

---

[18] DEFRA (n 16), 15.

[19] While the SWA now has the Scotch Whisky Industry Sustainability Strategy based on the concern for the protection of the environment (Scotch Whisky Association, 'Sustainability in the Scotch Whisky Industry' (Scotch Whisky Association) <https://www.scotch-whisky.org.uk/industry-insights/sustainability/ > accessed 9 October 2024), it does not have a strong link with the Scottish Greens, for instance. In fact, the Scottish Greens are seen to be attacking the Scotch Whisky industry by jointly proposing the ban on the use of peat with the SNP.

What is interesting in Scotland is that this image happens to correspond to an already well-established image of Scotland, 'the romantic view of ancient mists and braes'[20] created and propagated by Scottish Romantics including James Macpherson (1736–96), Robert Burns (1759–96) and Walter Scott (1771–1832), which has been continuously (and perhaps relentlessly) commodified and commercialized since then. Among others, Murray Pittock has pointed out the importance of Scotland's Romanticism in the creation of a national brand.[21] He draws attention to the context in which a Romantic view of Scotland emerged and propagated: until sometime after the defeat of the Jacobite rebellion in 1746, the last military challenge to the sitting power on the British mainland, the inaccessible landscapes of Scotland were seen as a source of internal threat. Scotland, in particular as represented by the Highlands, was seen a wild place where militant savages resided and would challenge the civilized way of life in England. However, with the expansion of the British Empire they were increasingly seen as a source of its external military power that would confront the hostile forces at the frontier. The emergence, acceptance, and propagation of a Romantic view of Scotland therefore reflected certain power relationship in the eighteenth century where the militant and uncivilized Scots (= the Highlanders) were subjugated by the civilized English and made to work for the benefit of the Empire: the taming of the Scots. Once Scotland ceased to be seen as a source of internal threat, a particular image of Scotland defined by its landscape was produced and projected domestically as well as globally, therefore stimulating inbound tourism to Scotland.[22] In Pittock's words, the Scottish landscape:

> … was a magical landscape full of mighty men, a countryside as violent, sudden, torrential, and dark as the moods and valour of its inhabitants. To many across the world, Scotland remains this country of bagpipes and tartan, mountain and flood, castles, clans and conflict, whisky and golf, a territory simultaneously rural and organic, long associated with the supernatural'.[23]

---

[20] Gillian Black, Rachael Craufurd Smith, Smita Kheria and Gerard Porter, 'Scotland the Brand: Marketing the Myth?' (2015) 24(1) Scottish Affairs 47,49.

[21] Murray Pittock, *Scotland: The Global History: 1603 to the Present* (Yale University Press 2022).

[22] There are many comments on the relationship between the consumption of food and tourism in modern society. See, for instance, Ian Cook and Philip Crang, 'The World on a Plate: Culinary Culture, Displacement and Geographical Knowledges' (1996) 1(2) Journal of Material Culture 131.

[23] Pittock (n 21), 199.

The Scottishness of Scotch Whisky outlined and secured by the IP system is therefore that of a Romantic Scotland with a focus on pristine, and often unforgiving, nature, that produces the pure and authentic ingredients of Scotch Whisky, namely, water, yeast and grains. The same climate also creates a just-right climate for its maturation. In line with their contemporaries, the Scottish Romantics sought unspoilt places, an embodiment of authenticity, in Scotland, which they found in the Highlands, a place of wilderness with rugged terrain and largely emptied of people. The place was emptied because the 'old way' of life in the Highlands was defeated by a modern one, and because people were either left or removed due to changes in power as well as industrial structures in the form of the Clearances.[24] The Scottish Romantics went about making this image as *the* image of Scotland, and one of the consequences of this was the making of the Highlands as an essentially imagined place.[25] Sociologically speaking, the image of Scotland that is evoked by Scotch Whisky reflects a particular phase of Scottish history in which certain power relationships produced a place which was devoid of people, and which was cultivated for the entertainment of the moneyed class – a space with particular meanings.

THE PROTECTION OF THE SCOTTISHNESS OF SCOTCH WHISKY

The IP does not have agency, and someone has to work on its behalf. The main agent that defends the Scottishness of Scotch Whisky that has been secured by the current IP regime is the SWA, the Scotch Whisky Association. The SWA is widely seen as a most effective trade body in exerting influence on taxation and trade.[26] The SWA was founded in 1942 but its predecessor, the Wine & Spirit Brand Association, was formed in 1912 in order to protect the sector against the potential fallout of the threat of tax hike proposed by the then Chancellor Lloyd George.[27] The Association changed its name to the

---

[24] The Highland Clearances refer to forced evictions of inhabitants of the Highlands and Western Isles that started in the mid-eighteenth century. It is one of the contentious points in Scottish history, and often seen as embodying the tradition of emigration from Scotland. David McCrone, *The New Sociology of Scotland* (SAGE 2017), 91–4.

[25] Ibid., Ch 16.

[26] Julie Bower and David Higgins, 'Litigation and Lobbying in Support of the Marque: The Scotch Whisky Association, c. 1945–c. 1990' (2023) 24(1) Enterprise & Society 286.

[27] The history of the SWA draws from the SWA's website: Scotch Whisky Association <https:// www .scotch -whisky .org .uk> accessed 9 October 2024,

Whisky Association in 1917 to champion Scotch and Irish whiskies' interest and has been working to protect and promote Scotch Whisky since 1942. The SWA has been effective in exerting influence on UK legislation on taxation on alcohol and the definition of the product, not only at the domestic level but also at the European and international levels. The SWA is credited with having successfully lobbied the UK legislature to provide statutory definition of Scotch Whisky as an appellation so that legislation would be extended to consumer protection.[28] At the international level, too, the SWA is seen as one of the major participants in securing three victories in the World Trade Organization (WTO) panel in reference to differentiated taxation on imported spirits in the 1990s.[29]

The SWA, a representative of individual producers, who are sometimes at odds with each other,[30] has proven to be a skilled political operator in protecting and promoting the Scottishness of Scotch Whisky. One recent occasion in which the SWA had to tread very carefully was the Scottish independence referendum of 2014.[31] Being a strong territorial brand, the association with Scotland is at the heart of Scotch Whisky the brand. It follows that an independent Scotland could further enhance the brand of Scotch Whisky, a point the then Chief Executive David Frost acknowledged in the SWA's annual review of 2013. Rather than coming out as a strong supporter for independence in order to further strengthen the Scottishness of Scotch Whisky, however, the SWA as a trade body played a 'good citizen' card by pledging they would respect the referendum outcome because it was a democratic exercise while citing their concern with ensuring stability and predictability in economy. As soon as the referendum result came through, the SWA first reiterated the inseparable link between Scotland and Scotch Whisky and vowed to continue working for the future success of Scotch Whisky and the Scottish nation. It also expressed its willingness to empower the Scottish Parliament in respect to tax-raising, spending and policy making in its submission to the Smith Commission on Devolution, using a type of language that the Scottish National Party (SNP) would use. Despite not aligning itself with the pro-independence

---

Ronald Ranta and Atsuko Ichijo, *Food, National Identity and Nationalism* (2nd edn, Springer Nature Switzerland AG 2022), Ch 3, and Bower and Higgins (n 26).

[28] Bower and Higgins (n 26).

[29] Andy Smith, 'How the WTO Matters to Industry: The Case of Scotch Whisky' (2009) 3(2) International Political Sociology 176.

[30] As for conflict among Scotch Whisky producers, see Bower and Higgins (n 26).

[31] Ranta and Ichijo (n 27), 98–101.

side, the SWA managed to emerge from the 2014 referendum with its reputation of the defender of Scotch Whisky unscathed.[32]

Two years later, in the run-up to the EU membership referendum of 2016, the SWA was, like many other business organizations and in line with some major players in the industry such as Diageo and Pernod Richard, firmly in the pro-Remain camp.[33] They argued that the UK's EU membership was central to the healthy development of the Scotch Whisky industry. Still, as in the case of the Scottish independence referendum of 2014, David Frost, the then Chief Executive of the SWA, who later was appointed as the UK's Brexit negotiator, did not forget to add that the SWA would respect the outcome of the referendum, which was a democratic exercise, and that Scotch Whisky would continue to thrive regardless of the referendum outcome. When the referendum result was confirmed, the SWA was quick to urge UK politicians to act swiftly to secure certainty about Scotch Whisky trade in particular with respect to the protection of Scotch Whisky the brand (that is, its GI status) and fair taxation. The concern over the future of Scottish protected food names, including Scotch Whisky's GI, was aired by the Scottish Government, which, together with various trade bodies, attempted to exert pressure on the UK Government to maintain protected food names and GIs by setting up a UK GI system compatible with the EU one as quickly as possible.[34]

The Brexit negotiation has highlighted the importance of GIs in trade in today's world. By 31 January 2021 when the UK formally left the EU in accordance with the European Union (Withdrawal Agreement) Act 2020, the Department of Food, Environment and Rural Affairs (DEFRA) had set up the UK GI scheme, largely replicating the EU system, to ensure the continuity of the protection of GIs.[35] As Scotch Whisky had been registered as a GI with the EU prior to the date of the UK's withdrawal, Scotch Whisky was automatically given the same protection under the newly set up UK GI scheme in Great Britain (England, Wales and Scotland) and the protection under the EU

---

[32] This may not be surprising as the Scottish independence referendum mainly revolved on the question of democracy rather than of securing the Scottishness of the Scottish nation.

[33] Atsuko Ichijo, 'What Has the Brexit Process Done to Scotch Whisky?' (2019) 90(4) Political Quarterly 637.

[34] The Scottish Government, 'News: Protected Food Names Under Threat' (The Scottish Government 2018) <https:// www .gov .scot/ news/ protected -food -names-under-threat/> accessed 4 October 2024.

[35] See: Department for Environment, Food & Rural Affairs, 'Protected Geographical Food and Drink Names: UK GI Schemes' (Department for Environment, Food and Rural Affairs 2020) <www .gov .uk/ guidance/ protected -geographical-food-and-drink-names-uk-gi-schemes> accessed 4 October 2024.

scheme in Northern Ireland and the EU territories continued unlike those products which had not been registered as GIs prior to 31 January 2021. Legally speaking, the SWA's concern with the protection of Scotch Whisky's GI was satisfactorily addressed at the time of the UK's withdrawal. However, the SWA raised its concern regarding some EU member states requesting further certification of Scotch Whisky as explained in the Scottish Government's letter to the Secretary of State for Environment, Food and Rural Affairs on 8 February 2021.[36] While the SWA continues to speak up to defend the Scotch Whisky industry's interests, their concern regarding the fallout of Brexit has moved from the protection of Scotch Whisky's GI to ensuring unhindered and fair trade of Scotch Whisky.

In the Brexit negotiation, the SWA intensely lobbied both the Scottish and UK Governments in order to secure the continued protection of Scotch Whisky's GI and to maintain a level playing field in terms of taxation. Elsewhere, it has been noted that, prior to Brexit, the SWA was engaged with frequent litigation in order to protect Scotch Whisky's GI and the SWA's activity is not confined to the UK level but extends to the international one.[37] One of the recent cases, which sheds light on how the SWA protects the Scottishness of Scotch Whisky, is that of Glen Buchenbach, a whisky produced by a German distiller, Waldhorn Distillery. In 2013, the SWA took the distillery represented by Michael Klotz to the Hamburg Regional Court arguing the distillery's use of 'Glen' in the name of its product was in breach of Scotch Whisky's EU GI, as the word 'Glen' was closely associated with Scotland and therefore, Scotch Whisky. The Hamburg Regional Court then referred the case to the Court of Justice of the European Union (CJEU) for the clarification of the EU's Spirits Regulation in ruling on the case, and the CJEU's judgment was delivered on 7 June 2018.[38] The CJEU clarified the Hamburg Regional Court needed to decide whether consumers would think directly of the geographical indication, Scotch Whisky, when they saw a similar product using the term 'Glen' and articulated that the evocation criterion of the law could be considered in the absence of a visual or phonetic similarity.[39] Following the judgment by the

---

[36] Fergus Ewing Cabinet Secretary for Rural Economy and Tourism, 'Letter to George Eustice: Whisky Trade Issues: Post-Brexit'(The Scottish Government 2021).

[37] Bowers and Higgins (n 26); Smith (n 29).

[38] C-44/17 *Scotch Whisky Association v Michael Klotz* [2018] ECR I-415; Vadim Mantrov, 'Do You Prefer Scotch or German Whisky? CJEU Judgment in the Scotch Whisky and Glen Buchenbach Dispute' (2018) 9(4) European Journal of Risk Regulation 719.

[39] Michael Loney, 'Does "Glen" Make Consumers Think of GI Protected Scotch Whisky?', 7 June 2018 Managing Intellectual Properties.

CJEU, the Hamburg Regional Court ruled in 2019 that the distillery breached Scotch Whisky's GI since the use of 'Glen' in the name of its product could imply that it was produced in Scotland and that the distillery had to drop the word from the product's name. The distillery appealed to the Hanseatic Higher Regional Court in Hamburg, which, in 2022, upheld the original ruling by the lower court. The SWA announced its victory in the case on 20 January 2022.[40]

When the appeal court upheld the lower court's original ruling, Waldhorn Distillery dropped the case and the SWA won praise from the industry. 'We'll give it to the Scotch Whisky Association: they're nothing if not determined' is how one industry press has described the court case that lasted for nine years.[41] The SWA's work to protect the Scottishness of Scotch Whisky is therefore widely recognized by the industry. As pointed out earlier, the image of Scotland that is associated with Scotch Whisky via its GI is that of a Romantic Scotland with its historical baggage. In the case of Glen Buchenbach, therefore, the SWA fought tooth and nail to preserve this particular image of Scotland in order to protect the brand of Scotch Whisky.

Moreover, the case against Glen Buchenbach has led to further legal clarification, in particular, the evocation criterion in determining if a GI has been breached or not, which experts on IP protection are interested in. Before the Glen Buchenbach case, the evocation was found in the partial incorporation of a GI in the sign or a visual or phonetic similarity such as the designation, 'Cambozola', given to a blue cheese made in Austria. However, in its judgment in the case of Glen Buchenbach, the CJEU stated that a breach of a GI through evocation could occur if there is close conceptual proximity even if there was no partial incorporation of a GI nor a visual or phonetic similarity. In other words, the CJEU ruled what was decisive was 'whether, when the consumer is confronted with a disputed designation, the image triggered directly in his or her mind is that of the product whose geographical indication is protected'.[42] The court found 'glen', a Gaelic word for a deep valley in the Highlands, was conceptually sufficiently close to what was associated with

---

[40] Scotch Whisky Association, 'Decision Over Glen Buchenbach Upheld by the Appeal Court' (Scotch Whisky Association 2022) <www.scotch-whisky.org.uk/newsroom/decision-over-glen-buchenbach-upheld-by-appeal-court/> accessed 4 October 2024.

[41] Jelisa Castrodale, 'Don't Put the Word "Glen" on a Whisky Bottle if it's Not Actually From Scotland, European Court Rules' (*Food and Wine Newsletter*, 15 February 2022) <https:// money .yahoo .com/ dont -put -word -glen -whisky -152352785.html?guccounter=1> accessed 9 October 2024.

[42] Manon Verbeeren and Olivier Vrins, 'The Protection of PDOs and PGIs Against Evocation: A "Grand Cru" in the CJEU's Cellar?' (2021) 16(4-5) Journal of Intellectual Property Law & Practice 316, 320.

Scotland and Scotch Whisky. In ruling this way, the CJEU effectively authenticated the Romantic image of Scotland as being entitled to legal protection, thus affording inadvertent support for the propagation of this particular image of Scotland. This is an example in which what appears to be a purely legal action could have unexpected ramification in society. In other words, this is yet another case to demonstrate that law is never consigned to the isolated courtroom but is part and parcel of society.

SCOTCH WHISKY AND THE PROJECTION OF SCOTLAND

As we have seen, the SWA's efforts to protect the Scottishness of Scotch Whisky through lobbying and ensuring legal protection of Scotch Whisky's GI have firmly established the Romantic view of Scotland, a land of rugged and wild landscape, of pristine nature and of a mystic past, as the image of Scotland. However, this is not the only image of Scotland that is currently projected, to state the obvious. At the opening of the Scottish Parliament on 1 July 1999, for instance, the First Minister of Scotland, Donald Dewar waxed lyrical about Scotland's past:

> The shout of the welder in the din of the great Clyde shipyards:
> The speak of the Mearns, with its soul in the land;
> The discourse of the enlightenment, when Edinburgh and Glasgow were a light held to the intellectual life of Europe;
> The wild cry of the Great Pipes;
> And back to the distant cries of the battles of Bruce and Wallace.[43]

Scotland's past described in his speech encompasses its shipbuilding industry, life in a rural village in Scotland, intellectual achievement during the Enlightenment and conflict with England, each of which can be mobilized to brand Scotland the place with a different flavor. In fact, the Scottish Government has been monitoring 'Scotland's Reputation' in respect of six dimensions (exports, governance, culture, people, tourism and immigration/investment) using the Anholt-Ipsos Nation Brands Index since 2008.[44] The

---

[43] The Scottish Parliament, 'Donald Dewar's Speech at the Opening of the Scottish Parliament 1 July 1999' <www.parliament.scot/-/media/files/history/donalddewarsspeech1july1999.pdf> accessed 4 October 2024.

[44] Scottish Government, *The Anholt-Ipsos Nation Brands Index: 2022 Report for Scotland* (Scottish Government 2023). It finds 'natural beauty' continues to be perceived as the strongest attribute of Scotland.

question therefore is where the Romantic view of Scotland that Scotch Whisky projects is situated in a wider endeavor of branding Scotland, the place.

It is evident that Scotch Whisky plays a prominent role in the promotion of inbound tourism both by the Scottish Government and relevant industries. In 2018, Scotland Food & Drink Partnership, a collaboration between industry organizations, research institutes, Scottish Government, and its agencies, published *Ambition 2030: A Growth Strategy for Farming, Fishing, Food and Drink*, and presented what they call 'the Scottish brand in 2030' as follows: 'It's 2030 and Scotland is famous as a Land of Food and Drink. We are known not just for our diversity of world-class products but as champions of responsible and sustainable production'.[45] In order to achieve annual turnover of £30 billion by 2030, the document proposes working with the tourism industry to increase the number of visitors to Scotland from the rest of the UK and internationally. The Scotch Whisky sector's success in increasing export on the back of its strong brand is also singled out as a model to emulate.[46] In response to *Ambition 2030*, the Scottish Tourism Alliance, representing 250 organizations involved in tourism in Scotland, published *Food Tourism Scotland: Creating a Global Tourism Destination and Unlocking a £1 Billion Growth Opportunity*, its action plan in 2019.[47] The action plan highlights visits to whisky distilleries as an example of food tourism, which is already thriving and, quotes an industry insider: 'Scotland's natural larder combined with its enviable reputation for whisky, makes it ideally placed to becoming the next must-explore food tourism destination'.[48] In these policy documents, the strength of the brand of Scotch Whisky in evoking authenticity as well as a wholesome environment which is indispensable in producing quality food is well recognized.

Scotch Whisky is also valued in these strategies for its capacity to produce a story line. Food Tourism Scotland suggests 'a visit to a castle becomes more meaningful with a dram of whisky in hand'[49] because of Scotch Whisky's evocation of the Romantic or mystic past of Scotland. Another report on the

---

[45] Scotland Food & Drink Partnership, *Ambition 2030: A Growth Strategy for Farming, Fishing, Food and Drink* (Scotland Food & Drink Partnership 2018), 7.
[46] Ibid., 8.
[47] Scottish Tourism Alliance, *Food Tourism Scotland: Creating a Global Food Tourism Destination and Unlocking a £1 Billion Growth Opportunity* (Scottish Tourism Alliance 2019).
[48] Ibid., 16.
[49] Ibid., 20.

impact of Robert Burns, Scotland's national bard, on the Scottish economy also points out:

> that because of the strong association between Burns, described as "Scotland's most famous tax collector" by the SWA,[50] and Scotch whisky, a strong story line could be created to encourage food tourism to Ayrshire as well as Scotland.[51] Scotch whisky, the brand which projects the Romantic view of Scotland, is therefore highly valued in efforts to grow the economy through encouraging inbound tourism.

There is plenty of evidence that Scotch Whisky has established itself as one of the chief attractions of Scotland. Surveys on visitors and potential visitors to Scotland frequently refer to Scotch Whisky. For example, VisitScotland's analysis of the 2015 and 2016 visitor surveys has found that a visit to a whisky distillery is one of the 20 top activities for tourists to engage in in Scotland and that these visits are most popular among overseas visitors, who are most likely on their first visit to Scotland.[52]

VisitScotland has also been carrying out a 'social listening' with online conversations to capture first-hand views of visitors and potential visitors to Scotland, and its 2022 report analyzes their 2019 exercise.[53] It has found in all regions the analysis has been carried out, consisting of Aberdeen and Aberdeenshire, Ayrshire and Arran, Cairngorm National Park, Glasgow and Orkney, the words whisky and distillery make frequent appearance suggesting a strong interest in Scotch Whisky among the actual and potential visitors to Scotland.

The brief survey of the role Scotch Whisky plays in the promotion of inbound tourism shows that the Scottishness of Scotch Whisky is well established and well recognized, and it facilitates attracting more tourists to Scotland. This is supported by solid legal protection. However, the image of Scotland that Scotch Whisky evokes is, as it has been repeatedly pointed out in the chapter, that of a Romantic Scotland with an emphasis on the savage beauty of wilderness, which could be problematic at certain levels. As noted earlier, the Scottish Government monitors its national reputation in respect to six dimen-

---

[50] Scotch Whisky Association, 'Story of Scotch' (Scotch Whisky Association) <www.scotch-whisky.org.uk/discover/story-of-scotch/> accessed 4 October 2024.

[51] Murray Pittock, *Robert Burns and Scottish Economy: Final Report* (University of Glasgow funded by Scottish Government's Economic Development Directorate 2019).

[52] 'Insight Department: Whisky Tourism – Facts and Insights' (*VisitScotland* 2018).

[53] 'Regional Social Listening Analysis: Insights Into Whisky' *(VisitScotland 2022).*

sions: exports, governance, culture, people, tourism, and immigration/investment, which, somewhat awkwardly, summarize the images of Scotland the Scottish Government wants to project to the outside world. At first glance, it is rather obvious that Scotch Whisky's contribution to the promotion of Scotland as a place of good governance or a desirable destination for migrants would be limited. In fact, if we recall the Romantic view of Scotland is entrenched with certain outcomes of changes in the power and industrial structures of the late eighteenth century Scotland, this is not surprising. A close look at the latest report provides interesting material to consider.[54] For instance, it finds that Scotland's ranking in the panel of 60 countries is lowest in 'export', a category that attempts to capture 'a sense of the economic strength and potential of a country'. Scotland's overall ranking out of 60 participating countries is 21st despite the *Ambition 2030* project discussed above.[55] Moreover, in regard to the question about the contribution to innovation and science, Scotland ranks 26th. It is not too surprising if the strong brand of Scotch Whisky, drawing heavily from the Romantic view of Scotland, does not translate into a high evaluation of Scotland's prowess in science and innovation, and this is where there is a potential pitfall in the strong brand of Scotch Whisky exists in what it could bring to the national branding of Scotland. Scotch Whisky the brand could interfere with or occlude other images of Scotland that various actors are trying to promote. Humza Yousaf, the then recently appointed First Minister, articulated his vision for Scotland as 'equality, opportunity and community', which respectively stands for 'tackling poverty and protecting people from harm', 'a fair, green and growing economy' and 'prioritising our public service'.[56] While this vision primarily targets the domestic audience, that is, Scottish voters, images of Scotland taking on and getting rid of poverty or bumping up public service are not conveyed by Scotch Whisky.[57]

The focus on natural beauty has the potential to tie in with the environmental movement. However, rather troublingly, the promotion and entrenchment of the image of Scotland associated with Scotch Whisky could conceal certain

---

[54] Scottish Government (n 44).

[55] Interestingly, the respondents associated 'agriculture', 'food' and 'craft' with Scottish export, which suggests that while Scottish export's association with agriculture and food is well established in line with the governmental efforts, the image of Scotland as a place of science and innovation has not caught on.

[56] Scottish Government, *Equality, Opportunity, Community: New Leadership – A Fresh Start* (Scottish Government 2023).

[57] There are conscious efforts on the part of the industry to address the questions of climate change and sustainability as seen in the SWA's strategy for 2023-2025, 'People. Planet. Prosperity'. See: 'Who We Are' (Scotch Whisky Association) <https://www.scotch-whisky.org.uk/who-we-are/>.

realities of Scottish history and society. In relation to Scotch Whisky, the image of Scotland that is evoked is that of the Romanticized Highlands. There is plenty of literature on how this version of the Highlands has been manufactured and reproduced.[58] Behind the Romanticized view of the Highlands as Scotland thus produced, the rugged, wild, and pristine landscape with very few people, is the pattern of land ownership, which meant a large sway of the Highlands was kept as a play (hunting) ground for aristocrats. What was required in such a space was wildlife – stags and grouses – not peasants. Cairngorms National Park, the largest national park in the UK, was established as recently as in 2003, after the establishment of the devolved Scottish Parliament, though the campaign to open up access to the wider public started in late 1920s.[59] The delay is usually attributed to problems in Scotland's system of land ownership, on which the Scottish Government has been working.[60] In short, the Scottish land ownership system is seen as highly problematic and undemocratic, entrenching ancient privileges. Moreover, the Romanticized view of Scotland, the imaginary Highlands, is what the outsiders, usually from a comfortable background, would see and what has been reproduced in literature, painting and music, not a view of those who lived there. As such, the Romanticized view of Scotland is a product of a certain power relationship of the late eighteenth century when a certain group of people, usually with assets, had power to define what was important and what was not and impose it on the rest of the population. This relationship has been continuously reproduced. These days, what is reproduced is perhaps not so much for the maintenance of the class relationship but for sustaining economic growth or the development of capitalist economy. 'Natural beauty', an image Scotch Whisky's GI conveys, brings tourists to Scotland and sells its products, thus bringing positive economic impact in Scotland while the underlying realities such as inequality remain hidden. Obviously, it is not the role of a territorial brand to be the flag bearer of social improvement. The main role of GIs is to protect consumers by providing trustworthy information about the product. However, as with any other institution, GIs are social constructs, which means that they could have impact beyond trade and commerce.

---

[58] For example, Hugh Trevor-Roper, 'The Invention of Tradition: The Highland Tradition of Scotland' in Eric Hobsbaum and Terence Ranger (eds), *The Invention of Tradition* (Cambridge University Press 1983); McCrone (n 24), Chs 15–17; Pittock (n 51), Ch 4.

[59] Melisa Butcher and Andy Morris, 'Mapping Home' in Karim Murji (ed), *Investigating the Social World 1* (Open University 2015).

[60] 'Land Reform' (Scottish Government) <https://www.gov.scot/policies/land-reform/> accessed on 9 October 2024.

CONCLUSION: GIS AND PLACE-BRANDING IN SCOTLAND

Scotch Whisky is a powerful place-based or territorial brand, and its GI has been effectively used to promote the product as well as Scotland with which it is associated. The Scotch Whisky industry has a skilled political operator to defend its interest through the protection of Scotch Whisky's GI in the form of the SWA, and the SWA has been effective in lobbying governments at various levels and using litigation to protect the Scottishness of Scotch Whisky. However, the image of Scotland associated with Scotch Whisky is of a particular kind, the Romanticized Highlands of Scotland, which can be at odds with other images of Scotland the Scottish Government and other industries might wish to project. Moreover, the image Scotch Whisky conveys could work to gloss over long-standing problems in land ownership and inequality in general in Scotland. Place-branding is not a means of social improvement but a marketing tool. Still, a close examination of what is being projected by a place brand can serve as a window to understanding social realities of the place.

7. Building Brand Napa
Ian Malcolm Taplin

How did a remote, predominantly agricultural area known for nuts and fruits for 150 years become a world-famous site for fine wine by the beginning of the twenty-first century? This chapter tells the story of how a fine wine market emerged in the region through the purposeful behavior of key individuals who recognized the area's potential and brought resources and, eventually, expertise to achieve this goal. They were abetted in this endeavor by leveraging the growth of a scientific and technical approach to viticulture and oenology spearheaded by formal institutional support in California, and a group of expert critics who were able to demystify wine for consumers who lacked knowledge and confidence in making purchasing decisions. I will also show how informal groups of winemakers initially shared tacit information about winemaking and then were complemented by governance organizations that helped protect the emerging reputation of the region. As wine quality in Napa improved, and signature grapes that garnered a premium price were acknowledged, wineries assiduously fought to protect the integrity of their evolving brand. The elevation of Napa wines to the level of a luxury product was the final part of the brand building effort as new wealthy winery owners established what have come to be known as 'cult wines': limited availability, high price, excellent quality wines. Not only has much of this been achieved in the past half-century, but it also occurred in a country initially with limited interest in wine consumption.

Since part of the business model for wineries has been to offer onsite tastings, visitors to the valley have increased dramatically. Catering to these large numbers of tourists has led to the development of ancillary hospitality industries (hotels and restaurants plus VIP transportation companies), successfully leveraging the region's wine reputation to charge high prices for what are considered elevated experiences. This has further cemented the distinct identity of Napa wines from other areas in California since it is now unambiguously seen as a luxury destination.

INTRODUCTION

In 1821, when Mexico gained independence from Spain, the Napa Valley, northeast of San Francisco was a sparsely populated agricultural backwater with a few farms that grew nuts and fruit. The area had barely attracted the attention of the Franciscan missionaries who established their northernmost mission in the nearby town of Sonoma in 1823 (*Mission San Francisco Solana*) as part of their proselytizing efforts with the Indigenous population. Since wine was central to many of their activities, the friars planted vineyards with 'mission grapes', the origins of which date back to sixteenth-century Europe. They also encouraged sedentary agricultural practices amongst the Indigenous inhabitants because they thought such a lifestyle would help 'civilize' them. What the wine tasted like and how much was produced is difficult to determine. One can only assume that it sufficed the mission's sacramental and social needs since accounts by secular travelers who frequented the mission were favorably disposed to both quantity and quality.[1]

Just over a decade after gaining independence, Mexico secularized the missions in 1833 and their lands were sold off. The large clerical estates north of San Francisco were distributed by Mariano Vallejo, a lieutenant from the San Francisco Presidio, who was responsible for allocating property to the local Indigenous population. Most of it, however, went to his friends. For example, large tracts of land in Napa were granted to individuals such as North Carolina mountain man George Yount, who had helped Vallejo turn Sonoma into a vibrant social and political administrative center. Yount was given the 12,000-acre Rancho Caymus in what is now the central part of Napa. He set about farming it as well as breaking it up into lots to be sold to individuals who were interested in viticulture as well as growing fruits and nuts. Others who went on to start wineries were similarly the recipients of Vallejo's generosity. The Indigenous population were less fortunate.

When Mexico ceded what they called 'Alta California' to the United States (US) in 1848, other intrepid newcomers entered the region eager to take advantage of more land giveaways.[2] Viticulture proved popular since it provided alcohol to the miners following the 1849 gold rush in California. Such miners were possibly not discriminating in their taste if the alcohol was sufficient to dull their senses after a day mining. Given this less than discerning demand, there was little pressure on winemakers to perfect an excellent product. When

---

[1] See Charles Sullivan, *Napa Wine: A History* (The Wine Appreciation Guild 2008), 20.

[2] Ian M Taplin, *The Napa Valley Wine Industry* (Cambridge Scholars Press 2022), 49.

the gold ran out, miners flocked to San Francisco and its adjacent areas, and the growing population continued to provide a market for wine and other alcoholic beverages.

In the next decade a continued influx of newcomers to Napa and Sonoma, some with winemaking backgrounds but most with unmitigated enthusiasm for what they saw as a new product, injected a more disciplined and informed approach to growing grapes. One such individual was the Hungarian Agostin Haraszthy who was commissioned by the California State Agricultural Society in 1858 to write a report providing practical notes on grape growing and general vineyard management.[3] Of particular importance was the fact that he addressed local grape-growing conditions rather than transfer what had been done on the east coast and even Europe where terrain and climates were different. He also acknowledged that growing conditions in Napa and Sonoma were perfect for wine and his efforts proved to be the first systematic attempt to apply a modicum of professionalism to this industry.

Additional California state support for the fledgling industry was forthcoming in the next few years. In an attempt to address financial problems faced by farmers because of the long cycle between planting and eventual crop harvests (typically a four-year period time frame), in 1859 the state legislature introduced a four-year tax exemption on all newly planted vineyards to allow wineries a realistic time frame to gain a sufficient revenue stream. This was followed in 1861 with the introduction of the Commission upon the Ways and Means best adapted to promote the Improvement and Growth of the Grape-vine in California.[4] Such endeavors were indicative of the state's awareness of the important role that agriculture could play in economic growth if potential farmers were given the requisite knowledge about best practices. This incipient institutional support proved vital in establishing parameters about what worked in an emerging wine industry.

For many of the early pioneers in wine, their skills were nonetheless rudimentary. It was a time of trial and error with no clear sense of what a quality product might taste like. But the soil and climate were conducive to grape growing and people experimented with what varietals grew best even though most relied upon mission grapes since that was a proven product.

---

[3] See Thomas Pinney, *A History of Wine in America: From the Beginnings to Prohibition* (University of California Press 1989) 262–3.

[4] Vincent P Carosso, *The California Wine Industry, 1830-1895* (University of California Press 1951), 50.

EARLY SUCCESSES[5]

In 1856 Haraszthy bought a 560-acre property northeast of Sonoma and planted 14,000 vines imported from Europe. He developed his own nursery on the site and helped two other immigrants, Charles Krug and Jacob Schram, develop their vineyards in Napa. They and other newcomers gradually replaced mission vines with European varietals such as Riesling, Zinfandel and Sylvaner and experimented with plantings on hillside slopes rather than the valley floor.

By the 1860s several vintages had demonstrated that one could make good quality wine in Napa if one had the requisite resources (money to acquire land and patience in seeking a return on the investment plus viticultural skill sets). Unfortunately demand for quality wine remained poor, especially during the recession years of the late 1870s. The market remained largely regional (California), and wine was still very much a commodity product that could not attract a price premium. It was a beverage consumed in saloons rather than as a complement to meals.

Wineries used rudimentary equipment to make the wine and it was placed in redwood casks then sold to merchants in San Francisco where it was often mixed with other wines in bigger barrels for eventual resale. This supply-and-demand disequilibrium encouraged quantity over quality for most producers; their small size limited their marketing opportunities, and they lacked production-scale economies. As with any agricultural product, high crop yield was seen as the norm, but this often came at the expense of quality. The result was often negative comments made about Napa wine although some Napa producers persisted in their attempts to craft a quality wine and eschewed the high yield viticulture method.[6]

By the 1880s the wine market was beginning to change. Evidence from local newspapers of the time indicated that merchants were beginning to be willing to pay higher prices for Napa wines over those from Sonoma, presumably because they felt the quality was better.[7] Winemakers in Napa, meanwhile, were establishing informal exchanges of information about growing practices which led to better quality. One such group was the newly formed St Helena Winegrowers Association that pledged to discourage the use of chaptalisation (adding sugar in the production process to increase alcohol levels). They also met informally and shared best practices. Cognizant of the need to protect the

---

[5] Taplin (n 2), 50.
[6] Sullivan (n 1), 74.
[7] 'Viticulture' (*Daily Alta California* California, March 15 1880).

embryonic reputation of Napa, they recognized that individual wineries would ultimately be judged by the collective image.

One owner who was at the forefront of this endeavor was the aforementioned Charles Krug who assiduously worked to build a consensus about best practices as well as transform the Association into a formal governance body.[8] Not only was this the first objective evidence of Napa wines' potential but also that producers in the region were beginning to meaningfully differentiate their wine from adjacent counties. They also realized that if they could consistently make a quality product, they needed to market it beyond California and especially to the east coast of the US where demand might be highest and more people willing to pay a premium price. To achieve this, producers began to articulate a variant of the French terroir argument, claiming the distinctive characteristics of the Valley in producing a quality wine. They also sought more support from the state, arguing that their industry was commercially viable and could play a role in the state's economic development. The pressure resulted in the creation of the Board of State Viticultural Commissioners in 1880 (part of the California State Agricultural Society) that was tasked with promoting viticulture in the state and providing resources to help growers mitigate problems.

In 1875 the University of California at Berkeley appointed Eugene Hilgard as professor of agriculture. He was a viticulture specialist who built a vineyard and cellar at the university and was a prominent voice in advocating geographic origin demarcations that would help local producers gain wider credibility. He also embraced a rigorous and systematic scientific and technical approach to winemaking, arguing, amongst other things, for a more thorough application of chemistry in the fermentation process. He demonstrated that wines from the region could be of good quality but only if scrupulous attention to detail was maintained. He opposed blending with mission grapes, which many still did, and urged growers to experiment with mainstream European varietals that would produce quality wines that reflected their place of origin. This entailed understanding soil types, micro-climates and other site-specific issues that had often been ignored in the past. In sum, he added a technocratic legitimacy to winemaking that endorsed the efforts of those in Napa who had been pushing for more rigor in their focus upon quality over quantity. He echoed their concerns but, crucially, also provided resources at the university that could help advance professionalism in winemaking.[9]

Hilgard's approaches were further endorsed by Board of State Viticultural Commissioner, Charles Wetmore, who tirelessly collected data on wine

---

[8] Sullivan (n 1), 70.
[9] Taplin (n 2), 56.

production, wrote reports and instructions for winemaking and argued that growers should plant Bordeaux varietals such as Cabernet Sauvignon.[10] The latter had not been considered seriously in the past but those that planted it following his advice discovered that it thrived in the region.

BRAND BEGINNINGS

The first notable recognition of Napa's potential to produce quality wines came at the 1888 State Viticultural Convention in San Franscisco in which professional wine judges evaluated red and white wines from throughout the state. Napa producers came out on top, receiving 21 first place awards, and the judges particularly commended the Cabernet Sauvignon from that region. When the results were widely publicized, it demonstrated that quality wine could be made in that area and that Cabernet Sauvignon could be a signature grape.[11]

One producer who was in the forefront of a heightened commitment to quality was former sea captain Gustav Niebaum. He bought land for a winery near Rutherford in 1880, pulled out the mission vines that had been planted earlier and replaced them with Bordeaux varietals as well as Riesling and Zinfandel. He hired capable, experienced managers to oversee production, rebuilt the existing winery to meet his stringent cleanliness requirements and the result was a state-of-the-art winery named Inglenook when it opened in 1891.[12] He recognized the potential benefits of brand building by bottling his wines as estate wines, putting a distinctive diamond trademark on the label, and selling them direct to consumers rather than going through merchant channels that others used. He focused upon east coast markets where he believed wine lovers could be persuaded to buy a Napa wine if it had demonstrable quality. His showmanship and embrace of publicity helped disseminate his message and clearly helped sales. But like others who shared his passion for making a quality wine, it often proved difficult to sell that wine at a premium price, mainly because California was still not associated with consistent fine production, despite Napa's success in winning local awards. His efforts were further dampened when productive harvests in the 1890s coincided with a recession and resulted in an oversupply of wine which put further downward pricing pressure on producers which led to bankruptcies for some. Selling direct to consumers was also difficult since a powerful group of merchants

---

[10] Pinney (n 3), 350.
[11] Sullivan (n 1), 133.
[12] Taplin (n 2), 58.

dominated the wine distribution and sales channels, effectively constraining smaller wineries which lacked resources to bypass such channels.[13]

THE POWER OF MERCHANTS

In 1894 seven of the state's largest merchants formed the California Wine Association (CWA). Their aim was to manage price and quantity fluctuations and to act as an umbrella group for many of the large producers (which included them). They would buy wine from growers, blend it, and then ship it for sale in barrels. There was a modicum of quality control, but since the final product was a blend, it often contained juice from well-made wineries as well as those that made sub-par quality wine.[14] This proved a disincentive for some growers to focus on quality rather than quantity and thus hindered the growing reputation of Napa even though the wine sold had a generic California demarcation. Napa still struggled to differentiate itself from California as a whole. Because the CWA was so powerful it was difficult for individual wineries that did have a commitment to quality to find ways of bypassing the Association's sales and distribution channels. This tension between a growing realisation that one could make a quality wine but find it difficult to sell under the existing rubric, constrained Napa's growth during the last decade of the nineteenth century.

Much of the wine sold by the CWA came from the central valley – an area known for producing high yields and average quality wines. The CWA's marketing muscle was predicated on producing a certain style of wine that could be easily transported and was sufficiently generic in taste for a consumer base that was not particularly discerning. Finally, the CWA provided consistent buyers for wine so even some Napa producers were seduced by the prospect of reliable sales rather than trying to market their wine by themselves.

Two events would gradually change the marketing power of the CWA. First, the late 1880s and 1890s had witnessed outbreaks of phylloxera which resulted in many vines being destroyed and ripped up. Subsequent plantings were based upon disease-resistant rootstocks (the product of technical advances promulgated by the universities) and focused upon Bordeaux varietals such as Cabernet Sauvignon. This set the stage for newcomers such as George de Latour to concentrate on Cabernet Sauvignon in his new vineyards (BV #1 and BV #2) as a varietal that would produce good quality/yield ratios and a wine on a par with Left Bank Bordeaux. In 1903 the US Department of Agriculture established an experimental vineyard called To Kalon near Oakville in

---

[13] Taplin (n 2), 61.
[14] Taplin (n 2), 63.

Napa where resistant rootstocks were also planted. The impetus behind this controlled experiment was to discern how a site-specific area could produce notable characteristics in a wine.

George de Latour and other newcomers with similar visions of managing yields to make a quality wine, developed alternative direct distribution channels to sell their wines to discerning consumers outside of the CWA framework. Whilst not always successful, they nonetheless established an embryonic network and developed a customer base who were prepared to pay a price premium for a wine that had a Napa designation rather than a generic California wine.[15]

Secondly, Napa's reputation was significantly enhanced by the 1915 Panama-Pacific International Exhibition (PPIE) where an international panel of judges enthusiastically awarded many of the prizes to Napa wine, including 20 gold medals for Inglenook. Some have questioned whether the awards were truly based on the quality of wine or more on the higher price points charged by Napa producers.[16] Price was thus equated with quality: high price equals high quality. A similar scenario had unfolded in France half a century earlier. The 1855 Bordeaux classification was based upon wine price and reputation rather than a truly objective evaluation of actual quality. Did the judges at the PPIE behave similarly? One will never know but what does emerge is the growing acknowledgement that apparently quality wines were being made in Napa and discerning consumers were willing to pay more for it than a generic California wine. This was a milestone in the area's reputation building.

Unfortunately, this progress came to a rather abrupt halt following social movements to limit alcohol consumption that eventually led to nationwide Prohibition. Wineries had thought they might be absolved from the growing condemnation of hard liquor and its destructive consequences for family life, but ultimately this proved to be an illusory hope.

COLLAPSE THEN REGENERATION

For the next five decades, Napa remained in hiatus: Prohibition (1919–33) effectively shut down most of the industry. This was followed by the struggle to rebuild in the 1940s and 1950s because of a dearth of skilled winemakers and a shift in American consumers' drinking habits.

---

[15] Taplin (n 2), 64–5.
[16] Taplin (n 2), 64.

Just prior to Prohibition there were approximately 700 wineries in the region but only 130 existed upon its repeal.[17] Those that reopened often lacked trained staff, the cellar conditions were derelict or unsanitary and vines deteriorated and had to be pulled out. The market for wine had also changed. Many consumers had become accustomed to poor-quality and often home-made wines so there was a limited demand for a refined product. What interest existed in alcohol was also focused upon fortified drinks like brandy. The recession years of the 1930s further compounded these problems as they restricted the spending power of many Americans. It was not until the 1960s that circumstances changed, in part because of improved prosperity and a rekindled enthusiasm for wine consumption but also, yet again, because of an influx of determined newcomers with winemaking experience or the resources and enthusiasm to start a winery.

Some of the notable figures in this new era were John Daniel Jr (who took over Inglenook), Andre Tchelistcheff (Beaulieu), Croation immigrant Mike Grgich (Souverain) and Robert Mondavi who built his now iconic mission-style winery in 1966. All had varying degrees of experience in winemaking, and they were followed in the next decade by others such as Warren Winiarski, Cathy Corison, Tony Soter and John Shafer. At the same time more detailed technical information about viticulture and oenology had become available at University of California, Davis where research into techniques for fine winemaking had been introduced into formal degree programs.[18]

Whilst knowledgeable about many of the details behind winemaking, these newcomers recognized the need to learn best practices from each other if they were to fully understand the growing conditions in Napa. To accomplish this, they formed informal networks to share information and revived the Napa Valley Technical Group (started in the 1940s by Tchelitscheff).[19] This group was in the forefront of advocating varietal and geographical labeling to distinguish their wines from those elsewhere in California. But above all they met and critiqued their wines, recognizing that the only way the region could be known for fine wines was if everyone were making them. This collective organizational learning proved crucial in addressing issues that otherwise had been dealt with via trial and error. Site-specific knowledge (planting and spacing distances plus canopy management) on both hillsides and the valley

---

[17] Thomas Pinney, *A History of Wine in America: From Prohibition to the Present* (University of California Press 2005).
[18] Pinney (n 17).
[19] Taplin (n 2), 80.

floor as well as varietal harvesting differences, enabled practical experiences to become aggregated into a collective good.[20]

Several major winery owners had earlier recognized the utility of organizational unity and in 1944 founded the Napa Valley Vintners (see Chapter 3 by Rex Stults in this volume for further historical details of this organization). Its membership expanded in the 1970s and it became involved in marketing the region's wines as well as developing the brand. The Napa Valley Grape Growers Association was formed in 1975 with the aim of fostering best practices amongst growers and re-emphasizing that quality wine begins in the vineyard.[21]

These formal and informal groups brought together individuals who believed that Napa could consistently produce fine wine if collectively they worked together to share tacit knowledge and provide a structure for information transfer. The impetus behind this was to legitimize the collective identity of the industry, encourage further professionalism amongst the actors, and integrate scientific and technical proficiencies into winemaking. Their aim was to benchmark quality as a product of scientific training. To do this necessitated a minimal amount of de facto governance if quality wines were to be consistently produced. The results might be formulaic and involve standardized production methods, but these were demonstrably the way to maximize the potential of the area's soil types and climate. The resulting wines, as I have argued elsewhere, increasingly became, 'uniform expressions of a long, hot, and dry growing season, supplemented by irrigation when necessary'.[22] In other words they were robust, fruit-forward wines that would stand out in a blind tasting.

CONSOLIDATING THE REPUTATION

Having established that fine quality wines could be made in Napa, the next stage was to determine the varietals that would not only grow best but also command a premium price. From the 1960s onwards most Bordeaux varietals had been planted as had Chardonnay, Syrah, Zinfandel and even Riesling. Most did well although Cabernet Sauvignon and Chardonnay's pedigrees, as

---

[20] GT Guthey, 'Agro-Industrial Conventions: Some Evidence From Northern California's Wine Industry' (2008) 174(2) The Geographic Journal 1, 38; see also Doug Shafer, *A Vineyard in Napa* (University of California Press 2012).

[21] Taplin (n 2), 102.

[22] Ian M Taplin, 'Bottling Luxury: Napa Valley and the Transformation of an Agricultural Backwater Into a World-Class Wine Region' (2015) 2(1) Luxury 81, 92.

fine French wines, helped persuade many growers that these grapes might be their signature wines in terms of oenological credentialing. But how could growers convince people on the east coast and elsewhere that Napa wines were in fact a credible alternative to their French counterparts? Two things occurred that successfully addressed these issues. One was a seminal event in Paris in 1976 that proved decisive in elevating Napa to the world wine stage. The second was a group of influential wine critics who further legitimated some of the varietals by developing a scoring system that would help novices understand the purported quality of the wine.

When a Paris-based English wine merchant named Stephen Spurrier, seeking to gain attention for some of his projects and bring California wines to a European audience, organized an official tasting of French and California wines in Paris, he selected 20 wines from the two countries and brought together a panel of expert French judges. The wines were blind tasted and to the astonishment of almost everybody, two Napa wines were chosen as best – Chateau Montelena's Chardonnay and Stag's Leap's Cabernet Sauvignon. These two wines were judged to be better than the French classified growths whose wines were now relegated to a secondary status behind the California upstarts. Much has been written (and filmed) about the Paris tasting and controversies surrounding the skewed methodology and even whether the judges were as competent as Spurrier contended.[23] Nevertheless, the results elevated Napa as an area producing not just fine wines but excellent ones. It also undermined French arguments about the salience of terroir, that the essence of place unique to their regions could be the *sine qua non* for fine wine. This myth was finally exploded for, as Taber noted, 'the Californians had demystified wine'.

When the Paris Judgment was publicized, it coincided with the growth of wine critics in the US who were helping neophyte consumers better understand wine. The two principal industry critics were Robert Parker's *Wine Advocate* magazine and *Wine Spectator*. They simplified buying by awarding scores (out of 100) that indicated their assessment of the quality of the wine. Wines with superior quality were scored 90–4; those described as a classic or exceptional wine, 95–100. Numerical scoring afforded a quasi-scientific evaluation of wine quality and was a hit with the American public, many of whom were new to wine and felt overwhelmed choosing a bottle. This was especially the case with more expensive wines that needed expert validation. Over subsequent decades, these critics have duly recognized the high quality of wine from Napa by awarding very high scores, thus further cementing the region's reputation.

---

[23] The definitive work on the tasting was written by the only journalist who bothered to turn up for the event, *Time Magazine*'s George Taber. See George Taber, *The Judgment of Paris* (Scribner 2005).

It has been argued that critics such as Robert Parker liked a certain style of wine from California —ones that were big and bold.[24] These wines stood out in blind tastings but were also stylistically rich and full of flavor and often with high alcohol content (often around 15%) because the grapes had been left on the vines for longer than normal. Napa, with its long, hot, dry, and sunny summers, was conducive to making this type of wine and many producers did just that. Finally, the wines were designed to be drunk upon purchase, unlike more tannic French wines that needed ageing. This satisfied impatient consumers who wanted instant gratification from their purchase.

Critics were effectively organizing the wine market into categories based on quality and Napa producers realized that Cabernet Sauvignon and Chardonnay could consistently deliver a style that fit into the 'best' category. This became their focus and such wines have become synonymous with Napa in recent decades. High critic scores subsequently enabled wineries to charge a higher price for their wine and market it as an ultra-premium product. As more newcomers entered the valley to make wine, their focus was typically on such varietals and high price points.

TAKING THE BRAND TO THE NEXT LEVEL

As Napa's reputation grew it attracted more industry entrants in the late 1980s and early 1990s, some of whom had extensive financial resources from an earlier successful business. As before such individuals were enthusiastic about wine and owning a winery but they had the capital to acquire the increasingly expensive land in the valley, hire the best winemakers and vineyard managers. They also took advantage of a new breed of consultant winemakers, such as the Frenchman, Michel Roland, to help them craft their wine.[25] The new entrants applied scrupulous detail and diligence to every aspect of the vineyard management and winery and were determined to make the highest quality wine possible from the area. Production was limited (often under 2,000 cases) and the wines were sold on allocation to a list of subscribers who were able to purchase three to six bottles a year. The wines were expensive (often close to or more than $1,000 per bottle) and typically were awarded very high scores from the critics. The latter's endorsement was important for their market validation.

---

[24] One such critic is English wine writer, Jancis Robinson who argued that such wines overwhelm others in tastings and 'muscle out finesse'. Producers, for their part, simply claim their wines are merely an expression of the vineyard and growing conditions. See Sullivan (n 1), 390.

[25] Taplin (n 2), 149.

Some of the best-known examples of such wines are Screaming Eagle (1992 debut vintage of 200 cases), Harlan Estate, Bryant Family, and Colgin.

Such an approach embodies all the features of a luxury branded product – highest level of quality, scarcity, high price – which conveys a sense of privilege and exclusivity, and comes from a special place.[26] Such wineries were able to build upon the growing reputation of Napa and deploy resources to ensure that their wine would be exceptional, distinctive and a true expression of what the region was capable of doing. The fact that these wines were opulent, rich, and often with high alcohol level, further demarcated them from their old-world counterparts, even where the same grapes were used. They also personified an American vision of winemaking that was immersed in scientific expertise and technical rigor. It was, as wine writer Matt Kramer notes, 'quantitative, methodical, and verifiable'.[27] Wineries and winemakers developed rigorous technically-mediated approaches that systematized all facets of fermentation and winemaking to guarantee a predictable outcome. Since the climate was perfect for growing vinifera grapes, such operational improvements enhanced consistency and allowed owners to balance any harvest variations. When a series of excellent vintages occurred in the late 1980s, this merely added to the growing reputation of the region.

Most Napa Valley wineries remained small (under 4,000 cases) even though the numbers were rising (more than 200 by the late 1980s). Collectively their reputation had grown as had the distinctive brands that secured most attention by critics. The so called 'cult wines' as they have come to be known embodied the essentialism of Napa Valley as a place and what it was capable of producing in its wines.[28] Critics lavished praise and prices rose. One winery owner captured the essence of what was happening in the valley:[29]

> Our goal was to make a series of single-estate, limited production, world-class wines. We had great hillside locations and fantastic soils. We aimed to produce several hundred cases from three estates. We built a small mailing list with information from restaurant owners, wine merchants, and people we knew who were passionate about fine wines. Our first release was limited to three bottles per customer. Most wanted more, perhaps a case or two, but we had neither the capacity not the inclination to meet his demand. We created an immediate perception of

---

[26] Peter Yeung and Liz Thach, *Luxury wine Marketing* (Infinite Ideas Press 2019), 6.

[27] Matt Kramer, *New California Wine* (Running Press 2004), 29.

[28] See Ian M Taplin, 'Crafting an Iconic Wine: The Rise of "Cult" Napa' (2016) 28(2) International Journal of Wine Business Research 105, for a more extensive discussion of this growth.

[29] Note: these interviews in footnotes 30 and 31 were carried out in conjunction with the author's own independent ongoing research into Napa wines.

scarcity which has helped us develop our reputation. The harder it is to get, the more people seem to want it. The biggest challenge has been saying "no" to very wealthy individuals who are used to getting what they want.[30]

Another owner said:

> What we are doing is an artisanal business that is selling an experience. Once you've drunk it, it's gone, so much of the value comes in anticipation. In many respects, we are the least business like in what we do because we're trying to limit sales. So, what wine we sell is basically the experience of being part of a bigger project that has to be expensive. The average person doesn't get it, and that's fine. They're not our customers.[31]

In my interviews with winery owners over the past decades, most have said that critic scores have been important for their brand building.[32] Many buyers, even of fine wine, are insecure in their own judgement and look for heuristic markers to judge quality. Some buyers admit to only buying wine with top scores, partly because they want to display such wines in their elaborately constructed cellars.[33] Such wines become status markers, communicating an aura of sophistication as well as wealth for the owners.

Wine has become a Veblen good (a product that is used as a positional or status marker) as Napa Valley wine has gained currency as an indication of success. Others are buying Napa Valley wine as an investment instrument that might be drunk at some stage or simply sit as part of a diversified portfolio of assets – what economist Robert Frank aptly noted as the ultimate liquid asset.[34] This heightened demand, often from ultra-high-net-worth individuals, further solidified Napa Valley's brand reputation.

CABERNET BECOMES KING

Vineyard acreage expanded during the 1980s and 1990s with most of it devoted to two varietals – Cabernet Sauvignon and Chardonnay. The former

---

[30] Personal interview (2010).
[31] Personal interview (2006).
[32] See Taplin (n 2), 161.
[33] See the special issue of *Wine Spectator* on the art of collecting wine. *Wine Spectator*, 'The Art of Collecting: Expert Advice on Creating a Great Wine Cellar' (*Wine Spectator*, 31 July 2017).
[34] Robert T Frank, 'A Cellar Full of Collateral, By the Bottle or by the Case' (*New York Times,* New York, 26 July 2015) <www.nytimes.com/2015/07/26/business/a-cellar-full-of-collateral-by-the-bottle-or-the-case.html> accessed 3 May 2024.

offered wineries the premium pricing they desired and by 1989 Bordeaux varietals (Cabernet Sauvignon, Cabernet Franc, Petit Verdot and Merlot which were used as blends) comprised most of the vineyard acreage in the valley.[35] Demand for fine wine was increasing in the US at this time and more Americans were trying California wines, especially those from Napa Valley. As noted earlier, stylistically these wines were different from their old-world counterparts but as critics continued to laud them, consumers were prepared to pay a premium price for them. Small production, limited availability and high-priced wines had this distinctive style and they frequently sold out.

In 1961 Cabernet Sauvignon accounted for 6% of total acreage whereas today it is just over 50%. This is followed by Chardonnay and then at smaller percentages the other Bordeaux varietals. Stand-alone Merlot sales collapsed because of the 'Sideways' phenomenon (a 2004 film in which the key character excoriated Merlot in favor of Pinot Noir) and have not recovered.[36] Since the highest priced wines were Cabernet, that became not only the varietal to plant but also the signature grape for Napa Valley. It commanded the highest price and wineries that had other varietals planted replaced them with Cabernet.

There are currently just over 450 wineries in Napa Valley, but most remain small (approximately 80% are still under 4,000 cases annual production). As wine scholar Charles Sullivan aptly noted, 'The idea that one can make fine wine, and lots of wine, but not lots of fine wine, has probably been laid to rest'.[37] Napa Valley is the case in point, and this is reflected in ever rising price points charged for wine from Napa.

In recent decades vintners have assiduously protected their reputation by forestalling efforts by some to use the Napa Valley label to sell inexpensive wine that came from grapes in other parts of California. The most famous example of this resulted in the lawsuit against Fred Franzia whose winery under the name of Napa Ridge was in Napa but processed inexpensive grapes from the central valley of California. He was leveraging the Napa name to sell a cheap commodity wine (sold for $1.99 a bottle as Charles Shaw, better known as 'two buck Chuck'). To stop his activities, the Napa Valley Vintners (NVV) lobbied the California State Legislature in 2000 to require any wine with a Napa designation to be made from at least 75% Napa grapes. After a series of appeals and new rulings that went all the way to the Supreme Court, the case was decided in favor of the NVV,[38] and that percentage rule exists today. The rationale behind the lawsuit was for 'the truth in labelling and not

---

[35] Sullivan (n 1), 386.
[36] Taplin (n 2), 146.
[37] Sullivan (n 1), 424.
[38] California Business and Professions Code §25241 (The Napa Name Law).

90 *Place-branding experiences*

allowing the Napa name to be misrepresented on the labels of wine'[39] that did not meet the required level of Napa grape contents in the winemaking.

The Napa Valley American Viticultural Area (AVA) that had been formed in 1981 and the sub-appellations that have been created since, bestowed a geographic identity not dissimilar to that of French appellations but without the restrictive governance. Talk of terroir in Napa is less evocative of a mythical Arcadian past such as that of Burgundy, but it does resonate with those who argue for further demarcations associated with estate demarcations.[40] It is also tempered by the invocation of technical efficiency and scientific rationales that maximize the vineyard's potential in ways that historical tradition cannot do in California. This viticultural rationalism also plays into the rhetoric of identity and credibility that has been purposefully used by producers to leverage their product as a super-premium good.

CONCLUSION

Napa Valley has firmly established itself on the world wine stage as a purveyor of exceptional quality wines. The cooperative framework that facilitated information sharing amongst winemakers in the 1970s and 1980s has been somewhat replaced by a more competitive environment where information is more likely to be hoarded than shared. Many individuals whom I interviewed said that much is shared but as the winery numbers have grown it is more difficult to informally collaborate than in the past.[41] This does not mean a cutthroat competitive environment – more a modicum of secrecy that has become pervasive. Nonetheless there remains a strong commitment to protecting the brand amongst incumbent winery owners.

Increased attention to environmental concerns over the past years includes mitigation of fire, drought, and pesticide use. Wineries have also faced labor shortages and consequently rising labor costs. Collective efforts to deal with this have included subsidized accommodation for workers. The valley's reputation inevitably attracted non-winery owners who bought land and built large houses, which pushed housing prices above what could be afforded by local workers, most of whom now drive long distances to work. Various attempts to constrain the suburbanization of the valley have been successful, such as those

---

[39] Interview with Rex Stults, Vice President of Industry Relations, Napa Valley Vinters (8 November 2023).

[40] See J Bonné, *The New California Wine* (Ten Speed Press 2013) and Steve Heimoff, *New Classic winemakers of California* (University of California Press 2018).

[41] Taplin (n 28).

limiting the minimum size of lots. Again, this was an effort spearheaded by the NVV and major winery owners. But it remains an expensive place to live for all but the very wealthy. In one sense this endorses the exclusiveness of the valley, lending legitimacy to the luxury aura the industry has so assiduously sought to evoke.

Napa Valley's success also begets a range of ancillary industries, particularly those in hospitality. Luxury hotels have been built that cater to tourists who want the full luxury wine experience. Charges at tasting rooms where people can try wine in a curated setting have risen dramatically. As one winery owner told me,[42] 'We cater to a small subset of wealthy individuals who want to celebrate a special occasion or create a remarkable event. If you pay $150-200 for a tasting, $500 for dinner and $800 plus for a hotel room, you are only attracting certain types'.[43] Other owners have said that they deliberately raised their tasting fees to discourage people who just want to come and drink but might not buy wine. When press coverage sometimes complains about the high prices and that Napa is becoming unaffordable for most people, it is missing the point. Napa no longer provides a commodity product. It is offering an ultra-premium wine in a luxurious setting where the experience is an integral part of the package. It is not designed for everybody, merely a select few.

Over the decades winery owners have worked hard in a purposeful manner to build a brand that is distinct from other regions in California (as well as other global wine regions). In doing this they benefitted from wine critics who liked their product and awarded top scores which reduced the insecurity that many wine consumers have about buying wine. They have also developed a product that is the embodiment of scientific and technical efficiency, which when combined with a climate that is undoubtedly very favorable for grape growing, results in a distinctive style of wine. And finally, by providing a comprehensive educational infrastructure, the state continues to support the industry, both in Napa Valley and other California wine growing regions.

---

[42] See Taplin (n 2) for descriptions of these interviews.
[43] Personal interview by author on own independent research (2021).

8. The Commercial Power of Place-Branding

Henry Farr, Rosie Mallory and Penny Erricker

INTRODUCTION

At their most basic levels, brands are heuristics. They allow consumers to make swift purchasing decisions based on previous experience and knowledge of the brand. If a consumer has used the products or services of a given brand before, and they see their logo, they are reminded of this previous experience, making them either more or less likely to purchase. Place-branding designation is a way to protect and exploit this effect regarding the place that a given brand is associated.

Geographical Indication (GI) is used by brands to demonstrate to consumers their quality, their heritage, and their authenticity. These are often shown prominently on packaging, allowing leverage of the strong brand equity of the geography that they indicate, with the aim of this therefore improving sales.

GIs can vary in rigor. Some, such as Protected Designations of Origin (PDO), require strict conditions on the part of producers. They reflect not only the strong brand equity of the region they represent, but also the highest standards in production. Strict entry requirements are therefore necessary so as not to tarnish or dilute their strong reputations.

However, brands can also use place-branding more casually, often evoking similar consumer reaction. This may be done through brand name, such as *New York Bakery Co*, through a brand character, such as *Dolmio's Dolmio Family*, or through promotional materials, such as *Fosters*. In each of these examples, the product in question is produced in the United Kingdom (UK), rather than the place that the brand relates to – New York, Italy, and Australia respectively.

Given the continued commercial success of these brands despite not possessing a rigorous GI or PDO, the question raised concerns the extent to which consumers understand or care about the specific protected status. We can be very confident that place-branding does impact consumer decision making.

The more prescient question lies in the level of understanding that consumers hold, and whether they distinguish between different levels of GI.

MARKET ASSESSMENT

Understanding of Place-Name Protections

As a form of intellectual property (IP) rights, GIs offer a powerful differentiation tool to products deeply defined by geographical areas. The distinctive characteristics of GI products can arise from the combination of specific geographic conditions, including natural elements like soil and climate, along with traditional production techniques and cultural influences that are particular to those regions. Through well executed GIs, the quality and tradition of such goods are protected and preserved, creating value for millions of producers, processors, and distributors around the world, while also benefitting consumers who can trust the authenticity and origin of these products.

GIs also serve as a significant developmental resource for countries that produce commodities. However, without adequate legal protection, there is potential for encouraging counterfeit products, which deceptively label products through the misuse of GIs.[1] This can harm the reputation of authentic goods, despite them not being responsible for the production and distribution of counterfeit goods. This could result in GI operators being forced out of business. As such, a large majority of national laws consider GIs as an independent category of IP rights, with precise criteria concerning registration, oppositions, and length of protection. To protect GIs in foreign jurisdictions, countries have undertaken mutual recognition via bilateral agreements since 1970.[2]

A 2019 study conducted by Brand Dialogue, a public relations agency and part of the Brand Finance Plc group, on British GI brands substantiates the view that location branding (associating products and services with a geographic location) can drive positive perceptions about brands. Let us firstly introduce a definition of place-branding to enhance our understanding of the connection between GI brands and their origins. Place-branding can be defined as the DNA of a place, encapsulating its distinctive characteristics, which are

---

[1] *Combating GI Product Counterfeiting in China* (Chinabrand IP Consulting GmbH, 2019) <www.origin-gi.com/wp-content/uploads/2019/10/CHINABRAND_Whitepaper_GI_China_EN.PDF> accessed 30 November 2023.

[2] Massimo Vittori, 'GIs: Between Tradition and Model Challenges' in *British GI Brands 2019* (Brand Dialogue 2019) <https://brandirectory.com/reports/british-gi-brands-2019/> accessed 20 September 2023.

Table 8.1   Phrases Associated with Protected Status

Metric	%
Authentic	66.2%
Premium Quality	62.2%
Preserve Traditional Methods and Culture	50.6%
Something to be Proud of	49.6%

Source: Brand Finance British GI Brands 2019 (April 2019) <https://brandirectory.com/reports/british-gi-brands-2019> accessed 5 June 2024

defined by what we (as consumers) perceive as its personality and identity.[3] Place-branding serves as a platform for showcasing what makes a place unique, empowering nations to discover and articulate these distinctive elements.[4] As such, it can be said that place-branding contributes powerfully to stakeholder perceptions of GI brands, given their close association with consumer perceptions of the nation brand, its distinctive traits, and cultural attributes.

Consumer Perceptions

Brand Dialogue's 2019 study found that British consumers respond positively to GI brands that feature geographical indications. Phrases associated with protected status skew positive with 'Authentic' (66.2%) and 'Premium Quality' (62.2%) receiving the highest scores, followed by 'Preserve Traditional Methods and Culture' (50.6%) and 'Something to be Proud of' (49.6%).[5] Brand origin can serve as a powerful differentiator for a brand and can help establish the desired reputation and product associations.[6] Typically, these associations pertain to trust and quality. This effect is strongest in sectors like fresh foods, packaged foods, coffee, tea, and water, where freshness, localized tastes, and flavors play a significant role in consumer preferences.[7]

---

[3] Florian Kaefer, *An Insider's Guide to Place Branding: Shaping the Identity and Reputation of Cities, Regions, and Countries* (Springer Nature Switzerland AG 2021) 7.

[4] Kaefer (n 3), 12.

[5] 'National Branding: How to Build an Effective Location Brand Identity' (Brand Finance, 21 October 2019) <https:// brandfinance .com/ insights/ nation -branding #location -branding -geographic -clustering -for -corporate -brands> accessed 20 September 2023.

[6] *British GI Brands 2019* (Brand Dialogue, 2019) <https://brandirectory.com/reports/british-gi-brands-2019/> accessed 20 September 2023.

[7] Ibid.

Scotch Whisky follows a set of shared factors, such as the cool and humid climate, which plays a crucial role in the spirit's maturation process in oak casks for a minimum of three years.[8] This combination of elements gives Scotch Whisky its distinctive Scottish character, designating it as a GI.[9] The earliest written mention of Scotch Whisky, dating back to the late 1400s, contributes to the perception of tradition and heritage associated with the product, which in turn supports its GI status. For its consumers, this substantiates the notion that Scotch Whisky distilleries know what they're doing and are experts in their craft. This, in turn, evokes a level of trust amongst stakeholders, assuring them that they are investing in products made in a specific way in accordance with UK law.

Parmigiano and PDO

Italian hard cheese Parmigiano Reggiano is another such brand which benefits from its PDO (Product of Origin) Status. Italy's reputation and influence is strongly attached to its food tradition, and consumers across the globe express positive perceptions towards Italy's cuisine and culinary heritage. Brand Finance research conducted in 2023 on global perceptions of 'soft power' found that Italian food is the most loved globally.[10] As such, when brands distinguish themselves as uniquely Italian, consumers almost instantaneously trust them, associating the brand with its Italian heritage, production techniques, and, consequently, perceived quality. The characteristics that are linked to products from geographical locations like Italy provide consumers with the guarantee that they are buying authentic produce steeped in rich heritage, as well as enhancing the work of local producers and protecting the product against imitations and unfair competition.

Through past use of these products, consumers learn to trust the PDO mark, making repeat purchase and recommendation more likely.

The PDO status is awarded to products of excellence that express a close tie to their territory of origin and follow specific production regulations to create

---

[8] 'Legal Protection in the UK' (Scotch Whisky Association) <www.scotch-whisky.org.uk/insights/protecting-scotch-whisky/legal-protection-in-the-uk/> accessed 30 November 2023.

[9] Lindesay Low, 'Scotch Whisky Association' in *British GI Brands 2019* (Brand Dialogue 2019) <https://brandirectory.com/reports/british-gi-brands-2019/> accessed 20 September 2023.

[10] Massimo Pizzo, 'Italy' in *Global Soft Power Index 2023* (Brand Finance, 2023) <https://static.brandirectory.com/reports/brand-finance-soft-power-index-2023-digital.pdf> accessed 20 September 2023.

quality.[11] Italian PDO products play a hugely significant role in Italy's nation brand value. They also play a role in bolstering Italy's soft power by spreading global appreciation for authentic Italian foods, thus showcasing the nation's rich and diverse culinary heritage.[12] Italy has the highest amount of GI and PDO products in Europe, with 906 products with a GI status.[13] These products contribute to 21% of exports in the Italian food-farming industry – a historical record in exports in 2021.[14]

Parmigiano Reggiano has a unique brand profile due to its PDO status. This protection ensures that the cheese can only be produced in designated regions, where specific environmental factors play a crucial role in shaping the cheese's unique flavor profile. The PDO status also guarantees traditional methods, stringent quality standards, and protects the distinctive aging process, resulting in the cheese's iconic nutty aroma and rich flavor. Finally, the PDO status is also important for traceability purposes. The PDO symbols displayed on packaging provide consumers with assurance of the cheese's genuine, high-quality production and its place of origin. Overall, recognizing Parmigiano's PDO status is vital at every stage, safeguarding its cultural heritage, outstanding reputation, and unique flavor, making it an iconic cheese.

The Mutual Benefits of Place-Branding

Napa Valley, nestled in Northern California, has also harnessed the commercial power of place-branding to become synonymous with premium wine production. This includes the area's rich history of tradition and expertise. Napa Valley's location is unique in that it is home to different soil types and microclimates which alters the taste of the region's grapes, creating multiple different types of wine. Furthermore, the Napa Valley reputation has been cemented through strict regulations, mandating that at least 85% of a wine's grapes must bear Napa Valley GI status, as the grapes originate from the region.[15] This commitment to quality control ensures that Napa Valley wines

---

[11] 'Italian Trade Agency: The Power of Italy's Food Tradition and Sustainability' (Brand Finance, 2 March 2023) <https://brandfinance.com/insights/italian-trade-agency-the-power-of-italys-food-tradition> accessed 20 September 2023.

[12] Ibid.

[13] 'eAmbrosia: The EU Geographical Indications Register' (European Commission) <https:// ec .europa .eu/ agriculture/ eambrosia/ geographical-indications-reGIster/> accessed 30 November 2023.

[14] 'Italian Trade Agency …' (n 11).

[15] 'California: Wine Law & Official Classifications' (Capstone California) <https:// capstonecalifornia .com/ study -guides/ regions/ california/ california/ wine _law> accessed 30 November 2023.

consistently deliver on their promise of excellence, further elevating their status in the global wine market. Beyond terroir and regulations, Napa Valley's commercial success of its GI status is also driven by tourism. In 2018, Napa Valley welcomed approximately 3.85 million visitors,[16] to sample the region's wines as well as enjoy fine dining experiences and picturesque vineyard landscapes. Napa Valley's multifaceted appeal has created a compelling place brand, embodying high-quality wine and craftsmanship which consumers are flocking to. This is a mutually beneficial effect for both place and brand. One can introduce a consumer to the other, and they can build up collective brand equity.

In essence, a GI can act as an advocate for a brand. Therefore, brands that register for GI status are likely to fight to obtain and keep that status. All products sold under a GI description must meet strict definitions and clear criteria, providing a strong foundation for producers to build their brands and prevent unfair competition from foreign imitations.[17] This allows consumers to have a level of confidence in the quality of their products, which cannot be conveyed in the same way by non-GI brands. For example, it is highly important for a product like Scotch Whisky to be protected from counterfeiting or imitation. Illegal imitations, which often lack quality control and standards, can negatively impact Scotch Whisky brands, whereby negative associations with the 'fake' are translated across to brands true to the name. If consumers think the 'fake' is low quality, they will be deterred from the real thing. Further, GI is positive for Scotland. It is a great ambassador for the country – 2.2 million people from across the globe visited Scotland's distilleries in 2019 as more and more people enjoyed the heritage of Scotch Whisky.[18] The whisky sector generates a reported £3.3 billion directly to the UK economy.[19]

Similarly, for brands like Parmigiano Reggiano, GI can play an important role in generating value. In 2021, the Parmigiano Reggiano supply chain generated a value of €1.7 billion for dairies and breeders, a community of about 50,000 people spread over the provinces of Parma, Reggio Emilia, Modena, and a part of Bologna and Mantua.[20] Its taste and its nutritional qualities, its

---

[16] 'Travel Research & Statistics' (Visit Napa Valley) <https:// www .visitnapavalley.com/about-us/research/> accessed 20 September 2023.

[17] Low (n 9).

[18] 'Facts and Figures' (Scotch Whisky Association) <https:// www .scotch -whisky.org.uk/insights/facts-figures/> accessed on 30 November 2023.

[19] 'Whisky Tourism Facts and Insights' (VisitScotland) <https:// pedagogie .ac -lille .fr/ histoire -geographie// wp -content/ uploads/ sites/ 8/ 2020/ 09/ ECOSSE -Whisky-Tourism-Facts-and-Insights2.pdf> accessed 9 October 2024.

[20] Massimo Pizzo, 'Italy: Enhancing its Soft Power with Parmigiano Reggiano' (Brand Finance, 15 March 2023) <https:// brandfinance .com/ insights/ 2022 -gsps -parmigiano-reggiano> accessed 20 September 2023.

millenary history and the Area of Origin attract hundreds of thousands of tourists every year. This tourist flow generates value not only for the dairies but for the whole region.[21] Additionally, the GI system also benefits the rural economy by boosting farmers' income and creating an incentive for people to live in more remote areas.[22]

For Kenya's coffee industry, securing official GI status would be a game-changer. In 2015, the Coffee Directorate (CD) in Kenya introduced the 'SO RICH SO KENYAN' Coffee Kenya Mark of Origin to highlight the richness and distinct flavour of Kenyan coffee. Unfortunately, due to a lack of local agreement and enforcement, this branding effort hasn't had the positive impact it could have. The failure to effectively market Kenyan coffee as a high-quality and reputable product has led to sluggish demand and limited coffee production in Kenya.[23]

Kenyan coffee already enjoys a reputation for its exceptional quality and unique flavor profiles. However, if Kenyan coffees were granted the GI status, it would bring several benefits. First, it would provide official recognition for the product and create a sense of loyalty among customers. Additionally, it would add value to Kenyan coffee, allowing producers to charge premium prices for origin-guaranteed products. GIs are known to fetch higher retail prices than similar non-GI products, and this could significantly boost production and increase the value of Kenyan coffee-producing land. These economic benefits could have a ripple effect on rural communities, potentially boosting job creation and contributing to improved living standards. GI status could also boost tourism, generating additional income for local communities and supporting the growth of the coffee sector. Ultimately, obtaining GI status has the potential to unlock the true value of Kenyan coffee and reinject energy into the industry.[24]

---

[21] Pizzo (n 20).

[22] Massimo Pizzo, 'Italy: Mismanagement of the Pandemic and Attempts to Relaunch Country's Image' (Brand Finance, 25 February 2021) <https://brandfinance.com/insights/italy-mismanagement-of-pandemic> accessed 20 September 2023.

[23] Ken Waweru, 'Kenya Seeks to Revive Coffee Sector After Years of Neglect' (The Africa Report, 12 September 2023) <https://www.theafricareport.com/321604/kenya-seeks-to-revive-coffee-sector-after-years-of-neglect/#:~:text=Coffee%20production%20has%20shrunk%20from,to%20less%20than%20100%2C000%20hectares> accessed 9 October 2024.

[24] Loise W Njeru, 'GIs and the Rural Development in Kenya' (oriGIn) <https://www.origin-gi.com/wp-content/uploads/2011/10/2_GIs_and_Rural_dvpt_in_Kenya.pdf> accessed 9 October 2024.

Proven Authenticity

In the UK, having a GI status resonates well with British consumers who prioritize authenticity and quality.[25] The term 'authentic' is closely linked to protected status, and it significantly influences consumer preferences, with about 71.4% of British consumers expressing a greater likelihood to purchase GI products.[26] This preference is even more pronounced among British food enthusiasts, reportedly totaling 7.3 million individuals, who exhibit a strong inclination towards investing in quality and actively seek to uncover the stories and origins behind brands. Consequently, this leads to heightened brand loyalty.[27] Food enthusiasts, in particular, place great importance on ingredient sourcing and are willing to pay extra for premium products. For brands with unique geographical narratives, there exists a substantial opportunity to engage this influential and dedicated community of advocates.

The Cornish pasty is the top GI product in the UK. Given its rich history, distinctive characteristics, and significant role in the Cornish economy, it is unsurprising that the Cornish pasty scores the highest for familiarity amongst British consumers, at 88%, while over half of consumers are also aware of its PGI (Protected Geographical Indication) status. Behind the Cornish pasty, in second and third place, we have Jersey Royal Potatoes and Scotch Whisky. The place-name association instantly highlights these brands' origins, which shapes their distinctive and unique identities. Further, the study highlighted the importance of effective marketing and public relations strategies in enhancing consumer familiarity of these brands' GI status. Finally, another British classic included in the study is Yorkshire Tea, earning the third-highest familiarity score. Research found that effective marketing campaigns, particularly on social media, have significantly contributed to the recognition of the product's protected status.

Sustainability Credentials

Research also finds that sustainability is becoming an increasingly important driver in consumer decision-making, which is in turn driving positive perceptions of GI brands. Studies find that consumer spending is increasingly reflective of sustainability concerns, and products with environmental, social and governance (ESG)-related claims have averaged 28% cumulative growth

---

[25] *British GI Brands 2019* (n 6).
[26] *British GI Brands 2019* (n 6).
[27] *British GI Brands 2019* (n 6).

over five years, outperforming products without such claims.[28] Yorkshire Tea is one such GI brand that is taking steps to improve its ethical and environmental footprint.[29] The brand is focused on building strong relationships with its suppliers and investing in its supply chain to ensure the long-term quality of its tea blends. This quality assurance is critical for maintaining the brand's GI status, which is associated with the unique quality and characteristics of the tea produced in the Yorkshire region. Further, all Yorkshire Tea products are now CarbonNeutral® certified, and the certification process has led to the planting of over 1.5 million trees in Kenya.[30] Such initiatives have the potential to enhance the appeal of Yorkshire Tea's GI-protected products to consumers who value not only the tea's authenticity but also the brand's commitment to ethical and sustainable practices.

Consumer Understanding

While the GI status held by Parmigiano Reggiano has bolstered its reputation as a premium product, in 2019 Brand Dialogue conducted consumer market research in partnership with Consorzio del Formaggio Parmigiano Reggiano, which found that genuine awareness is relatively lacking amongst UK consumers, at only 65–75%. The study also found that there is high knowledge confusion amongst consumers. As a GI brand, Parmigiano Reggiano is the only hard cheese legally allowed to be called Parmesan because of its PDO but, there remains confusion between Parmigiano and other hard cheeses that lack the PDO status, despite Parmigiano's strong heritage, distinctive characteristics, and unique flavor profile. This serves to show the element of confusion in consumer's minds, and the lack of distinction between different levels of GI. Although other Italian hard cheeses, such as Grana Padana, do not merit official PDO status, they are still perceived as high quality by consumers.

The study then analyzed the impact of Parmigiano packaging on consumer choice. Of the UK category buyers surveyed, 64% said that the message that Parmigiano is made 'according to PDO regulations' would 'impact them a lot or a fair amount.' As such, the product's PDO status alone doesn't appear as

---

[28] Sherry Frey, Jordan Bar Am, Vinit Doshi, Anandi Malik, and Steve Noble, 'Consumers Care About Sustainability – and Back it Up With Their Wallets' (McKinsey Company, 6 February 2023) <www.mckinsey.com/industries/consumer-packaged-goods/our-insights/consumers-care-about-sustainability-and-back-it-up-with-their-wallets> accessed 20 September 2023.

[29] *British GI Brands 2019* (n 6).

[30] 'People and Planet' (Yorkshire Tea) <www.yorkshiretea.co.uk/about-us/people-and-planet> accessed 20 September 2023.

strong an argument for driving consumer interest in the product. That said, the study found that consumers were more receptive to messaging around provenance and the product's natural, additive-free characteristics. They also loved the flavor and easy usability of the cheese, and the fact that it is synonymous with Italian cuisine and cooking. Moreover, the fact that Parmigiano Reggiano has been produced for over 900 years using the same techniques was seen as impressive by consumers. All this suggests that, while its GI status may not be the most important fact driving consumer preference for the hard cheese, it does play a significant role in enhancing positive consumer perceptions.

Another driver of commercialization of GI brands and products is achieving a price premium. Food enthusiasts buy into brands more than any other group, but need to be convinced of the value of the brand, as higher price does not necessarily mean higher quality. However, food enthusiasts care about where ingredients come from and are therefore prepared to pay extra for quality products. This helps GI brands achieve a price premium due to their associations with superior quality and excellency, based on tradition and uniqueness, as well as the criteria required of products to meet legally required criteria. A Nielsen study on how perceptions about brand origin shape purchasing intentions around the world reveals similar results. Nearly three-quarters of global respondents say brand origin is as important or more important than other purchase drivers including price.[31] It is estimated that, on average, products protected by GIs in the European Union (EU) are sold at a price 2.23 times higher than of a similar quantity of non-GI product.[32]

Obtaining GI status unquestionably provides brands with a competitive advantage in the market. This advantage lies in the need for clear and easy demonstrable connections between a product and its geographical origin or region-specific characteristics. To meet strict regulatory requirements for GI status, brands must establish and maintain this connection effectively, which sets high barriers for entry for non-GI brands. Brands without GI status may find it challenging to comply with a country's requirements, automatically placing GI brands in a position of control over the standards in their respective markets. This control not only enhances brand familiarity and recognition but

---

[31] 'Nation Branding: How to Build an Effective Location Brand Identity' (Brand Finance, 21 October 2019) <https:// brandfinance .com/ insights/ nation -branding #location -branding -geographic -clustering -for -corporate -brands> accessed 20 September 2023.

[32] 'Fact Sheet: The Value of Geographical Indicators for Business' (European IPR Helpdesk, 2016) <https:// www .yumpu .com/ en/ document/ read/ 55980842/ fact -sheet -the -value -of -geographical -indications -for -businesses> accessed 20 September 2023.

also fosters trust among consumers who associate the GI status with quality and authenticity.

However, obtaining and protecting the official GI label is an ongoing commitment. Non-GI brands may attempt to target GI products through counterfeiting or imitations in trying to piggy-back off the positive associations of the GI. At the same time, if these imitations fall short in terms of quality, it can damage the reputation of both the imitator and the authentic GI brand. In turn, this can tarnish trust among consumers for both parties.

Another significant barrier to entry is the need for consensus within the community of producers and additional stakeholders. Building a consensus involves farmers, distillers, regulators, and more to come to an agreement on the origin and quality of products associated with the GI.

GI as a Barrier to Entry

In terms of branding and market share, GI status holds immense power. When brands or products lack GI status and attempt to enter a market already dominated by GI brands with strong reputations and dominant market shares, it can pose a challenge. GI status brings forward associations of quality, tradition, and pride in a product. It also often directly ties these brands to the nation or region from which the GI originates.

As a result, the market dominance by GI brands may appear to be a net negative, especially when these brands need to maintain high sustainability standards and face increased environmental pressures to consistently yield natural and native-produced ingredients each year. However, this monopoly effect can have highly positive repercussions for the region's economy. For instance, using Scotch Whisky as an example: a 2015 article reported it boasted 128 distilleries, contributed to 24% of the UK's food and drink exports and supported 40,000 jobs across the UK.[33] This illustrates the significant economic benefits that strong GI brands can bring to a region, highlighting the potential for both economic growth and cultural preservation.

---

[33] 'Scotch Whisky "worth £5bn to UK economy"' (BBC, 28 January 2015) <https:// www .bbc .co .uk/ news/ uk -scotland -scotland -business -31003387> accessed 3 May 2024.

Table 8.2   Nike Awareness and Familiarity

Brand	Awareness	Familiarity
Nike (USA)	96%	77%
Apparel USA Average	63%	39%

Source: Brand Finance Global Brand Equity Monitor 2023 (October 2023) https://brandirectory.com/research (accessed 5 June 2024)

BEST PRACTICE FOR EXPLOITING COMMERCIAL BENEFIT FROM PLACE-BRANDING

We have established that there are many commercial benefits to having a product strongly associated to a place, be it legally protected or not. Marketers must therefore be sure to make best use of these associations.

Every brand has specific assets that make it unique and enable it to establish a competitive advantage over equivalent products or services. Brands look for their point of distinctiveness and make this prominent to and understood by the customer to drive commercial performance.

For example, Nike's distinctive 'Swoosh' logo is one of the most recognizable and iconic logos in the world. The 'Swoosh' is a simple design made up of a curved checkmark shape, typically displayed in black. It was created by Carolyn Davidson in 1971 and represented the wing of the Greek goddess Nike, who personified victory. The logo became associated with athleticism, motion, and speed.

The Nike logo is used in all the company's marketing campaigns and is often the center of attention in them as this reinforces the visual identity of the logo in the audience watching the advertisements. Brand recognition of the logo is worldwide especially with the association and sponsorship of high-profile athletes and events which help create an emotional connection between the brand and its target audience. Also, the Swoosh logo is consistent with all the brand's messages and is used extensively in their digital marketing. Lastly, the logo is integrated into the design of all apparel and footwear design of the brand.

This effect is also seen in the Global Brand Equity Monitor Research of Brand Finance as shown in Table 8.2.

Higher levels of brand awareness and brand familiarity have been proven to drive higher revenues for a brand as they provide various advantages such as premium pricing, increased consumer trust and loyalty, word of mouth marketing, cross selling, and upselling.

For those brands with a strong place association, this should be seen as importantly as any other brand asset, such as a logo or patented technology, as it can generate higher commercial benefit, give a competitive advantage, and be associated with the country's community, culture, and tourism promotion.

To talk about what makes a place brand strong and capable of driving commercial benefits, it is important to remind ourselves of what we mean by 'brand' in this commercial context.

When we speak about brands in the context of accounting or law, we consider brands to be 'trademarks and their associate intellectual property' with this IP being designs, domains, art works etc. that are linked to the use of the trademarks.

Trademarks themselves are defined by the World Intellectual Property Organization (WIPO) as 'a sign capable of distinguishing the goods or services of one enterprise from those of other enterprises.'[34] In other words, in legal terms, trademarks are simply a signpost distinguishing one company, product or service from another.

However, the ability to trademark a brand or protect a brand's GI does not necessarily mean that that brand is 'strong'.

Rather the strength of the place brand lies in its ability to impact stakeholders' actions: whether to buy the product, what price to pay, whether to work for an organization, etc.

What this means is that place brands are more than signposts. In reality, they are a unit of storage for the cumulative familiarity, reputation and appeal among all stakeholders (customers, employees, suppliers, investors and the external public) and a method for exploiting that familiarity, reputation and appeal through the use of clear, distinctive signposting.

Crucially therefore, we must acknowledge, in the commercial context, place brands are there to convince consumers that a given product will satisfy their needs better than the competition, thereby driving up sales and generating a return for the brand owner. The way they make money is to influence stakeholders to make decisions that are favorable to person, business, nation, organization etc. that they wouldn't make for the same entity if it had a less strong place brand.

Among customers, the aim of brands is to make money and a strong place brand can be used to stimulate the expansion of the demand curve versus an equivalent product that lacks such a place brand association. By stimulating additional demand, the place brand has the effect of raising revenue and profit by either allowing for an increase in volume sold or price point or both.

Brands do this by having a higher level of penetration and awareness, and by stimulating a higher rate of conversion among non-customers (trial) and

---

[34] 'Trademarks' (WIPO) <https://www.wipo.int/en/web/trademarks> accessed 9 October 2024.

customers (loyalty) than other brands. In other words, they get more people to buy more (preferably at a higher price).

This effect is well summarized within the 'marketing funnel'. The marketing funnel is a key construct when analyzing the impact of brands on business performance. Customers and other stakeholders need to be aware of brands to consider them. Following this, the features of the product, service, price, availability, image etc., as well as in some cases the nature of promotional activities, lead people to consider and ultimately purchase branded products and services. The marketing funnel encompasses these effects into a simplified structure which provides an overview of strength.

Brand Finance analysis shows that,[35] when combined, familiarity and consideration conversion explain over 80% of variance in market share.

We therefore begin our Place-Branding Best Practice principles by looking at how brands can raise awareness of their associated place brand.

Make it Prominent in Marketing

Successful brands are driven by strong awareness among consumers, both current and potential. With the market funnel as the basis of demand for any brand, we observe awareness as the foundation for encouraging a consumer down the purchase path.

A brand is not able to make full commercial use of their place brand if the consumer base is not sufficiently aware of the product's connection to a certain place.

For instance, given Scotland's rich heritage of whisky production, it makes strong commercial sense for whisky brands to emphasize their product's Scottish origin, as this will elevate the product above an alternative non-Scottish whisky in the eyes of the consumer.

The most prominent way in which this can be done is through brand name and nomenclature. To continue with the example of Scotch Whisky, ensuring that the brand is referred to by consumers and suppliers as such – as '*Scotch*' whisky. By extension, all brand literature (website copy, packaging, etc.) should also refer to the place brand when describing the brand.

Visual assets also raise awareness of a brand's geographic roots. Distinctively Scottish imagery on packaging presents the place brand link to the consumer at the point of purchase. This can elevate a given whisky brand above a non-Scottish equivalent.

---

[35] Alex Haigh, 'Brand Beta: Analysing Brand Strength and Why it Matters' (Brand Finance, 29 August 2023) <https://brandfinance.com/insights/brand-beta-analysing-brand-strength-and-why-it-matters> accessed 20 September 2023.

Geographic themes through advertising and activations perpetuate this perception among consumers and create a narrative for the consumer to understand the story, history, and tradition of the product and brand.

By raising awareness of the place brand connection, the brand can become synonymous with the region/product. This allows the product to leverage equity around the given place's produce, thereby increasing sale likelihood and subsequently revenue.

Explain to Customers (Customers become Protectors of GI)

Beyond simply presenting the place brand, consumers may need to be educated of the place brand and its meaning for the product. Ultimately, a brand is a 'mental shortcut' used to guide consumer decision making. Educating consumers of benefits will help the product to build reputation and trust.

In the case of Kenyan coffee, for instance, it would be important to educate customers of the relative benefits of Kenyan coffee versus other commonly place-branded coffee varieties, such as Colombian or Ethiopian coffee.

It is beneficial to generate a distinctive positioning versus these 'competitor place brands' to create a loyal customer base that specifically prefers the Kenyan variety. This would help a Kenyan coffee brand stand above a crowded product segment and generate increased commercial returns.

Educating consumers of place-branded benefits is also important where the place brand product is relatively new or less well known, with consumers therefore less likely to understand the benefits without support.

Scotch Whisky is steeped in years of tradition and hence consumers are very likely to understand the relative strength of Scotch Whisky above a whiskey from another country. Conversely, Napa Valley is a far more recent point of distinction for high quality wine. Consequently, it was important for Napa Valley wineries to educate consumers about the quality of their wine, to elevate it towards the heights of traditional wineries in France, Germany, etc.

A strong example of this successful consumer education is the Paris Wine Tasting of 1975, where a series of Napa Valley wines outscored French equivalents in a blind tasting. This recast the reputation of Napa Valley wine in the wine community and elevated the region's reputation for high quality wine production.

By educating consumers, an area can build and maintain a strong reputation. Such reputations are built over time, persisting and compounding in consumer's minds. As a result, consumers understand the benefits of purchasing from a given region thus generating a price and/or volume premium above equivalent products from other regions.

Consumers also build up loyalty and pride in certain place brands, either through their personal heritage or through an affinity for the product. This means that, when the product is threatened or imitated, these consumers become advocates for the brand and can help to maintain barriers to entry on behalf of the place and product.

Understanding What these Perceptions Are

Brands should use market research to track the perceptions surrounding their place brand. This can be done through a combination of qualitative focus groups and quantitative equity studies. Market research will help brands to understand the drivers of value for their place brand, as well as identifying potential threats.

Understanding the strengths of both the product brand and the place brand it is associated with help a marketing team to focus their marketing efforts on the places where it is most likely to drive value. Where strengths are identified, these can be fed to brand teams to form the basis for packaging and communications.

Conversely, market research will identify weaknesses in brand equity. Where perceptions have dropped, marketing efforts can be used to realign these. Such research can also identify threats from competitor place brands that may need to be addressed.

Very often, marketing efforts are stretched and not sufficiently large to cover all possible avenues. Market research analytics can be used to identify the areas where money will be best spent to extract greater return on marketing investment.

Challenge Pretenders, Expand Barriers to Entry

Finally, brands with strong place brand associations should challenge pretenders and establish strong barriers to entry for their industry.

As with any product brand, place brands are bound to face competition from new entrants. The most likely competitor on this front would be another region producing a similar product. For instance, Indian whiskeys have long tried to compete with more traditional Scotch Whiskies.

In 2021,[36] an Indian whiskey producer, Unibev Ltd, was alleged to have marketed its whiskey 'STROTTS' 'with the motive to benefit from the reputation and goodwill of Scotch whisky'. The Scotch Whisky Association raised a legal challenge to this, and the case was settled in their favor by the Delhi Court. The ruling prevented Unibev from using the 'STROTTS' brand or 'any

---

[36] *Scotch Whisky Association v Unibev Ltd*, 1 February 2021 <https://indiankanoon.org/doc/72539493/> accessed 3 May 2024.

other mark, image, statement, expression or description which is indicative, suggestive or evocative of the United Kingdom or Scotch Whisky'.

By lodging and subsequently winning this case, the Scotch Whisky Association have sent a message to other would-be pretenders that they will be challenged and prevented from doing so. This legal challenge establishes a strong barrier to entry for the Scotch Whisky market.

Such legal cases are also a means for the incumbent place brand to assert their prestige and superiority to consumers. Where consumer loyalty has been established, the consumers themselves can become vocal defenders and advocates of the place brand. Successfully challenging competitors will only serve to increase the status and grandeur around a given place brand.

CONCLUSION

Place-branding holds vast commercial power. Indeed, its widespread use by corporate brands, inherently profit-driven entities, should serve as primary evidence of this.

Places and regions hold strong equity among consumers. Commercial brands use place-branding and GIs to appeal to this equity among their consumers. In turn, they hope that this increases consumers' likelihood to purchase, thereby earning increased revenue.

Place-branding's commercial power is one reason behind the legal protections that are put in place. These protections are established to uphold quality in production, and to ensure that only products from that certain region can bear the GI. They also act as barriers to entry, thereby restricting supply and allowing producers to maintain high prices and protect their profit margins.

However, place-branding remains more common than place-branding protections, and there exists varying degrees of protection. This raises the question of how important protecting a place brand actually is. Do consumers really care? If brands continue to use place-branding without protection then it must still provide some commercial benefit?

Clearly, there is still benefit to be borne from use of any place brand, if the connection is strong enough. However, the strongest place-branding protections remain the gold standard. For those brands with strong legal status, their brand equity lies not just in their own brand but in the shared brand equity of their region.

This brand equity is evidenced in the legal case of *Scotch Whisky Association v Unibev Ltd*.[37] The final ruling in the SWA's successful challenge prevented Unibev not only from using the 'STROTTS' brand name, but also 'any other

---

[37] *Scotch Whisky Association v Unibev Ltd*, ibid.

mark, image, statement, expression or description which is indicative, suggestive or evocative of the United Kingdom'. This demonstrates that the brand equity of the traditional Scotch Whiskies lies not purely in their individual name or brand, but in their collective association with the brand equity of the UK, specifically Scotland.

While legal challenges are lodged for reasons of heritage and national pride, they are also lodged on commercial bases, and as long as place brands continue to hold commercial power, they will be protected by the companies and places that use and benefit from them.

9. Authentic Place-Branding of Kenya's Coffee Through Certification Mark: Practice and Prospects

Tom Kabau

INTRODUCTION

The Chapter evaluates Kenya's approach to authentic and credible place-branding of its premium coffee in the local and international market through the Coffee Kenya certification mark of origin, as a strategy of increasing the visibility, popularity, and sales of the produce. As discussed in the Chapter, where there has been prevalent use of the name 'Kenya' in a generic context by various coffee processors, both locally and internationally, the unverified produce purported to be from the country, that is also characterized by extensive blending with coffee from other sources, has resulted in skepticism and distrust regarding the alleged origin and content. As such, Kenya has failed to gain a substantive competitive edge and obtain higher economic benefits for its premium coffee. The utilization of the Coffee Kenya certification mark of origin for berries solely sourced from the country offered the prospect of authenticity and credibility to coffee marketed by approved processors, which would in turn translate to its greater preference and consumer loyalty, and economic benefits to the country.

Increased trade in coffee has immense potential economic benefits for Kenya. Coffee is the most extensively traded product of the tropical regions of the globe, with the unique characteristic that it is generally produced in developing and least developed states of the Global South.[1] According to the International Coffee Organization (ICO), Kenya ranks as the third largest producer of arabica coffee in Africa, though there was a decrease in output in

---

[1] Elmamoun Amrouk, 'Depressed International Coffee Prices: Insights into the Nature of the Price Decline' (Food and Agriculture Organisation, July 2018) <www.fao.org/fileadmin/templates/est/COMM_MARKETS_MONITORING/Coffee_Cocoa/Documents/coffee_prices_2018.pdf> accessed 8 October 2024.

the year 2022–3, from 0.76 million bags to 0.73 million which amounted to a variance of 4.6%.[2] The decrease in Kenya's output was partly attributed to prolonged drought and the coffee berry infection in the Central Highlands of the state.[3]

Kenya's mild arabica coffee has a niche in the international sphere due to its unique quality and characteristics that are not found in such products from other countries.[4] In particular, Kenya's 2016 *Report of the National Task Force on Coffee Sub-Sector Reforms* highlighted the potential competitive edge of coffee from the country as follows:

> Kenya coffee has a sharp pointed acidity, heavy winey characteristic, chocolatey, caramel flavours, a black currant aftertaste and a soft and smooth finish. It is because of these unique characteristics that Kenya coffee stands out in the world market.[5]

As is the case with wine, coffee has flavor profiles that are unique and distinctive depending on the soil and altitude conditions of its geographical origin.[6] Most of the coffee growing parts of Kenya are within the ranges of 1,400 to 2,100 metres above sea level in altitude, and have rich volcanic soils, which provide their beans with the stated unique flavor profiles associated with the Kenyan produce.[7] The counties in which coffee is grown in Kenya include Kiambu, Nyeri, Kirinyaga, Murang'a, Meru, Embu, Machakos, Kericho, West-Pokot, Uasin-Gishu, Vihiga, Trans-Nzoia, Tharaka-Nithi, Taita-Taveta, Siaya, Nyamira, Nandi, Nakuru, Migori, Marsabit, Makueni, Laikipia, Kisumu,

---

[2] 'Coffee Report and Outlook' (International Coffee Organization, December 2023) <https://icocoffee.org/documents/cy2023-24/Coffee_Report_and_Outlook_December_2023_ICO.pdf> accessed 8 October 2024.

[3] Ibid.

[4] Willy Bett, Cabinet Secretary, Ministry of Agriculture, Livestock and Fisheries, 'Speech During the Welcoming Breakfast Meeting with Global Coffee Buyers for Origin Trip to Kenya' (28 November 2016, Nairobi), 2 <https://www.yumpu.com/en/document/view/56444553/speech-by-mr-willy-bett-cabinet-secretary-ministry-of-agriculture-livestock-and-fisheries-during-the-welcoming-breakfast-meeting-with-global-coffee> accessed 8 October 2024.

[5] *Report of the National Task Force on Coffee Sub-Sector Reforms* (Republic of Kenya, May 2016), 26.

[6] Ibid., 23.

[7] See generally, Grenville K Melli, 'Coffee Kenya Mark of Origin' (Coffee Directorate, Agriculture Fisheries and Food Authority, Republic of Kenya, 2015) <www.ico.org/documents/cy2014-15/Presentations/115-pmdc-coffee-kenya-mark-of-origin.pdf> accessed 8 October 2024.

Kisii, Kericho, Kakamega, Homa-Bay, Elgeyo-Marakwet, Busia, Bungoma, Bomet, and Baringo.[8]

The classification of Kenya's coffee is on the basis of bean size rather than its various flavor profiles, and no state-sponsored or formal cataloguing of tastes exists.[9] Nonetheless, industry-inspired profiling indicates that the cup profiles for the Central Kenya region are well-rounded acidity with a grapefruit taste for Murang'a and Kiambu counties, and full bodies that have sharp citrus acidity with blackcurrant and chocolate hints for the counties of Kirinyaga and Nyeri.[10] With regard to the counties that constitute the highlands west of the Rift Valley, among them Nandi, Nakuru, Kericho, Trans Nzoia, and Baringo, the taste profiles of the regions' cups are medium acidity, with some fruity overtones and rich chocolate tastes.[11] The cup profiles for the Western region counties of Bungoma, Vihiga and Kakamega are bright acidity with fruity overtones.[12] The Kisii, Nyamira, Migori, and Kisumu counties of the Nyanza region are associated with medium acidity, smooth and creamy bodies that have sweet, nutty, and toasty fruity hints.[13]

It is noteworthy that the name 'Kenya' is commonly and generically added to various brand names by both domestic and foreign processors, usually as 'Kenyan Coffee' and 'Kenya AA'.[14] Nonetheless, the unregulated common and generic usage of the name 'Kenya' in various unverified and unauthenticated coffee brands opens such place-branding to consumer skepticism regarding the validity and purity of alleged origin and content. Further, Kenya's coffee is prevalently used to blend with other inferior products from other countries due to the premium quality and tasty flavours of the country's berries.[15] As had been pointed out in 2016 by Willy Bett, the then Cabinet Secretary in the Ministry of Agriculture, Livestock and Fisheries, the prevalent blending activities had rendered it difficult to find 100% pure Kenyan coffee both locally and internationally.[16] Consequently, the prevalent blending signif-

---

[8] *Report of the National Task Force on Coffee Sub-Sector Reforms* (n 5), 65.
[9] See ibid., 24.
[10] Kenya Co-operative Coffee Exporters Ltd, 'Coffee Growing Regions in Kenya' (2022) <www .kencaffee .coop/ coffee -growing -regions -in -kenya/ > accessed 8 October 2024.
[11] Ibid.
[12] Ibid.
[13] Ibid.
[14] 'Kenya AA' is the most premium and preferred category of the various classifications of the coffee from the country, which also include AB, C, E, PB, T and TT.
[15] Bett (n 4), 2–3.
[16] Ibid.

icantly aggravates consumer skepticism and distrust of the alleged genuineness of unverified and uncertified brands that regard their produce as being 'Kenyan Coffee' or 'Kenya AA', eroding potential competitiveness and visibility of the country's produce in the international market on the basis of origin and content.

Based on the above realities, the use of the 'Coffee Kenya' certified national mark of origin was thus deemed to be one of the mechanisms of establishing greater visibility and prominence of the premium produce on the local and international market, creating authenticity based on the Kenyan origin and content, and removing existing skepticism regarding products bearing the name 'Kenya', or even 'Kenya AA'. It is noteworthy that some of the core problems that characterize coffee farming in Kenya include low earnings and delayed payments in the coffee despite its premium quality.[17] Greater visibility and preference for pure Kenyan coffee in the local and international market was expected to translate to higher sales and increased income for the country's farmers.

Consequently, the Coffee Kenya mark of origin that signifies authentic and unblended Kenyan coffee was registered in 2009 by the then Coffee Board of Kenya (succeeded by the Coffee Directorate) with the objective of promoting the distinctiveness of Kenyan coffee, and fostering product loyalty from global consumers.[18] The sale and consumption of unblended, 100% Kenyan coffee would likely translate to greater volumes of sales of the produce from the country.[19] As such, the Coffee Kenya brand was a marketing strategy anticipated to provide the product with the much sought visibility in the global market.[20] In 2015, when the Coffee Kenya brand had just been officially launched (which was subsequent to earlier local registration in 2009), coffee was approximated to contribute to 1% of Kenya's gross domestic product (GDP), and was engaging up to 30% of the labor force involved in agricultural activities.[21]

Contrary to the expectations, and as discussed in this Chapter, the utilization of the Coffee Kenya certification mark has had some limitations especially internationally, and has not successfully resulted in effective branding, visibility, and optimisation of Kenya's premium coffee in the local and international market, resulting in continued low returns for farmers. Nonetheless, it is about the various state and non-state actors building upon the minimal flickers of preference of authentically and credibly place-branded

---

[17] *Report of the National Task Force on Coffee Sub-Sector Reforms* (n 5), xx.
[18] Melli (n 7).
[19] Ibid.
[20] Ibid.
[21] Ibid.

Kenyan coffee to achieve higher popularity, visibility, and optimization of Kenya's premium produce on the local and international market for greater economic returns. Further, it is on the basis of such realities that this Chapter advocates for adoption of broader legislation domestically, in addition to Kenya becoming party to international instruments that enable a more robust approach to place-branding of coffee through implementation of additional mechanisms such as geographical indications (GIs) and appellations of origin. Further, the emerging practice of certification of sustainably and organically produced coffee should be incorporated into Kenya's mainstream authentic place-branding initiatives as it presents an international market segment that has immense potential for growth.

SELECTING THE COFFEE KENYA CERTIFICATION MARK AS THE PLACE-BRANDING MECHANISM

The Coffee Kenya brand consists of a logo with the slogan 'so rich, so Kenyan'. The 'so rich' part of the slogan exemplifies Coffee Kenya's richness in acidity and flavor, which includes a pleasing fragrance and hints of chocolate, floral, and citric tastes.[22] In addition, the 'so Kenyan' part of the slogan typifies the fact that 'Coffee Kenya belongs to the Arabica variety and is grown on rich volcanic soils, found in the highlands of Kenya between 1,400 and 2,100 metres above sea level.'[23] Nonetheless, the logo fails to also include vital market authentication and validation statements such as '100% Kenyan coffee', or 'pure Kenyan coffee', or 'unblended Kenyan coffee'.

The use of a certification mark rather than a GI as the mechanism for protecting the place brand of Kenya's coffee internationally may have been informed by the realities on the ground. First, Kenya does not have GI legislation. As defined under Article 22(1) of the Agreement on Trade-Related Aspects of Intellectual Property Rights (TRIPS Agreement), a GI implies 'indications which identify a good as originating in the territory of a member, or a region or locality in that territory, where a given quality, reputation or other characteristic of the good is essentially attributable to its geographical origin.'[24] A draft Geographical Indications Bill, conceptualized in 2009, is yet to be adopted into law.[25] The undesirable prolonged delay in the enactment of the Geographical

---

[22] Melli (n 7).

[23] Ibid.

[24] Agreement on Trade-Related Aspects of Intellectual Property Rights (adopted 15 April 1994, entry into force 1 January 1995) 1869 UNTS 299.

[25] See generally, Titilayo Adebola, 'The Legal Construction of Geographical Indications in Africa' (2023) 26 Journal of World Intellectual Property 3, 20–1.

Indications Bill into law has been attributed to the congested legislative agenda of the Kenyan Government, the state's common law tradition for which a *sui generis* mechanism for protecting GIs seems unusual, and James Otieno-Odek's end of tenure as the Managing Director of the Kenya Industrial Property Institute (KIPI).[26] It has been argued that James Otieno-Odek was a strong proponent of the adoption of GI law in Kenya through various initiatives, including pushing for the conceptualization of the Bill and publicizing the potential role and value of GI legislation in various forums.[27]

In the absence of a substantive law relating to GI, Kenya fulfils its obligations relating to the protection of GIs under the TRIPS Agreement through registration and protection of certification marks and collective marks in accordance with its Trade Marks Act.[28] Section 40(1) of the Trade Marks Act is relied upon to protect some GI-like aspects, through certification marks.[29] Section 40(1) of the Trade Marks Act defines and provides for the registration of a certification trade mark as a 'mark adapted in relation to any goods to distinguish in the course of trade goods certified by any person in respect of origin, material, mode of manufacture, quality, accuracy or other characteristic from goods not so certified'.[30] Place-branding and protection of GI aspects such as origin through certification marks is not unique to Kenya, and has been utilized in other jurisdictions. For instance, in the United States (US), GI aspects may be protected though the use of trade marks, certification marks, or even collective marks.[31]

In sum, a certification mark is a distinctive sign utilized to indicate that particular goods comply with certain standards and characteristics that have been predetermined by the proprietor of the mark, in the context of their origin,

---

[26] Getachew Mengistie and Michael Blakeney, 'Geographical Indications and the Scramble for Africa' (2017) 25(2) African Journal of International and Comparative Law 199, 213–4.

[27] See ibid.

[28] Adebola (n 25), 20. See, Trade Marks Act, Chapter 506, Laws of Kenya.

[29] Joshua Kitili, 'A Case for Geographical Indication? An Overview of the Tinderet Case' (Centre for Intellectual Property and Information Technology Law, Strathmore University, 20 September 2023) <https://cipit.strathmore.edu/a-case-for-geographical-indication-an-overview-of-the-tinderet-case/#:~:text='4%20Kenya%20does%20not%20yet,collective%20trademarks%20or%20service%20marks> accessed 8 October 2024.

[30] Trade Marks Act, Chapter 506, Laws of Kenya.

[31] Inessa Shalevich, 'Protection of Trademarks and Geographical Indications' (2008) 6 Buffalo Intellectual Property Law Journal 67, 68.

mode of manufacture, quality, materials, accuracy, or other characteristics.[32] The proprietor of the certification mark is usually not the producer or manufacturer of the goods but rather an independent enterprise, institution, governmental entity that has the competence and capacity to certify the applicable goods.[33] In the case of Kenya, the proprietor of the Coffee Kenya certification mark is the Coffee Directorate, which in turn licences coffee processors.

There was place-branding merit and benefits in the use of the Coffee Kenya certification mark of origin. Such a certification mark conveyed to the international market that the product was tested for certified standards by an entity that was not the producer, thus guaranteeing quality.[34] The Coffee Kenya mark of origin certification indicated that the product originated from Kenya, and its production and processing were within standards of it having the 'rich' attributes associated with coffee from country, as it had not been blended with products from other countries.

Nonetheless, there are distinctions between certification marks and GIs, which can affect the effectiveness of one over the other as a place-branding mechanism for Kenya's coffee, given potential differences in appreciation of each approach by the consumers of the product. For instance, a certification mark is not necessarily based on naturally occurring characteristics, and could be a result of artificial modification provided the set standards are sustained, which can negate consumer preferences and market loyalty. On the other hand, a GI is usually based on natural distinctiveness of a product such as coffee, as naturally affected by weather or soils, among other natural phenomenon. Consequently, consumers may have the notion that a certified product such as Coffee Kenya does not guarantee 100% natural occurrence of its characteristics, and thus negate their preference for the product.

Registration and the Scope of Protection

The Coffee Kenya certification mark was registered at KIPI by the then Coffee Board of Kenya (CBK) in 2009 as number 66945. The registration at the World Intellectual Property Organization (WIPO) was made by the CBK

---

[32] Anil Sinha, 'Collective Marketing: Adding Value through Geographical Indications, Certification Marks and Collective Marks' (Training of Trainers Program on Effective Intellectual Property Asset Management by Small and Medium-sized Enterprises, World Intellectual Property Organization, Phnom Penh, 20–3 May 2013) <www.wipo.int/edocs/mdocs/sme/en/wipo_smes_pnh_13/wipo_smes_pnh_13_g_sinha.pdf> accessed 8 October 2024.
[33] Ibid.
[34] See generally Sinha (n 32).

on 20 December 2010, and was due for renewal on 20 December 2020.[35] The certification mark was then licenced to various coffee processors and dealers, to utilize on their products that were within the established standards in their domestic and international sales.[36] The entities originally licenced to use the mark included C Dormans, Kenya Nut Company, Gibsons Coffee, and Kimathi University of Technology.[37] The Coffee Research Institute (CRI) has the role of testing to ensure that the standards and contents of the products to be sold under the Coffee Kenya brand are complied with.[38]

Relying on the Madrid System, Kenya sought to have the registration at WIPO granted recognition and protection in Australia, the European Union (EU), Japan, Switzerland, Iran, Sudan, and Republic of Korea.[39] One of the setbacks in the effectiveness of the protection of the certification mark of origin was the notification of refusal of provisional protection by Australia, the EU, Republic of Korea, Japan, Iran, and Switzerland, with only Sudan failing to file a refusal to offer provisional protection before the expiry of the applicable period.[40] A provisional refusal of protection under the Madrid System is an interim communication by the state in which a mark is proposed to be protected that it will not offer the sought protection due to legal factors in its jurisdiction, pending final determination of the issue.[41] If there is no successful appeal by the state seeking protection within the applicable period, the provisional refusal of protection by the foreign country becomes a final rejection.[42]

It is noteworthy that the registration of the Coffee Kenya certification mark at WIPO under the auspices of the defunct CBK eventually expired on 20 December 2020, and was taken over by two currently valid registrations by

---

[35] World Intellectual Property Organization, 'WIPO-ROMARIN: International Registration Details' (15 January 2015).

[36] Melli (n 7).

[37] 'Kenya Bets on Origin Mark to Boost Coffee Sales' (*Daily Nation,* Nairobi, 14 January 2015 updated 28 June 2020) <https:// nation .africa/ kenya/ business/ Kenya-bets-on-origin-mark-to-boost-coffee-sales/996-2589500-kmmm4h/index .html> accessed 8 October 2024.

[38] The mandate of the Coffee Research Institute includes conducting research on coffee production, processing and marketing. See 'Our Services' (Coffee Research Institute, 2023) <www.kalro.org/coffee/?q=node/30> accessed 8 October 2024.

[39] World Intellectual Property Organization (n 35).

[40] Ibid.

[41] 'Madrid System: Frequently Asked Questions' (World Intellectual Property Organization, September 2023) <www .wipo .int/ madrid/ en/ faq/ #accordion _ _collapse__08> accessed 8 October 2024.

[42] Ibid.

the successor Coffee Directorate, under registration numbers 1250302 and 1598320.[43]

With regard to registration number 1250302 that was issued 25 March 2015, the Coffee Directorate had sought recognition and protection of Coffee Kenya in Australia, Switzerland, the European Union Intellectual Property Office, Iran, Japan, Republic of Korea, and Sudan.[44] While Australia, Switzerland, the European Union Intellectual Property Office, and Japan filed provisional refusal of protection communications at WIPO, Iran, Republic of Korea, and Sudan did not file for such refusal of protection.[45] Germany was the only foreign country designated to have the second registration number 1598320 that is dated 20 April 2021 apply, but the subject country opposed by issuing a provisional refusal to grant such protection in 2022.[46] Consequently, the Coffee Kenya certification mark is internationally protected only in Iran, Republic of Korea and Sudan.[47]

Coffee Kenya Certification as Necessitated by Realities of Generic Exploitation of 'Kenya' Brand

Other non-Kenyan entities and actors in the coffee industry internationally have demonstrated their keenness to include the 'Kenya' brand name in their products. They include 'Kenya Bean', applied for registration as a national trade mark at WIPO by the Republic of Korea, but which is now terminated.[48] Other similar applications or registrations at WIPO include 'Kenya Espresso', and 'Kenya Coffee & Sweet Dessert' by the Republic of Korea.[49] There was also the 'Kenya Coffee' national trade mark registration application at WIPO by George Kimemiah of the US that terminated in 17 September 2004.[50] The stated international trade mark registrations at WIPO are through the Madrid

---

[43] 'Madrid Monitor' (World Intellectual Property Organization) <https://www3.wipo.int/madrid/monitor/en/> accessed 8 October 2024.
[44] Ibid.
[45] Ibid.
[46] Ibid.
[47] Ibid.
[48] 'Global Brand Database' (World Intellectual Property Organization) <https:// branddb .wipo .int/ en/ quicksearch/ results ?sort = score %20desc & start = 0 & rows = 30 & asStructure = %7B %22_id %22: %22f95b %22 , %22boolean %22: %22AND%22,%22bricks%22:%5B%7B%22_id%22:%22f95c%22,%22key%22: %22brandName%22,%22value%22:%22kenya%22,%22strategy%22:%22Simple %22%7D%5D%7D&_=1700116575428&fg=_void_> accessed 8 October 2024.
[49] Ibid.
[50] Ibid.

System, which is premised on the 1891 Madrid Agreement Concerning the International Registration of Marks, and the 1989 Protocol Relating to the Madrid Agreement Concerning the International Registration of Marks.[51] The Madrid System provides an expedient system for registering and managing trade marks globally, in which only a single international trade mark application is made by a state for purposes of protection in up to 130 different jurisdictions.[52]

Further, a review of coffee stocked in Kenyan sale outlets and online stores demonstrates that the word 'Kenya' is widely used, in addition to the specific brand names of particular coffee products, as demonstrative of origin of the produce and in order to tap from the global goodwill of the country's berries. In that context, the country's name is affixed to the brand names in the forms such as 'Kenya AA' (based on the classification of the berries) and 'Kenyan coffee'. For instance, an entity by the brand name Screen 18, based in Florida, US, markets its 'Kenya AA' coffee as being 'consistently rich fruit and berry flavour' and as having a 'deep, wine-like acidity, and pleasing aroma', besides being 'full-bodied, bold and juicy'.[53] Ajiri markets its 'Kenyan AA Whole Bean Coffee' as constituting 'rich burgundy undertones and pleasant notes of citrus and berry' that is allegedly 'sourced from the lush high-altitude volcanic soils of Kenya'.[54] According to Willoughbys Coffee, the cup characteristic of its 'Kenya AA Barichu' is hints of 'cinnamon, sugar cane and vanilla'.[55] Carpe Diem Coffee and Tea Company has a 'Kenya AA' brand that it markets by highlighting that 'Kenyan coffee has ... a deeply satisfying aroma, an excellent balance of acidity and body, and excellent fruit'.[56] The Kahawa Company

---

[51] Madrid Agreement Concerning the International Registration of Marks (adopted 14 April 1891, revised at Brussels 14 December 1900, at Washington 2 June 1911, at The Hague 6 November 1925, at London 2 June 1934, at Nice 15 June 1957, and at Stockholm 14 July 1967) 828 UNTS 389; Protocol Relating to the Madrid Agreement Concerning the International Registration of Marks (adopted at Madrid on 27 June 1989, as amended on 3 October 2006 and on 12 November 2007) WIPO Lex No TRT/MADRIDP-GP/001.

[52] 'Madrid System – The International Trademark System' (World Intellectual Property Organization) <www.wipo.int/madrid/en/> accessed 8 October 2024.

[53] 'Kenya AA' (Screen 18, 2022) <https://screen18coffee.com/product/kenya-aa/> accessed 8 October 2024.

[54] 'Kenyan AA Whole Bean Coffee'(Ajiri) <https:// ajiritea .com/ products/ kenyan-aa-whole-bean-coffee> accessed 8 October 2024.

[55] 'Kenya AA Barichu' (Willoughbys Coffee, 2023) <www.willoughbyscoffee.com/KEST.html> accessed 8 October 2024.

[56] 'Kenya AA' (Carpe Diem Coffee and Tea Company, 2022) <www.carpe-coffee.com/coffee-beans/kenya-aa> accessed 8 October 2024.

states that its 'Kenya Kiboko AA' sourced from Nyeri, Kenya, 'features a slight acidity with chocolate and cherry notes'.[57]

As highlighted above, the marketing and sale of Kenyan coffee is primarily on the basis of the bean size descriptions rather than other potentially more lucrative classifications such as flavors.[58] Depending on size, the classifications are essentially AA, AB, C, E, PB, T and TT.[59] Whereas the primary focus of the classifications is the size of the green berries, there are nonetheless some minimal connection with the amount of flavor content. For instance, 'Kenya AA' constitute broad coffee beans that are expected to contain the largest amount of flavourful oils and nuances.[60] This classification is unique to Kenyan coffee, as other states have their particular and distinctive modes of categorizing their berries. Despite the above designations being associated with Kenyan coffee, they are open to abuse and misrepresentation as there lacks effective restriction or limitation on their use, and any local or foreign processor can use any of the designations such as 'Kenya AA' to brand their ground berries for the market, even without compliance with the bean size.[61]

There is no market evidence to indicate that the use of particular designations such as 'Kenya AA' is legally restricted, protected or enforced. A survey of the coffee marketed both in Kenya's retail shops and in online portals targeting international consumers indicates that the 'Kenya AA' designation is utilized freely, without restrictions, and in the absence of any mechanisms of verifying the authenticity of compliance by the particular coffee producer. As such, it is plausible to state that the classification of Kenya's coffee on the basis of brand size, including the purported premium 'Kenya AA' designation, is prevalent, common and generic, and thus lacks authentic place-branding value that is protected or enforceable as intellectual property (IP). The unverified, unrestricted and generic use of the 'Kenya AA' brand by both local and foreign coffee processors has eroded its value as a means of authentically and genuinely place-branding premium coffee from Kenya in the international market. In addition, Kenya's coffee is highly blended with other low-grade berries from other states, and, as explained in the introductory section of the Chapter, this renders it hard to find 100% pure Kenyan coffee. Consequently,

---

[57] 'Kenya Kiboko AA' (Kahawa Company) <https://kahawa-company.com/product/kenya-kiboko-aa-coffee/> accessed 8 October 2024.
[58] *Report of the National Task Force on Coffee Sub-Sector Reforms* (n 5), 24.
[59] Dave Hoch, 'Kenyan Coffee Beans: Everything You Need to Know' (*Big Cup of Coffee*, 31 July 2023) <https://bigcupofcoffee.com/kenyan-coffee/> accessed 8 October 2024.
[60] Ibid.
[61] See generally, ibid.

coffee products branded as 'Kenya AA' and such similar variations of the country's name are open to reasonable consumer skepticism and distrust about the wholesomeness of the alleged origin and content. As such, the Coffee Kenya certification mark of origin that is registered at KIPI and WTO and licensed to processors who trade only in pure Kenyan coffee that complies with requisite standards provides prospects for authentic and verifiable place-branding of the country's berries.

It is noteworthy that from an IP rights perspective, 'Kenya' is also a common and generic name and as long as there are no complaints to relevant Kenya state agencies such as KIPI or the Anti-Counterfeit Agency (ACA), or a legal suit premised on allegations of a coffee producer infringing a protected mark and symbol, or commission of the tort of passing off or misrepresentation, coffee dealers and processors can use the country's name. Further, any of the stated purported infringement claims or actions would still require proof, and be open to applicable exemptions and defences, such as the name 'Kenya' being generic and common, and 'Kenya AA' being a prevalent acceptable description and generic designation of the coffee in accordance with the applicable country's classification schedule.

The use of 'Kenya' in coffee brands, including by non-Kenyans and through the above-discussed unverified and unauthenticated mechanisms, is nonetheless indicative of the potential economic value of the country as the place of origin for coffee products in the international market. It essentially exemplifies the tapping of the outstanding international goodwill of Kenyan coffee. Given the prevalent use of the name Kenya in various coffee brands, it may be queried whether there was any tangible value and merit in the conceptualization, and registration at both KIPI and WIPO, of the Coffee Kenya certification mark of national origin. The potential economic value of the Coffee Kenya certification mark is by providing an authentic and credible indication of Kenya's coffee in an international and local market flooded by unverified and unsubstantiated Kenyan brands, in an environment in which such other products have their origin and content further distrusted by the prevalent practice of blending.

Thus the certification was a strategic effort at confronting some of the drawbacks that arose from the previous failure to authentically and suitably brand Kenyan coffee both locally and internationally.[62] The 2016 *Report of the National Task Force on Coffee* acknowledged that Kenya had not properly positioned itself by branding pure coffee from the country.[63] It regretted that Kenya preferred a blending approach in the sale of its coffee, rather than pro-

---

[62] *Report of the National Task Force on Coffee Sub-Sector Reforms* (n 5), 24.
[63] Ibid.

moting the sale and marketing of coffee that was authentically and verifiably internationally branded as being Kenyan.[64]

CUSTODY OF THE COFFEE KENYA MARK IN THE INSTITUTIONAL SHIFT FROM CBK TO DIRECTORATE

As discussed above, the original applications for the protection of the Coffee Kenya national mark of origin at both KIPI and WIPO was by the now defunct CBK in 2009 and 2010 respectively. However, institutional reforms in the agricultural sector resulted in the abolition of the CBK and the establishment of the Coffee Directorate as a department of the Agriculture, Food and Fisheries Authority (AFFA). As anticipated under the Agricultural Sector Development Strategy (ASDS) for the period 2010–20, Kenya enacted the AFFA Act and the Crops Act of 2013, which repealed the Coffee Act of 2001.[65] Through the stated legislative changes, the CBK became the Coffee Directorate under the AFFA, with regulatory oversight of the coffee sub-sector.[66] The Coffee (General) Regulations 2016 were subsequently enacted by the relevant Cabinet Secretary for the purposes of implementation of the Crops Act 2013.[67] Clause 4(2)(h) of the Coffee (General) Regulations 2016 requires the AFFA (under whose auspices the Coffee Directorate operates) 'to promote the application of the National Coffee Kenya Mark of Origin by local and international industry players'.[68] It is noteworthy, that as discussed, the Coffee Directorate has sustained the protection of the Coffee Kenya certification mark at WIPO, including through subsequent registration application that expanded protection to Iran, Republic of Korea and Sudan, but not Australia, Switzerland, Germany, the European Union Intellectual Property Office, and Japan (as protection was opposed and declined there).[69]

---

[64] Ibid.
[65] Ibid, 7. See, Agriculture, Fisheries and Food Authority Act, No 13 of 2013; Crops Act, No 16 of 2013.
[66] *Report of the National Task Force on Coffee Sub-Sector Reforms* (n 5), 7–8.
[67] Coffee (General) Regulations of 2016, Legal Notice No 120 of 27 June 2016.
[68] Ibid.
[69] 'Madrid Monitor' (n 43).

CONTEMPORARY PRACTICES RELATING TO OTHER CERTIFICATIONS IN KENYA'S COFFEE SECTOR

Other contemporary certification approaches are not essentially place-branding, and mostly focus on both the farmers' production methods, and the shortening of the supply chain rather than the nature of processing and branding for the market as is the case with Coffee Kenya. Such certifications are often undertaken as strategies of strengthening the economic significance of coffee smallholder farmers in the value chain.[70] They are generally premised on the idea of encouraging 'supply chain partners to engage in direct sales transactions under long term contractual arrangements based on trust regarding product quality and delivery reliability'.[71]

These other certifications are within three major categorizations, comprising: voluntary ones such as Fair Trade (FLO – Fair Trade Labelling Organisation), responsible trade (Utz certified) and sustainable trade (Rainforest Alliance); company standards ones like Coffee and Farmer Equity (CAFÉ) Practices by Starbucks and Nespresso AAA; and sector-wide standards ones, like the Common Code for the Coffee Community (4C Association) that is a collaboration between various actors including non-governmental organisations (NGOs), coffee associations and trade unions.[72]

The objective of the Fair Trade certification is to create a coffee trading partnership that will establish greater equity.[73] The Fair Trade Labelling Organisations International (FLO-Cert) undertakes inspection and certification of producer organizations and traders, with the core requirement being that they be smallholders that majorly depend on family labor, and are part of cooperatives that are managed through democratic ethos.[74] The Fair Trade initiative is aimed at minimizing the significance of middle men along the coffee supply chain, in addition to creating positive social conscience amongst retailers and consumers.[75] Utz certification focuses on 'improved farm management, input efficiency and coffee traceability, while also demanding good performance on

---

[70] Ruerd Ruben and Paul Hoebink, 'Introduction: Coffee Certification in East Africa – Searching for Impact' in Ruerd Ruben and Paul Hoebink (eds), *Coffee Certification in East Africa: Impact on Farms, Families and Cooperatives* (Wageningen Academic Publishers 2015). 23, 26.
[71] Ibid.
[72] Ibid., 27.
[73] Ibid., 29.
[74] Ruben and Hoebink (n 70), 29.
[75] Ibid., 29–30.

social and environmental issues'.[76] CAFÉ Practices certification seeks to guarantee that Starbucks obtains coffee that is sustainably grown and processed.[77]

The German Coffee Association and the German Government's international development agency (GTZ) developed the 4C Association that utilizes a verification standard that builds on basic good agricultural practices and sustainable coffee production.[78] The Rainforest Alliance certification that is supported by the United Nations Development Program and the Global Environment Facility promotes, among coffee farmers, improved financial benefits, decent working conditions, gender equity, biodiversity protection, and access to education for children in farm communities.[79]

It is noteworthy that there is an emerging and vital fourth approach to certification, which is premised on organic farming methods, and the spiralling need for such agricultural produce, including coffee. For instance, the Traceable Organic Coffee from Kenya (TRACE Kenya) was launched in September 2020 and promotes organic farming through certification.[80] Financed by the Ministry of Foreign Affairs of Denmark (DANIDA) and implemented by Solidaridad in partnership with African Coffee Roasters (ACR), the TRACE Kenya project has the objective of building the capacity of small-scale farmers to produce coffee that satisfies the global organic market standards.[81] Further collaboration in the certification project is with the Coffee Research Institute (CRI) and the county governments of Kericho, Nandi and Bungoma which are in the geographical areas that the scheme targets.[82] The TRACE Kenya project is also envisioned to support coffee cooperatives across Kenya to develop the necessary requisite internal control systems for the purposes of expanding organic certification in the country.[83] The TRACE Kenya project aim is to open up organically certified Kenyan coffee to numerous market opportunities in Europe and the US, where organic products have gained immense

---

[76] Ibid., 30.
[77] Ibid.
[78] Ibid., 30–1.
[79] 'What Does "Rainforest Alliance Certified" Mean?' (Rainforest Alliance, 25 April 2024) <https://www.rainforest-alliance.org/insights/what-does-rainforest-alliance-certified-mean/> accessed 8 October 2024.
[80] 'Bridging the Gaps Towards Organic Coffee Certification in Kenya' (Solidaridad, 13 November 2020) <www.solidaridadnetwork.org/news/bridging-the-gaps-towards-organic-coffee-certification-in-kenya/#:~:text=Launched%20in%20September%202020%2C%20the,Bungoma%2C%20Kericho%20and%20Nandi%20counties> accessed 8 October 2024.
[81] Ibid.
[82] Ibid.
[83] Ibid.

popularity.[84] The reduction of health risks, and minimization of environmental degradation that is linked to use of chemicals and pesticides, will be beneficial to both the farm workers and the consumers.[85]

ENDURING SECTORAL PROBLEMS DESPITE THE COFFEE KENYA CERTIFICATION MARK

Problems relating to poor earnings for farmers are still prevalent despite the place-branding of Coffee Kenya through the certification mark both at KIPI and WIPO, as an avenue of increasing visibility of and demand for Kenya's premium product. This is in addition to other forms of voluntary, sustainable trade and company standards certification that have been discussed, and, more particularly, the emerging practice of organic coffee farming through the TRACE Kenya project. With regard to poor earnings by farmers that in no doubt discourage coffee farming, the payments from the Nairobi Coffee Exchange in May 2023 were US dollars (USD) 4 per kilogram of clean coffee, which was a 50% drop from USD 8 in 2022.[86] The significant drop in prices may be attributed to progressively decreasing international demand for the product in light of surpluses resulting from increased yields of coffee in other countries such as Brazil and Colombia.[87]

Limitations of the Coffee Kenya Certification Mark and a Case for More Robust Practice of Authentic Place-Branding

The challenges that result from poor financial returns for coffee farmers in Kenya are not solely premised on poor international branding or visibility, and are multifaceted in nature. Among the predicaments is the 'long coffee value chain' from the producers of the berries to the coffee consumers, the consequence of which include the meagre economic benefits that accrue to the farmers.[88] Global oversupply of coffee by core producing states has also

---

[84] Ibid.
[85] Ibid.
[86] 'What the Future Holds for Thousands of Coffee Farmers' (*Daily Nation*, Nairobi, 16 May 2023) <https://nation.africa/kenya/counties/nyeri/what-the-future-hold-for-thousands-of-coffee-farmers-4236704> accessed 8 October 2024.
[87] Gerald Andae, 'Coffee Prices Decline on Low Demand, Expected Surplus' (*Business Daily*, Nairobi, 4 November 2022) accessed 8 October 2024.
[88] Chelsea Bruce-Lockhart and Emiko Terazono, 'From Bean to Cup, What Goes into the Cost of Your Coffee?' (*Financial Times*, London, 4 June 2019) <https:// www .ft .com/ content/ 44bd6a8e -83a5 -11e9 -9935 -ad75bb96c849> accessed 8 October 2024.

contributed to unsustainable prices for farmers.[89] The ICO estimates that the global coffee supply further increased by 0.1% to 168.2 million bags in the 2022–3 period, and even predicts that there will be a surplus of a million bags in the 2023–4 period.[90] Further, the major coffee roasters and processors have increasingly exercised excessive market power,[91] including regulation of pricing.

Nonetheless, despite the multifaceted nature of the challenges of increasing Kenyan coffee sales both internationally and locally, and ensuring higher economic returns for the farmers and produces, it is inevitable that one of the core solutions remains the enhanced, robust, and optimum branding of Kenyan coffee. Indeed, the 2016 *Report of the National Task Force on Coffee Sub-Sector Reforms* had credibly established that there still existed an untapped market both locally and internationally.[92] Based on the discussed value of the distinctiveness and uniqueness of Kenyan coffee, and the existence of an untapped market, a more robust approach to optimum and broad international place-branding is necessary, and should be a core part of addressing the problem of poor economic returns in the coffee sector.

A limitation of the contemporary narrow approach to place-branding through certification include the opposition and refusal to offer protection by Australia, Switzerland, Germany, European Union Intellectual Property Office and Japan.[93] In particular, a certification mark is premised on the trade marks legal regime, which is territorial in nature. It implies that trade mark protection and rights exist in each state according to the legal and regulatory regime of that particular country, and as evaluated and accepted for protection by that subject state. Article 6(3) of the Paris Convention for the Protection of Industrial Property provides that '[a] mark duly registered in a country of the Union shall be regarded as independent of marks registered in the other countries of the Union, including the country of origin'.[94] Consequently, with the exception of 'well-known trade marks',[95] a mark registered in one state

---

[89] Peter Kettler, 'We Love Coffee. Are We Willing to Pay the Price?' (*FairTrade International*, 5 June 2019) <https://www.fairtrade.net/news/we-love-coffee-are-we-willing-to-pay-the-price> accessed 8 October 2024.

[90] International Coffee Organization (n 2).

[91] Amrouk (n 1).

[92] *Report of the National Task Force on Coffee Sub-Sector Reforms* (n 5), 11.

[93] 'Madrid Monitor' (n 43).

[94] Paris Convention for the Protection of Industrial Property (adopted 20 March 1883, as amended on 28 September 1979) 828 UNTS 305.

[95] Well known trade marks are protected in other states even if not registered in that subject country. See, ibid., Article 6bis; Articles 16(2) and (3) of the Agreement on Trade-Related Aspects of Intellectual Property Rights (n 24).

confers no rights in another jurisdiction unless by consent, or by subsequent registration in accordance with the legal or regulatory scheme in that other state. Connie Nichols observes that:

> The requirement to protect trademarks through use and registration in multiple counties is due largely to the territoriality principle of trademark law. As will be discussed in-depth below, this principle advances the theory that trademarks are governed and protected *only* by the jurisdiction granting the rights as opposed to the competing "universality" doctrine, which provides that once a trademark "[is] lawfully affixed to merchandise in one country, the merchandise would carry that mark lawfully wherever it went and could not be deemed an infringer." ... The universality doctrine presents difficulty in administration and has been rejected by most nations, with the principles of territoriality prevailing.[96]

Consequently, there is a need for Kenya to enact domestic legislation, and ratify or accede to, international legal instruments that not only reinforce protection through certification, but enable additional vital forms of authentic place-branding of its coffee, including GIs and appellations of origin. Though there is similarity between GIs and appellations of origin, the basic distinction between the two concepts is the extent of the link of the protected product with the place of origin, which must be stronger in the case of an appellation of origin.[97] As such, the characteristics of an item to be protected as an appellation of origin must arise, exclusively or principally, from its geographical origin.

Indeed, the 2016 *Report of the National Task Force on Coffee* recommended that the country enacts GI legislation for the purposes of providing a legal framework for the registration and protection of the coffee origin brands locally and internationally. In making the recommendation, the 2016 Report noted that there was demonstrable evidence that the registration of GIs

---

Nonetheless, the test whether a trade mark is well known is still determined by the subject state in accordance with local factors, rather than universal standards or criteria.

[96] Connie Davis Powell Nichols, 'Article 6bis of the Paris Convention for Well-Known Marks: Does it Require Use or a Likelihood of Consumer Confusion for Protection? Did *Belmora LLC v Bayer Consumer Care Ag* Resolve this Question?' (2020) 30(2) Indiana International and Comparative Law Review 235, 236.

[97] 'Frequently Asked Questions: Geographical Indications' (World Intellectual Property Organization) <www .wipo .int/ geo _indications/ en/ faq _geo graphicali ndications .html #: ~: text = The %20basic %20difference %20between %20the ,essentially %20from %20its %20geographical %20origin> accessed 8 October 2024.

increases production output, and that the 'certainty afforded by legal protection' would enhance opportunities for investment in the coffee sector.[98]

By having a strong domestic legislation, and being a party to vital international legal instruments relating to place-branding through certification marks, GIs and appellations of origin, and prohibition of misrepresentation of origin and content, Kenya would be able to undertake robust and optimal protection of the premium coffee produce and have its farmers reap higher economic benefits. Such international agreements that Kenya has not acceded to or ratified, and as such is not a bearer of place-branding rights and obligations enunciated in the instruments, include: the 1958 Lisbon Agreement for the Protection of Appellations of Origin and Their International Registration;[99] and the 1891 Madrid Agreement for the Repression of False or Deceptive Indications of Source on Goods.[100] The 1958 Lisbon Agreement for the Protection of Appellations of Origin enables state parties to protect, through a harmonized application at WIPO, the GIs and appellations of origin in the context of the source of goods having contributed to their unique quality or characteristics. The 1891 Madrid Agreement for the Repression of False or Deceptive Indications requires that any goods bearing a false or deceptive indication of source be seized, the importation of such goods be prohibited, and suitable sanctions be applied in connection with their importation.

Through the suggested domestic legislation and membership of the vital international legal instruments, Kenya would be placed to implement some of the authentic place-branding suggestions made by the *Report of the National Task Force on Coffee*. The Report recommended that the prevalent description and sale of Kenyan coffee based on bean-size and grade be terminated, and be replaced by one that focuses on flavor profiles that would be part of origin branding of its premium tastes.[101] The target areas can be mapped based on the natural factors that result in particular flavors, and the dominant tastes would be established and named for purposes of place-branding.[102] Some of the flavors that have been associated with Kenyan coffee include piercing acidity, thick

---

[98] *Report of the National Task Force on Coffee Sub-Sector Reforms* (n 5), 27.

[99] Lisbon Agreement for the Protection of Appellations of Origin and Their International Registration (adopted 31 October 1958, entry into force 25 September 1966, and as revised 14 July 1967 (Stockholm) and 21 May 2015 (Geneva)) 923 UNTS 205.

[100] Madrid Agreement for the Repression of False or Deceptive Indications of Source on Goods (adopted 14 April 1891, as revised 31 October 1958, with the Additional Act of Stockholm of 14 July 1967) 828 UNTS 163.

[101] *Report of the National Task Force on Coffee Sub-Sector Reforms* (n 5), 26.

[102] Ibid.

winey, chocolatey, caramel, and blackcurrant, among others.[103] Consequently, localities that produce coffee with similar flavours can be grouped together to establish origin appellations and clusters.[104] Further, naming can be done on the basis of favourable local names, or well-known geographical features.[105] Such features of the coffee can then be subject to more robust authentic and credible place-branding and enforcement of standards through certification, GIs and appellations of origin. Further, the place-branding should include essential market authentication and validation statements such as 'pure Kenyan coffee', or '100% Kenyan coffee', or 'unblended Kenyan coffee'.

Kenya may then also obtain some valuable comparative lessons regarding prospects, merits and returns of robust, authentic, and credible place-branding of coffee from Colombia, particularly given the state's immense success with the Juan Valdez brand. Colombia's National Federation of Coffee Growers created and popularized a fictional coffee grower by the name of Juan Valdez, who was represented alongside his mule, Conchita, and whose name and images were used to brand the country's coffee.[106] As pointed out, Juan Valdez, with his characteristic moustache, straw hat and mule, has become an international icon through his constant media presence, whilst Colombia's coffee farmers continue to reap immense economic benefits from the brand.[107] The introduction of the Juan Valdez brand in 1960 resulted in 'a 300% increase in Americans identifying Colombian coffee as the world's finest within 5 months of its introduction in 1960, pressurizing many companies into introducing "all Colombian" brands'.[108] Colombia has maintained robust branding of its coffee through the Juan Valdez fictional character in premium markets, particularly the US, in the subsequent decades and thus maintained a high reputation with premium economic benefits.[109] Consequently, Colombia's Juan Valdez brand

---

[103] Ibid.

[104] Ibid.

[105] Ibid.

[106] Narcís Bassols, 'Branding and Promoting a Country amidst a Long-term Conflict: The Case of Colombia' (2016) 5(4) Journal of Destination Marketing and Management 314.

[107] Magdalena Florek and Francisco Conejo, 'Export Flagships in Branding Small Developing Countries: The Cases of Costa Rica and Moldova' (2007) 3 Place Branding and Public Diplomacy 53, 67.

[108] Jonathan Morris, 'We Consumers - Tastes, Rituals, and Waves' in Britta Folmer (ed), *The Craft and Science of Coffee* (Elsevier 2017), 457, 468.

[109] Florek and Conejo (n 107), 67. See also, José Marcio Carvalho, Ely Laureano Paiva and Luciana Marques Vieira, 'Quality Attributes of a High Specification Product: Evidences from the Speciality Coffee Business' (2006) 118(1) British Food Journal 132, 136.

was regarded as being the US's best-known brand in 2005.[110] As is the case with Colombia, successful rebranding of Kenya's coffee should incorporate immense advertising and marketing, an aspect that has been missing with respect to the Coffee Kenya certification mark.

The discussed emerging practice of sustainable organic coffee farming certification through TRACE Kenya (including the traceable non-use of harmful pesticides and herbicides) should also be supported, and entrenched in the formal structures of authentic and credible place-branding through mechanisms such as state-supported certification, GIs and appellations of origin to prevent abuse and misrepresentation both domestically and internationally, and to reinforce their economic utility. It is apparent that some of the greatest potential for increasing the value of Kenya's premium coffee product both locally and internationally is through the inclusion and mainstreaming of sustainable organic certification, including the traceable non-use of harmful pesticides and herbicides. Solidaridad has credibly opined that:

> Within the Kenyan coffee sector, the trend towards organic and sustainable practices is a strategic move that allows more local farmers to access the competitive high value markets while contributing to reduction of the associated health risks and negative environmental impacts and promoting sustainable use of the earth's resources.[111]

Reinforcing robust place-branding with direct sales and diversified markets

It is noteworthy that Kenya inherited the colonial legacy of highly regulated processing and sale of coffee through restrictive licencing mechanisms. Kenya's colonial legacy of high regulation of the coffee sector has also resulted in economically unsustainable long coffee value chains between coffee farmers and consumers that include middle men and logistics entities thriving. The highly government-regulated sale of Kenya's coffee has further traditionally required that the produce be traded through the Nairobi Coffee Exchange (NCE).[112]

It is thus apparent that robust authentic place-branding initiatives for Kenya's premium coffee must be supplemented by cutting the lengthy value chain and by directly linking the farmers with the market; initiatives that the Kenyan Government is commendably undertaking. For instance, the government supported the November 2023 Nyeri Coffee Exposition that included

---

[110] Bassols (n 106), 314.
[111] 'Bridging the Gaps Towards Organic Coffee Certification in Kenya' (n 80).
[112] 'Who We Are and Our Mandate' (Nairobi Coffee Exchange, 2023) <www.nairobicoffeeexchange.co.ke/about> accessed 8 October 2024.

the participation of various international coffee buyers as an initiative aimed at opening up new markets that directly link with the farmers, and eliminate the role and significance of middle men and logistics entities.[113] Kenya's Deputy President, Rigathi Gachagua, who hails from the coffee growing Nyeri County, has explicitly stated that the government will reform the coffee sector and has undertaken diverse initiatives relating to the opening up of direct sales by farmers in new markets in countries such as Germany, China, and US, among others.[114] Making reference to the ongoing reform under the post-2022 government regime, the New KPCU Managing Director, Timothy Mirugi, stated that 'the auction and the direct market' are being opened 'so that the farmer can get the very best price that ... the international market can offer'.[115]

The robust marketing of Kenyan coffee that is authentically and credibly place-branded should also target exploiting potential markets in the Africa regional and sub-regional trading blocs, including the East African Community (EAC), the Common Market for Eastern and Southern Africa (COMESA), and the Africa Continental Free Trade Area. The Kenya Export Promotion and Branding Agency is commendably targeting the Africa Continental Free Trade Area in its marketing of the Kenyan coffee, a bloc that is touted to constitute 'the world's biggest free trade area since the formation of the World Trade Organization (WTO)'.[116]

The government should aggressively open up and promote Coffee Kenya certification and other forms of authenticated and credible place-branding of Kenyan coffee to diverse processors, particularly farmers' cooperative unions and groups, which may require state support to ensure compliance with requisite standards.

---

[113] 'Nyeri Coffee Expo: Direct Coffee Sales is a Move in the Right Direction for Kenyan Coffee' (Kenya Export Promotion and Branding Agency, Nairobi, 8 November 2023) <www.makeitkenya.go.ke/about-keproba/news-room/latest-news/nyeri-coffee-expo-direct-coffee-sales-is-a-move-in-the-right-direction-for-kenyan-coffee> accessed 8 October 2024.

[114] 'Kenya Eyes Direct Coffee Sales to US and Other Lucrative Markets - DP Gachagua' (*Citizen Digital*, Nairobi, 6 October 2023) <https://www.citizen.digital/news/kenya-eyes-direct-coffee-sales-to-us-and-other-lucrative-markets-dp-gachagua-n328858> accessed 8 October 2024.

[115] Sarah Njoroge, 'Win for Coffee Farmers as Government Opens Direct International Market' (*Citizen Digital*, Nairobi, 15 November 2023) <https://www.citizen.digital/business/win-for-coffee-farmers-as-govt-opens-direct-international-market-n331397> accessed 8 October 2024.

[116] 'Nyeri Coffee Expo: Direct Coffee Sales is a Move in the Right Direction for Kenyan Coffee'(n 113).

Various state and non-state actors in the coffee sector should also focus on expanding the local market for the authenticated and credibly place-branded Kenyan produce by promoting a domestic coffee culture particularly among its upper and middle class segments of the population. There is minimal consumption of coffee in Kenya, including among the middle and upper class segments of society, which denies the country a vital potential local market when compared to countries such as Ethiopia. Kenya's coffee is export-oriented, with the state trading more than 95% of its coffee to the world market.[117] According to ICO statistics, Kenya does not even feature among the top 16 consumers of coffee in Africa in the 2021–3 period that comprises Ethiopia, Algeria, Egypt, Morocco, South Africa, Tunisia, Nigeria, Sudan, Madagascar, Ivory Coast, Libya, Uganda, Democratic Republic of Congo, Senegal, Burkina Faso, and Cameroon.[118] Kenya thus does not benefit from a vibrant local market, unlike its neighbour Ethiopia, Africa's largest consumer according to ICO statistics,[119] or even Uganda.

CONCLUSION

The registration of the Coffee Kenya certification mark of origin at KIPI and WIPO by the CBK (and subsequently by the Coffee Directorate) signified vital progress towards authentic place-branding as a mechanism of tapping the international goodwill accorded Kenya's premium coffee. Nonetheless, the largely narrow approach to place-branding of Kenya's coffee through only the certification mark has limitations that negate the country's capacity to effectively tap the domestic and global market, optimally benefit from its premium product, and provide its farmers with increased economic returns. Consequently, robust, broad, and optimal place-branding of Kenya's coffee though additional mechanisms that include GIs and appellations of origin is essential, and they require backing up by appropriate domestic and international legal regimes. In addition, the emerging practice of certification of organically produced coffee should be assimilated into Kenya's mainstream authentic place-branding activities, as it presents an international market segment that has enormous potential for growth. Further, a robust, authentic, and credible place-branding of Kenya's premium berries should be reinforced by the aggressive opening up of direct processing and sale of coffee to consumers by farmers, and by the elimination of the economically unsustainable

---

[117] Andae (n 87).
[118] International Coffee Organization (n 2).
[119] See Ibid.

long value chain, in addition to the diversification into emerging and prospective international and local markets.

PART IV

Intellectual Property Law in Practice

10. The Legal Protection of Geographical Indications in the United States: Following the Footsteps of Napa Valley

J. Scott Gerien

In 1979, before any wine appellation had received legal recognition in the United States (US), the wine author Richard Paul Hinkle observed '[t]he Napa Valley is the spiritual center of American winegrowing. It was not the first of America's wine-growing regions, nor is it the largest. But, bestowed with a touch of magic, it has always been the best known.'[1] Such reputation continues today as succinctly stated by *San Francisco Chronicle* senior wine critic Esther Mobley in 2023: 'Napa Valley is the great American wine region'.[2]

The reason for this critical recognition of the region is the quality of its wine. As a result of this, the wine industry is the overwhelming economic engine of Napa County. According to studies conducted by Napa Valley Vintners, the Napa wine industry provides an annual economic impact of more than $9.4 billion locally and nearly $34 billion in the US, creating 44,000 jobs in Napa County and nearly 190,000 throughout the US.[3] While, like most wine regions throughout the world, Napa Valley is dealing with the impacts of climate change on its industry, the recognition of the Napa Valley brand, the geographical indication (GI), allows it to do so in an effective and thoughtful manner as to do so is critical to future success.

As one of the US's best known GIs, today the Napa Valley is also one of the most protected GIs in America. However, despite its fame, the vintners and the

---

[1] Richard Paul Hinkle, *Napa Valley Wine Book* (Vintage Image 1979) 11.
[2] Esther Mobley, 'Top Wineries in Napa Valley, Where to go tasting in America's most iconic wine region' *San Francisco Chronicle* (San Francisco, 13 June 2023).
[3] 'Napa Valley Fast Facts' (Napa Vinters) <https://napavintners.com/press/docs/napa_valley_fast_facts.pdf> accessed 4 October 2024.

community, which benefit from the Napa Valley GI did not always realize the importance of obtaining legal protection for the GI.

Unlike Europe, where governments have long recognized the importance of GIs to the agriculture industry and their communities through *sui generis* protection of GIs, the US historically has commoditized agriculture, which emphasizes production over sustainability and local quality.[4] Such commoditization of agriculture has no need for GIs, which do not serve the purpose of increased industrial production. As a result, the legal concept of 'geographical indications' is still fairly foreign to most Americans. There is no specific GI protection system in the US similar to that of Europe,[5] and instead GIs are protected pursuant to the trademark system under the federal Lanham Act (Trademark Act of 1946) and through an appellation system and consumer protection laws specific to the alcohol beverage industry under the Federal Alcohol Administration (FAA) of 1935.

The story of the legal recognition of Napa Valley as an appellation for wine and 'geographical indication' begins with the FAA Act, so that is where this next section will begin in its review of the legal protection of GIs in the US.

PROTECTION OF GEOGRAPHICAL INDICATIONS PURSUANT TO THE FEDERAL ALCOHOL ADMINISTRATION ACT (FAA ACT)

Following the end of Prohibition in the US in 1933, the US Congress adopted the FAA Act in 1935 to protect US consumers and ensure that they received truthful and accurate information in relation to their purchase of alcohol beverage products.[6] During the re-establishment of the US wine industry after Prohibition, since appellations did not exist as a legal or practical construct, wineries generally referenced states and counties that had pre-established boundaries when indicating the geographic origin of the wine.

During the 1970s, this practice changed when the US wine industry, particularly in California, began focusing on higher quality wines rather than commodity wines. Wine labels increasingly referred to places and regions that

---

[4] See Gerardo Patron-Cano, 'Modern Capitalism and Food Commoditization: The Limitations of Industrial Agriculture and the Challenges of Sustainable Alternatives' (MA thesis, University of Denver 2015).

[5] Given the disproportionate political and marketplace influence of industry agriculture conglomerates in the US, there also does not appear to be any governmental or popular interest in a European-like GI protection system in the US.

[6] The FAA Act is found at 27 USC §§201–219.

had no clear boundaries. Examples include Northern California, Napa Valley, Howell Mountain, and North Coast.

Creation of the US Appellation System for Wine

Recognizing that the use of undefined geographical names could mislead consumers and be abused by producers, the Bureau of Alcohol, Tobacco and Firearms (ATF),[7] the US government agency responsible for enforcing the FAA Act at the time, proceeded to adopt a formal wine appellation system in the US in 1978. The framework allows for different types of wine appellations, each of which has a prescribed requirement of a minimum percentage of grapes from that area used to make the particular wine carrying the appellation. This framework only applies to wine appellations located in the US.

As was the case before the creation of the formal framework, state and county names (for example, California or Sonoma County) continue to be used as appellations, except that now at least 75 percent of the wine bearing such an appellation must be derived from grapes grown in the identified state or county, and the wine has to be fully finished within the identified state or an adjacent state in the case of a state appellation, or within the state in which the identified county is located.[8] The use of multi-county and multi-state appellations on a wine label is also permitted so long as no more than three counties in a state or three contiguous states are listed on the label and the percentage of grapes from each respective county or state is exactly identified, with the total adding up to 100 percent (plus or minus 2 percent).[9] As US states and counties already existed pursuant to political boundaries, there is no process by which these appellations must be established or recognized under the appellation framework.

A new type of appellation known as the 'American Viticultural Area' (AVA) was also established for geographic areas that were not previously defined. The law defines AVAs as 'delimited grape growing regions distinguished by geographical features, the boundaries of which have been recognized and defined' by the agency.[10] An AVA can be identified on a wine label

---

[7] The Homeland Security Act of 2002 (See Reorganization of Title 27, Code of Federal Regulations, 68 Fed Reg 3744 (Jan 24, 2003)) transferred responsibility for enforcement of the FAA Act from the ATF to the newly-formed US Alcohol and Tobacco Tax and Trade Bureau (TTB), where it remains today. The ATF was, and TTB now is, part of the US Treasury Department.

[8] 27 CFR §4.25(b)(1)(i) (2021).

[9] 27 CFR §4.25(c)–(d) (2021).

[10] 27 CFR §4.25(a)(1)(vi), (e) (2021).

if at least 85 percent of the wine is made from grapes grown inside that AVA and the wine is fully finished in the state in which the AVA is located (or in *a* state in which the AVA is located where the AVA straddles more than one state).[11] The process for obtaining agency recognition of an AVA is further discussed below.

The wine appellation framework also allows for the use of foreign wine appellations on imported wine sold in the US. There are two types of foreign appellations recognized under the rules. The first, like the US political appellation, includes a country, state, province, territory, or other political subdivision of a country equivalent to a state or county.[12] Such foreign political appellations can be used on wine imported into the US if at least 75 percent of the wine is derived from grapes grown in the named appellation, and the wine conforms to the requirements for the use of that appellation in the country of origin.[13]

The second type of foreign appellation is a foreign viticultural area, defined as a 'delimited place or region', other than a political appellation, 'the boundaries of which have been recognized and defined by the country of origin for use on labels of wine available for consumption within the country of origin'.[14] Like an AVA, a foreign viticultural area can only be used on wine derived at least 85 percent from grapes grown in that foreign viticultural area, and the wine must also conform to the production, composition, and designation requirements of the country of origin.[15]

Unlike an AVA, there is no process by which the Alcohol, Tobacco and Tax Bureau (TTB) (formerly the ATF) officially recognizes a foreign viticultural area. According to the TTB, in order to determine what is an acceptable foreign appellation or foreign viticultural area, an inquiry should be made of the appropriate foreign government, and inquiries may also be directed to the TTB International Affairs Division.[16]

Process for Recognition of an AVA

The process by which an AVA is recognized by the TTB was established in 1978 by the ATF under its authority granted by the FAA Act. Any party may

---

[11] 27 CFR §4.25(e)(3) (2021).
[12] 27 CFR §4.25(a)(2) (2021).
[13] 27 CFR §4.25(b)(2) (2021).
[14] 27 CFR §4.25(e)(1)(ii) (2021).
[15] 27 CFR §4.25(e)(3) (2021).
[16] 'Wine Labelling: Appellation of Origin' (TTB) <www.ttb.gov/labeling-wine/wine-labeling-appellation-of-origin> accessed 4 October 2024.

submit a petition to the TTB to establish an AVA. An AVA petition must contain the following information:

1. independent evidence that the name of the proposed AVA is currently and directly associated with the area and that the area is nationally or locally known by such name;
2. evidence in support of the boundaries of the viticultural area, including commonalities within the boundary, and how such common elements are different in areas outside of the boundary;
3. a description of the geographical features of the proposed area affecting the viticulture, such as climate, geology, soil, and topography, including how such features distinguish the viticultural area from surrounding areas; and
4. the exact boundaries of the area based on discernible reference points found on the topographic maps of the US Geological Survey.[17]

Once the completed petition is received from the petitioner, the TTB commences a public rulemaking process under the Federal Administrative Procedure Act.[18] However, the TTB is not under any legal obligation to proceed with rulemaking upon receipt of a petition.[19] The rulemaking process typically includes at least one Notice of Proposed Rulemaking (NPRM), a public comment period, and a Final Rule creating or rejecting the proposed AVA. Thereafter, the AVA, consisting of the name of the viticultural area and its boundaries, is set forth in Title 27, Part 9, Subpart C of the Code of Federal Regulations.[20] There is no official appellation or AVA register in the US, although the TTB does maintain a website listing recognized AVAs.[21]

Unlike wine appellations in Europe, AVAs only designate the origin of the grapes pursuant to the minimum 85 percent threshold, and the location of the production of the wine. Other than the origin and percentage composition requirements, there are no requirements that certain grape varieties must be used, that the wine must be of a certain quality, or that certain viticultural practices must be employed.

---

[17] 27 CFR §9.12 (2011).
[18] 5 USC §§551-559 (2018).
[19] 27 CFR §9.11(c) (2011).
[20] 27 CFR §§9.21–9.289 (2011).
[21] 'Established American Viticultural Areas' (TTB) <www.ttb.gov/wine/established-avas> accessed 4 October 2024.

The Napa Valley AVA

The Final Rule establishing the system for appellations of origin for wine was published by the ATF in 1978. The Napa Valley name was already in use on wine labels in the 1970s, and the Napa Valley wine industry was active in the process of providing input to the ATF for the creation of the US appellation system for wine. So, shortly after the Final Rule issued, the Napa Valley Vintners Association (NVV) and the Napa Valley Grape Growers Association (NVG) submitted a combined petition to establish the Napa Valley AVA in January of 1979.[22]

However, the process of determining the boundaries of an AVA can be contentious. Parties included within the boundaries of the AVA can be perceived as having a market advantage over those parties found to be outside of the boundaries. This was demonstrated by the process by which the Napa Valley AVA petition was reviewed and established.[23] Two years after the original AVA petition was submitted, and after much industry input, the Napa Valley AVA was established in 1981 with boundaries larger than the original 1979 proposal.[24] In the meantime, the less controversial Augusta AVA, located in the State of Missouri, became America's first AVA, established in 1980, with Napa Valley then becoming America's second AVA.[25]

With the establishment of the Napa Valley AVA, what more was necessary to protect the Napa Valley name? Any party wanting to use Napa Valley on a label needed to comply with the origin and production requirements of the AVA. All wine labels used in the US must first be submitted to the TTB for approval.[26] If an AVA is misused on a wine label, the approval for such label may be denied or revoked such that the product cannot be sold.[27] Thus, the Napa Valley name was safe. Vintners could rely on the TTB's authority to control the market to prevent misuse of the Napa Valley name. Or could they?

---

[22] Richard Mendelson, *Appellation Napa Valley: Building and Protecting an American Treasure* (Val de Grace Books 2016) 34–42.

[23] For a detailed history of the contentious nature of the creation of the Napa Valley AVA, see, ibid.

[24] Ibid. at 43–9, 56; 27 CFR §9.23 (1985).

[25] 27 CFR §§9.22-23 (1985).

[26] 27 CFR §13.21 (2021).

[27] 27 CFR §§13.23, 13.41 (2021).

Napa Ridge and the AVA Brand Name Loophole

As part of the labeling regulations for wine, 'a brand name of viticultural significance may not be used unless the wine meets the appellation of origin requirements for the geographic area named'.[28] In other words, where a brand name for wine encompasses an appellation, then the wine labeled with such brand name must comply with the appellation requirements, thereby providing further protection for appellations. However, certain labels for brands encompassing appellations had been approved before the appellation system was in place or before certain AVAs were officially recognized.

In 1986 this issue came before the ATF, and they established an exception, or grandfather provision, for pre-existing brand names of viticultural significance. Under this exception, wineries that obtained label approval from the TTB for a brand name of viticultural significance prior to 7 July 1986, were allowed to continue to use that brand name, so long as the label included an appropriate appellation of origin for the wine or a label disclaimer.[29] Such pre-existing label approvals were treated as a property and could also be sold by the original owner to other parties.[30]

This exception was a non-issue for many years. Then, beginning in the 1990s, a California winery called Bronco Wine Company (Bronco) began purchasing grandfathered label approvals, most notably for the brand NAPA RIDGE. Bronco proceeded to use this brand for wine made from grapes sourced outside of Napa Valley, from regions where grapes were much less expensive and of an arguably lower quality. However, the label clearly stated the names of these lesser-known appellations from which the grapes were sourced, albeit in a much smaller size than the NAPA RIDGE brand name. Thus, this use of NAPA RIDGE complied with the federal label requirements for wine and was legal under the grandfather provisions of the law.[31]

Bronco then proceeded to purchase a winery facility in Napa County with the capacity to produce 18 million cases of wine annually, more than the total annual production of all wine made from Napa Valley grapes. The Napa Valley wine industry, led by NVV, became concerned and realized that the protection of the AVA was not enough and that the value of the Napa Valley brand was in jeopardy.[32]

---

[28] 27 CFR §4.39(i)(1) (2021).
[29] 27 CFR §4.39(i) (2021).
[30] Richard Mendelson (n 22), 144.
[31] Ibid., 143–6.
[32] Ibid.

After looking for numerous political solutions, NVV determined that its best recourse could be found before the California state legislature.[33] NVV commissioned a consumer confusion survey that demonstrated that over 80 percent of consumers surveyed believed that wine with a 'NAPA' brand name was made from grapes grown in Napa Valley.[34] This was presented to the California legislature which recognized the potential for harm to the reputation and economy of Napa Valley.[35] In response, the legislature passed 'truth in labeling' legislation which prohibited the use of the word 'Napa' on the label, packaging material, or advertising of wine produced, bottled, labeled, offered for sale, or sold in California, unless at least 75 percent of the grapes used to make the wine were from Napa County.[36] In 2000, the law was signed into law by California's governor.

As the law would prevent Bronco from producing wine in California with the misleading, grandfathered Napa brand name, Bronco immediately challenged the state law claiming violation of its First Amendment freedom of speech, and that federal law preempted the more restrictive California legislation.[37] Bronco lost the appeal at the California Supreme Court, as well as at the US Supreme Court. The Court found that Bronco was not precluded from using the NAPA RIDGE mark on wine from Napa, and as such, the only speech being restricted was deceptive commercial speech.[38] Furthermore, because the federal law did not expressly address the issue addressed in the state law, the state law was complementary and not conflicting with the federal law.[39] The Napa truth-in-labeling law would go into effect. Shortly thereafter, Bronco ceased production of non-Napa wine under the Napa brand names. NVV had prevailed and Napa Valley was again protected in the US.

However, NVV learned that it is not enough to rely on the government to protect an industry's GI rights. If parties are allowed to misuse an appellation, then such loss of control risks dilution and genericide of the valuable name and brand. With protection secured in the US, NVV turned its focus to the legal protection of Napa Valley in foreign jurisdictions.

---

[33] Ibid., 148.
[34] Ibid., 149.
[35] Ibid., 149–50.
[36] California Business & Professional Code §25241(a) (2009).
[37] *Bronco Wine Co v Jolly*, 33 Cal 4th 943, 956 (2004).
[38] Ibid.
[39] Ibid.

NAPA VALLEY'S JOURNEY ABROAD BRINGS IT BACK TO THE US

In the early 2000s, following the Bronco victory, NVV began looking to protect the Napa Valley name outside of the US The first target was the European Union (EU). In 2006, the US and the EU signed the Agreement on the Trade in Wine, in which the jurisdictions agreed to mutually recognize certain 'names of origin' for wine, which included Napa Valley.[40] However, NVV had learned its lesson, it could not simply rely on governments to protect its rights, it needed to affirmatively seek protection for Napa Valley under all available protection systems.

In the early 2000s, the EU had an appellation protection system for wine, but it did not protect non-EU appellations or have a process for doing so. So, NVV prepared a letter supported by evidence to the Directorate General for Agriculture and Rural Development at the European Commission requesting protection of Napa Valley as an appellation for wine in the EU. The EU worked with NVV, and in 2007 Napa Valley became one of the first non-EU wine appellations registered in the EU.[41]

However, during the course of applying for recognition in the EU and other countries, NVV learned that the US appellation system for wine, with its different treatment of what constitutes an appellation and the manner in which appellations are recognized, did not 'translate' into recognition in other jurisdictions. NVV also learned that if there was registration of Napa Valley at the US Patent and Trademark Office (USPTO), this would assist NVV in its journey for protection abroad. So, it was back to the US to get registration at the USPTO.

PROTECTION OF GEOGRAPHICAL INDICATIONS UNDER THE US TRADEMARK SYSTEM

Other than the wine appellation system established pursuant to the FAA Act, GIs are protected under US trademark laws pursuant to the Lanham Act. As a signatory to the Agreement on Trade-Related Aspects of Intellectual Property Rights (TRIPS), the US takes the position that its obligations pursu-

---

[40] Agreement Between the United States of America and the European Community on Trade in Wine (TTB) <www.ttb.gov/images/pdfs/us-eu-wine-agreement.pdf> accessed 4 October 2024.

[41] 'eAmbrosia: the EU Geographical Indications Register' (European Commission) <https://ec.europa.eu/agriculture/eambrosia/geographical-indications-register/> accessed 4 October 2024.

ant to Articles 22–4 of TRIPS related to GIs are satisfied by the provisions of the Lanham Act.[42] While TRIPS does not obligate countries to provide a registration system for GIs, the US is also of the position that GIs may be registered in the US pursuant to the trademark registration system:

> Geographical indications can be viewed as a subset of trademarks. Geographical indications serve the same functions as trademarks, because like trademarks they are: 1) source-identifiers, 2) guarantees of quality, and 3) valuable business interests. The United States has found that by protecting geographical indications through the trademark system – usually as certification and collective marks -- the United States can provide TRIPS-plus levels of protection to GIs, of either domestic or foreign origin.[43]

The US protects all types of marks pursuant to federal registration or through common law unregistered use.[44] However, registration provides several benefits, including the presumption of distinctiveness[45] and exclusivity.[46] Additionally, since common law trademark rights are not recognized in most countries, US registration facilitates registration outside of the US. This was the principal reason that NVV sought US registration of NAPA VALLEY as a geographical certification mark since the wine appellation system already provided the majority of the protection for Napa Valley within the US.

So, if GIs may be protected under the US trademark system, into which category of marks would they be classified, trademarks/service marks, certification marks or collective marks? Well, it depends. Below we will review each type of mark relative to treatment of a GI in that category.

Geographical Certification Marks

Certification marks are terms or symbols that certify the quality and/or origin of a particular good or service.[47] Some certification marks are intended solely

---

[42] 'Geographical Indications Protection in the United States' (United States Patent and Trademark Office) <www.uspto.gov/sites/default/files/web/offices/dcom/olia/globalip/pdf/gi_system.pdf> accessed 4 October 2024 ("Protecting GIs as trademarks, collective or certification marks employs the existing trademark regime, a regime that is already familiar to businesses, both foreign and domestic"); see 15 USC §§1052, 1054 (1999).

[43] Ibid.

[44] 15 USC § 1114 (2005); 15 USC § 1125(a) (2012).

[45] *Brooklyn Brewery Corporation v Brooklyn Brew Shop*, 17 F.4th 129, 146 (Fed. Cir. 2021).

[46] 15 USC § 1057(b) (2010).

[47] 15 USC §1054 (1999).

to indicate that a product or service has met certain quality requirements. For instance, the certification mark FM APPROVED indicates and certifies that cleanroom materials bearing that mark have met certain product performance and safety standards.[48] Geographical certification marks certify the origin of goods. They can also certify the quality of the goods, although that is not required.[49] Examples of geographical certification marks include PARMA HAM,[50] IDAHO for potatoes,[51] and RIOJA for wine.[52]

While a trademark owner must use or license use of the mark to obtain rights, the owner of a certification mark *cannot* use the certification mark. The mark can only be used to certify the goods of other parties who are then allowed to use the mark on the certified goods.[53] This prevents the owner from directly benefitting from the mark and maintains the integrity of the certification process. Furthermore, use of the certification mark must be made available to any party whose products meet the certification standards.[54] The certification standards must be applied to all parties equally.[55] The certifier must also exert control over the mark and ensure that the certification standards are being met by any users of the mark.[56]

For geographical certification marks, the certifier must also demonstrate that it has the authority to control the geographical term that is the subject of the certification mark.[57] The certifier may be the government itself, one of the departments of a government, or a body with governmental authorization that is not formally a part of the government. There may also be an interrelationship between bodies in more than one of these categories.[58]

Rights in a geographical certification mark may also be asserted without registration of the mark with the USPTO. In fact, much of the US case law addressing geographical certification marks involves the mark COGNAC,

---

[48] US Registration No. 3, 896,437.
[49] 15 USC §1127 (2006); TMEP §1306.02 (July 2022).
[50] US Registration No. 2,014,628.
[51] US Registration No. 802,418.
[52] US Registration No. 692,578.
[53] 15 USC §1127 (2006).
[54] All that is required under the law is that there be certification standards. The owner of the certification mark has complete discretion in determining the standards. See, 27 CFR §§2.45, 2.76 and 2.88 ('A copy of the certification standards governing use of the certification mark on or in connection with the goods or services specified in the application.').
[55] *Trademark Manual of Examining Procedure* (TMEP) (May 2024), §1306.04.
[56] Ibid.
[57] TMEP §1306.05(b).
[58] Ibid.

which has never been registered with the USPTO. Case law involving the COGNAC geographic certification mark spans from 1944,[59] to as recent as 2020.[60]

As the preceding demonstrates, there are numerous burdens in maintaining the validity of a geographical certification mark. So why not protect a GI as a trademark? If a trademark encompasses a term that is geographically descriptive, it cannot be registered absent a showing that the geographically descriptive term has become recognized by consumers as a brand.[61] For example, in the US there is a very well-known brand of cream cheese called PHILADELPHIA. While that term is geographic, the owner of the brand was able to demonstrate that consumers had come to recognize it as a brand rather than just the geographic origin of the product. As a result, the term was registered as a trademark for cream cheese. However, this is a very high burden to meet.

A geographical certification mark may be registered by the certifier with the name of the specific geographical area, and that name will receive instant protection and exclusivity without showing that consumers have come to recognize the term as a distinctive geographical identifier.[62] Geographical certification marks under the Lanham Act also do not need to meet the TRIPS definition of GIs in order to be registered.[63] Accordingly, while GIs may be protected through use as geographical certification marks, not all geographical certification marks are necessarily geographical indications.

Thus, in pursuing protection under the Lanham Act, NVV applied to register NAPA VALLEY as a geographical certification mark for wine. The process was long, and NVV needed to demonstrate that all of the trademarks registered for wine encompassing the word 'NAPA' (of which there were many) were actually compliant with geographic origin standards. In 2015, NAPA VALLEY was registered with the USPTO as a geographical certification mark for wine.[64]

---

[59] Otard, Inc v Italian Swiss Colony et al., 141 F.2d 706, 61 USPQ 131 (CCPA 1944).

[60] *Bureau Nat'l Interprofessionnel Du Cognac*, No. 91242020, 2020 WL 1528535, at *7 (13 March 2020).

[61] TMEP §1210.09.

[62] See TMEP §1306.05(d); *Luxco, Inc v Consejo Regulador del Tequila, A.C.*, 121 USPQ 2d 1477, 1482 (TTAB 2017).

[63] See TMEP §1300 et seq..

[64] US Registration No. 4,853,438.

Geographical Collective Marks

Pursuant to the Lanham Act, collective marks are exclusively used on goods or services by members of an association or organization.[65] A certification process or standard is not required for a collective mark, although the organization may elect to set standards for its members. Compared to certification marks, the rules related to the use and availability of collective marks are less strict, making collective marks easier to maintain. On the other hand, the owner of a collective mark with geographical significance, for example, a regional trade association, may not claim exclusive use in the geographical term absent some evidence of fame or acquired distinctiveness, and absent such acquired distinctiveness, others may also use the geographic term.

For example, the mark RONES DE GUATEMALA and Design is registered by the Asociación Nacional de Fabricantes de Alcoholes y Licoresas of Guatemala as a collective mark for 'rums from Guatemala'.[66] The registration disclaims exclusive rights to the words 'RONES DE GUATEMALA' as 'rones', or 'rum' is generic, and 'Guatemala' is geographically descriptive. Thus, based on the registration, the Asociación has no right to preclude others from using the term 'Guatemala' on rum, only the logo design mark. Had the Asociación registered the mark as a geographical certification mark, it could have stopped others from using or registering 'Guatemala' for rum as it would have been granted exclusive rights in that geographic term for rum.

Geographical Indications – or rather Geographical Designations – as Trademarks in the US

Since a trademark right is exclusive, that is, it can only be used or licensed for use by its owner, it is a protection structure generally unsuitable for the protection of GIs. The Lanham Act provides that a geographically descriptive trademark, a mark that encompasses the name of the place from which the goods emanate, may not be registered as an inherently distinctive trademark.[67] However, such a mark may be entitled to registration and the associated protections if it can be shown that the mark 'has become distinctive of the applicant's goods in commerce'.[68]

When a geographic term becomes distinctive of one party's product, however, it is functioning as a brand name, such as PHILADELPHIA for cream

---

[65] 15 USC §1127 (2022).
[66] US Registration No. 3884367.
[67] 15 USC §1052(e) (2021).
[68] 15 USC §1052(f) (2021).

cheese, rather than as a symbol of geographic origin, such as NAPA VALLEY for wine. However, if the owner of the trademark is a government-sanctioned entity, and that entity can prove a geographic term has acquired distinctiveness with goods controlled by the entity, and the entity wants to treat the GI as a trademark, the USPTO has held that this is acceptable.

In the US, the Ethiopian Intellectual Property Office (EIPO) sought to register three geographic designations for Ethiopian coffee, Harrar/Harar, Sidamo and Yirgacheffe, as trademarks. EIPO's plan was to offer royalty-free licenses of the trademarks to US coffee companies to create a network of licensed distributors, who in return, would actively promote Harrar/Harar, Sidamo and Yirgacheffe to consumers in the specialty coffee market.[69] However, the National Coffee Association, the leading trade association for the US coffee industry, objected to the registration of Harrar/Harar and Sidamo on the basis they were generic. In response, EIPO submitted evidence demonstrating that the geographic terms had acquired distinctiveness and prevailed in obtaining trademark registrations.[70]

Thus, the monopolization of a geographic term as a trademark that may otherwise function as a GI is possible in the US. However, given that trademarks may be restricted in their use by the owner and are not available to all that may otherwise qualify for use of the geographic term to show geographic origin, the protection of 'GIs' as trademarks is less common than their protection as geographical certification marks.

That one party can control a geographical term as a certification mark is controversial, which is why the law requires that the certification mark be available to any party that can meet the certification standards. More controversial is allowing a single party to own a monopoly in a geographical term that is descriptive of product origin as a trademark, thereby having the right to exclude others. It is for this reason that GIs are not generally registered as trademarks under US law.

CONCLUSION

Geographical indications can be protected under US law, albeit without one clear path to do so. In the case of Napa Valley, protection has been maximized in the US as both an AVA and geographical certification mark. With the registration of NAPA VALLEY with the USPTO, NVV was better able to protect

---

[69] Daphne Zographos Johnson, 'Using Intellectual Property Rights to Create Value in the Coffee Industry' (2012) 16(2) Marquette Intellectual Property Law Review 303–4.

[70] Ibid.

the name abroad and now has registration as a GI or geographical certification mark in 44 countries, with several applications currently pending.

11. Protection of Place Brands in Germany: Opportunities, Challenges and Strategies from a Practitioner's Perspective

Katharina Hendrike Reuer and Wiebke Baars

OVERVIEW: PROTECTION OF PLACE BRANDS IN GERMANY AND THE EU

In Germany today, the generic term 'place brands' for labelling products is connected with the legally anchored terms 'indications of geographical origin' ('*geografische Herkunftsangaben*' – 'GIs') and 'designations of origin' ('*Ursprungsangaben*' – 'DOs'), which originate from European Union (EU) law. German consumers are familiar with GIs, such as in connection with regional foodstuffs (for example Nürnberger Lebkuchen, Schwarzwälder Schinken and also for German beer like Bayerisches Bier and Kölsch). The indication that the product originates from a certain region or a certain place implies to the consumer, on the one hand, that the product corresponds to other products of the same type with an identical indication of origin in the way it is produced or its composition. On the other hand, the GI awakens the consumer's perception of the product and increases its value. The intention of German consumers to strengthen the local economy by purchasing a product from their 'own' region and to act in a particularly responsible manner in terms of 'sustainability' is also becoming increasingly important, for example because long transportation routes are avoided and the product is particularly fresh as a result.[1] 'Place brands' and names which have a link with place can be protected in a variety of ways, based on different foundations in the EU.

In Germany, names and signs protected as GIs are regarded as a separate concept of rights – independent of the protection for registered trademarks –

---

[1] Thomas Schulteis, § 126 Rn. 1 MarkenG, para. 1, in BeckOK MarkenR, 36. Ed. 1.1.2024.

and are subject to their own protection regime, which is however integrated into the German Trademark Act (ss. 126–129 of the German Trademark Act ('MarkenG')). This is essentially a protection against being misled by false indications of origin for goods or services, that is consumers and competitors are protected against misleading product designations for foodstuffs and spirit drinks as to their origin. This protection arises solely through the use of the GI and – unlike trademark rights – does not require an entry in the trademark register. In addition, GIs can also obtain trademark protection in Germany as a so-called collective trademark (MarkenG, s. 99) and – only in exceptional cases – as a registered individual trademark. In contrast to registered trademarks, there is no 'proprietor' in the sense of a person entitled in rem to the (unregistered) GI under the Trademark Act. The right to use the GI is independent of legal declarations, acts of the authorities or courts, and so on, but is based exclusively on purely factual circumstances, namely the geographical origin of the products on the one hand and the public perception on the other. If a company moves its registered office out of the geographical area, it may no longer use the indication of origin. Conversely, any newcomer may use the indication without express permission, even if it is a collective mark (s. 100(1)).

In addition, protection for GIs and DOs comes from German and EU legislation targeted at specific sectors. The EU regulations provide for protection for foodstuffs and alcoholic beverages to be obtained by entry in the EU Commission's register within the framework of a separate protection system in each case.[2] As will be seen below, German law had partly already implemented EU obligations while the remaining EU Regulations are directly applicable in Germany (and all other member states, within the meaning of Art. 288(2) of the Treaty on the Functioning of the European Union ('TFEU'), without the necessity of implementation by national legislation).

German Law

German law provided protection for competitors, and later also for consumers, against the misleading use of GIs according to the principles of the protection against misleading statements under section 3 of the Law against Unfair Competition ('UWG') (old version). Since the MarkenG implemented the First Council Directive 89/104/EEC of 21 December 1988 to approximate the laws of the Member States relating to trademarks, GIs have also been declared

---

[2] All GIs and DOs registered at EU level can be searched in the EU Commission's eAmbrosia register <https:// ec .europa .eu/ agriculture/ eambrosia/ geographical-indications-register/> accessed 3 May 2024.

to be signs and subjected to the protection of their own law regime and, in this respect, placed alongside the protection of trademarks and commercial designations (MarkenG, ss. 1(3) and 126 et seq.).

Product-specific EU Regulations for GIs and DOs
Unlike the MarkenG, the EU Trade Mark Regulation[3] ('EUTMR') does not provide for protection of GIs. However, like in Germany, according to Art. 74(2) EUTMR, GIs can be protected as so-called EU collective marks. Product-specific EU regulations are decisive for the protection of GIs and DOs.

There are product-specific regulations at EU level on the protection of designations for wines,[4] for aromatized wine products,[5] and for spirit drinks ('Spirit Drinks Regulation' ('SDR'))[6] that have direct effect in Germany. These provisions are aligned with the fourth product-specific regulation on the protection of GIs and DOs for agricultural products and foodstuffs ('Quality Schemes Regulation' ('QSR')),[7] which does not fall under the scope of one of the other three more specific regulations. The MarkenG in turn contains supplementary provisions for the implementation of the QSR (MarkenG, ss. 130–136). Accordingly, all products that are labelled with GIs or DOs protected under these EU regulations and are to be distributed on the German market must meet the requirements of these EU regulations.

---

[3] Regulation (EU) 2017/1001 of the European Parliament and of the Council of 14 June 2017 on the European Union trade mark (codification) [2017] OJ L154/1.

[4] Regulation (EU) No 1308/2013 of the European Parliament and of the Council of 17 December 2013 establishing a common organisation of the markets in agricultural products and repealing Council Regulations (EEC) No 922/72, (EEC) No 234/79, (EC) No 1037/2001 and (EC) No 1234/2007 [2013] OJ L347/671, Arts 92 et seq.

[5] Regulation (EU) No 251/2014 of the European Parliament and of the Council of 26 February 2014 on the definition, description, presentation, labelling and the protection of geographical indications of aromatised wine products and repealing Council Regulation (EEC) No 1601/91 [2014] OJ L84/14, Arts 10 et seq.

[6] Regulation (EU) 2019/787 of the European Parliament and of the Council of 17 April 2019 on the definition, description, presentation and labelling of spirit drinks, the use of the names of spirit drinks in the presentation and labelling of other foodstuffs, the protection of geographical indications for spirit drinks, the use of ethyl alcohol and distillates of agricultural origin in alcoholic beverages, and repealing Regulation (EC) No 110/2008 [2019] OJ L130/1.

[7] Regulation (EU) No 1151/2012 of the European Parliament and of the Council of 21 November 2012 on quality schemes for agricultural products and foodstuffs [2012] OJ L343/1.

Stricter requirements are placed on a DO than on a GI, as it can only be used to designate a product that originates in a specific place, or a specific region, but only in exceptional cases in a specific country. The quality or characteristic of the product must be essentially or exclusively due to a particular geographical environment with its inherent natural and human factors, and its production steps must all take place in the defined area (QSR, Art. 5(1)). In contrast, the product marked with a GI can also – and not only exceptionally – originate in a specific country. Furthermore, it is sufficient if the quality, reputation, or other characteristic is essentially attributable to its geographical origin, and that at least one production step took place in the defined geographical area (QSR, Art. 5(2)).

PROTECTION FOR PLACE BRANDS – CREATION, SCOPE, AND OBSTACLES

Creation of Protection as GI under German Law

GIs are separate from registered trademarks and differ from them in function in that they do not refer to the commercial origin of goods or services or to the business owner or the business itself, but to the geographical origin of a good or service and its specific characteristics based on that origin. According to MarkenG, s. 126(1), GIs include (1) the names of places, regions, territories, or countries as well as (2) other indications or signs *used* in the course of trade to designate the geographical origin of goods or services (3) German law thus equates *direct* GIs with the 'other indications or signs', that is the so-called *indirect* GIs, where the local reference of a product or service is conveyed other than by the use of the geographical names. For example, special landmarks of a place,[8] provided they have not found their way into the vernacular, and the designations of vineyard sites are considered as indirect GIs.[9] The use of the indication to identify the geographical origin of goods and services must take place in the course of trade in Germany. Registration is not required.

According to the MarkenG, all GIs *used* in the course of trade, are protected against any use of them for goods or services of a different origin, if such use is likely to mislead as to the geographical origin (MarkenG, s. 127(1)).

---

[8] Case *Frankfurter Römer (Mouson)*, BGH [1954] I ZR 174/52, GRUR 1955, 91, 92.

[9] Case *Stich den Buben*, BGH [2000] I ZR 126/98, GRUR 2001, 73, 75; Franz Hacker § 126 MarkenG, para. 67 in Paul Ströbele, Franz Hacker and Frederik Thiering (eds), (14th edn, 2024).

Scope of Protection as GI under German Law

Pursuant to MarkenG, s. 127(1), the consumer is protected against being misled in relation to goods or services which use a GI although the goods or services in question do not originate from the geographically designated place, territory, or country. The decisive factor here is the perception of the trade, that is in the case of GIs for goods or services aimed at the general public, the perspective of an averagely informed and reasonable consumer who pays attention to the GI in a manner appropriate to the situation must be taken into account.[10] For example, the German Federal Court of Justice (Bundesgerichtshof (BGH)) has confirmed that the word 'Himalaya' constitutes a GI and that salt advertised as 'Himalayan salt', which in fact does not come from the Himalayan mountains, misleads the consumer as to the geographical origin of the product.[11] MarkenG, s. 127(2) provides protection in the case of a qualified GI against the use of such an indication even though the goods or services do not have the quality or characteristic that such a GI has.

MarkenG, s. 127(3) guarantees the protection of GIs with a 'special reputation' – even without a risk of misleading – against exploitation of reputation or dilution. Thereby, the qualitative element of a special reputation can be based either on the objective characteristics and quality features of a product (primary benefit) or on its pure prestige value or reputation (secondary benefit).[12] For example, case law has assumed an infringement of the indication of origin 'Champagne' in case of use for IT devices,[13] and for household water treatment devices.[14]

Loss of Protection as a GI Under German Law

A GI may lose its protection under MarkenG, s 126(2) if the understanding of the public concerned has changed in such a way that the GI is only perceived as a designation or indication of the kind, quality, variety and other properties or characteristics of products. This is so when only a very insignificant part of

---

[10] Case *Warsteiner III,* BGH [2001] I ZR 54/96, GRUR 2002, 160, 162; Case *Original Oettinger,* BGH [2002] I ZR 72/99, GRUR 2002, 1074, 1076.

[11] Case *Himalaya-Salz,* BGH [2016] I ZR 86/13, GRUR 2016, 741.

[12] Franz Hacker Hacker § 127 MarkenG, para. 38 in Paul Ströbele, Franz Hacker and Frederik Thiering (eds), (14th edn, 2024); Case *Bayerisches Bier II,* BGH [2012] I ZR 69/04, GRUR 2012, 394, para 38.

[13] Case *Champagner bekommen, Sekt bezahlen,* BGH [2002] I ZR 290/99, GRUR 2002, 426.

[14] Case *ChamPearl,* OLG Munich [2003] 29 U 4011/03, GRUR-RR 2004, 17, 18.

the public sees the indication as an indication of the geographical origin of the product.[15] MarkenG, s. 126(2) also prevents GIs from being protected for any one party if they are generic designations which never indicated a geographical source in the first place or which are perceived by the public as having no understandable link with a place. Examples are 'Hamburger', 'Italienischer Salat' ('Italian Salad'), 'Wiener Schnitzel', or 'Wiener Würstchen' ('Viennese sausage').[16] There are also legally defined generic names, identified by the legislator, such as the 'standard cheeses' set out in s. 7 and Appendix 1 of the Cheese Ordinance such as 'Gouda', 'Edam', 'Brie', 'Provolone', or 'Mozzarella'.[17]

Protection of Place Brands as Registered Trademarks under German Law

The protection of simple place names via a trademark registration is difficult under German law as these often fulfill an absolute ground for refusal for the registration of trademarks. According to MarkenG, s 8(2) No 2 such designations are excluded from registration as trademarks which consist exclusively of signs and indications which may serve in trade to designate the geographical origin of the goods or services. Pursuant to MarkenG, s 8(2) No 4, trademarks are excluded from registration if they are liable to deceive the public, in particular as to the geographical origin of the goods or services.

The current German case law on the ground for refusal of signs being purely descriptive of geographical origin was largely based on the 'Chiemsee' ruling of the Court of Justice of the European Union (CJEU). According to the CJEU, there is a general presumption that place names can be considered as GIs and there must be concrete evidence that the place name is exceptionally not suitable to serve in trade as an indication of the geographical origin of the goods or services concerned. Therefore, a reality-based prognosis must be made, which is not merely based on the current circumstances, but also takes into account possible future economic developments, which are not beyond the realms of

---

[15] Settled case law of the BGH, for example, Case *Warsteiner II*, BGH [1998] I ZR 55/96, GRUR 1999, 252, 255; Case *SPA*, BGH [2001] I ZR 120/98, GRUR 2001, 420, 421; in order to maintain the understanding of origin, it may be sufficient if 10–5% of the relevant public still see an indication of the geographical origin of the product in the claim.

[16] See also Franz Hacker Hacker § 127 MarkenG, para. 83 in Paul Ströbele, Franz Hacker and Frederik Thiering (eds), (14th edn, 2024).

[17] 'Kaeseverordnung' 14 April 1986, (*German Federal Law Gazette* (BGBl)), I, 412 <https://www.gesetze-im-internet.de/k_sev/K%C3%A4seV.pdf> accessed 7 October 2024.

probability and could reasonably be expected to lead to a descriptive use of the place name in question.[18]

Following this, according to the case law of the BGH and the German Federal Patent Court (Bundespatentgericht (BPatG)), a German trademark registration can be considered for such place names if there are concrete indications which make a descriptive use as an indication of origin appear completely improbable.[19] In the case of names of countries, regions, large cities, or other economically significant localities, there is a basic presumption that these terms should be available for free use by anyone for goods.[20] Application can, however, be difficult. For example, the names PEKING[21] and MADRID[22] were rejected because of a need to keep them free. However, the BPatG considered the designation КРМЕЛЁВСКАЯ (Kremlevskaja) for the goods 'meat, sausage and pasta products, fish and delicatessen salads' to be registrable as a trademark. The word was an adjective of 'Kremlin' and meant 'Kremlin-like' or 'castle-like'. Therefore, no descriptive meaning was conveyed to the domestic public in connection with the goods claimed. There was also no GI, since the Kremlin could not be considered as a place of manufacture or distribution of the goods claimed and it was not apparent that this would be the case in the future.[23]

Protection for Place Brands according to Product-Specific EU Regulations

Agricultural products and foodstuffs
Agricultural products and foodstuffs may be entered in the EU Register of Protected Designations of Origin and Protected Geographical Indications pursuant to QSR, Art. 11. This register was introduced by the EU in 1992 as a system for the protection and promotion of traditional and regional food

---

[18] Case C-108/97 and C-109/97 *Windsurfing Chiemsee Produktions- und Vertriebs GmbH (WSC) v Boots- und Segelzubehör Walter Huber (C-108/97) and Franz Attenberger (C-109/97)* [1999] ECR I-2810, paras 25, 37; Case C-488/16 P *Bundesverband Souvenir – Geschenke – Ehrenpreise e. V. v European Union Intellectual Property Office (EUIPO)* [2018] ECLI:EU:C:2018:673, paras 37 et seq; Paul Ströbele in § 8 MarkenG, para. 456 in Paul Ströbele, Franz Hacker and Frederik Thiering (eds), *Markengesetz* (14th edn, 2024).

[19] Case *PEKING*, BPatG [2022] 28 W (pat) 541/20, GRUR-RS 2022, 4615.

[20] Case *Madrid*, BPatG [2011] 27 W (pat) 518/10, BeckRS 2011, 7243; Paul Ströbele (n 18), § 8 para. 521.

[21] Case *PEKING*, BPatG [2022] 28 W (pat) 541/20, GRUR-RS 2022, 4615.

[22] Case *Madrid*, BPatG [2011] 27 W (pat) 518/10, BeckRS 2011, 7243.

[23] Case *Kreml*, BPatG [2020] 28 W (pat) 21/18, GRUR-RS 2020, 22757.

products and today also includes so-called 'traditional specialties guaranteed' (cf QSR, Title III) in addition to the protected DOs and protected GIs. The production process is not bound to any area, the only decisive factor is that the traditional recipe or production method is followed. This category includes, for example, 'Heumilch' ('hay milk'), which is produced in Germany. With the entry onto the register, the protected designation acquires EU-wide protection against the unlawful use of the protected name. The registered indications are provided with EU-wide standardized pictograms and are based on the respective national language.[24] The core element for protection is a 'product specification' which prescribes exactly how the respective product is to be manufactured.

Currently, 93 German food products are protected by this register,[25] such as 'Schwäbische Spätzle' which was registered as a protected GI in 2012. They must be produced in Swabia according to the conditions prescribed in the product specification in order to ensure a consistently high quality.

Also, the EU Regulations stipulate that generic names are not registrable as a GI (QSR, Art. 6(1)).[26] A generic designation can be assumed if the designation in question is used to a greater extent for similar products in other states which do not originate from the designated region. A development towards a generic designation is even more likely if products that do not meet the requirements of a DO or GI are exported to the original region of origin without any objection.[27]

---

[24] Details as well as the information in the national languages can be found in Annex X of the Commission Implementing Regulation (EU) No. 668/2014 for the application of Regulation (EU) No. 1151/2012 of the European Parliament and of the Council on quality schemes for agricultural products and foodstuffs [2014] OJ L179/36 and in the Annex of the Commission Delegated Regulation (EU) No. 664/2014 with regard to the establishment of the Union symbols for protected designations of origin, protected geographical indications and traditional specialties guaranteed and with regard to certain rules on sourcing, certain procedural rules and certain additional transitional rules [2014] OJ L179/17.

[25] 'Schutz von geografischen Angaben und Namen traditioneller Spezialitäten' (Federal Ministry of Food and Agriculture, 8 May 2023) <https:// www .bmel .de/ DE/ themen/ landwirtschaft/ agrarmaerkte/ geschuetzte -bezeichnungen .html> accessed 7 October 2024; overview of the individual products is available at <https://www.dpma.de/digitaler_jahresbericht/2021/jb21_de/geo_herkunft.html> accessed 7 October 2024.

[26] Cf Regulation (EU) No 1308/2013 (n 6), Art. 101 for wines and Art. 3(7) in conjunction with Art. 35 SDR for spirit drinks.

[27] Case C-465/02 and C-466/02, *Federal Republic of Germany (Case C-465/02) and Kingdom of Denmark (Case C-466/02) v Commission of the European*

The scope of protection provided for agricultural products and foodstuffs is governed by QSR, Art. 13(1). Accordingly, registered names are protected against commercial use for comparable products that are not covered by the registration or when the name exploits the reputation of the protected name, as well as against misuse, imitation or evocation notwithstanding the presence of words indicating the true origin of the products and also against false or misleading indication as to origin.

A similar system exists for the protection of GIs for wines and spirits as for agricultural products and foodstuffs.

Spirits drinks
For spirits drinks, under the SDR, a GI is 'an indication identifying a spirit drink as originating in the territory of a country, region or locality within that territory, where a given quality, reputation or other characteristic is essentially attributable to that geographical origin' (SDR, Art. 3(4)).

An application for registration of the GI must be submitted to the EU Commission (cf SDR, Art. 22 et seq.). The Commission then examines the application and makes the list of designations for which registration has been requested public for at least one month (SDR, Art. 26). If no objection is received or if an objection to the application is unsuccessful, the GI is registered and entered onto the register (SDR, Art. 33).

The scope of protection of GIs for spirit drinks under the SDR
The scope of protection provided for spirit drinks in SDR, Art. 21(2) SDR is almost identical to that of agricultural products and foodstuffs under QSR, Art. 13 mentioned earlier. The EU has provided for very wide-ranging protection for GIs.[28] Firstly, where there is the clear case that the name of a GI is used directly for products that do not meet the requirements for this GI. This is the case, for example, when a spirit produced in Germany is sold as 'Scotch Whisky', as only products produced in Scotland may bear the GI (cf. Scotch Whisky Regulations 2009 (SI 2009/2890), reg. 3). Secondly, when there is '*any misuse, imitation or evocation*'. In this context, an infringement also exists if the protected designation is used in translation or with additions such as '*-style*'. In the German version of the SDR, the term '*any misuse*' is translated with the term 'appropriation' which requires that the infringer uses

---

Communities [2005] ECR I-9178, paras 77 et seq; Case T-291/03, *Consorzio per la tutela del formaggio Grana Padano v Office for Harmonisation in the Internal Market* [2007] ECR II-3086, para. 65.

[28] See also Case C-44/17 *Scotch Whisky Association v Michael Klotz* [2018] ECLI:EU:C:2018:111, para. 54.

the designation as if it belonged to the infringer, that is that it is protected by property or quasi-property rights. The concepts of *imitation* and *evocation* differ insofar as in the case of evocation a different wording is used than that of the protected designation, but there is a recognizable reference to the registered designation.[29] Consequently, an evocation can also be made by figurative signs.[30]

An example from protection of the GI 'Scotch Whisky'
From a practical as well as legal point of view, the most interesting infringements are those of SDR, Art. 21(2)(b), in particular the infringing act of *evocation*, which has gained considerable contour in recent years due to several landmark CJEU preliminary rulings as well as follow-up rulings by German courts. In Germany, we have learned in recent years that there is a danger not only from imitators who deliberately exploit the reputation of protected GIs with counterfeit products, but also from whisky enthusiasts, for example, who want to express their enthusiasm for the original product by referring to the GI Scotch Whisky in the product name or labelling and who are thereby causing an illegal evocation of the protected GI.

According to the case law of the CJEU, the concept of *evocation* essentially covers a situation in which the term used to designate a product incorporates part of a protected GI, so that when the consumer is confronted with the name of the product in question, the image triggered in the mind of the consumer is that of the product whose indication is protected. The national courts must therefore primarily rely on the presumed reaction of consumers in the light of the term used to designate the product at issue, it being essential that those consumers establish a link between that term and the protected GI.[31] In doing so, the national court must consider the perception of an average European consumer who is reasonably well informed and reasonably observant and circumspect. In this respect, the CJEU has already referred to various criteria

---

[29] Kurt-Dietrich Rathke, No. 134. Verordnung (EU) Nr. 1151/2012 des Europäischen Parlaments und des Rates über Qualitätsregelungen für Agrarerzeugnisse und Lebensmittel, Art 13 para. 19 and 21 in Olaf Sosnitza and Andreas Meisterernst (eds), *Lebensmittelrecht*, Werkstand: 189. EL April 2024 (Food law, current version 189th edn, April 2024).

[30] Cf Case C-614/17 *Fundación Consejo Regulador de la Denominación de Origen Protegida Queso Manchego/Industrial Quesera Cuquerella SL* [2019] ECLI:EU:C:2019:344, para. 22; Case *The Glen Els,* OLG Hamburg [2019] 3 U 262/16, GRUR-RR 2020, 351 para. 44.

[31] Case C-75/15 *Viiniverla Oy v Sosiaali- ja terveysalan lupa- ja valvontavirasto* [2016] ECLI:EU:C:2016:35, paras 21, 22; Case C-44/17 *Scotch Whisky Association v Michael Klotz* [2018] ECLI:EU:C:2018:111, paras 44–6.

that can justify an evocation. However, these do not necessarily have to be present; rather, the criteria are defined by a (non-exhaustive) group of cases. One of those cases covers the situation in which the term used to designate the product in question includes part of a protected GI. Furthermore, the CJEU has ruled that products which are similar in appearance can be presumed to allude to a protected GI if the sales names have a phonetic and visual similarity. If the criteria are not met, it is particularly important to take account of the criterion of 'conceptual proximity' between the disputed name and the protected GI.[32]

In the leading Scotch Whisky case *Glen Buchenbach*, (in which the authors' firm TaylorWessing was involved) the issue was not the impermissible use of the GI 'Scotch Whisky' for a German whisky, but the use of the designation 'Glen' in the name 'Glen Buchenbach'. The CJEU therefore ordered the referring German court to examine whether the average European consumer, thinks directly of (not just associate with) the protected GI 'Scotch Whisky', when the consumer is confronted with a comparable product bearing the disputed designation 'Glen', in the absence of (i) any phonetic and/or visual similarity between the disputed designation and the protected GI and (ii) any partial incorporation of that indication in that designation, a conceptual proximity between the protected GI and the disputed designation.

The Hanseatic Higher Regional Court of Hamburg affirmed that there was an evocation with the designation 'Glen' in the name 'Glen Buchenbach' for whisky that is not Scotch Whisky. In particular, the court has clarified that the assessment of an evocation does not require that 'Glen' be a synonym for Scotch Whisky. Rather, it requires a conceptual similarity within the understanding of the relevant consumer which does not constitute merely distant associations with Scotland as a 'region', for example, with depictions of landscapes which may refer to Scotland as a geographical origin – or even to a completely different region – or with the use of the English language. In this context, the court also attributed an indicative effect according to the consumer survey that confirmed that essentially only Scotch whiskies with the designation 'Glen' in the name had been represented in the relevant marketing area, as well as in the trademark register in its determination that the relevant consumer would perceive a whisky with 'Glen' in its name as originating from Scotland.[33] Furthermore, the Court found that the defendant had *deliberately*

---

[32] Case C-75/15 *Viiniverla Oy v Sosiaali- ja terveysalan lupa- ja valvontavirasto* [2016] ECLI:EU:C:2016:35, paras 22, 25, 28, 33–5; Case C-44/17 *Scotch Whisky Association v Michael Klotz* [2018] ECLI:EU:C:2018:111, paras 45–51.

[33] Case *Glen Buchenbach*, OLG Hamburg [2022] 5 U 43/19, GRUR 2022, 1535 paras 80, 84–6; cf Case *The Glen Els*, OLG Hamburg [2019] 3 U 262/16, GRUR-RR 2020, 351 para. 46.

chosen a reference to the Gaelic term 'Glen' and that the *lack of coincidence* in the selection of this indication allowed the conclusion that a direct conceptual reference to Scotch Whisky and not only to the Gaelic language word for valley, was established.[34]

The *Glen Buchenbach* decisions of the CJEU and the Hanseatic Higher Regional Court are milestones for the protection of GIs and emphasized that an infringing evocation of the protected GI Scotch Whisky can also be caused by the using product names with 'merely' a Scottish reference such as Glen, Mac/Mc or Highland, or by using design elements typical of the country such as the tartan pattern.[35] The judgment therefore significantly extends the protection of GIs and thus at the same time the possibilities of a successful defense.

Wines

For wines, German Wine Act ('WeinG'), ss. 22b et seq. contain national regulations on the protection of geographical designations. Section 22b(1) defines geographical designations within the meaning of the WeinG.[36] On the one hand, the definitions refer to the DO and GI protections under EU law. On the other hand, the definitions refer to smaller and larger geographical wine-growing areas and wine-growing regions as well as names of municipalities and parts of municipalities that are not covered by EU law.

The scope of protection of indications for wines according to Regulation (EU) No 1308/2013, Art. 103(2) is regulated with formulations that differ in detail from the regulations for agricultural products and foodstuffs and spirits presented above. However, similar to those regulations, protected DOs and GIs and the wines using these protected names in accordance with the product specification are protected against any direct or indirect commercial use, any misappropriation, imitation or evocation, or any other false or misleading indication as to the provenance, origin, nature, or essential qualities of the product which appear on the presentation or outer packaging, in advertising or in doc-

---

[34] Case *Glen Buchenbach*, OLG Hamburg [2022] 5 U 43/19, GRUR 2022, 1535 para. 930; cf Case C-75/15 *Viiniverla Oy/Sosiaali- ja terveysalan lupa- ja valvontavirasto* [2016] ECLI:EU:C:2016:35, para. 48.

[35] Cf. a very similar case *The Glen Els,* OLG Hamburg [2019] 3 U 262/16, GRUR-RR 2020, 351 paras 44–8, 61).

[36] Geographical designations within the meaning of this Act shall be (1.) designations of origin and geographical indications within the meaning of Article 93(1) (a) and (b) of Regulation (EU) No 1308/2013, (2.) the names of vineyard sites and areas entered in the vineyard register and names of smaller geographical units delimited in the real estate map, insofar as these names are entered in the vineyard register in a procedure regulated in the legal ordinance pursuant to § 23 paragraph 4, as well as, (3.) the names of municipalities and parts of municipalities used in the course of trade to designate a product.

uments relating to the wine products concerned, or the use of containers liable to convey a false impression as to origin, as well as against any other practice liable to mislead the consumer as to the true origin of the product.

The Protection of the GI 'Napa Valley' and 'Coffee Kenya' in Germany

As explained above, WeinG, s. 22b et seq. contains national regulations on the protection of geographical designations. 'Napa Valley' is protected as a DO under WeinG, s. 22b(1) No 1 in conjunction with Regulation (EU) No 1308/2013, Art. 93(1)(a) under file number PDO-US-17738. The enforcement of the EU-wide protection is therefore governed by Regulation (EU) No 1308/2013, Art. 103, which prevails over the provisions of the WeinG,[37] and also goes much further than the latter's s. 22b(2).[38]

The wording of that provision essentially corresponds to that of SDR, Art. 21(2). Therefore, in case of an unlawful use of the term 'Napa Valley' for a product that does not originate from the Napa Valley region, for example for a German wine, a claim for injunctive relief pursuant to MarkenG, s. 135(1) in conjunction with Regulation (EU) No 893/2004, Art. 103 may be claimed, for example, by a competitor or, if applicable, by an interest group of Napa Valley wine makers.

'Coffee Kenya' has not yet been registered as a GI; however, protection under MarkenG, ss. 126 et seq. is conceivable as because 'Coffee Kenya' establishes a direct geographical reference to the product bearing the name 'Kenya', the designation is to be qualified as a direct GI. It is also not apparent that it is a generic name which might exclude protection as a GI. However, there is a lack of judicial decision on whether Coffee Kenya meets all the requirements for a GI against this legal background.

If one wants certainty and broader protection, it makes sense to apply for registration as a GI under EU law. According to QSR, Annex I, coffee as a beverage based on plant extracts can in principle be registered as a DO if the other requirements for a DO under QSR, Art. 5 are met.

---

[37] Thomas Boch No. 400. Weingesetz, § 1 para 3 in Olaf Sosnitza and Andreas Meisterernst (eds), *Lebensmittelrecht* Werkstand: 189. EL April 2024 (Food law, current version: 189th edition April 2024).

[38] Thomas Boch, *Weingesetz* (8th online-edn, C H Beck 2021), 'WeinG § 22b para 2'.

Challenges in Practice of the Enforcement of GIs and DOs

The enforcement of GIs and DOs is associated with many challenges. The fact that there have been many landmark decisions by the CJEU in recent years on the interpretation of EU regulations that serve to protect GIs and DOs is due in particular to the commitment of associations such as the Scotch Whisky Association, which have pursued litigation all the way to national high courts and the CJEU in order to have outstanding issues relating to the interpretation of, for example, the SDR clarified.

Enforcement also requires close monitoring of the market to identify infringements and quickly stop trends of leaning on known GIs or DOs. This may be a difficult task, as some infringing products are sold via the internet. Establishing a good network of local traders who monitor the market is crucial. Another challenge is having the right infrastructure in place. Only the big trade associations have access to specialized laboratories that can analyze the ingredients of potentially infringing products in order to establish if the legally defined criteria of a protected GI or the production method are met. In practice, it is also important to document well the history and reputation of the GIs and DOs and their products. For example, in its *Glen Buchenbach* decision, the Hanseatic Higher Regional Court also relied on comprehensive documentation of the use of the designation 'Glen' for Scotch Whisky on the EU market and a survey on the European consumer's understanding of the designation 'Glen' as a reference to Scotch Whisky.

Furthermore, law enforcement is often a balancing act, especially when, in some cases, enthusiasts of the protected products want to express their appreciation by imitating or borrowing from the protected designations and do not realize that they are crossing the boundaries of the law. Here, the right balance must be found between a friendly approach and a sharp warning. Many conflicts can be resolved through dialogue. Even in cases where the infringer has already made substantial investments in its product, the parties may be able to find a commercially viable solution through settlement discussions that consider the interests of both parties.

12. Protection and Enforcement of 'Place Brands' in the United Kingdom

Gareth Jenkins, Kirsten Gilbert, Claire Keating, Elise Cant and Ann Lee

INTRODUCTION

In this chapter, we explore the options available for protection and enforcement of place brands in the United Kingdom (UK) (and the European Union (EU)), as well as the potential obstacles in securing these enforceable rights.

We start with an overview of the effect of the UK's withdrawal from the EU ('Brexit') on relevant intellectual property (IP) laws in the UK, then we proceed to look at the available rights protecting place brands, the possible grounds for refusal of registration and the strategies that are available for enforcing place brand rights in the UK.

BREXIT

On 1 January 2021, the UK Intellectual Property Office (UKIPO) created new national registered trade marks and designs to replicate rights that would otherwise have been lost upon the UK's withdrawal from the EU. These new rights provide holders of registered EU trade marks (and also registered community designs or international registrations designating the EU) with a corresponding national registration in the UK (unless the owner had opted out of receiving this right).

Trade marks that are registered in the UK and EU are therefore now independent from one another, albeit many will now be identically protected on both registers under separate registrations.

Prior to Brexit, the Trade Marks Act 1994 (UKTMA), governing trade mark law in the UK, was already harmonized with EU law.[1] As such Brexit changed

---

[1] Most recently the Commission Implementing Regulation (EU) 2018/626 of 5 March 2018 laying down detailed rules for implementing certain provisions

nothing in terms of procedures, requirements for registration and enforcement of traditional trade marks within the UK. Longer term, however, there is the possibility that UK and EU law will diverge as a result of new precedents set in future case law by the respective Courts.

From a broader perspective, however, particularly in relation to geographic indications (GIs) (discussed below) substantive changes have been necessary, because, prior to Brexit, GIs were protected in the UK only by virtue of its membership of the EU.[2] The UK's departure from the EU therefore necessitated the creation of a new UK-based GI scheme; and this has been further complicated by the post-Brexit Northern Ireland Protocol.[3] This means that in order for a GI to be protected in Northern Ireland in a way that is currently similar to that in the rest of the UK, it must be done through the European Commission's GI schemes. As a result, a GI can only be said to be protected throughout the *entire* UK (meaning England, Wales, Scotland *and* Northern Ireland) if it is protected in both the UK and EU.

The rights available under a protected GI will be discussed in more detail below.

OVERVIEW OF AVAILABLE UK RIGHTS WHICH MAY PROTECT PLACE BRANDS

Trade Marks

A trade mark's essential function is to guarantee the origin of the goods and services provided under it. It enables consumers to assume the goods and services originate from the right-holder, thus creating goodwill in relation to

---

of Regulation (EU) 2017/1001 of the European Parliament and of the Council on the European Union trade mark, and repealing Implementing Regulation (EU) 2017/1431 [2018] OJ L104/37.

[2] Under Regulation (EU) No 1151/2012 of the European Parliament and of the Council of 21 November 2012 on quality schemes for agricultural products and foodstuffs [2012] OJ L343/1 and other specific regulations for certain categories of products, for example Regulation (EU) 2019/787 of the European Parliament and of the Council of 17 April 2019 on the definition, description, presentation and labelling of spirit drinks, the use of the names of spirit drinks in the presentation and labelling of other foodstuffs, the protection of geographical indications for spirit drinks, the use of ethyl alcohol and distillates of agricultural origin in alcoholic beverages, and repealing Regulation (EC) No 110/2008 [2019] OJ L130/1.

[3] Protocol on Ireland/Norther Ireland (UK Government) <https:// assets .publishing.service.gov.uk/media/5da863ab40f0b659847e0184/Revised_Protocol _to_the_Withdrawal_Agreement.pdf> accessed 3 October 2024.

them. Resultantly, trade marks can create desire for a product on the basis that a consumer will believe it to be of a particular quality and thus endow the brand with financial value. If this guarantee of origin is not protected, the reputation and goodwill a mark carries can be damaged, and, as a result, will equally damage the brand's value, consumer loyalty, and alter consumer activity.

Almost any sign used in trade could potentially be a trade mark, including words, logos, slogans, shapes, or even sounds and smells so long as they can perform the essential function; this can include place names.[4] However, for a trade mark to be able to perform its essential function it may not be descriptive or devoid of any distinctive character so as to enable competing traders in the marketplace to use the descriptive or generic terms to describe or denote their goods. In other words, there must be something in the mark which is distinctive and sets it apart, thereby enabling consumers to distinguish goods/ services provided under the mark from those of other undertakings. For place brands this can be tricky, owing to the following exclusion for trade mark protection under the UKTMA 1994:

   3.(1) The following shall not be registered:
        3.(1)(c) Trade Marks which consist exclusively of signs or indications which may serve in trade, to designate the kind quality, quantity, intended purpose, value, *geographical origin*, the time of production of goods or of rendering of services, or other characteristics of goods or services (emphasis added).

---

[4] Trade Marks Act 1994, s. 1; for 'unconventional' marks such as smells, registrability would depend on the mark being capable of representation in such a way that the clear and precise subject matter of protection can be identified, see Trade Marks Act 1994, s. 1(1)(a) and Case C-273/00 *Ralf Sieckmann v Deutsches Patent- und Markenamt* [2002] ECR I-11737.

The question of whether a geographical name may be protected was discussed in the European Court of Justice[5] case *Nordmilch eG v OHIM*,[6] which concluded a sign could be registered:

> ...where the sign applied for designates a geographical place name which, in the minds of the relevant public, is already associated with the goods/services listed in the application;

Or:

> ...where there is no current association, but the name is liable to be used in the future by undertakings as an indication of the geographical origin of the goods/services concerned.

It will be interesting to see if, post-Brexit, courts in the UK take different approaches to this.

Registered trade marks are obtained through the UKIPO, and if granted, provide the owner with proprietary rights for an initial ten-year period running from the day that the application for registration was filed. The registration is renewable every ten years thereafter in perpetuity,[7] and assuming the trade mark is consistently being used, maintained and does not become generic, these rights could in theory last forever.

The Law of Passing Off

Unregistered rights can also be acquired in a sign under the common law tort of passing off; this relies upon goodwill generated through the use and marketing of the sign when used in respect of specific goods and services. Notably, in the absence of formalities, the scope of this action is slightly broader and the owner can claim rights in the goodwill relating to the overall 'get up' of

---

[5] The relevant UK and EU legislation, Trade Marks Act 1994, s. 3(1)(c) and EU Trade Mark Regulations (n 1), art. 7(1)(c) respectively, is phrased in the same terms. Therefore, ECJ cases remain persuasive post-Brexit though it is noted that there is increasing scope for UK courts to depart from this, see to that effect EU (Withdrawal) Act 2018, s. 6 as amended by the Retained EU Law (Revocation and Reform) Act 2023, s. 6.

[6] Case T-295/01 *Nordmilch eG v Office for Harmonisation in the Internal Market (Trade Marks and Designs) (OHIM)* [2001] ECR II-04365.

[7] Trade Marks Act 1994, s. 42.

their goods (including names, designs and packaging), beyond individual representations of a mark,[8] which could include place names.[9]

Certification Marks

Certification marks (certification trade marks) are a specific type of trade mark, obtained through registration. The function of these trade marks is to distinguish goods/services which are certified as being made using certain materials or by certain manufacturing processes, or that they are of a particular quality or possess certain characteristics.[10] These marks differ from ordinary trade marks, as the owner is unable to use the mark itself on the goods or services,[11] rather, they allow others to use the mark, as a means to confirm to consumers that their goods or services comply with the relevant characteristics of the certification trade mark. Regulations specifying these characteristics must be filed as part of the application process for registering a certification trade mark,[12] and these govern who may use the mark on their goods/services.[13]

The Scotch Whisky Association (SWA)[14] is the trade body for, and represents the producers of around 95% of the Scotch Whisky sold globally. It owns registered certification trade marks for the trade mark 'Scotch Whisky' in the US,[15] and Hong Kong.[16] This protection is particularly valuable in these territories as they do not have a specialized scheme of GIs in place, as will be discussed further below. These certification trade marks enable consumers in these territories to distinguish genuine Scotch Whisky products from those that do not adhere to the stringent standards dictating, among other things, the raw materials and production processes which can be used. In 2021, the estimated

---

[8] *Reckitt & Colman v Borden (Jif Lemon case)* [1990] RPC 341.
[9] The law of passing off is discussed in some detail in Chapter 16.
[10] Trade Marks Act 1994, s. 50(1).
[11] Ibid., Sch. 2 para. 4.
[12] Ibid., Sch. 2 para. 6(2).
[13] UKIPO, *Manual of Trade Marks Practice* (2019), 3.4.2.
[14] Scotch Whisky Association <www.scotch-whisky.org.uk/>.
[15] Louis Thomas, '"Scotch Whisky" granted certification Trade Mark in the US' (*The Drinks Business*, 24 June 2022) <https://www.thedrinksbusiness.com/2022/06/scotch-whisky-granted-certification-trademark-in-the-us/> accessed 3 October 2024; US registration no 6763223 (registered 21 June 2022).
[16] Jessica Broadbent, 'Scotch Whisky trademarked in Hong Kong' (*Just Drinks*, 22 August 2023) <https://www.just-drinks.com/news/scotch-whisky-trademarked-in-hong-kong/> accessed 3 October 2024; Hong Kong registration no 305457880 (registered 10 March 2023).

global sales of Scotch Whisky totaled £4.5 billion,[17] which emphasizes the value of quality control to curb the emergence of counterfeit goods.

Geographical Indications (GIs)

The trade mark regime is complemented by a scheme of GIs specifically applicable to goods which are characteristic of, or which have strong links to, certain territories or regions, such that they are expected meet particular standards.[18] As discussed above, the UK's scheme of GIs was established post-Brexit, and relies on the retained EU Regulation No 1151/2012 and other specific regulations for certain categories of products, for example EU Regulations Nos 110/2008 and 2019/787 for spirit drinks.

'Scotch Whisky' and 'Scotch' are protected GIs in the UK,[19] as well as in many overseas markets including China and the US (though in the US this is under the umbrella of certification trade marks, discussed above), and traders can only use these names to market their products if their characteristics, raw materials and manufacturing processes comply with the strict requirements specified in the GI's technical file.[20] Unlike trade marks, such rights are not owned by individual traders or businesses, and they can be used by *any* trader selling compliant products.[21]

Compliance with the Scotch Whisky GI is monitored by the HM Revenue & Customs (HMRC) in the UK,[22] which ensures that any products marketed as

---

[17] Scotch Whisky Association Newsroom, 'Scotch Whisky granted certification mark in the US' (Scotch Whisky Association, 21 June 2022) <https://www.scotch-whisky.org.uk/newsroom/scotch-whisky-granted-certification-trademark-in-the-united-states/> accessed 8 October 2024.

[18] Lionel Bently, Brad Sherman, Dav Gangjee and Phillip Johnson, *Intellectual Property Law* (6th edn, OUP 2022), 1214.

[19] Initially in the EU under Regulation (EC) No 110/2008 (n 2), art. 16(a)–(c), and subsequently in the UK under Agreement on the withdrawal of the United Kingdom of Great Britain and Northern Ireland from the European Union and the European Atomic Energy Community 2019/C 384 I/01 [2019] OJ C3841/1, art. 54(2).

[20] For an illustration, see Case-44/17 *Scotch Whisky Association v Michael Klotz (Glen Buchenbach case)* [2018] OJ C268/10.

[21] Department for Environment, Food and Rural Affairs, *Guidance – Protected geographical food and drink names: UK GI schemes* (Gov.UK, 2021) <https://www.gov.uk/guidance/protected-geographical-food-and-drink-names-uk-gi-schemes#logo-rules> accessed 8 October 2024.

[22] The Spirit Drinks Regulations 2008 (SI 2008/3206), reg. 6, enforcing EU Spirit Drinks Regulation 2019/787 (n 2). (NB the latter Regulation became retained EU law under the EU (Withdrawal) Act 2018.)

Scotch Whisky are in line with the requirements specified by the GI,[23] as well as by the UKIPO when new trade mark applications are filed incorporating these protected names (see available grounds for refusal, as discussed below).

Further, separate EU regulations[24] on spirit drinks (including Scotch Whisky) are also applicable, which primarily regulate the labelling and sugar content of such drinks.

CROSSOVER BETWEEN CERTIFICATION TRADE MARKS AND GIS

There are multiple ways in which a 'place brand' can be protected, and given variations in law and practice from country to country, the best routes of protection may vary. As discussed below, Scotch Whisky and Napa Valley are protected in a number of countries by way of a selection of registrations as certification trade marks, American viticultural areas ('AVA' in the US) and GIs (in the UK and EU).

The term 'Scotch Whisky' is not a registered certification trade mark in the UK, and the absolute grounds for refusal discussed below would mean this is not an available option in most cases. There are similarities between protected GIs and certification trade marks, in that both restrict the use of the protected term to goods which comply with the strict requirements of a certification trade mark's regulations or the GI technical file. It is possible for a certification trade mark to be obtained in relation to a designation of geographic origin.[25]

Not all countries offer GI schemes, and in these cases a certification trade mark may be an appropriate alternative, subject to local laws.

BENEFITS OF TRADE MARK REGISTRATION, WHERE AVAILABLE

Obtaining registered trade mark protection in the UK and the EU offers a wide range of benefits to the trade mark proprietor and their business. These benefits include: an automatic defence to trade mark infringement (in the UK),[26] provided that the registration could not be declared invalid, a wider range of

---

[23] Department for Environment, Food and Rural Affairs, *Guidance – Using a protected geographical food or drink name: UK GI scheme rules'* (Gov.UK, 2020) <https://www.gov.uk/guidance/using-a-protected-geographical-food-or-drink-name-in-the-uk-gi-scheme-rules> accessed 8 October 2024.

[24] Such as EU Regulation 2019/787 (n 2).

[25] Trade Marks Act 1994, Sch. 2, s. 3.

[26] Trade Marks Act 1994, s. 11(1).

enforcement options, including the ability to oppose a later application based on a likelihood of confusion or association with the earlier mark, licensing opportunities, the protection of brand equity, and the ability to record a registered mark with the UK and EU customs offices for enforcement purposes.

The benefits of trade mark protection equally apply to distinctive place brands and their accompanying sub-brands, discussed later in the chapter.

The principal benefit of obtaining a registered trade mark in the UK or the EU (which, as above, no longer covers the UK) is that the registration gives the proprietor a basis to prevent third parties from using, or seeking to register an identical or confusingly similar mark,[27] in that territory. Owning a registered trade mark is, therefore, a powerful tool to combat infringement and counterfeiting, whilst reducing the risk of, or preventing, reputation damage and revenue loss. A registered trade mark therefore allows a proprietor to safeguard the investments made in their brand.

In the UK, as set out in *Reckitt & Colman Ltd v Borden*, three factors must be proven in order to prove passing off: that the mark carries goodwill, that there has been a misrepresentation in the course of trade, and that damage has resulted.[28] The burden to prove the existence of goodwill in the UK is high and can often prove difficult and expensive. In contrast, the proprietor of a registered trade mark can start enforcing and defending its registration prior to its products or services even hitting the market. Also, unlike the protection conferred under the common law of passing off for each of the jurisdictions of England and Wales, Scotland and Northern Ireland, trade mark registration confers rights that are UK-wide.

In addition to providing a basis for enforcement, a registered trade mark can act as a deterrent. Once a trade mark is registered there is a presumption that it is valid until challenged;[29] this presumption alone can deter third parties from seeking to register or use an identical or confusingly similar mark, to avoid conflict. It is simple for third parties to understand that a registered right exists because the UK and EU Trade Mark registers are publicly available, and information about the scope of protection conferred by the registration is, therefore, easily accessible.

---

[27] Directive (EU) 2015/2436 of the European Parliament and of the Council to approximate the laws of the Member States relating to Trade Marks [2015] OJ L336/1, arts 5(1), (3)(a), 10(2); Trade Marks Act 1994, ss. 5(1)–(3) and 10(1)–(3).

[28] The Jif Lemon case – *Reckitt & Colman Ltd v Borden Inc* [1990] 1 All ER 873.

[29] Case C-196/11 *Formula One Licensing BV v OHIM and Global Sports Media Ltd* [2012] OJ C179/13 paras 40–1.

Trade mark registrations provide the proprietor with an exclusive property right,[30] which can be assigned,[31] and licensed.[32] Assigning or licensing a registration, as opposed to an unregistered trade mark, is clear cut, owing to the scope of protection being clearly specified on the Register, which is not the case with an unregistered right. This increased certainty allows a proprietor further control over its brand when licensing a trade mark.

Licensing enables expansion into further markets via third-party collaborations, which occurs not infrequently in the Scotch Whisky market, for instance, the whisky collaboration between Johnnie Walker and HBO coined 'White Walker', which displays both the John Walker & Sons Trade Mark and the Games of Thrones logo.[33] Collaborations such as this can increase a brand's reach and reputation amongst the public, which is desirable for business owners.

Specific Considerations for Place Brands like Scotch Whisky, Napa Valley and Coffee Kenya

A key difference where place brands are concerned is that they are essentially descriptive marks, and this makes protection of them in their 'pure' form as traditional trade marks extremely difficult in most jurisdictions.

As above, some territories, such as the EU and UK, operate systems for protection of GIs. Scotch Whisky (and Scotch Whisk*ey*) are protected in this way in the UK (meaning England, Scotland and Wales, but *not* Northern Ireland, as discussed above)[34], whilst an agreement between the UK and US means that

---

[30] Directive (EU) 2015/2436 of the European Parliament and of the Council to approximate the laws of the Member States relating to Trade Marks [2015] OJ L336/1, art 10(1); Trade Marks Act 1994, ss. 2(1), 9(1).

[31] Directive (EU) 2015/2436 of the European Parliament and of the Council to approximate the laws of the Member States relating to Trade Marks [2015] OJ L336/1, art. 22 (1); Trade Marks Act 1994, ss. 24(1), 25(2)(a).

[32] Directive (EU) 2015/2436 of the European Parliament and of the Council to approximate the laws of the Member States relating to Trade Marks [2015] OJ L336/1, art 25(1); Trade Marks Act 1994, s. 25(2)(b).

[33] Rosalind Erskine, 'The 8 best whisky collaborations for Father's day' (*The Scotsman food and drink*, 5 June 2019) <https:// foodanddrink .scotsman .com/ drink/ the-8-best-whisky -collaborations-ideal-for-fathers-days/> accessed 3 October 2024.

[34] Retained EU Regulation No 1151/2012 (n 2) and other specific regulations for certain categories of products, for example EU Regulation Nos 110/2008 and 2019/787 for spirit drinks (n 2).

over 700 wine names protected as AVAs in the US are also recognized and deemed to be protected in the UK,[35] including 'Napa Valley'.[36]

There does not appear to be any registered protection for the term Coffee Kenya in the UK at present, however, the UK-Kenya Economic Partnership Agreement (EPA),[37] was ratified on 22 March 2021. This includes an agreement to conclude negotiations in subject matters including IP rights, within five years of the Agreement entering into force. It is, therefore, to be expected that Coffee Kenya is likely to become a protected term in the UK in due course.

As mentioned above, for a GI to be protected in Northern Ireland, this has to be done under the European Commission's GI schemes,[38] as a result of the post-Brexit Northern Ireland Protocol. Scotch Whisky is protected in this way in Northern Ireland, and similarly, Napa Valley is protected in the EU (and therefore Northern Ireland) as a registered GI.

The descriptive nature of these types of marks does not necessarily mean that place brands cannot be registered as Trade Marks, but there may be stricter criteria that need to be met. In the UK, for example, a mark *containing* a GI can be registered, provided its specification is suitably limited to ensure that it only covers goods for which the GI is protected – this is to avoid the mark being used deceptively.

If the mark contains a GI, an objection to UK trade mark registration under ss. 3(4) and (3)(b) is appropriate. This objection can be overcome by limiting the goods to those protected by the GI. For example:

Mark – 'NESCO Cornish Clotted Cream'
Goods – cream

---

[35] Agreement between the United States of America and the United Kingdom of Great Britain and Northern Ireland on Trade in Wine (2019) <https://ustr.gov/sites/default/files/US-UK_Agreement_on_Trade_in_Wine_signed_Jan_31_2019.pdf> accessed 3 October 2024.

[36] 'Protected geographical food and drink names' (Department for Environment, Food and Rural Affairs) <www.gov.uk/protected-food-drink-names?register%5B%5D=american-viticultural-areas&status%5B%5D=registered> accessed 4 October 2024.

[37] The UK-Kenya Economic Partnership Agreement (Economic Partnership Agreement Between the United Kingdom of Great Britain and Northern Ireland, of the one part, and the Republic of Kenya, a Member of the East African Community, of the other part).

[38] Retained EU Regulation No 1151/2012 (n 2) and other specific regulations for certain categories of products, for example EU Regulation Nos 110/2008 and 2019/787 for spirit drinks (n 2).

An objection under s. 3(4) and (3)(b) UKTMA 1994 would be raised but would be overcome by limiting the specification to 'Cream complying with the specifications of the PDO Cornish Clotted Cream'.

Scotch Whisky brands are often named after the geographical region in which the distillery is based, and there are five Scottish regions whose names are also protected under the Scotch Whisky Regulations 2009, namely:

- Campbeltown;
- Islay;
- Highland;
- Lowland;
- Speyside.

In creating a distinctive brand, distilleries often combine the regional names alongside the distillery's name (if different), or otherwise with sub-brands which denote a specific bottling or special characteristic, and it is these 'combination brands' which can as a whole carry sufficient distinctiveness for registration as a trade mark. By way of example, 'Highland Shepherd Scotch Whisky'[39] and 'Isle of Barra Single Malt Scotch Whisky'[40] are both registered trade marks in the UK (both covering suitably restricted lists of goods).

Additionally, any trade mark application for whisky which is 'evocative' of Scotland may meet with an objection if the goods do not originate from Scotland. The UKIPO's *Manual of Trade Marks Practice* specifically states:[41]

> …Each provision will be considered on its own merits and it is possible that a Trade Mark which contains a word such as 'Highland', and which is intended for use in respect of alcoholic drinks, will attract both an objection under section 3(3)(b) on the basis that it is evocative of Scotland and would therefore be deceptive if used on whisky produced outside of Scotland and fall under the Protected Geographical Indications, as well as an objection under section 3(4) on account of it being one of the five protected localities and regions.

As previously mentioned, there are a range of IP rights that are available to Scotch Whisky producers, and of course to Napa Valley wine producers or Kenyan coffee producers, and these can be used as a valuable collection of

---

[39] UKTM No. UK00003587732 <https://trademarks.ipo.gov.uk/ipo-tmcase/page/Results/1/UK00003587732> accessed 4 October 2024.

[40] UKTM No. UK00003333309 <https://trademarks.ipo.gov.uk/ipo-tmcase/page/Results/1/UK00003333309> accessed 4 October 2024.

[41] *Manual of Trade Mark Practice* (Intellectual Property Office, 2018, updated 2024) <https:// www .gov .uk/ guidance/ trade -marks -manual/ the -examination -guide> accessed 4 October 2024.

rights, protecting various elements of the overall brand as well as the look and feel of the product.

CHALLENGES IN OBTAINING TRADE MARK REGISTRATION FOR PLACE BRANDS

There are various challenges involved in trying to obtain protection for geographical brands, both in the UK and further afield. As mentioned, both Scotch Whisky and Napa Valley are protected in the UK as GIs, and the existence of these rights has a direct impact on how related brands or sub-brands can be protected. The UKIPO's *Manual of Trade Marks Practice* provides a fairly detailed overview of the possible objections that could arise,[42] and the requirements that an application must meet in order to avoid or overcome such objections. These are discussed in more detail below.

Descriptiveness and Non-Distinctiveness

The most obvious ground for refusal of a geographical trade mark is that of descriptiveness under UKTMA 1994, s. 3(1)(c),[43] and resulting non-distinctiveness under s. 3(1)(b). These objections go hand in hand, because a mark which is descriptive is automatically devoid of distinctiveness, and a mark which consists solely of a geographic term will receive an objection on the basis it describes the geographical origin of the goods.

Geographic brands such as Scotch Whisky, Napa Valley and Coffee Kenya will, therefore, be objectionable, however, marks which *include* these terms *may* be registrable, provided they comply with other requirements, as discussed below or if they can establish distinctiveness through use.[44]

Deceptiveness

This ground for objection, under UKTMA 1994, s. 3(3), is also likely to be raised against a mark consisting solely of a geographic term or a term which describes a type of product, on the basis that if the goods or services do not in fact originate from that place, or are not the type of product identified by the term, then the mark will likely deceive consumers in leading them to incorrectly believe the goods have these characteristics when they do not. For example Savile Row Taylors for clothing per se.

---

[42] Ibid.
[43] Trade Marks Act 1994.
[44] Ibid., s. 3(1).

For this type of objection, UK Examiners will usually provide guidance as to how to overcome the refusal. This will often involve amending the specification to specifically identify the goods or services as originating from the geographic location, or otherwise narrowing the wording to cover only that category of goods.

Prohibition Under 'Any Enactment or Rule of Law' other than Relating to Trade Marks

Section 3(4) UKTMA 1994 effectively provides a cover-all, which prevents registration of a mark which is prohibited under any enactment or rule of law outside of the UKTMA 1994, including, but not limited to, international agreements. This includes signs such as plant varieties, the Olympic and Paralympic symbols, and, significantly, GIs.

As such, whilst terms such as Scotch Whisky and Napa Valley cannot actually be registered as traditional trade marks in the UK due to the above absolute grounds for refusal, as protected GIs they can in fact themselves form a basis for refusal under UKTMA 1994, s. 3(4). As above, this is likely to also apply to the term Coffee Kenya in due course, by virtue of UK-Kenya EPA, and any resulting agreement with regard to protection of IP rights.

ENFORCEMENT

If an association such as the SWA or individual producers of Scotch Whisky feel that the Scotch or Scotch Whisky name is not being used properly, or if they think words and labelling are being used that create a likelihood of confusion on the part of the public as to whether the drink is Scotch Whisky, then there are likely to be a number of enforcement options available to them. The exact tools available will depend on the jurisdiction in which the infringing use is taking place. In the UK the options would be:

- For an individual producer of Scotch Whisky acting on behalf of a group to take enforcement action on the basis of passing off. For example, the case involving Bollinger shows that it is possible to prevent the use of names that are distinctive of a discernible class of products under what is called the extended form of passing off.[45] The extended form of passing off

---

[45] *J Bollinger SA v Costa Brava Wine Co Ltd* [1960] Ch 262; *Erven Warnick BV v J Townend & Sons (Hull) Ltd* [1979] AC 731; *Chocosuisse Union des Fabricants Suisses de Chocolat v Cadbury Ltd* [1999] RPC 826 and *Diageo North America Inc v Intercontinental Brands (ICB) L*td [2010] EWCA Civ 920.

occurs where as a result of the quality or characteristic of the goods they have acquired goodwill in the name itself rather than as a result of the brand name associated with the goods.
- For the SWA or the individual producers of Scotch Whisky to alert the relevant government body, in this case HMRC, to the misuse of the protected GI and require enforcement action to be taken. The relevant enforcement authorities have been given powers of entry, inspection and search, the power to take samples and to seize goods as part of their general enforcement activities. They also have the power to bring follow-up actions against those responsible for the misuse. Cases where the use of words and labelling that create a likelihood of confusion on the part of the public as to whether the drink is Scotch Whisky can also be referred to HMRC for enforcement action. It may also be possible to refer the misuse to other administrative bodies such as the Advertising Standards Agency.
- The SWA could apply to record the protected GI with Customs Authorities, to bestow the ability to monitor goods crossing the borders on them, and prevent the import and export of products that are misusing the Scotch Whisky name. Customs recordals provide an effective means of halting the flow of counterfeit goods into UK and EU markets. The resultant reduction in counterfeit products further allows consumers to assume the consistency of quality of trade marked goods, and reduces the risk that poor quality counterfeit goods pose to a proprietor's reputation.
- There may also be special provisions in trade agreements between nations or other bilateral agreements with other nations to provide reciprocal protection of place brands.

It is important that the protected GIs and certification trade marks are properly enforced, as if the regulations are not enforced, then the certification trade marks and protected GIs can be cancelled where compliance with the requirements for the product specification can no longer be ensured.

CONCLUSION

Place brands can be protected and enforced in the UK. There are challenges.

The exact nature of the mark will determine what type of protection is available and the difficulty to register, in light of the various grounds of refusal available to the UKIPO.

Marks which contain a geographic term or even a protected GI are in theory registrable but likely to be subject to a specification of goods restriction, as required by the examiners of the UKIPO. However, once registered, the trade mark protection will be strong and a valuable asset to any owner.

With the advances in technology, access to goods and distribution of goods, the volume of counterfeits and infringing articles continue to rise. The additional legal protection of 'place brands' beyond the traditional trade mark registration can help brand owners to try and deal with these.

13. IP Law in Practice: the Case of Kenya
Chebet Koros and Melissa Omino[1]

LEGAL FRAMEWORK OF PLACE-BRANDING IN KENYA

Definition of Geographical Indications in Kenya

In Kenya, the protection of place-branding is commonly referred to as the protection of 'geographical indications' (GIs), and as such, this chapter will primarily employ the term 'GIs' when discussing place-branding protection. There is no universally accepted definition of GIs, and Kenya's current GI framework, falling under the Trade Marks rules, does not provide one either. However, in Kenya's Draft Geographical Indications Bill,[2] GI is defined as:

> a description or presentation used to indicate the geographical origin, in the territory of a country, or a region or locality in that territory, where a given quality, reputation or other characteristics of goods or services are exclusively or essentially attributable to the geographical environment, including natural factors, human factors or both.[3]

---

[1] The co-authors are both intellectual property practitioners and researchers, and this chapter's research received valuable assistance from research assistants, namely Joshua Kitili, Doreen Abiero, and Calvin Mulindwa.

[2] Ben Sihanya, *Intellectual Property and Innovation Law in Kenya and Africa Transferring Technology for Sustainable Develoment* (Sihanya Mentoring & Innovative Lawyering 2016) 412. In 2007, efforts to enact a Geographical Indication Act in Kenya culminated in the development of the Geographical Indications Bill. It remains in draft form as it was not officially published for parliamentary debate. The provisions of this bill have been incorporated into the recent Intellectual Property (IP) Bill of 2020, which is yet to undergo parliamentary proceedings.

[3] Draft Geographical Indications Bill 2007, s. 2, available online at <https://www.origin-gi.com/wp-content/uploads/2010/02/bill_geo_indications2007.pdf> accessed 9 October 2024.

In other words, GIs can function as certifications of specific qualities or reputation linked to the product's geographical origin, which may result from environmental advantages, uniqueness, or human factors like specialized manufacturing skills and traditions.[4] This definition under Kenya's GI Bill could benefit from further refinement by incorporating more specific criteria or standards to ascertain the locality or territoriality of the products.[5] Kenya predominantly relies on trade mark law, particularly utilizing collective trade marks, for GI protection. In contrast, Europe employs a distinct and dedicated GI system comprising Protected Designation of Origin, Protected Geographical Indication, and Traditional Specialties Guaranteed categories.[6] The key difference between these two systems lies in the nature of protection, as will be discussed in this chapter.

Protection of Geographical Indications in Kenya

GIs are recognized as intellectual property (IP) rights,[7] and the Kenyan Constitution mandates the state to safeguard, promote, and support the IP rights of its citizens.[8] For more than 15 years, Kenya has not enacted a dedicated GI law. Efforts, such as the Draft Geographical Indications Bill of 2007 ('the Draft GI Bill') and the recent Intellectual Property Bill of 2020 ('the IP Bill'), have been undertaken to address this gap. The Draft GI Bill's main features are the definition and administration of GIs in Kenya. However, the Draft GI Bill has not been assented to despite garnering comments and support from various stakeholders.[9] Additionally, Kenya abides by the general principles of international laws governing GI protection, to which it is a party,

---

[4] Sihanya (n 2).

[5] Sihanya (n 2), 413.

[6] Regulation (EU) No 1151/2012 of The European Parliament and of the Council of 21 November 2012 on quality schemes for agricultural products and foodstuffs [2012] OJ L323/1.

[7] Agreement on Trade-Related Aspects of Intellectual Property Rights (1994) Marrakesh Agreement Establishing the World Trade Organization, Annex 1C, 1869 U.N.T.S. 299, 33 I.L.M. 1197 (1994) (the TRIPS Agreement).

[8] Constitution of Kenya 2010, Art. 40(5).

[9] Saudin J Mwakaje, 'Protection of Geographical Indications and Cross-Border Trade: A Survey of Legal and Regulatory Frameworks in East Africa' (2022) 25(1) The Journal of World Intellectual Property 31; International Trademark Association (INTA), 'Comments on the Kenya Draft Bill on Geographical Indications' (2018) <http://www.inta.org/wp-content/uploads/public-files/advocacy/testimony-submissions/ COMMENTS -ON -THE -KENYA -DRAFT -BILL -GI -April -2018 .pdf> accessed 9 October 2024.

and these principles hold legal significance within the country.[10] Among these international laws is the Agreement on Trade-Related Aspects of Intellectual Property Rights ('the TRIPS Agreement'), which Kenya's current GI framework, within the Trade Marks Act, complies with. Both Kenya's IP Bill and GI Bill,[11] provide comparable exceptions to the TRIPS Agreement's exceptions to the general prohibitions on GIs.[12] For example, the provisions and exceptions in the Draft GI Bill pertaining to the registration of a misleading trade mark in conflict with a GI for wines, spirits, or other goods,[13] closely resemble those outlined in Articles 22(3) and 23 of the TRIPS Agreement.

Current protection: trade marks protection for GIs in Kenya
Kenya follows a common law legal system, with the Constitution of 2010 serving as the foundational law. The Trade Marks Act first commenced on 1 January 1957, and was subsequently amended until its current version in 2007. While the Act facilitates trade mark registration, legal recourse for unregistered trade mark infringement is unavailable. However, Trade Marks Act, s. 5 recognizes unregistered trade marks, enforceable through common law passing-off actions. To succeed, owners must prove the unregistered mark's sufficient reputation through public use. Furthermore, Trade Marks Act, s. 15A protects unregistered trade marks, contingent on substantial evidence of their reputation and well-known status in Kenya. The Trade Marks Act provides for the registration of three types of marks, namely 'ordinary' trade marks, certification marks, and collective marks. The latter two categories are discussed in this chapter.

In Kenya's existing legal framework, GIs are safeguarded through trade mark law, which is akin to the approach taken in the US. This protection is specifically provided through collective marks and certification marks. The Trade Marks Act of Kenya provides for the registration of geographical names or indications of geographical origin as collective marks, however, it does not provide for the criteria of GI protection.[14] A collective mark is a mark used in trade by members of an association to distinguish their goods or services from those of non-members.[15] On the other hand, certification marks are marks used in trade to distinguish certified goods from uncertified ones based

---

[10] Constitution of Kenya 2010, Art. 2(5).
[11] IP Bill of Kenya 2020, s. 194(c); Geographical Indications Bill 2007, s. 6(c).
[12] TRIPS Agreement, Art. 24(9).
[13] Draft GI Bill of Kenya 2007, ss. 21 and 22.
[14] Trade Marks Act CAP 506, s. 40A(5).
[15] Trade Marks Act CAP 506, s. 40A(1).

on their origin, material, manufacturing method, quality, accuracy, or other characteristics.[16]

Both the registration of GIs as collective marks and as certification marks share some common aspects. In both cases, the purpose is to distinguish goods or services based on their origin or other specific characteristics. Secondly, for collective marks, an association of members must apply in the prescribed manner, providing the rules that govern the mark's usage.[17] Similarly, for certification marks, the mark belongs to the person certifying the goods or services, and specific regulations regarding its use must be deposited with the Registrar.[18] Thirdly, in both cases, alterations must be reported. The registered owner must communicate any changes made to the rules governing the collective mark to the Registrar in writing,[19] or the change in ownership of the certification mark must be by consent from the court.[20]

However, there are some differences between the two registration types. For collective marks, the primary focus is on distinguishing goods or services of association members from those of non-members,[21] while certification marks focus on distinguishing certified goods from uncertified ones based on specific characteristics, including origin.[22] Additionally, collective marks involve the association controlling the mark's usage,[23] while certification marks involve a person or entity certifying the goods or services.[24] Further, certification marks have certain limitations and conditions. For example, to preserve the impartiality of the owner of a certification mark, using the mark personally is prohibited.[25] In contrast, owners of collective marks are typically allowed to use the mark themselves.[26] Furthermore, a certification mark's distinctiveness may be evaluated by the court or Registrar, who will assess whether the mark is inherently distinctive or has acquired distinctiveness through its use.[27] In the context of trade mark registration, 'distinctive' refers to the ability of the mark to differentiate goods or services associated with the trade mark owner

---

[16] Trade Marks Act CAP 506, s.40(1).
[17] Trade Marks Act CAP 506, s. 40A(2).
[18] Trade Marks Act CAP 506, s. 40(1) and (7).
[19] Trade Marks Act CAP 506, s. 40A(4).
[20] Trade Marks Act CAP 506, s. 40(8): the certification trade mark cannot be assigned or transferred without court consent.
[21] Trade Marks Act CAP 506, s. 40A(1).
[22] Trade Marks Act CAP 506, s. 40(1).
[23] Trade Marks Act CAP 506, s. 40A(3).
[24] Trade Marks Act CAP 506, s. 40(1).
[25] Trade Marks Act CAP 506, s. 40(1).
[26] Trade Marks Act CAP 506, s.40A.
[27] Trade Marks Act CAP 506, s. 40(2).

from those with no connection to the owner.[28] Lastly, where a certification mark is one of multiple registered trade marks that are identical or very similar, the use of any of those trade marks, as permitted by the registration, does not constitute an infringement on the rights of the other trade marks.[29] Overall, both types of registration serve the purpose of safeguarding and distinguishing products concerning their origin or quality, making them the current primary legal means of protecting GIs, and place brands, in Kenya.

Examples of protected GIs in Kenya
In August 2010, the Maasai Community Trust successfully registered 'Maasai/Masai' as a collective mark to ensure the authenticity of products originating from the Maasai/Masai community.[30] This registration serves the dual purpose of preventing any offensive use of the mark and empowering the community to oversee the management of their natural resources, environment, and products.[31] The collective mark registration includes provisions for licensing arrangements and the vigilant monitoring of any unauthorized use of the mark, specifically restricting its use to products closely associated with the Maasai/Masai community and providing a clear procedure for obtaining a license to utilize the mark.[32]

Another example is the 'Taita Basket', which is a registered collective mark safeguarding a GI. In February 2016, a workshop brought together 30 skilled basket weavers to impart knowledge about trade marks, quality standards, and branding.[33] This led to the establishment of the 'Taita Baskets Association' and their subsequent application for a collective trade mark with the Kenya Industrial Property Institute ('KIPI') in September 2016.[34] The Association's application included a representation of the collective trade mark, usage regulations, and the Association's constitution. On 3 April 2017, they successfully secured the 'Taita Basket' collective mark, a pivotal asset in protecting and

---

[28] Trade Marks Act CAP 506, s. 12(2).
[29] Trade Marks Act CAP 506, s. 40(6).
[30] Michael Blakeney, Thierry Coulet, Getachew Mengistie and Marcelin Tonye Mahop (eds), *Extending the Protection of Geographical Indications: Case Studies of Agricultural Products in Africa* (Routledge 2018).
[31] Ibid.
[32] Ibid.
[33] 'Japan FIT/IP Global Activities in Africa and LDCs'. (World Intellectual Property Organization 2019) <https://www.wipo.int/edocs/pubdocs/en/wipo_pub_flyer_fitjip_africa.pdf> accessed 9 October 2024.
[34] 'Taita Basket: A New Identity for Basket Weavers in Kenya' (World Intellectual Property Organization 2019) <http://www.wipo.int/ipadvantage/en/details.jsp?id=10875> accessed 9 October 2024.

promoting their products.[35] Beyond conferring rights, this mark also entails responsibilities, notably maintaining stringent quality standards.[36]

Additionally, the KIPI Trademarks Registry features several certification marks, including 'ECHUCHUKA', registered in September 2006 by the Turkana Bio Aloe Organization (Tubae) in Turkana County, Kenya.[37] This mark is dedicated to aloe vera products cultivated and produced by the Lake Turkana community. Its usage is exclusively limited to Tubae members, though membership is open to any organized and registered aloe group in Turkana.[38]

Another example is in April 2009, the Tea Board of Kenya ('TBK') registered a certification mark or 'Mark of Origin' under the name 'Finest Premium Kenyan Tea, Tea Board of Kenya'. It introduced specific usage requirements and demonstrated Kenya's dedication to preserving the authenticity and quality of its tea products while promoting their unique origin.[39]

Additionally, 'Coffee Kenya' was registered by the Coffee Board of Kenya, a state corporation, as a certification mark in November 2005 under class 30. Furthermore, 'Coffee Kenya so rich, so Kenyan' is registered by the Coffee Board of Kenya.[40] Usage guidelines for this mark mandate that any coffee packaging or containers bearing it must exclusively contain 100% coffee

---

[35] Kenya Industrial Property Institute (KIPI) Journal, Trademark Registration Number 94134.

[36] Kenya Industrial Property Institute (KIPI) Trademark Application for Registration Number 94134, Regulation for Use of Collective Trade Mark 'Taita Basket', Article 5.

[37] Blakeney et al. (n 30), 217.

[38] Ibid.

[39] Ibid. The specific usage requirements included: exclusive use granted by TBK upon meeting certification system requirements; tea packets and containers with the mark must contain 100% Kenyan-produced tea; adherence to the Tea Industry Code of Practice, with exceptions for tea bags or specific market demands; packaging quantities following Tea Regulations 2008; packaging meeting market standards, or, in the absence of specifications, complying with the Kenya standard for tea packets and containers (KS 1927:2005); and packaging exclusively conducted in TBK-registered premises.

[40] V Nzomo, 'Registration of the "COFFEE KENYA" Certification Mark by the Government' (15 January 2015); 'Kenya bets on origin mark to boost coffee sales' (*Nation Media Group*, Nairobi, 14 January 2015) <https:// nation .africa/ kenya/ business/ Kenya-bets-on-origin-mark-to-boost-coffee-sales/ 996-2589500 -kmmm4h/index.html> accessed 9 October 2024: the article refers to four companies that have met the requirements to use the certification mark.

produced in Kenya.[41] Moreover, coffee carrying this mark must meet the packaging standards outlined in the Coffee Regulations of the Coffee Act.[42]

Registration by individuals of trade marks that use geographical names

While GIs are primarily meant to indicate the geographical origin of a good or service, the KIPI Trade Mark Registry often records trade marks with geographical names that lack registration as collective or certification marks. In these cases, it is customary to include disclaimers, as per Trade Marks Act, s. 17, specifying that the registration of such names does not hinder others from using the same geographical name for similar goods. Registered trade marks with geographical names that are not certification or collective marks include *Meru* Arabica Coffee, *Mount Kenya* Infusions, *Mount Kenya* Milk, *Mount Kenya* Specialty, *Aberdare* Tea, *Aberdares* Fresh, *Changoi* Tea Farm, *Kaimosi* Tea Farm, *Kapchorua* Tea Farm among others. These trade marks have been registered with a disclaimer on the right to the exclusive use of the geographical name.[43] To qualify for registration, a trade mark, except certification marks, needs to include words that do not directly describe the product's features or quality and are not commonly associated with a specific geographical area. This raises concerns about the legitimacy of trade marks that have geographic names in them, an issue that IP practitioners need to address when working on place-branding.[44]

Potential National Legal Protection: Intellectual Property Bill of Kenya, 2020

The GI framework, within the Trade Marks Act, however, lacks sufficient regulation for GIs in Kenya, as it lacks specific provisions for the definition and administration of GIs. The Draft GI Bill, introduced in 2007 with specific regulations, was later incorporated into the IP Bill. The IP Bill's primary objective is to consolidate all existing IP laws and integrate the Kenya Copyright Board, KIPI, and the Anti-Counterfeit Authority into a unified IP office. However, there has been limited progress on the Bill following public participation initiated by the previous Kenyan Government. The IP Bill is yet to undergo

---

[41] Blakeney et al. (n 30), 217.

[42] Ibid; Coffee Act of Kenya CAP 333 and the Crops (Coffee) (General) Regulations 2019.

[43] Meru Arabica Coffee TMA No. 60346, Mount Kenya Infusions TMA No. 103072, Mount Kenya Milk TMA No. 74761, Mount Kenya Specialty TMA No. 97409, Aberdare Tea TMA No. 51320, Aberdares Fresh TMA No. 56807.

[44] Trade Marks Act CAP 506, s. 12(1)(d).

parliamentary proceedings. Part XVIII of the Bill proposes the establishment of a national GI law in Kenya, much of which replicates provisions from the 2007 GI Bill, with some minor enhancements. The Bill defines GIs, influenced by the TRIPS Agreement and World Intellectual Property Organization (WIPO) definitions,[45] emphasizing that certain qualities, reputation, or characteristics of the products are inherently tied to and influenced by geographic origin. Additionally, it outlines procedures for administration, registration, exclusions, and the duration of GI protection.

CHALLENGES IN THE CURRENT LEGAL GI FRAMEWORK IN KENYA

In the Kenyan context, a gap in the legal framework regarding GIs exists. The gap is felt first with the lack of definition of GI in the current statute. At most, the element of distinctiveness, as would be required for the registration of a mark, in the Trade Mark Act is the first attempt to capture GIs in the law. Section 12(1)(d) states that to qualify for registration a mark must contain or consist of 'a word or words having no direct reference to the character or quality of the goods, and *not being according to its ordinary signification a geographical name* or a surname'.

The challenge faced in the current legal framework was illustrated in practice through the *Tinderet* Case.[46] This case highlights the public interest, private interest, and government perspectives on current GI protection in Kenya, as will be discussed later in the chapter. The case involved an application for the expungement of a registered trade mark bearing a geographical area and demonstrates the lack of clarity around GIs in Kenya and the reluctance of the tribunal faced with a claim regarding GI protection through trade mark registration to un-muddy the waters. The matter involved the use of the term 'Tinderet' in the trade mark 'Tinderet Tea Farm' owned by George

---

[45] TRIPS Agreement, Art. 22: 'Indications which identify a good as originating in the territory of a Member, or a region or locality in that territory, where a given quality, reputation or other characteristic of the good is essentially attributable to its geographical origin.'; WIPO, *Geographical Indications: An Introduction* (2nd edn, World Intellectual Property Organization 2021) <http://www.wipo.int/publications/en/details.jsp?id=4562> accessed 9 October 2024: 'a sign used on products that have a specific geographical origin and possess qualities or a reputation that are due to that origin'.

[46] *The Matter of Trademark No. 100387 'Tinderet Tea Farm' in the Name of George Williamson & Co Ltd Private Co Ltd, Expungement Application by Dr Isaac Rutenberg & Caroline Wanjiru of the Centre for Intellectual Property and Information Technology Law (CIPIT)*, 26 June 2023.

Williamson & Co Ltd.[47] The argument put forward by the applicant was that 'Tinderet' was descriptive of the region in which tea was grown in the Kenyan tea highlands, referring specifically to the Tinderet Region in Nandi County. If the mark was not expunged it would hinder other tea farmers from the region from using the name Tinderet. Moreover, statements from the Kenya Tea Development Agency (KTDA), which pointed towards it being a GI, supported the geographical uniqueness of Tinderet as a tea-growing region. The quality of tea grown in Tinderet is unique and attributed to its climatic conditions, mineral-rich soils, and well-distributed rainfall. These factors contribute to the tea's distinct characteristics, which include its deep golden hue, rich body, and mild flavor.

Ultimately, the tribunal ruled in favor of the trade mark owner, affirming the mark's legal validity, acquired distinctiveness, and compliance with GI requirements.[48] However, the applicant achieved partial success in the case, with the respondent being required to record conditions of use of the trade mark. The tribunal held that the proprietors' trade mark was distinctive and compliant with s. 12 of the Trade Marks Act: this was because it had been in use in the Kenyan market since 2010, acquiring sufficient distinctiveness over approximately 13 years to become a badge of origin for the goods in class 30 of the Nice Classification. However, in bringing this issue to the tribunal, the applicant encountered several challenges, including the absence of a specific framework dealing with GIs in Kenya. Additionally, the Trade Marks Act, which is the default Act with the competence to handle GIs within the legal framework, does not provide a clear definition of GIs. Furthermore, there is frustration regarding the lack of progress in enacting and operationalizing the IP Bill 2020, which dedicates an entire part of the statute to the protection and registration of GIs. Lastly, there is a lack of regulations within the current legal framework to assist in the protection of GIs as collective marks.

GIs show the unique nature and contribution of a region to goods that collective marks do not, and as such, require a framework with the intention to showcase the distinctiveness of marks based on their origin. The latter challenge became evident when the applicants attempted to utilize the provision of collective marks in lieu of legislation on GIs, without the guidance of rules for implementing collective marks as GIs. With regards to the trade mark, 'Tinderet Tea Farm', the tribunal ruled that the mark is to be used only on the tea grown in the Tinderet area in Nandi Hills Region. Moreover, the mark is to be used to identify the origin of the proprietors' tea and the proprietors are not

---

[47] The trade mark 'Tinderet Tea Farm' was registered with a disclaimer on the exclusive use of the words 'Tinderet', 'Tea' and 'Farm'.
[48] Trade Marks Act CAP 508, s. 12(1)(d).

to use the mark in a manner that will cause a negative reputation of the Tinderet Area, especially in reference to tea growing and production. The Tribunal's ruling affirmed that GIs are only provided for within the Trade Marks Act in the context of registration as collective marks, but did not address the lacuna in the law regarding the criteria for the registration of GIs as collective marks. Section 40A(5) provides that 'Geographical names or other indications of geographical origin may be registered as collective marks or service marks'. It does not attempt to cover anything else to do with GIs beyond this scope, thus only succeeding in burdening the definition of GI with a connection to an association, which association is to determine the rules of use of the mark. The Tribunal declined to create a pathway towards the recognition of GIs, other than the meandering route of challenging the lack of distinctiveness of a mark based on s. 12(1)(d) or the strict adherence to the formation of an association that would determine the rules of use of a GI as a collective mark as envisioned by s. 40A(5). This, then, is the current state of practice of GIs in Kenya.

The attempt to bring GIs to the forefront of legislation is suspended in the fate of the IP Bill 2020. Place-branding is thus a matter that may continue to be litigated through the tribunals and courts. What should be concerning, however, is why redress begins at the tribunal and not at the point of the attempt to register a mark that is clearly GI. The examination of the Tinderet mark is something that should cause pause for thought at the KIPI, as, Kenya awaits the actual enactment of legislation on GIs, they are the first defense for GIs. It is also concerning that the statements by the KTDA did not seem to sway the tribunal on the issue of GIs. The applicants attached a copy of an extract from the KTDA website describing the quality of the tea directly associated with the geographical area where it is grown, including the Nandi Hills where Tinderet is located. This is indeed a competent body with expertise in goods on unique characteristics based on geographical parameters. Their expertise ought to have had more weight considering the subject matter at hand. Despite the absence of rules on GIs, a logical analysis would have weighed the statements as expert evidence on product quality based on the region.

It appears that place-branding has a long road to travel in legislative reforms and practice culture in Kenya. There is a clear need for capacity building as Kenya prepares to implement this form of IP directly within its legislation, not only for incoming legislative reforms but also to ensure a baseline understanding of GIs from the point of registration to the point of adjudication of disputes. This would ensure that the essence of the need for GIs is explained well to interested applicants to ensure that applicants are well placed to fully explore the unique geographical advantage of goods within Kenya's disposal as part of its development agenda. Kenya is currently not fully exploring the avenues available and thus finds itself vulnerable to possible scenarios such as those created by the Tinderet case.

VARIED PERSPECTIVES REGARDING GI PROTECTION IN KENYA

The *Tinderet* case exemplifies the threefold perspectives concerning current GI protection in Kenya: the public interest, private interest and government viewpoints. From the public interest standpoint, the applicants, who were IP practitioners and academics, engaged in public interest litigation, invoking Kenya's Constitution.[49] Public interest litigation serves various purposes, including establishing legal precedents, enforcing existing legal protections, prompting policy and statutory changes, and addressing historical injustices.[50] In this case, the applicants sought to uphold the integrity of the trade mark Register and Kenya's trademarks law. Furthermore, they argued that the true applicants were the people of Tinderet, who owned tea farms. They contended that 'Tinderet Tea Farm' failed to distinguish the proprietors' tea from others in Tinderet, potentially infringing on public rights. The applicants argued that the rights to the phrase 'Tinderet Tea Farm' should be public rights for anyone owning a tea farm in Tinderet, and contended that registering these rights as an ordinary trade mark converts public rights into private rights held by an individual.[51] The applicants further asserted that 'Tinderet' deserved GI protection under the Trade Marks Act,[52] highlighting GIs as communal rights managed by local communities, suggesting that the registration of the 'Tinderet' name should be for entities representing Tinderet's people or tea trade, rather than benefiting individuals.

From a private interest perspective, George Williamson & Co Ltd underscored their long-standing ownership of the Tinderet tea farm since the 1960s and their use of the 'Tinderet' term and elephant device since 2010. Their primary argument was that trade marks incorporating geographic names were permissible within Kenya's legal framework, provided they possessed distinctiveness. They asserted that their trade mark met this requirement and had no intention to appropriate public IP rights associated with the name 'Tinderet.' Furthermore, they drew attention to the absence of a GI statute in Kenya and emphasized the critical need for such a GI statute to establish clear criteria for evaluating and protecting GI attributes.

---

[49] Kenya Constitution 2010, Art. 22(2)(c).
[50] *Guide: Public Interest Litigation in Kenya* (KATIBA Institute 2023) <https://katibainstitute.org/download/guide-public-interest-litigation-in-kenya/#:~:text=Public%20Interest%20Litigation(PIL)%20has,the%20lives%20of%20many%20Kenyans> accessed 9 October 2024.
[51] KIPI Ruling on the *Tinderet* Case, 4.
[52] Trade Marks Act CAP 508, s. 12.

From the perspective of the Kenyan Government's Trade Mark Registry, the influence of international agreements on Kenyan legislation is recognized, particularly the necessity of introducing GI protection to comply with treaties such as the TRIPS Agreement. However, it is permissible to register trade marks that incorporate geographic names, provided that a disclaimer is included. This stance is consistent with the established practices of the Registry. In the *Tinderet* case, the Registry concluded that the trade mark proprietors were not required to include a disclaimer for the use of 'Tinderet Tea Farm' as a phrase. Furthermore, the Tribunal affirmed the legal entitlement of the trade mark proprietors to use the 'Tinderet Tea Farm' trade mark, as outlined in Trade Marks Act, s. 20. They also dismissed the applicants' request to register 'Tinderet Tea Farm' as a collective mark.

The contrasting opinions regarding the current legal framework for GIs in Kenya underscore the complexities and deficiencies within the law, emphasizing the urgent need for a dedicated GI legal framework. Such a framework would aim to provide clarity in terms of the protection and regulation of GIs in Kenya.

EXPLORING THE IMPLICATIONS OF IMPLEMENTING AN EU-STYLE GI PROTECTION IN KENYA

The *Tinderet* case highlights the difficulties in registering GIs in Kenya, primarily due to the absence of a well-defined legal framework. Under the TRIPS Agreement, specialized protection is already provided for GIs related to wines and spirits.[53] This presents an interesting opportunity, as several countries are advocating for an extension of this provision to cover all GI products, including agricultural products.[54] Given that agriculture is Kenya's primary economic activity, extending GI protection has the potential to enhance the value of vital products like Kenyan tea and coffee.[55] However, there is a counter-argument to this. Some contend that the costs of extending such protection may outweigh the benefits, especially for developing countries, as non-European Union (EU) nations would be required to protect over 700 registered GI products from the EU, with limited reciprocal benefits.[56]

---

[53] TRIPS Agreement, Art. 23.
[54] S C Srivastava, 'Protecting the Geographical Indication for Darjeeling Tea' in Peter Gallagher, Patrick Low and Andrew L. Stoler (eds), *Managing the Challenges of WTO Participation: 45 Case Studies* (CUP 2005), 231.
[55] Sihanya (n 2), 410.
[56] Ibid.

Should Kenya consider adopting a GI system like that of Europe, it is vital to analyze its potential and anticipated effects. It is crucial to distinguish between the nature of GI protection in Kenya and the *sui generis* GI system in Europe.[57] The success of GIs in one territory does not necessarily guarantee replicable success in others; it relies on factors such as investments and infrastructure.[58] Given that agriculture is a central economic activity in Kenya, our focus turns to the EU's Regulation No 1151/2012 concerning quality schemes for agricultural products and foodstuffs.[59]

Europe utilizes a unique GI system consisting of PDO (Protected Designation of Origin), PGI (Protected Geographical Indication), and TSG (Traditional Specialities Guaranteed) categories.[60] In contrast, Kenya relies on Trade Mark law, predominantly utilizing collective marks for GI protection. The primary distinction between the two systems lies in the nature of protection. Europe has a dedicated GI system with distinct categories, while Kenya incorporates GIs into its Trade Mark law framework. Europe's examination process focuses on production methods, whereas Kenya's emphasizes origin and specific characteristics. Where Europe provides more extensive protection through national and EU-wide registration, Kenya's protection is limited to the national level. Nevertheless, both regions have legal enforcement mechanisms in place.

Implementing EU-style GI protection in Kenya has diverse implications, one of which is the potential for increased international recognition. Currently, several countries, including some within the EU, as well as numerous non-African nations, have registered trade marks containing variations of

---

[57] S F Musungu, S Asfaha, S Balibrea, L Dore, M Gragnani and M Julia, 'The Protection of Geographical Indications and the Doha Round: Strategic and Policy Considerations for Africa' [2008] QUNO IP Issue Paper, 8.

[58] Susy Frankel, 'Geographical Indications and Mega-Regional Trade Agreements and Negotiations' in Irene Calboli and Wee Long Ng-Loy (eds), *Geographical Indications at the Crossroad of Trade, Development, and Culture* (CUP 2017), 147–67: this may indicate that the legal framework alone may be insufficient for fostering local industry development—additional factors like investments and infrastructure are crucial.

[59] Regulation (EU) No 1151/2012 of the European Parliament and of the Council of 21 November 2012 on quality schemes for agricultural products and foodstuffs [2012] OJ L343/1.

[60] Ibid.

'Kenya Coffee'[61] and 'Kenya Tea'.[62] This situation raises questions regarding the approval process carried out by the Tea and Coffee Boards of Kenya. These encompass inquiries into the thoroughness and efficacy of these approvals, emphasizing the need for a thorough examination and possible adjustments to safeguard the distinctiveness and unique qualities associated with Kenyan coffee and tea. However, embracing a GI protection system akin to that of the EU could elevate Kenyan GIs to global standards, thus enhancing their international reputation. Drawing from the EU's experience, such a system may enable GI producers to command higher prices for their distinctive products, potentially benefiting rural employment and promoting agro-tourism.[63]

Additionally, Kenya could benefit from adopting the EU's PDO, PGI, and TSG categories, which provide clear product categorization for consumers and producers. This enhanced clarity improves understanding of GI product characteristics and origins. Moreover, EU-style GI protection may enhance Kenyan exports to Europe, increasing competitiveness globally among consumers seeking unique, high-quality items. Implementing a dedicated GI protection system would also strengthen Kenya's legal framework, streamlining procedures for more effective GI protection and enforcement.

However, introducing an EU-style GI system in Kenya presents significant challenges. Primarily, such a transition requires substantial amendments to Kenya's legal and administrative frameworks. Developing essential regulations, providing training to officials, and establishing supervisory bodies

---

[61] WIPO, 'Global Brand Database': a search uncovers 'Kenya Coffee' trade marks registered in two EU countries and 18 non-African countries <https://branddb.wipo.int/en/quicksearch/results?sort=score%20desc&rows=30&asStructure=%7B%22_id%22:%22719a%22,%22boolean%22:%22AND%22,%22bricks%22:%5B%7B%22_id%22:%22719b%22,%22key%22:%22brandName%22,%22value%22:%22coffee%20kenya%22,%22strategy%22:%22Simple%22%7D%5D%7D&_=1694682928395> accessed 9 October 2024.

[62] WIPO, 'Global Brand Database': a search revealed 'Kenya Tea' trade marks registered in 15 non-African countries <https://branddb.wipo.int/en/quicksearch/results?sort=score%20desc&start=30&rows=30&asStructure=%7B%22_id%22:%221f62%22,%22boolean%22:%22AND%22,%22bricks%22:%5B%7B%22_id%22:%221f63%22,%22key%22:%22brandName%22,%22value%22:%22Kenya%20tea%22,%22strategy%22:%22Simple%22%7D%5D%7D&_=1694683172039> accessed 9 October 2024.

[63] European Commission, Directorate-General for Agriculture and Rural Development, *Evaluation support study on geographical indications and traditional specialities guaranteed protected in the EU: final report* (Publications Office 2021), 5 <https://data.europa.eu/doi/10.2762/891024> accessed 9 October 2024.

demand significant resources and time. Despite prior attempts to create a dedicated GI law in Kenya, including the most recent effort in 2020, progress has been elusive. Consequently, adopting an EU-style GI system would likely encounter comparable delays, if not stagnation.

Small-scale farmers and artisanal producers, who constitute most Kenyan GI producers, might encounter challenges in adapting to a complex EU-style system.[64] Meeting stringent criteria and navigating the application process could also be daunting. Furthermore, the EU-style approach involves thorough examination and verification, which could potentially increase costs and administrative burdens for Kenyan producers seeking GI protection.[65] Aligning Kenya's existing trade mark-based GI protection system with the new EU-style system could be intricate, given potential differences in the scope of protection and the criteria for product and region eligibility.

A significant challenge lies in the widespread lack of awareness and understanding regarding the value of GIs, not only in Kenya but also on a global scale. An illustrative case is a 1998 Eurobarometer study conducted among European consumers, which revealed that many either failed to notice GI labels or were unaware of their significance.[66] Kenya must prioritize capacity-building efforts for officials, producers, and stakeholders to ensure the successful implementation of an EU-style GI protection system. Additionally, the creation of a successful *sui generis* GI regime necessitates the existence of infrastructure and accompanying investments in development and capacity building.[67]

It is, therefore, crucial to address the complexities of safeguarding GIs and the concerns of developing nations when considering adopting an EU-style GI protection system in Kenya.

CONCLUSION

Kenya's unique geographic features and renowned agricultural products make a compelling case for GI protection. However, the absence of a dedicated GI

---

[64] Justin Hughes, 'The Limited Promise of Geographical Indications for Developing Country Farmers. Geographical Indications at the Crossroads of Trade, Development, and Culture in the Asia-Pacific' in Irene Calboli and Wee Long Ng-Loy (eds), *Geographical Indications at the Crossroad of Trade, Development, and Culture* (CUP 2017).

[65] The application and registration fees for substantive examination, verification, and registration of a GI are likely to be higher than those for an ordinary trade mark registration.

[66] Blakeney et al. (n 30).

[67] Frankel (n 58), 147–67.

law has resulted in the unclear utilization of Trade Mark law, mainly through collective and certification marks, as the primary means of safeguarding place-branding. Several examples of registered GIs, such as 'Maasai/Masai' and 'Taita Basket,' which are collective marks, shed light on the practical implementation of GI protection in the absence of a dedicated law.

Challenges within the current legal framework were vividly demonstrated through the *Tinderet* case, showcasing the complexities and ambiguities surrounding GI protection in Kenya. The case underscored the pressing need for legislative reforms and capacity-building initiatives to enhance the understanding of GIs among stakeholders and officials. Varied perspectives from the public, private, and government sectors on the current GI framework in Kenya highlighted the existing gaps and controversies within the legal framework, emphasizing the urgency of a dedicated GI legal framework.

While transitioning to an EU-style GI system could elevate the international recognition of Kenyan GIs and enhance their market value, it also presents significant challenges. These challenges include the need for legal and administrative amendments, potential barriers for small-scale producers, and the necessity for capacity-building on the value and use of GIs. Striking a balance between safeguarding valuable GIs and addressing the concerns of various stakeholders is, therefore, crucial. The road ahead requires careful consideration, legislative reforms, and capacity-building efforts to fully unlock the potential of Kenya's unique geographical advantages in the global market.

PART V

Intellectual Property Law in Policy Analysis

14. The International Legal Landscape for Geographical Indications
Titilayo Adebola

INTRODUCTION

Geographical (or place) names have perennially played pivotal roles in trade by serving as a means to position products competitively and signal reputation based on origin. These names have been instrumental in disseminating diverse products across the globe, including alcoholic beverages (Scotch Whisky and Napa Valley wines) and coffee (Coffee Kenya). This chapter presents a critical analysis of the international intellectual property (IP) landscape for geographical indications (GIs). While Article 22(1) of Agreement on Trade-Related Aspects of Intellectual Property Rights (TRIPS) defines GIs as indications which identify goods as originating in a territory, region or locality, where a given quality, reputation or other characteristic of the goods are essentially attributable to its geographical origin, it offers World Trade Organization (WTO) members flexible domestication choices.[1] The flexibility in the choice of legal systems for protecting GIs has engendered divergences in GI systems. For example, some WTO members such as the European Union (EU) have opted to introduce *sui generis* (which means special, unique, or literally 'of its own kind') GI systems. Conversely, others such as the United States (US) and Kenya protect GIs through certification or collective marks. The flexibility also introduces nuanced complexities in the conceptualization and governance of GIs.

This chapter argues that post-TRIPS, GI consensus setting has predominantly shifted from the multilateral to bilateral level. Stemming from the challenges in reaching a comprehensive multilateral consensus, countries

---

[1] For discussions on the inclusion of reputational link, see Dev Gangjee, 'From Geography to History: Geographical Indications and the Reputational Link' in Irene Calboli and Wee Loon Ng-Loy, *Geographical Indications at the Crossroads of Trade, Development, and Culture: Focus on Asia-Pacific* (Cambridge University Press 2017).

have increasingly turned to bilateral agreements, regional and national laws, to negotiate and establish their preferred GI standards. This shift has allowed countries to directly tailor agreements to suit their socio-economic priorities. For example, bilateral agreements could mandate the introduction of specific GI registration systems (such as *sui generis* or certification/collective mark systems) or provisions on sustainable development (such as those on labor, gender, environment, or climate protection). While bilateralism allows for nuanced negotiations, it fosters fragmentation in GI regimes. In other words, the divergences in domestic GI regimes complicate harmonization efforts and exacerbate the inconsistencies in the international GI architecture.

Accordingly, the chapter unpacks the complexities inherent in GI law-making. In doing so, it draws attention to the construction of pertinent GI provisions in TRIPS and World Intellectual Property Organization (WIPO) treaties alongside regional and national developments. Although GIs were once perceived as exclusively European, there is now a mosaic of GI registration systems globally. Nonetheless, the EU remains actively involved in shaping trade agreements relating to GIs, to preserve and promote its preferences. The chapter accentuates examples of GI registration systems from Europe, Africa, and the US, to uncover the politics, power asymmetries and contemporary challenges in GI regimes. This examination raises questions about the future trajectory of GI frameworks, prompting considerations regarding the implications of the diverse rules, and how they may evolve. Ultimately, the chapter underscores the reasons for the varied legal terminologies and regimes for GIs and place brands, including Scotch Whisky, Napa Valley wines, and Coffee Kenya, which are the central interests of this book.

CONTESTATIONS AND COMPROMISES: THE INTERNATIONAL STANDARDS FOR GEOGRAPHICAL INDICATIONS

Globalization, business expansions, cosmopolitan palates and exotic consumer choices triggered the proliferation of GIs. In seeking to govern GI trade across multiple jurisdictions, TRIPS establishes enforcement-backed minimum standards, while WIPO develops evolving legal norms for GIs.[2] GIs protected under international frameworks engender harmonized instruments amongst participating countries, enhancing market access, and potentially generating higher demands for the products. However, as discussed below, the

---

[2] The WTO currently has 166 member states <www.wto.org/english/thewto_e/whatis_e/tif_e/org6_e.htm> accessed 10 October 2024; WIPO has 193 member states <www.wipo.int/members/en/> accessed 10 October 2024.

international frameworks focus primarily on establishing legal rules for GIs, without addressing their implementation or impacts at regional and national levels. For instance, how do policy makers or producers ensure that continuous GI production does not harm biodiversity? How do they tackle concerns regarding the impact of GIs on climate change, from production and transportation to consumption? More still, how do they ensure fair compensation for all stakeholders along the product value chains, especially the often-marginalized local workers, while preventing the commercial benefits from flowing predominantly to the large entities, including the multinational companies often involved in GI businesses? Before proceeding, it is imperative to clarify that I will adopt the expression 'indication of geographical origin' (IGO) in this chapter to jointly refer to the multiple terms used internationally, regionally and nationally to indicate and protect the geographical origin of products, including 'certification marks', 'collective marks', 'indications of source', 'appellations of origin', 'protected designation of origin', 'protected geographical indication' and 'sui generis geographical indications'.[3] I will also refer to 'products' and 'goods' interchangeably.[4]

World Trade Organization: Enforcement-Backed Minimum Standards for Geographical Indications

TRIPS firmly established 'geographical indications' as a category of IP, along with copyright, trade marks, industrial designs and patents.[5] However, GIs starkly differ from other categories of IP in several ways. GIs are characterized by their geographical associations. As a result, they often evoke deep emotional connections, reflecting the reputation, cultural pride and heritage related to their origin. The intrinsic link between GIs and unique natural and human-made features tied to their geographical origins, including biodiversity, climate, genetic resources, soil topography, and traditional practices, distinguishes GIs from other IP rights. Unlike other IP rights, GIs are collectively

---

[3] See World Trade Organization, Council for Trade-Related Aspects of Intellectual Property Rights, *Review under Article 24.2 of the Application of the Provision of the Section of the TRIPS Agreement on Geographical Indications* (IP/C/W/253/Rev.1, 24 November 2003).

[4] For a discussion on the difference between products and goods, see: Dwijen Rangnekar, *Geographical Indications: A Review of Proposals at the TRIPS Council: Extending Article 23 to Products other than Wines and Spirits* (UNCTAD-ICSTD Project on IPRs and Sustainable Development Issue Paper No. 4 2003), 3..

[5] Section 3, Articles 22–4 of the Agreement on Trade Related Aspects of Intellectual Property Rights (TRIPS).

owned. Communities often play vital roles in preserving traditional practices, ensuring the authenticity of GIs, whereas other IP rights are usually owned by individuals or corporate entities. Beyond introducing GIs as a distinct category of IP, the multi-layered GI provisions in TRIPS reflect the delicate compromise agreed by negotiators based on their historical inclinations.[6] The GI provisions in TRIPS can be neatly divided into four segments, namely, the (i) definition of GIs, (ii) protection systems for GIs, (iii) additional provisions for wines and spirits, and (iv) exceptions and unresolved issues reserved for future negotiations.

Definition of geographical indications
Article 22(1) of TRIPS defines GIs as '*indications* which identify a good as originating in the territory of a Member, or a region or locality in that territory, where a given quality, reputation or other characteristic of the good is essentially attributable to its geographical origin' (emphasis added). In a broad sense, 'indications' encompass signs or information that show or point out specific features of products. Since this book is concerned with place-branding, I will briefly juxtapose GIs with place-branding. A place-brand refers to an image, perception or reputation associated with a specific location.[7] Place-branding involves a strategic effort to shape and manage how a location is perceived.[8] For example, 'incredible India' represents a branding campaign highlighting India's rich cultural heritage, diverse landscapes and historical significance.[9] Similarly, 'visit California' promotes California as a destination offering diverse experiences, from beaches to mountains and urban life.[10]

---

[6] International Center for Trade and Sustainable Development, *UNCTAD-ICTSD Project on IPRs and Sustainable Development: Resource Book on TRIPS and Development* (Cambridge University Press 2005), 267–321.

[7] Robert Govers and Frank Go, *Place Branding: Glocal, Virtual and Physical Identities, Constructed, Imagined and Experienced* (Palgrave Macmillan 2009); Pantea Foroudi, Suraksha Gupta, Philip J. Kitchen and Mohammad Mahdi Foroudi, 'A Framework of Place Branding, Place Image, and Place Reputation: Antecedents and Moderators' (2016) 19(2) Qualitative Market Research 241.

[8] See World Intellectual Property Organization (WIPO), *Standing Committee on the Law of Trademarks, Industrial Designs and Geographical Indications: The Protection of Country Names Against Registration and Use as Trademark* (WIPO/STrad/INF/7, 23 November 2015).

[9] Finola Kerrigan, Jyotsna Shivanandan and Anne-Marie Hede, 'Nation Branding: A Critical Appraisal of Incredible India' (2012) 32(2) Journal of Macromarketing 319; David Geary, 'Incredible India in a Global Age: The Cultural Politics of Image Branding in Tourism' (2013) 13(1) Tourist Studies 36.

[10] *Corporate Brand Guidelines* (Visit California 2022).

GIs can serve to promote place-branding and vice versa. Put differently, a GI has the potential to enhance and support the place-branding efforts of its place of origin. For instance, Scotland's place-branding and its GI for whisky are mutually reinforcing. Scotland's place-branding revolves around highlighting its rich cultural heritage, stunning landscapes, dynamic cities and authentic whisky.[11] The GI for Scotch Whisky emphasizes its historical place of origin, quality standards, and traditional techniques.[12] Both the place-branding for Scotland and GI for Scotch Whisky celebrate Scottish heritage, culture, and quality craftsmanship, positioning Scotch Whisky as a cornerstone of Scotland's global identity and inviting visitors to experience its rich cultural legacy first-hand.

The broad definition of GIs in TRIPS encompasses 'indications of source' and 'appellations of origin', which are pre-existing terms for protecting place-based products as provided for in the Paris Convention for the Protection of Industrial Property of 1883 (Paris Convention), the Madrid Agreement for the Repression of False or Deceptive Indications of Source on Goods of 1891 (Madrid Agreement), and the Lisbon Agreement for the Protection of Appellations of Origin and their International Registration of 1958 (Lisbon Agreement).[13] An indication of source is a sign, or an expression, employed to specify that goods or products originate in a specific place, country or region, without confirming claims of quality or reputation.[14] To be sure, although an indication of source establishes the origin of products, it does not denote that any special qualities, characteristics or reputation of the product are attributable to the place of origin identified. Examples of indications of source include

---

[11] David McCrone, *Scotland – The Brand: The Making of Scottish Heritage* (Edinburgh University Press 1995); Alastair Durie, Ian S Yeoman and Una McMahon-Beattie, 'How the History of Scotland Creates a Sense of Place' (2005) 2(1) Place Branding 43, Gillian Black, Rachel Craufurd Smith, Smita Kheria and Gerard Porter, 'Scotland the Brand – Marketing the Myth?' (2015) 24(1) Scottish Affairs 47.

[12] Niall G MacKenzie, Andrew Perchard, David Mackay and George Burt, 'Unlocking Dynamic Capabilities in the Scotch Whisky Industry, 1945 – Present' [2022] Business History 1; Julie Bower and David M Higgins, 'Litigation and Lobbying in Support of the Marque: The Scotch Whisky Association, c.1945 – c. 1990' (2023) 24(1) Enterprise & Society 286.

[13] Irene Calboli, 'Expanding the Protection of Geographical Indications of Origin under TRIPS: "Old" Debate or "New" Opportunity?' (2006) 10(2) Marquette Intellectual Property Law Review 182.

[14] Latha R Nair and Rajendra Kumar, *Geographical Indications: A Search for Identity* (LexisNexis Butterworths 2005), 11–20.

mentioning the name of a country on a product, such as 'made in Kenya' and using a symbol such as Tartan to identify products from Scotland.

The Lisbon Agreement defines an appellation of origin as a geographical name of a country, region or locality, which serves to designate a product originating therein, the quality and characteristics of which are due exclusively or essentially to the geographical environment, including natural and human influences.[15] Under the Lisbon Agreement, products protected by appellations of origin are required to be direct geographical names of countries, regions or localities where distinguishing qualities and characteristics of the products exclusively or essentially result from the said geographical environments.[16] For example, Tequila is the first appellation of origin from Mexico.[17] A commonly cited rationale for appellations of origin is *terroir*, a concept deeply rooted in the world of wine and loosely interpreted to cover the 'total elements of a vineyard' or 'the interplay of natural elements that make up the myriad environments in which vines grow'.[18] *Terroir* connotes the essence of a geographic area's influence on agricultural products.[19] In the context of GIs, it extends beyond the wine industry, and embodies the collection of environmental factors, including soil, climate, topography, and human practices that uniquely shape the character and quality of products grown in a particular region.[20] However, it is important to highlight that changing climatic conditions pose challenges to maintaining traditional *terroir* characteristics, urging producers to consider adaptation while preserving authenticity.[21]

---

[15] Lisbon Agreement for the Protection of Appellations of Origin and their International Registration of 1958, Article 2.

[16] Marsha A Echols, *Geographical Indications for Food Products: International Legal and Regulatory Perspectives* (Kluwer Law International 2008), 52–5.

[17] Sarah Bowen and Ana Valenzuela Zapata, 'Geographical Indications, Terroir and Socioeconomic and Ecological Sustainability: The Case of Tequila' (2009) 25(1) Journal of Rural Studies 108.

[18] James E Wilson, *Terroir: The Role of Geology, Climate, and Culture in the Making of French Wines* (Octopus Publishing Ltd 1998); Tim Josling, 'The War on Terroir: Geographical Indications as a Transatlantic Trade Conflict' (2006) 57(3) Journal of Agricultural Economics 337.

[19] Laurence Berard and Philippe Marchenay, *From Localized Products to Geographical Indications: Awareness and Action* (CNRS 2008), 18.

[20] Ibid.

[21] Lisa F Clark and William A Kerr, 'Climate Change and Terroir: The Challenge of Adapting Geographical Indications' (2017) 20(3–4) Journal of World Intellectual Property 88; Lisa F Clark and William A Kerr, 'Are Geographical Indications Sustainable in the Face of Climate Change?' (2022) 12(2) Queen Mary Journal of Intellectual Property 226; Andrea Borghini, Nicola Piras and Beatrice

Legal protection systems for geographical indications

In establishing the policy space for translating its provisions into domestic legal architecture, TRIPS allows WTO member states to protect GIs through any legal means they deem fit, including *sui generis* GI rights (special or unique laws tailored for GIs), collective marks (marks indicating membership of an association), certification marks (marks certifying product quality or specific characteristics that conform to established standards), and utilizing unfair competition laws including passing off laws to protect against deceptive practices.[22] The breadth of options mirror the diversity in legal systems and the nature of products associated with specific areas.[23] It allows WTO members to configure the most suitable means to protect GIs that correspond with their contexts, needs, and realities. However, this policy space precipitated the shift to bilateralism and the emergence of contests when countries seek to impose their preferences. The outcome of such contests usually depends on the relative power or influence of the parties involved. As Dev Gangjee notes, the US and EU have spent significant political and economic capital in advocating their preferred models.[24] The US strongly prefers protecting IGOs through collective or certification mark systems, while the EU prefers *sui generis* GI systems.[25]

Nonetheless, TRIPS specifically provides for member states to establish legal mechanisms for interested parties to prevent: (i) the use of any means in labelling or presenting a product that implies the product originates from a geographical area that is different from its true place of origin in a manner that misleads the public about its geographical origin and (ii) any use that constitutes unfair competition.[26] This provision intends to curtail misleading practices, limit consumer deception and maintain the integrity of IGOs. TRIPS further provides that WTO members must refuse or invalidate the registration

---

Serini, 'Hot Grapes: How to Locally Redesign Geographical Indications to Address the Impact of Climate Change' (2023) 2 World Development Sustainability 10043.

[22] Justin Hughes, 'Champagne, Feta, and Bourbon: The Spirited Debate about Geographical Indications' (2006) 58(2) Hastings Law Journal 299.

[23] Irina Kireeva and Bernard O'Connor, 'Geographical Indications and the TRIPS Agreement: What Protection is Provided to Geographical Indications in WTO Members?' (2010) 13(2) Journal of World Intellectual Property 275.

[24] Dev Gangjee, *Relocating the Law of Geographical Indications* (Cambridge University Press 2012), 201.

[25] Paul J Heald, 'Trademarks and Geographical Indications: Exploring the Contours of the TRIPS Agreement' (1996) 29 Vanderbilt Journal of Transnational Law 635.

[26] TRIPS, Article 22(2). Unfair competition as defined in Article 10bis of the Paris Convention for the Protection of Industrial Property 1967.

of trade marks that consist of GIs if (i) the products do not originate in the territory indicated and (ii) the use of the indication in the trade mark for such products in that member state misleads the public regarding its true place of origin.[27] This provision aims to ensure that trade marks incorporating GIs accurately represent the origin of the products they signify. It prohibits the registration of trade marks that falsely suggest a specific geographical origin for products that do not originate from that indicated territory, preventing misleading practices that could deceive consumers about the true source of the products.

Additional provisions for wines and spirits
As two of the case studies in this book, Napa Valley wines and Scotch Whisky, fall under this category, I shall investigate the rationales and contours of the additional provisions for wines and spirits in TRIPS. TRIPS does not explicitly provide an explanation for carving out special provisions for wines and spirits.[28] The drafting history and negotiation records of TRIPS also fail to explain the enhanced provisions. However, the bifurcation can be traced to the EU's strategic advocacy. The EU had initially proposed higher levels of protection for all products during the negotiations, and when this was rejected, it firmly bargained for the additional protection for wines and spirits, due to their susceptibility to imitation, misrepresentation, deceptive labelling practices and unfair trade in countries that did not have appellation of origin systems.[29] Article 23(1) provides for WTO members to introduce the legal mechanisms for interested parties to stop the use of a GI that identifies wines or spirits from a specific place for wines or spirits that do not originate from that indicated place. This requirement stands, even if the true origin of the product is mentioned or the GI is used in translation or accompanied by expressions such as 'kind', 'type', 'style', 'imitation' or the like. Its objective is to guarantee that GIs for wines and spirits accurately denote their origin.[30] For instance, labelling a wine 'Napa Valley-like Tuscan wine' is prohibited.

Article 23(2) provides that the registration of a trade mark for wines or spirits that contains or consists of a GI identifying wines or spirits will be refused or invalidated. This can occur based on a member's legislation if it so permits or at the request of an interested party.[31] This provision differs from Article 22(3)

---

[27] TRIPS, Article 22(3).
[28] Aaron C Lang, 'On the Need to Expand Article 23 of the TRIPS Agreement' (2006) 16 Duke Journal of Contemporary and International Law 487, 494.
[29] Bernard O'Connor, *The Law of Geographical Indications* (Cameron May 2004); Gangjee (n 24), 239.
[30] For more on this, see Rangnekar (n 4).
[31] Ibid.

above because there is no requirement for deception. In other words, misleading the public as to the true place of origin is not a prerequisite for the refusal or invalidation.[32] For example, if a company in Kenya attempts to register a trade mark 'Glen Highland' for a whisky produced outside the recognized Scottish region for Scotch Whisky, the provision would enable the Scottish authorities or an interested party, such as the Scotch Whisky Association, to request the refusal or invalidation of the trade mark 'Glen Highland' for whisky not originating from Scotland, despite the absence of explicit deception or misleading practices. Even if the company is not explicitly trying to deceive consumers into believing their product is Scotch Whisky, Article 23(2) allows for refusal or invalidation of the trade mark. The use of 'Glen', a common indicator in Scotch Whisky, in the trade mark for a non-Scottish whisky can be contested under this provision.

In addition, Article 23(3) provides for the protection of homonymous GIs for wines subject to ensuring that (i) the indications are not misleading, (ii) the indications will be differentiated from each other, and (iii) the producers are treated equitably. For example, Pisco from Peru and Chile are protected under the EU's GI system as a Protected Geographical Indication (PGI) and Protected Designation of Origin (PDO) respectively. PGIs and PDOs are specific categories of protection mechanisms within the EU's *sui generis* framework, emphasizing different characteristics of the product. To comply with TRIPS, when homonymous GIs like Pisco from Peru and Chile exist, it is crucial to ensure that the indications are not misleading, they are differentiated and that producers are treated fairly and equitably within the EU GI system.

Exceptions and unresolved issues reserved for future negotiations
While TRIPS offers several exceptions to its GI provisions and reserves issues for future negotiations, I focus here on the conflicts between *sui generis* GI systems and trade mark systems because these are the systems often used to protect Scotch Whisky, Napa Valley wines and Coffee Kenya. Article 24(5) preserves the rights of a trade mark holder where a trade mark has been applied for or registered in good faith, or where rights to a trade mark have been acquired through use in good faith either before the date of application for a GI or before the GI is protected in its country of origin. If an application for a trade mark is in conflict with a GI, by being identical with it or similar to it, an opposition to the trade mark must be presented within five years after the

---

[32] Felix Addor and Alexandra Grazioli, 'Geographical Indications Beyond Wines and Spirits: A Roadmap for a Better Protection for Geographical Indications in the WTO/TRIPS Agreement' (2002) 5 Journal of World Intellectual Property 865, 879–81.

adverse use or date of publication, whichever is earlier, and provided the GI is not used or registered in bad faith.[33]

For example, if a cheese producing company, Sayof Foods, unaware of the existing Roquefort GI, applies to register a trade mark 'Roquefort Delicacies' for their cheese products in France, the trade mark will be deemed to be identical or similar to the established Roquefort GI. Even if Sayof Foods, in good faith and before the protection of the Roquefort GI, has utilized and established rights to their trade mark, according to Article 24(5) of TRIPS, the holder of the Roquefort GI has the right to oppose the trade mark application within a five-year period. This opposition period begins upon their awareness of the adverse use or the publication of the trade mark, whichever occurs earlier. For the opposition to be effective, the stakeholders of the Roquefort GI must demonstrate that the trade mark application conflicts with their GI, being either identical or similar, and that the GI was not used or registered in bad faith. If the opposition meets these specified conditions and the trade mark was indeed acquired in good faith, the rights of the trade mark holder might be preserved despite the conflict with the Roquefort GI. This demonstrates how Article 24(5) of TRIPS operates to protect the rights of a trade mark holder who, in good faith and before the GI protection, acquired rights to a conflicting trade mark, while also outlining conditions and timelines for opposition by GI stakeholders.

In *European Communities - Protection of Trademarks and Geographical Indications for Agricultural Products and Foodstuffs,* the US and Australia requested consultations with the EC to determine whether the EC's methods of protecting GIs were consistent with TRIPS (including but not limited to Articles 3, 16, 24, 63, and 65).[34] The US contended inter alia that EC Regulation 2081/92 (as amended) failed to provide national treatment in relation to GIs and that it did not provide sufficient protection to pre-existing trade marks that were similar to or identical to protected GIs. Addressing the multi-part doctrinal issues raised, a panel found the EC Regulation did not provide national treatment to other WTO members right holders and products because the registration of a GI from countries outside the EC was contingent upon the government of that country adopting a system of GI protection equivalent to the EC's system and offering reciprocal protection to EC GIs. In addition, unlike EC nationals, a foreign national did not have guaranteed access to

---

[33] TRIPS, Articles 5 and 6.

[34] 'DS174: European Communities – Protection of Trademarks and Geographical Indications for Agricultural Products and Foodstuffs' (World Trade Organization) <www.wto.org/english/tratop_e/dispu_e/cases_e/ds174_e.htm> accessed 10 October 2024.

the EC's system for their GIs. This decision triggered revisions to the GI laws in Europe. However, on the second point of not providing sufficient protection to pre-existing trade marks that were similar to or identical to protected GIs, the panel decided that the EC's treatment of the relationship between GIs and trade marks was not inconsistent with TRIPS.

As Michael Handler points out, the case represents a symbolic retaliatory retort by the US and Australia to the EU's expansionist agenda and protectionism, often seen as barriers to trade.[35] The US and Australia sought to draw attention to the consequences of non-compliance with TRIPS. At its core, the dispute reflects one of the perennial power struggles in the GI discourse. It accentuates the broader global discussions around the delicate balance between protecting IP rights, fostering fair trade practices and limiting undue barriers that hinder free market access.[36]

In its final article on GIs, Article 24 of TRIPS reaffirms members' commitment to negotiating and exploring enhanced protection for GIs related to wines and spirits. This article also tasks the Council for TRIPS with routinely reviewing the application of GI provisions.[37] Initially, the Council was slated to conduct its first review within two years of the entry into force of the WTO Agreement. Moreover, it stipulates that if any compliance issue arises concerning GIs, a member can escalate it to the Council. At the request of a member, the Council must engage in consultations when bilateral or plurilateral discussions fail to resolve the matter among concerned members. Dwijen Rangnekar comprehensively maps the reviews and proposals at the TRIPS Council in *A Review of Proposals at the TRIPS Council: Extending Article 23 to Products other than Wines and Spirits*.[38] These proposals should contribute to possible future GI negotiations at the TRIPS Council.

---

[35] Michael Handler, 'The WTO Geographical Indications Dispute' (2006) Modern Law Review 70; Michael Handler and Robert Burrell, 'GI Blues: The Global Disagreement over Geographical Indications' in Kathy Bowrey, Michael Handler and Dianne Nicol (eds), *Emerging Challenges in Intellectual Property* (Oxford University Press 2011), 126–44.

[36] Dev S Gangjee, 'Proving Provenance? Geographical Indications Certifications and its Ambiguities' (2017) 98 World Development 12.

[37] For the Doha Mandate on Geographical Indications, See 'TRIPS: Geographical Indications' (World Trade Organisation) <www.wto.org/english/tratop_e/trips_e/gi_background_e.htm> 10 October 2024.

[38] Rangnekar (n 4); For the up-to-date developments on the reviews and submissions, see 'TRIPS: Geographical Indications' (World Trade Organization) <www.wto.org/english/tratop_e/trips_e/gi_background_e.htm> accessed 10 October 2024.

World Intellectual Property Organization: Evolving Norm Setting for Geographical Indications

As exhibited by the growing membership of its agreements including the Geneva Act of the Lisbon Agreement, WIPO's role in shaping the international protection and registration systems for GIs has gained prominence and increased in significance, particularly with the stalled negotiations on enhanced GI protection in the TRIPS Council.[39] Even though it does not have a dispute settlement body akin to TRIPS, WIPO has been pivotal in the construction and dissemination of the legal rules for GIs. Its efforts have focused on fostering international agreements, registration systems and norms for GIs. Nevertheless, it is worth noting that even before the TRIPS Agreement came into force, WIPO played a primary role in shaping discussions and policies surrounding GIs. Its historical involvement has contributed significantly to the conceptualization and creation of GIs as a distinct category of IP rights.[40]

This part of the chapter is dedicated to the Lisbon System, which represents WIPO's latest advancements on GIs. Understanding the Lisbon System is crucial because it shapes the GI systems of its members at national or regional levels. It also typifies the underlying power dynamics and strategies adopted in international GI law-making. While TRIPS negotiators failed to reach consensus on the establishment of a multilateral system for notifying and registering GIs for wines and spirits and left it as a topic for further negotiations as provided in Article 23(4) of TRIPS, the core consortium of European actors interested in creating the international register strategically shifted to WIPO to push their position.[41] This strategic forum/regime shifting is an example of the maneuvering and legal tactics adopted by state actors in the IP law-making game, when faced with limitations within a negotiating platform.[42] The Lisbon System, comprising the Lisbon Agreement and its Geneva Act, sets

---

[39] Sao Tome and Principe (10 October 2023), Senegal (10 October 2023) and Portugal (19 October 2023) are the latest contracting parties to the Geneva Act. The Geneva Act now offers protection in 21 contracting parties, covering up to 57 countries.

[40] Ruth Okediji, 'The International Intellectual Property Roots of Geographical Indications' (2007) 82(3) Chicago-Kent Law Review 1329.

[41] Dev Gangjee, 'Making a Place for Place-Based IP: WIPO and Geographical Indications' in Sam Ricketson (ed), *Research Handbook on the World Intellectual Property Organization: The First 50 Years and Beyond* (Edward Elgar, 2020), 150–69.

[42] On forum/regime shifting, see Laurence Helfer, 'Regime Shifting: The TRIPS Agreement and New Dynamics of International Intellectual Property Lawmaking' (2004) 29 Yale Journal of International Law 1; Laurence Helfer,

the legal framework to facilitate the international protection and registration of Appellations of Origin (AOs) and GIs in its 43 contracting parties, spanning 72 countries.

The Lisbon Agreement established an international registration system for AOs. In an attempt to increase its membership and reflect the recent developments, including the introduction of GIs as distinct category of IP rights in TRIPS, the Geneva Act of the Lisbon Agreement provides for the international protection and registration of both AOs and GIs.[43] With the Geneva Act, producers get enhanced market access and access to a global database on appellations of origins and GIs, while consumers gain access to traceable unique products from different parts of the world. Interestingly, unlike the TRIPS negotiations for GIs where the differing positions of the EU and US were considered, non-Lisbon Agreement contracting parties, such as the US, had no voting rights and held no leverage in the negotiations for the Geneva Act.[44] This raised questions about the fairness, inclusivity and transparency of the entire negotiations.

The Geneva Act provides for the protection of indications that include the name of a geographical area, or any designation associated with the area, effectively identifying a product as originating from that geographical area, where a given quality, reputation or other characteristic of the product is essentially attributable to its geographical origin. It introduces flexibility with regard to the implementation of its protection standards.[45] Similar to the policy space introduced in TRIPS, the Geneva Act provides for the protection of AOs and GIs through *sui generis* AOs, GI systems, trade mark systems, administrative systems or any legal means.[46] In particular, Article 13(1) of the Geneva Act safeguards prior trade marks that were applied for or registered in good faith

---

'Regime Shifting in the International Intellectual Property System' (2009) 7(1) Perspectives on Politics 39.

[43] Geneva Act, Article 2.1(ii).

[44] Daniel Gervais and Matthew Slider, 'The Geneva Act of the Lisbon Agreement: Controversial Negotiations and Controversial Results' in William van Caenegem and Jen Cleary (eds), *The Importance of Place: Geographical Indications as a Tool for Local and Regional Development* (Springer 2017), 15–46.

[45] For a detailed analysis of the Geneva Act, see Matthijs Geuze, 'Protecting Geographical Origin Brands Abroad: The Geneva Act of the Lisbon Agreement' in William van Caenegem and Jen Cleary (eds) *The Importance of Place: Geographical Indications as a Tool for Local and Regional Development* (Springer 2017), 4–13.

[46] Daniel Gervais, 'A Look at the Geneva Act of the Lisbon Agreement: A Missed Opportunity?' in Irene Calboli and Ng-Loy Wee Loon, *Geographical*

or acquired through use in good faith in a contracting party. The Geneva Act also allows for the protection and registration of trans-border AOs and GIs. If a product originates from a geographical area that extends over the territory of two adjacent contracting parties, they are allowed to file joint or separate applications to protect such products as AOs or GIs. For example, if Nigeria was a contracting party to the Lisbon System, it could file joint or separate applications with Niger under the Lisbon System to protect 'Kilishi' as an AO or GI. Kilishi is a spicy dried meat snack made from beef and infused with spices, produced in both Northern Nigeria and neighboring Niger.

Tripartite advantages of the Lisbon System are: (i) it offers a streamlined central management of AOs and GIs for all goods with a single application with WIPO in one language and one set of fees; (ii) an AO or GI remains valid as long as it is protected in the contracting party of origin with no renewal requirements and no renewal fees; (iii) it provides strong protection standards as contracting parties are required to protect registered AOs and GIs against any usurpation, imitation or accompanying terms such as 'type', 'kind', 'make', 'imitation' or the like. Furthermore, the Lisbon System prohibits any misleading practice as to the true origin of or nature of the goods.

Unlike other contested IP subject matters like plant and pharmaceutical patents, which attract global attention, IGOs do not command public attention or interventions.[47] The relative lack of public prominence in the IGO discourse can be attributed to the nature of the issues they present. Unlike topics such as access to essential food, medicines, vaccines and therapeutics which directly impact lives and health, IGOs may not typically appear to pose immediate life-threatening effects. Consequently, there tends to be a reduced sense of urgency and widespread activism surrounding GIs.[48] However, this is far from the reality as the IGO landscape not only raises crucial questions about the politics of international law-making, it also reveals contemporary social,

---

Indications at the Crossroads of Trade, Development, and Culture (Cambridge University Press 2017), 122–44.

[47] Dwijen Rangnekar, *Demanding Stronger Protection for Geographical Indications: The Relationship between Local Knowledge, Information and Reputation* (INTECH 2004), 1, 7.

[48] oriGIn (Organization for an International Geographical Indications Network) is a leading GI network. It is a global alliance of GIs from a large variety of sectors, representing about 600 associations of producers and other GI-related institutions from 40 countries. Massimo Vittori, 'The International Debate on Geographical Indications (GIs): The Point of View of the Global Coalition of GI Producers – origin' (2010) 13(2) Journal of World Intellectual Property 304.

economic, and environmental concerns, including gender roles, power asymmetries, inequalities, and climatic impacts of GI-related activities.[49]

For example, in drawing attention to the intersections of GIs and gender, the Food and Agriculture Organization of the United Nations (FAO) in its *Lessons Learned from 15 Years of FAO Work on Geographical Indications* notes that GI systems could act as a catalyst for gender equality.[50] It maintains that stakeholders could define the role of women producers and give them positions with greater decision-making power in GI value chains.[51] Similarly, it is axiomatic that climate change has profound implications on GIs.[52] It affects every stage in the cycle of GI products, from production to consumption. Changes in temperature, precipitation patterns and extreme weather events can alter the traditional growing conditions of crops, challenging the quality and unique characteristics of crop-related GI products. Variations in climate patterns can also elicit the emergence of pests and diseases threatening the sustainability of crop-related GI products. Furthermore, the production, processing and transportation of certain GI products can contribute to greenhouse gas emissions and climate change. As climate change adaptation and mitigation are global priorities, the GI sector faces the dual challenge of adjusting to a changing climate while simultaneously addressing its environmental impacts. Although these vital issues are not addressed at the international level, there is a growing trend of attempts to tackle them at regional and national levels.

---

[49] Fabio Parasecoli, 'The Gender of Geographical Indications: Women, Place and the Marketing of Identities' (2010) 10(6) Cultural Studies 467, 469; Sarah Bowen, 'Embedding Local Places in Global Spaces: Geographical Indications as a Territorial Development Strategy' (2010) 75(2) Rural Sociology 209; Rosemary Coombe and S Ali Malik, 'Transforming the Work of Geographical Indications to Decolonise Racialised Labor and Support Agroecology' (2018) 8 UC Irvine Law Review 363.

[50] Food and Agriculture Organization of the United Nations, *Using Geographical Indications to Improve Sustainability, Lessons Learned from 15 Years of FAO Work on Geographical Indications* (Rome, FAO 2023) <http://www.fao.org/3/cc3891en/cc3891en.pdf> accessed 10 October 2024.

[51] Ibid.

[52] Andrea Borghini, Nicola Piras and Beatrice Serini (n. 21).

RHETORIC VERSUS REALITY: THE POLITICS OF INTRODUCING AND MAINTAINING GEOGRAPHICAL INDICATIONS AT REGIONAL AND NATIONAL LEVELS

Amidst the ongoing contestations surrounding the international legal architecture for GIs, there is a notable shift towards regional and national arenas. Advocates of GIs, especially European actors, unswervingly endorse GIs as instrumental tools for the preservation and promotion of cultural identities, living traditions, gastronomic heritages, and socio-economic development. This narrative portrays a harmonious coexistence between cultural heritage and socio-economic development. However, the reality is manifestly different.[53] For instance, although European, African, and Asian countries are *demandeurs* for strong GI systems at the international level, the social and economic impacts of GIs on the three continents are incomparable.[54] Notably, unlike other IP rights debates, which often involve opposing stances between the Global North and Global South, the polarization on GIs is Old World versus New World.[55] Here we see the European countries as 'Old World' *demandeurs* for stronger GI systems.[56] Conversely, 'New World' countries like the US, Australia and New Zealand push back as opponents of stronger GI systems.[57] Scotland falls under the Old World category, while the US falls under the New World category. Old World typically refers to countries

---

[53] Susy Frankel, 'Geographical Indications and Mega-Regional Trade Agreements and Negotiations' in Irene Calboli and Ng-Loy Wee Loon (eds) *Geographical Indications at the Crossroads of Trade, Development and Culture: Focus on Asia-Pacific* (Cambridge University Press 2017), 147–167.

[54] Dwijen Rangnekar, 'The Pros and Cons of Stronger Geographical Indications' (2002) 6(3) Bridges 3–6; Dwijen Rangnekar, *International Protection of Geographical Indications: The Asian Experience* (Innovation and Sustainable Development Final Technical Report 2004).

[55] Jose Manuel Cortes Martin, 'The WTO TRIPS Agreement: The Battle between the Old and the New World over the Protection of Geographical Indications' (2004) 7(3) Journal of World Intellectual Property 287; Daniel Gervais, 'Irreconcilable Differences? The Geneva Act of the Lisbon Agreement and the Common Law' (2015) 53(2) Houston Law Review 341; Shujie Feng, 'Geographical Indications: Can China Reconcile the Irreconcilable Intellectual Property Issue between the EU and US?' (2020) 19 World Trade Review 424.

[56] Kal Raustiala and Stephen R Munzer, 'The Global Struggle over Geographic Indications' (2007) 18(2) European Journal of International Law 337.

[57] Dev Gangjee, 'Quibbling Siblings: Conflicts between Trade Marks and GIs' (2007) 82(3) Chicago-Kent Law Review 1253.

with long-established production traditions rooted in historical expertise and cultural heritage, while the New World refers to countries newer to the production of particular products. Producers in these countries may adopt innovative approaches or techniques, resulting in products that may have distinct characteristics, as influenced by local contexts.

As we approach the 30th anniversary of the conclusion of the Uruguay Round, the contrasting socio-economic rewards of *demandeurs* is evident at national levels.[58] The New World countries have also experienced varying degrees of socio-economic growth.[59] One of the central points to excavate from this is that 'place' and 'contextual realities' in GI sites matter.[60] Domestic contexts influence the outcomes of GI systems. Put differently, there are manifold factors required for the full realisation of the promises and risks of GIs.[61] For example, while the EU has now expanded its legal landscape for GIs to incorporate crafts and industrial products following success with the protection

---

[58] Oliver Gergaud, Florine Livat, Bradley Rickard and Frederic Warzynski, 'Evaluating the Net Benefit of Collective Reputation: The Case of Bordeaux Wine' [2017] Food Policy 8; Giulia Meloni and Johan Swinnen, 'Trade and Terroir: The Political Economy of the World's First Geographical Indication' (2018) 81 Food Policy 1; Riccardo Crescenzi, Fabrizio De Filippis, Mara Giua and Cristina Vaquero-Pinero, 'Geographical Indications and Local Development: The Strength of Territorial Embeddedness' (2022) 56(3) Regional Studies 381. See for examples around the Asia-Pacific, Irene Calboli and Ng-Loy Wee Loon, *Geographical Indications at the Crossroads of Trade, Development, and Culture* (Cambridge University Press 2017).

[59] See for example, John Overton and Warwick E Murray, 'GI Blues: Geographical Indications and Wine in New Zealand' in William van Caenegem and Jen Cleary (eds), *The Importance of Place: Geographical Indications as a Tool for Local and Regional Development* (Springer 2017), 197–220; Peter Drahos, 'Sunshine in a Bottle? Geographical Indications, the Australian Wine Industry, and the Promise of Rural Development' in Irene Calboli and Ng-Loy Wee Loon, *Geographical Indications at the Crossroads of Trade, Development, and Culture: Focus on Asia Pacific* (Cambridge University Press 2017), 259–80.

[60] Sarah Bowen, 'Development from Within? The Potential for Geographical Indications in the Global South' (2010) 13(2) Journal of World Intellectual Property; Delphine Marie-Vivien and Estelle Bienabe, 'The Multifaceted Role of the State in the Protection of Geographical Indications: A Worldwide Review' (2017) 98 World Development 1–11; Justin Hughes, 'The Limited Promise of Geographical Indications for Farmers in Developing Countries' in Irene Calboli and Ng-Loy Wee Loon (eds), *Geographical Indications at the Crossroads of Trade, Development and Culture: Focus on Asia-Pacific* (Cambridge University Press 2017), 61–86.

[61] Frankel (n. 53), 147–67.

of its food/agricultural goods and beverages, many African and Asian countries are still at nascent stages in the construction of GI laws and policies.[62]

Europe: Flourishing Geographical Indication Framework

Reflecting the increasing inclination towards regional and national law-making for GIs, particularly when there are impasses at the international level, the EU translates its international aspirations for GIs into domestic law through its multi-layered *sui generis* GI framework. The EU's GI framework includes Protected Designation of Origin (PDO) and Protected Geographical Indication (PGI) systems, which cover food, agricultural products and wines. The framework also includes a Geographical Indications of Spirit Drinks (GI) system, which as the name implies, covers spirit drinks.[63]

Products registered as PDOs are those with the strongest links to the places they are made; every part of the production, processing and preparation process must take place in a specific region. For instance, for wines to be registered as PDOs, the grapes have to be sourced exclusively from the geographical area where the wine is made. Porto or Port is a sweet, fortified wine registered as a PDO in Portugal. Only wines produced in the Douro Valley can be referred to as 'Porto'. In Case T-417/20 *Joaquim Jose Estves Lopes Granja v European Union Intellectual Property Office (EUIPO)*, the General Court considered whether a trade mark application for the registration of 'Portwo Gin' consti-

---

[62] The EU's new Regulation 2023/2411 on the Protection of Geographical Indications for Crafts and Industrial Products and amending Regulations (EU) 2017/1001 and (EU) 2019/1753 [2023] OJ L2411 entered into force on 16 November 2023.

[63] (i) Regulation (EU) No 1151/2012 on Quality Schemes for Agricultural Products and Foodstuffs [2012] OJ L343/1 (ii) Regulation (EU) 2021/2117 of the European Parliament and of the Council of 2 December 2021 amending Regulations (EU) no 1308/2013 establishing a Common Organisation of the Markets in Agricultural Products, (EU) No 1151/2012 on Quality Schemes for Agricultural Products and Foodstuffs, (EU) No 251/2014 on the Definition, Description, Presentation, Labelling and the Protection of Geographical Indications of Aromatised Wine Products and (EU) No 228/2013 Laying down Specific Measures for Agriculture in the Outermost Regions of the Union [2021] OJ L435/262, (iii) Regulation (EU) 2019/787 on the Definition, Description, Presentation and Labelling of Spirit Drinks, the Use of Names of Spirit Drinks in the Presentation and Labelling of Other Foodstuffs the Protection of Geographical Indications for Spirit Drinks, the Use of Ethyl Alcohol and Distillates of Agricultural Origin in Alcoholic Beverages, and Repealing Regulation (EC) No 110/2008 [2019] OJ L130/1.

tuted an exploitation of the reputation of the 'Porto' PDO.[64] The Court held that there was a close connection between the signs, from phonetic and visual perspective and that the Portwo sign, which Joaquim sought to register, was clearly indissociable from the earlier PDO.

PGIs emphasize the relationship between a geographic region and the name of a product, where a particular quality, reputation or other characteristic is essentially attributable to its geographical origin. To qualify as a PGI, at least one of the stages of production, processing or preparation must take place in the region. Continuing with the example of wines, a PGI status can only be granted if at least 85 per cent of the grapes used come exclusively from the geographical area where the wine is made. An example of a PGI is Dorset Blue Vinney Cheese. Dorset Blue Vinney Cheese is a lightly pressed cheese made from unpasteurized milk in the county of Dorset, England.

Geographical Indication of Spirit drinks protects the name of a spirit drink originating in a country, region or locality where the product's particular quality, reputation or other characteristic is essentially attributable to its geographical origin. Raw products do not need to come from the region, but at least one of the stages of distillation or preparation must take place in the region. For example, Scotch Whisky is registered as a Geographical Indication of Spirit in the EU. In Case C-44/17 *The Scotch Whisky Association, The Registered Office v Michael Klotz,* the Scotch Whisky Association instituted an action against Michael Klotz for marketing a whisky produced by the Waldhorn distillery in Berglen, Buchenbach valley in Swabia, Germany under the designation 'Glen Buchenbach'.[65] The label on the bottles included the following: 'Waldhornbrennerie [Waldhorn distillery], Glen Buchenbach, Swabian Single Malt Whisky, Deutsches Erzeugnis [German product], Hergestelt in den Berglen [produced in the Berglen]'. The Scotch Whisky Association asserted that the use of the term 'Glen' for the German whisky infringed the registered GI 'Scotch Whisky' as it was liable to cause consumers to make an inappropriate connection to the registered GI, and to mislead them as to the true origin of the whisky. Following referral from the Landegricht Hamburg, the Court of Justice of the European Union held that in order to decide whether there is an evocation prohibited by the EU law, the national court must determine

---

[64] Judgment of the General Court (Fifth Chamber) 6 October 2021, ECLI:EU:T:2021:663.

[65] Judgment of the Court (Fifth Chamber) 7 June 2018 in Case C-44/17, ECLI:EU:C:2018:415, Request for a Preliminary Ruling under Article 267 TFEU from Landgericht Hamburg (Regional Court, Hamburg, Germany), made by decision of 19 January 2017, received at the Court on 27 January 2017, in the proceedings *Scotch Whisky Association v Michaek Klotz.*

whether a consumer thinks directly of the protected GI 'Scotch Whisky' when they see a comparable product with the designation 'Glen'. In interpreting the scope of Geographical Indication of Spirit drinks, this case broke new ground by establishing that the conceptual proximity between a GI and the contested name can engender an evocation.[66]

The EU also has several quality schemes for food and agricultural products, with the most prominent being the Traditional Speciality Guaranteed (TSG) that highlights the traditional aspects of products, including the way the product is made or its composition, without being linked to a specific geographical area. The key function of the TSG is to safeguard traditional methods of production and recipes by helping producers of traditional products in marketing and communicating the value-adding attributes of their traditional recipes and products to consumers.[67] The registration of a product as a TSG protects it against falsification and misuse.[68] For example, Gueuze TSG is a traditional beer made mainly through spontaneous fermentation and is produced in and around Brussels, Belgium. However, as a TSG, it can be produced elsewhere.

Beyond introducing effective frameworks, the EU remains actively involved in developing its GI strategies through internal measures (within the EU) and external measures (engagement with the rest of the world). This materially contributes to the success of its GI systems. Its internal measures include supporting producers and other stakeholders in the GI value chains. Its external measures include exporting its GI preferences through bilateral and multilateral trade and economic agreements, to ensure its products are adequately protected and enforced in foreign jurisdictions. For example, at the internal level, the EU's Common Agricultural Policy (CAP) gives European farmers a competitive advantage in global markets for food/agriculture related GIs and other agricultural products.[69] CAP has a strong budget and robust funding to support its agricultural producers (€387 billion, 2021–7).[70] CAP supports farmers through three mechanisms, namely Income Support, Market Measures and Rural Development Measures.[71] Income support involves paying farmers directly to ensure income stability and renumeration for environmentally

---

[66] Ibid.
[67] EU Regulation 1151/2012 (n. 63), Article 17.
[68] Andrea Zappalaglio, 'Anatomy of Traditional Specialities Guaranteed: An Analysis of the Functioning, Limitations and (Possible) Future of the Forgotten EU Quality Scheme' (2022) 71(12) GRUR International 1147.
[69] European Commission, 'Common Agricultural Policy' <https://agriculture.ec.europa.eu/common-agricultural-policy_en> accessed 10 October 2024.
[70] Ibid.
[71] Ibid.

friendly farming. Market measures include addressing adverse market situations such as a sudden drop in demand due to health scares or fall in prices due to a temporary oversupply on the market. Rural Development Measures in national and regional programs address the needs and challenges faced in rural areas. In 2019, the EU supported its famers with €41.43 billion under income support, €2.37 billion under Market Measures and €14. 18 billion under rural development.

At the external level, strong GI protection is often a priority in EU trade talks, agreement policies and international relations. Rationales for promoting these EU GIs include market access, cultural heritage preservation and gastronationalism.[72] According to Michaela DeSoucey, gastronationalism signals 'the use of food production, distribution, and consumption to demarcate and sustain the emotive power of national attachment, as well as the use of national sentiments to produce and market food'.[73] Most EU countries have at least one GI. Nevertheless, five Southern countries: France, Greece, Italy, Portugal, and Spain, have registered the majority of EU GIs. The European Commission registered its 3,500th registered GI (Correze wines from France) in February 2023.[74] Considering the TRIPS provisions in Article 22 to 24, and the pending negotiations on extensions, in addition to forum-shifting back to WIPO, the EU incorporates its GI preferences in bilateral agreements and free trade agreements (also referred to as TRIPS Plus agreements).

The US objections to the EU's TRIPS Plus agreements includes its disagreement with the scope and type of protection afforded to IGOs, concerns regarding market access limitations or restrictions due to GI protection and debates over the validity or genericity of certain IGOs. For example, the US considers some EU GIs like Feta Cheese as generic. A product becomes generic when the name initially employed to denote it as originating from a particular

---

[72] Martijn Huysman, 'Exporting Protection: EU Trade Agreements, Geographical Indications, and Gastronationalism' (2020) 29(3) Review of International Political Economy 979; Atsujo Ichijo and Raonald Ranta, *Food, National Identity and Nationalism: From Everyday to Global Politics* (Palgrave Macmillan 2016); Atsuko Ichiji, *Food and Nationalism: Gastronationalism Revisited* (Cambridge University Press 2020).

[73] Michaela DeSoucey, 'Gastronationalism: Food Traditions and Authenticity Politics in the European Union' (2010) 75(3) American Sociological Review 432.

[74] European Commission, 'Protecting Local Food and Drinks: 3,500 Geographical Indications Registered' (23 February 2023) <https://agriculture.ec.europa.eu/news/protecting-local-food-and-drinks-3-500-geographical-indications-registered-2023-02-23_en#> accessed 20 October 2023.

geographic region can no longer be exclusively used for that product.[75] This occurs when such a name becomes customary or widely adopted, implying that it is no longer restricted to products originating from its initial place of origin. Having EU-style GI protection would affect US producers and exporters who consider EU GIs as generic. The deep divisions between the EU and US positions contributed to the crumbling of the Transatlantic Trade and Investment Partnership (TTIP). Nonetheless the EU and US have a bilateral agreement that governs trade in wine, including GIs such as Napa Valley wines.[76] The Agreement facilitates trade in wine between the parties and seeks to improve cooperation in the development and transparency of regulations affecting the trade.[77] This reflects how countries often adjust their stance on IGOs in line with parties that they seek to build trade and business partnerships with.[78]

Existing EU trade agreements that protect GIs include the EU - South Korea FTA, EU - South Africa EPA, EU - Canada CETA, and EU - Japan EPA. The EU - South Korea FTA was a watershed agreement, as it was the most comprehensive that the EU had negotiated. Importantly, its extensive coverage caters to some of the contemporary challenges associated with GIs through the introduction of a chapter on Trade and Sustainable Development that incorporates labor, environment and climate protection.[79] In the chapter, the parties commit to promoting the development of international trade in ways that contribute to sustainable development, and to integrating this commitment into every level of their trade relationship. The FTA was the EU's first trade deal with an Asian country. Similarly, the recently concluded EU - Kenya EPA on 19 June 2023, is set to be the most comprehensive and ambitious EU deal with an African country. The EPA also recognizes the importance of GIs for sustainable agriculture and rural development. Parties commit to cooperate on facilitating the

---

[75] Deborah J Kem and Lynn M Forsythe, 'Trademarks and Geographical Indications: A Case of California Champagne' (2006) 10 Chapman Law Review 257, 266.

[76] Consolidated Text: Agreement between the European Community and the United States of America on Trade in Wine (1 June 2012).

[77] Consolidated Text: Agreement between the European Community and the United States of America on Trade in Wine (1 June 2012), Article 1.

[78] Bernard O'Connor and Giulia de Bosio, 'The Global Struggle Between Europe and United States Over Geographical Indications in South Korea and in the TPP Economies' in William van Caenegem and Jen Cleary (eds), *The Importance of Place: Geographical Indications as a Tool for Local and Regional Development* (Springer 2017), 47–8.

[79] Free Trade Agreement between the European Union and its Member States, of the One Part, and the Republic of Korea of the Other Part [2011] OJ L127, Chapter 13.

identification, recognition and registration of products that could benefit from protection as GIs, including coffee and tea from Kenya.[80]

The EU promotes the effective enforcement of its GIs globally as part of its 'Strategy for the Enforcement of Intellectual Property Rights in Third Countries' through bilateral agreements.[81] This is manifest in its position in WTO-TRIPS and WIPO as discussed above. The EU consistently emphasizes the significance of GIs to its economy and the importance of ensuring market access for EU GI products worldwide and extending additional GI protection to diverse products. In contrast, countries like the US often advocate for a more cautious and limited approach to IGOs. For instance, the US disputes the protection of generic products. The EU also provides technical cooperation programs to 'help third countries *improve* their IPR systems' (emphasis added).[82] 'Improve' here means to align these countries' IGO systems with EU preferences. The EU adopts economic pressure (for example, through trade and economic partnership agreements as discussed above) and ideational power (technical cooperation programs, epistemic knowledge creation, knowledge circulation and capacity building, especially in African and Asian countries). To be sure, the EU remains crystal clear about its position on GIs. It emphasizes that GIs are key to the EU economy, and it seeks these threefold GI outcomes: (i) a multilateral register for GIs – that enhances a simple, cost-effective system of worldwide registration for GIs, (ii) the extension of additional GI protection to all products – to prohibit copying (use of style, like, type and so on), and (iii) to ensure market access for EU GI products.[83]

United Kingdom: Emerging Geographical Indication Framework

The transition period for the United Kingdom's (UK's) withdrawal from the EU (Brexit) officially ended on 31 December 2020. One of the immediate effects of this was that the EU GI system ceased to have effect in Great Britain (England, Scotland, and Wales – the EU GI regulations continue to apply in Northern Ireland due to the Northern Ireland Protocol).[84] The EU

---

[80] Economic Partnership Agreement between the Republic of Kenya, Member of the East African Community of the One Part, and the European Union and its Member States of the Other Part OJ L, 2024/1648, Articles 74 and 83.

[81] Strategy for the Enforcement of Intellectual Property Rights in Third Countries [2005] OJ C129/03.

[82] Ibid.

[83] 'Why Do Geographical Indications Matter to Us?' (European Commission, 30 July 2003) <https://ec.europa.eu/commission/presscorner/detail/en/MEMO_03 _160> accessed 10 October 2024.

[84] The EU GI system still covers GIs from Northern Ireland.

Commission also ceased oversight of the protection of GIs in Great Britain. In response, the UK established its GI system, which is managed by Department for Environment, Food and Rural Affairs (DEFRA).[85] Beyond the territorial carve-out, there are no crucial differences between the UK and EU systems. The UK Government introduced three protection schemes similar to the EU schemes outlined above: (i) PDO, (ii) PGI, and (iii) TSG. Scotch Whisky was registered as a GI under Class 2 (Whisky or Whiskey) in the UK on 31 December 2020.[86]

Similar to the EU's bilateral agreement with the US as outlined above, the UK and US have a bilateral agreement to protect certain wines (including Napa County and Oak Knoll District of Napa Valley American viticultural areas) and spirit drinks names in the UK.[87] Although these beverages are not protected as GIs, the UK committed to protecting the use of the relevant product names of these US products, enabling them to retain authenticity in the UK market. By committing to safeguarding the use of these product names, the UK ensures that only products that meet certain defined criteria or originate from specific regions in the US can use these names within the UK market. This protection serves to maintain the reputation and distinctiveness of these products, preventing unauthorized use by other producers and promoting consumer confidence in them.

Africa: Nascent Geographical Indication Framework

Despite aligning with Old World *demandeurs,* African countries have not experienced the levels of commercial successes with IGOs that their European

---

[85] Department for Environment, Food and Rural Affairs, 'Protected Geographical Food and Drink Names: UK GI Schemes' (31 December 2020) <www.gov.uk/guidance/protected-geographical-food-and-drink-names-uk-gi-schemes> accessed 10 October 2024.

[86] Department for Environment, Food and Rural Affairs, 'Scotch Whisky: Protected Spirit Drink Name' <https://www.gov.uk/protected-food-drink-names/scotch-whisky> accessed 10 October 2024.

[87] Napa County (Atlas Peak, Calistoga, Chiles Valley, Diamond Mountain District, Howell Mountain, Los Carneros, Mt. Veeder, Napa Valley, North Coast, Oak Knoll District of Napa Valley, Oakville, Rutherford, Spring Mountain District, St. Helena, Stags Leap District, Wild Horse Valley, Yountville) American Viticultural Area and Oak Knoll District of Napa Valley American Viticultural Area. Over 700 wines and 2 spirits (Bourbon Whiskey and Tennessee Whiskey) are protected in the UK <www.gov.uk/protected-food-drink-names?register%5B%5D=american-viticultural-areas&status%5B%5D=registered> accessed 10 October 2024.

counterparts have.[88] IP regimes in Africa are mainly governed through intergovernmental institutions, the two main ones being the African Intellectual Property Organisation (OAPI) and African Regional Intellectual Property Organisation (ARIPO).[89] OAPI is a member of the Geneva Act of the Lisbon Agreement (it acceded to the Geneva Act on 15 December 2022, the Act entered into force on 15 March 2023).[90] OAPI's Bangui Agreement Relating to the Creation of an African Intellectual Property Organisation (Bangui Agreement) provides two options for the protection of GIs: collective marks and *sui generis* GI systems.[91] Under the provisions of the Bangui Agreement, groups or associations of producers within OAPI member states can collectively register and protect a mark that signifies a certain geographical origin and specific qualities or reputation associated with products originating from that region.[92] This method allows these groups to collectively promote and protect their products' geographical identity. Additionally, the Bangui Agreement offers the option of a *sui generis* system for the protection of GIs. Like the EU GI framework, this alternative involves the establishment of a unique system tailored to the protection of GIs within OAPI member states. OAPI operates a single regional registration system through its office in Yaounde, Cameroon. Violet de Galmi and Tchoukou du Niger (from Niger) are protected as collective marks; Poivre de Penja and Miel blanc d'Oku (from Cameroon) are protected as *sui generis* GIs.

On the other hand, ARIPO's Banjul Protocol on Marks provides for the protection of GIs through certification or collective marks.[93] While ARIPO does

---

[88] Titilayo Adebola, 'The Legal Construction of Geographical Indications in Africa' (2023) 26(1) Journal of World Intellectual Property 3.

[89] Caroline Ncube, *Intellectual Property in Africa: Harmonising Administration and Policy* (2nd edn, Routledge 2023).

[90] However, not all African countries are members of these organizations. For example, Nigeria and South Africa are not members of either organisation.

[91] Bangui Agreement Relating to the Creation of an African Intellectual Property Organisation, Constituting a Revision to the Agreement Relating to the Creation of an African and Malagasy Office of Industrial Property (Bangui Central African Republic, 2 March 1977), Articles 2.2 and Annex VI on Geographical Indications.

[92] Ibid.

[93] Banjul Protocol on Marks Adopted by the Administrative Council at Banjul, the Gambia on 19 November 1993 and amended on 28 November 1997, 26 May 1998, 26 November 1999, 21 November 2003, 25 November 2013, 17 November 2015, 22 November 2017, 23 November 2018, 20 November 2019, 26 August 2021, 8 December 2021 and 25 November 2022. There are 13 contracting parties to the Banjul Protocol on Marks: Botswana, Cape Verde, Eswatini, The Gambia,

not have a *sui generis* GI system in force, with the support of the EU, ARIPO has commenced discussions on designing and introducing its *sui generis* GI Protocol.[94] Applicants seeking to protect GIs through certification or collective marks can file a single application either through a Banjul Protocol contracting state or through the ARIPO Office in Harare, Zimbabwe. Mukono Vanilla is registered as an IGO through Uganda's Trade Marks system.

Although African countries have a plethora of unique place-based products that could be successfully marketed globally, many of these products are not formally protected as GIs for several reasons including underdeveloped or inadequately enforced legal frameworks for GIs, lack of awareness of the potential benefits of GIs, limited financial resources to develop and maintain GI regimes and prioritization of other pressing socio-economic challenges such as poverty, healthcare, and infrastructure development.[95] Indeed, in many African countries, unique place-based products are socially named after their origins. For example, *Dodo Ikire*, a conically shaped savory snack made with plantains, pepper, oil and salt, is named after the town where it originated – Ikire, in Osun State, South West Nigeria. However, *Dodo Ikire* is not a registered IGO. In fact, like 70 per cent of African countries, Nigeria does not have any registered IGOs. There are only about 200 registered African GIs around the continent.[96] These IGOs are registered through (certification and collective) marks and *sui generis* systems. Argane (from Morocco), registered in 2021, was the first registered African GI. About 15 other countries have gone on to register diverse unique food, agricultural products, crafts and beverages, including Kenya which has three for coffee, tea, and Taita baskets registered under its trade marks system.[97] The few products that are protected have not

---

Lesotho, Liberia, Malawi, Mozambique, Namibia, Sao Tome and Principe, Uganda, United Republic of Tanzania and Zimbabwe.

[94] African Regional Intellectual Property Organisation (ARIPO), 'ARIPO Member States Discuss GI Protection Approach' (ARIPO 2023) <https:// www .aripo .org/ success -stories/ aripo -member -states -discuss -gi -protection -approach -2927> accessed 10 October 2024.

[95] Chidi Oguamanam and Teshager Dagne, 'Geographical Indication (GI) Options for Ethiopian Coffee and Ghanaian Cocoa' in Jeremy De Beer, Chris Armstrong, Chidi Oguamanam and Tobias Schonwetter, *Innovation and Intellectual Property: Collaborative Dynamics in Africa* (UCT Press and GIZ 2014), 77–108.

[96] Monique Bagal, Massimo Vittori and Luis Fernando Samper, *Manual for Geographical Indications in Africa* (Intellectual Property Rights and Innovation in Africa AfrIPI, EUIPO European Union Intellectual Property Office April 2023).

[97] Ibid.

generated the full potential of endogenous social and economic development that GI protagonists promise, and there are several reasons for this.

While as WTO members, many African countries have shifted to registration-based forms of protection based on obligations to protect GIs as established under TRIPS. IP rights were not the priority for these countries when they joined the WTO. Many African countries joined the WTO to gain improved market access conditions for agricultural products, amongst others.[98] Indeed, many of these countries inherited IP right systems from colonial administrations and had limited expertise (especially in government institutions responsible for law and policy making) of the foreign IP systems foisted on them during the colonial era.[99] In the years following the end of formal colonization, although African decolonization activists pushed for Pan-Africanism, which led to the establishment of the Organisation for African Unity (now African Union), many former colonial administrators retained strong control to safeguard the commercial benefits derived from their former colonies. As Carolyn Deere notes, 'the legacy of French influence on the structure and legal systems in general, and on IP laws specifically, continued'.[100] France also encouraged the establishment of a regional IP institution for Francophone Africa – OAPI – which prompted the fragmentation of IP rights governance in Africa. ARIPO was subsequently established to provide a platform for collaborations and cooperation for Anglophone African countries. This division, based on linguistic affiliations, has created separate but parallel structures for IP management and cooperation among Francophone and Anglophone African nations.

With support from the EU and other international organizations like the FAO, the African Union adopted a Continental Strategy on Geographical Indications in Africa 2018 – 2023 (Continental Strategy).[101] The Continental Strategy sets out a roadmap to support African countries and intergovernmental institutions with the development, protection and promotion of GIs in Africa.[102] Its vision for the future of GIs in Africa is an improved enabling environment

---

[98] Multilateral Trade Negotiations Uruguay Round, 'Communication from Nigeria' (MTN.TNC/W/86 28 August 1991) <https://docs.wto.org/gattdocs/q/UR/TNC/W86.PDF> accessed 10 October 2023.

[99] Adebola (n. 88).

[100] Carolyn Deere, *The Implementation Game: The TRIPS Agreement and the Global Politics of Intellectual Property Reform in Developing Countries* (Oxford University Press 2009), 250.

[101] African Union Commission Department of Rural Economy and Agriculture, 'Continental Strategy for Geographical Indications in Africa 2018 – 2023' (African Union 2018).

[102] Ibid.

for GIs that fosters sustainable rural development and increases food security.[103] As I argue elsewhere, African countries can benefit immensely from GI protection.[104] Although they were not active formulators of the GI orthodoxies, African countries can effectively participate in the GI implementation game by tailoring it to suit their interests. As an illustration, several countries across the continent produce traditional alcoholic beverages; examples include Apeteshi from Ghana and Ogogoro from Nigeria. These beverages could be standardized, branded, and protected as GIs. Similarly, several African countries cultivate and produce coffee beans. In addition to Kenya, notable coffee-producing countries in Africa include Ethiopia, Uganda, Tanzania, Rwanda, Ivory Coast and Burundi.

Furthermore, the recently established African Continent Free Trade Area(AfCFTA), which seeks to promote economic integration and create a unified market for Africa offers a platform for African countries to leverage GIs as a tool for socio-economic development and to support local industries, while preserving and promoting Africa's rich heritage and diverse products.[105] As African countries are in the early stages of realizing the socio-economic promises of GIs, they can draw valuable lessons on the subject from their European counterparts and apply them in ways that are contextually appropriate. In light of the AfCFTA and its extensive continent-wide free trade area, African countries can strategically integrate GIs as a fundamental component of bilateral agreements.

CONCLUSION

Thanks to globalization, advertising and marketing, consumers are increasingly willing to pay a premium for GIs. Consumer choices are influenced by wide-ranging factors, including the desire for authentic products and the traceability of these products. Modern consumers are especially curious about 'where' and 'how' products are produced. Moreover, international trade has contributed to de-localizing consumer choices and facilitating access to products in distant places.[106] The recognition and valorization of provenance are driven by IP and related frameworks at international, regional, and national levels. In particular, WIPO plays a crucial role as the principal international

---

[103] Ibid.
[104] Titilayo Adebola, 'Geographical Indications in the Era of the African Continental Free Trade Area (AfCFTA)' (2022) 17(9) Journal of Intellectual Property Law and Practice 748.
[105] Ibid.
[106] Hughes (n. 22), 300.

organization for proselytizing GIs. Through WIPO's norm setting, GIs have evolved from an arcane French and European concept to a firmly entrenched registration-based and enforcement-backed category of IP rights in the WTO's TRIPS. Yet, unlike other categories of IP rights in TRIPS such as patents, trade marks and copyright, which generally have similar legal rules at national levels, national GI regimes vary. As collective rights anchored on 'place' (or origin of products), state and international actors usually facilitate the introduction and implementation of GI regimes at national levels. This chapter critically examines the current GI architecture at international, regional and national levels, and highlights key contemporary developments therein.

15. Legal Protection of Scotch Whisky, Napa Valley AVA and Coffee Kenya by Distinctive Signs in the Digital Market[1]

Pilar Montero

PRELIMINARY CONSIDERATIONS

We are currently living in an economy in which consumers are more concerned about the products they buy, and they require more information about the composition of the products, their production processes and other characteristics. Therefore, certain products with a tradition and special characteristics, such as Scotch Whisky, Napa Valley AVA wines and Coffee Kenya, need to inform consumers about the specific characteristics, in order to avoid consumers being disappointed and to assure them that they are paying for a product that respects a certain production process linked to a tradition and traditional know-how. The geographical origin of products is very important for consumers, as they do not want to be misled about the production areas of the products they purchase. The reasons may be, for example, to support a region, a country, or a particular community. Frequently, the desire to buy products from a certain region is also driven by the knowledge that some regions preserve ancestral experience and know-how regarding particular production techniques. This is usually known by consumers, who want to obtain a product with the characteristics and quality they expect. In this regard, a European Union Intellectual Property Office (EUIPO) study shows that Scotch Whisky is among the top

---

[1] The work for this chapter has been financed by the research project for groups recognized as research groups of excellence, entitled: 'Protection of innovation in agriculture in the digital age' (Gen. Valenciana Prometeo Excellence Research Group Projects: CIPROM/2021/57). Lead Professors: Esperanza Gallego and Nuria Fernandez.

10 Geographical Indications (GIs), representing 28% of the sales in European Union (EU).[2]

For these unique products it is important to communicate their characteristics to consumers, and to avoid intellectual property (IP) infringements, both in the physical world and especially in the digital environment. A good system to help communicate this information to consumers is through the use of distinctive signs that are incorporated into products to indicate not just their commercial origin but also the quality, geographical origin and other related information. In this regard it is interesting to consider the possibility of using trade marks, namely certification and/or collective marks, and also GIs, depending on the countries and the legal tools provided by the different legislations.

Even if we have different definitions in each country, we can see that certification or guarantee marks are signs capable of distinguishing goods or services which are certified by the proprietor of the mark regarding characteristics (such as material, mode of manufacture of goods or performance of services, quality, accuracy and so on) from goods and services which are not so certified.[3] Collective marks are signs capable of distinguishing the goods or services of the members of the association, owner of the mark, from those of other undertakings.[4] GIs are a distinctive sign with more differences between countries. First of all because GIs are not specifically protected in all the countries at the international level, yet in the last ten years we can see important development of this kind of protection in several countries. See for instance the last Philippines Law.[5] Considering a common legal definition, a GI is a distinctive sign consisting in a name which identifies a product originating in a specific geographical place whose given quality, reputation or other characteristic is essentially attributable to its geographical origin, and some of the production steps of which take place in the defined geographical area.

Those signs refer to characteristics particularly important for products coming from particular places, and with specific characteristics. This quality is largely determined by the production process, the raw materials, the geographical origin, the controls carried out, the accepted and prohibited techniques,

---

[2] European Union Intellectual Property Office, 'Infringement of Protected Geographical Indications for Wine, Spirits, Agricultural Products and Foodstuffs in the European Union' (2016), 28.

[3] Regulation (EU) 2017/1001 of the European Parliament and of the Council of 14 June 2017 on the European Union trade mark (codification) [2017] OJ L154/1 (EUTMR). Definition of a collective mark, art. 83(1).

[4] EUTMR (n 3), Definition of a collective mark, art. 74(1).

[5] 'Rules and Regulations on Geographical Indications in Philippines' (GI-RR) issued on 5 October 2022.

packaging requirements and other characteristics that make it possible to offer consumers a final product in which the consumer has the guarantee that they are buying a unique product.

The rationale for protecting this type of product is based on the convenience of protecting the collective investment made by certain communities in enhancing the value of their traditions, as well as their adaptation to the modern marketplace. In order to be able to identify these products with added value in the market, it is appropriate for them to be marked with signs that differentiate them from others that do not meet these certified quality requirements and therefore lack this added value.

The need to promote distinctive quality signs is an increasing trend, both in the interest of consumers and producers and additionally to avoid unjustified distortions in international trade,[6] in a real and digital environment. A key question may be to determine whether the digital market raises new challenges or has particular characteristics to which the rules of the physical market may not always be suitable.

With the aim of identifying the best strategies for protecting these unique products, Scotch Whisky, Napa Valley AVA wines and Coffee Kenya coffees, in the digital market, it is useful to review the main existing distinctive signs as quality indicators, their legal regime, as well as the challenges they face in the digital market.

TYPES OF DISTINCTIVE SIGNS THAT IDENTIFY TRADITIONAL AND UNIQUE PRODUCTS

The definition of quality is not easy, as it is a broad concept with different meanings and can be both objective and subjective.[7] Quality can refer to the nature, characteristics, or requirements of a product. Furthermore, this definition can take into consideration the composition of the products, the tradition,

---

[6] Pilar Montero García-Noblejas, 'Towards a core unitary legal regime for Geographical Indications in the European Union digital market' (2021) 14(4-5) Journal of Intellectual Property Law & Practice 427; Dominique P Barjolle, 'Geographical Indications and protected designations of origin: intellectual property tools for rural development objectives' in Dev S Gangjee (ed), *Research Handbook on Intellectual Property and Geographical Indications* (Edward Elgar 2016), 440; Stefano Sandri, *La nuova disciplina della Proprietà Industriale dopo i GATT-TRIPS* (Cedam 1996), 47.

[7] Norbert Olszak, *Droit des appellations d'origine et indications de provenance* (Tec et Doc 2001), 70.

their origin, safety, or health characteristics.[8] In this chapter we will consider quality in its first meaning, that is referring to the conformity of a product to certified characteristics.[9] Therefore, distinctive signs of quality must have as a common denominator that the products using the signs must fulfil specific certified common characteristics, and consequently their quality will also be uniform and guaranteed. Quality is often linked to reputation or renown, but the two terms should not be confused, although they are clearly related.[10] Reputation is not always determined by higher quality, nor does quality alone lead to reputation.

The aim of this chapter is to analyze the best system to protect special products with a particular quality and a unique reputation due to their history and tradition, such as Scotch Whisky, Napa Valley AVA wines, and Coffee Kenya coffee, in the market and particularly in the digital market. Those special products typically eligible for protection by GIs deserve particular protection, because they embody an added value that cannot be replaced.[11] Those products are the result of a cultural heritage, in which the roots of the people are manifested, and this is something that cannot be invented.

The story of Scotch Whisky begins as early as the 15th century, and the earliest documented record of distilling in Scotland occurred in 1494 in the tax records of the day, the Exchequer Rolls. Scotch Whisky is world-renowned

---

[8] Giovanni Antonia Grippiotti, 'Designazioni d'origine, indicazioni geografiche e attestazioni di specificita' [1994] Riv dir ind 553.

[9] ISO 9000 Standard definition: *'Quality: degree to which a set of inherent characteristics (differentiating feature) meets the requirements (established need or expectation, usually implicit or mandatory)'*.

[10] The different meanings of the term quality in the Dictionary of the Royal Spanish Academy, are: 1. Property or set of properties inherent to something, which allow its value to be judged; 2. Good quality, superiority or excellence. According to the Oxford English Dictionary the definition is: (originally) 'the nature, kind, or character (of something)'; (later) 'the standard or nature of something as measured against other things of a similar…'

[11] Regulation (EU) No 1151/2012 of 21 November 2012 on quality schemes for agricultural products and foodstuffs [2012] OJ L343/1 Recital 1:
> The quality and diversity of the Union's agricultural, fisheries and aquaculture production is one of its important strengths, giving a competitive advantage to the Union's producers and making a major contribution to its living cultural and gastronomic heritage. This is due to the skills and determination of Union farmers and producers who have kept traditions alive while taking into account the developments of new production methods and material.

See also Recital 6 Regulation (EU) 2024/1143 of 11 April 2024 on geographical indications for wine, spirit drinks and agricultural products, as well as traditional specialities guaranteed and optional quality terms for agricultural products.

for its unique flavour and the key to its success lies in the fact that has been produced and matured in Scotland in oak casks for a minimum of three years, from distilleries located in the designated regions.[12] The Napa Valley has always had grapevines, although it was not until 1824 that the area began to be used to grow grapes for wine production.[13] Napa Valley is one of the most famous wine regions in the United States (US). Finally, the history of Kenya coffee began in the late 1800s thanks to the activities of the missionaries. This coffee is ranked as one of the best coffees in the world. Nowadays, approximately six million Kenyans make their livelihoods in the coffee sector.[14]

If we look at the existing distinctive signs, we can see that quality as a function is protected and required by regulation and can be found in guarantee or certification marks and in GIs. In these signs, quality guarantee is not a de facto function or a possible function, but a function required and protected by the regulations.[15] Quality is the element determining the protection. In these distinctive signs, quality will have positive and negative content. Therefore, the goods must fulfil controlled characteristics. Quality derives directly from compliance with a set of rules of use or specifications that must be met during production.[16] And the information transmitted to the consumer is exactly the existence of a certain quality that derives from the unique characteristics and history. The information provided will not inform the consumer of the commercial origin of the product, but the geographical origin that is the basis for this quality. In this regard, the aroma and flavour of Scotch Whisky derive from the distillation of a fermented substrate, made from malted barley with or without other cereals, followed by maturation in oak casks. The characteristics are dependent on the specific distillery processes used and the subsequent maturation. There is a wide range of aromas and flavors in individual Scotch Whiskies. The main factors which distinguish Scotch Whisky are: the differences in the production process, including differences reflected in the legal definitions; the geography, geology and climate of Scotland; and the skills and

---

[12] Julie Bower, 'Scotch Whisky: History, Heritage and the Stock Cycle' (2016) 2(11) Beverages 3-4.

[13] Anil Hira and Tim Swartz, 'What Makes Napa Napa? The Roots of Success in the Wine Industry' (2014) 3(1) Wine Economics and Policy 14.

[14] Monique Bagal et al., *Study on the potential of marketing of Kenyan Coffee as Geographical Indication* (iram and European Commission 2013), 1.

[15] Carlos Fernández Novoa, *Tratado sobre derecho de marcas* (Marcial Pons 2004), 679.

[16] Alberto Francisco Ribeiro De Almeida, *Autonomia Jurídica da Denominação de Origem. Uma perspectiva transnacional. Uma garantia de qualidade* (Wolters Kluwer Coimbra editora 2010), 735 and 750.

know-how of the distiller and the blender.[17] Coffee from Kenya has specific characteristics because coffee requires specific temperature, rainfall, and altitude conditions that limit the growing region to tropical areas. Kenya has the reputation to grow one of the finest Arabica coffees in the world. Basic natural factors explain the typicality of this coffee resulting in a unique national coffee. The main regulatory body (Coffee Board of Kenya) is implementing a national branding strategy aimed at gaining value from this comparative advantage. Additionally, distinctive qualities appear at the regional levels depending on the type of soils, the altitude, and human practices.[18] Within the Napa Valley AVA, regions have been recognized that possess distinct microclimates and terrain that imprint recognizable characteristics on the grapes grown there.[19]

Sometimes operators make the choice to use individual trade marks to protect unique and quality products. But this is not the best choice because it is not aligned with the main trade mark function as an indicator of commercial origin. The use of an individual trade mark for Scotch Whisky or Coffee Kenya as a guarantee sign may not ensure the real and effective use of the sign required for the trade mark enforcement.[20] This is because, in order to preserve the trade mark right, the law requires proof of genuine use, and this use should be in connection with the essential function of the trade mark. In addition, there may be disadvantages in trying to register such a sign, because it is very likely to fall foul of one of the grounds for refusal set out in trade mark law, in particular as regards restrictions on the registration of misleading, descriptive or generic signs. Absolute grounds for trade mark refusal are designed to protect the public interest, and to prevent the appropriation of words that should be freely available to all competitors. For this reason, in Spain the word mark 'Canar Y Wine' for wines from the Canary Islands has been cancelled. The judge considered that this trade mark infringes the absolute grounds for refusal, and that it is not possible to grant such a broad monopoly, which would be contrary to competition law, as it would otherwise grant a very strong competitive advantage to a single economic operator.[21]

Collective marks are similar to individual marks since they identify a commercial origin. However, in this case, the commercial origin must always

---

[17] Geographical indication to be registered: 'Scotch Whisky', Technical document.
[18] Bagal et al. (n 14), 20.
[19] 'Napa Valley Appellations' (Visit Napa Valley) <http://www.visitnapavalley.com/wineries/appellations/> accessed 3 May 2024.
[20] Case C-689/15 *W.F. Gözze Frottierweberei GmbH, Wolfgang Gözze v Verein Bremer Baumwollbörse* ECLI:EU:C:2017:434.
[21] Case of the Commercial Law Court of Las Palmas de Gran Canaria, Number 372, 19 November 2021.

be a collective.[22] That is why they are trade marks in which the owner is usually an association. But this will depend on the tradition of each country with regard to legal persons. These trade marks, in addition to identifying the business origin, generally also communicate common characteristics of the products or services, which are the result of the fact of belonging to that collective. For instance, the EU collective mark 'fnsea' (000861120) registered for services relating to the protection of the professional interests of farmers. Collective marks can be a good complement to GIs, since they differentiate the products that come from a producer association. A collective mark could differentiate products fulfilling the product specification of a GI and coming from a particular producer's association. As for instance the EU collective mark: 'QUESO MANCHEGO Consejo Regulador de la Denominación de Origen' (014260293) for cheeses protected with the registered designation of origin queso manchego. In these cases, it is very important to avoid any confusion between the GI and the collective mark, as they have different functions.

Guarantee or certification marks are a distinctive sign having particular characteristics compared to individual trade marks, as the function indicating the commercial origin is secondary to the function indicating the quality of the products or services, which is more prominent.[23] However, this function as an indicator of quality is different from the function that can be found in individual trade marks.[24] Certification marks fulfil the function of giving certainty or a guarantee to third parties as to compliance with certain characteristics or attributes present in the goods or services. It is this primacy of the certifying function that explains why they are known as 'certification marks' or 'guarantee marks'.[25]

Certification or guarantee marks have some similarities with collective marks, however, both types of signs must be differentiated. Otherwise, there is a risk of misuse of these IP rights, creating problems for protection.

---

[22] EUTMR (n 3), art. 74 and UK Trade Mark Act 1994, s. 49.

[23] Jeffrey Belson, *Certification Marks* (Sweet & Maxwell 2002), 5; Giulio Enrico Sironi, 'Marchio colletivo' in Adriano Vanzetti and Giulio Enrico Sironi (eds), *Codice della Proprieta Industriale* (Giuffré Editore 2013),163.

[24] Fernández Novoa (n 15), 679.

[25] Directive (EU) 2015/2436 of the European Parliament and of the Council of 16 December 2015 to approximate the laws of the Member States relating to trade marks (recast) [2015] OJ L336/1, art. 27:
> "guarantee or certification mark" means a trade mark which is described as such when the mark is applied for and is capable of distinguishing goods or services which are certified by the proprietor of the mark in respect of material, mode of manufacture of goods or performance of services, quality, accuracy or other characteristics, from goods and services which are not so certified.

As far as similarities are concerned, both types of trade marks have a common denominator, namely the fact that they are signs intended to be used in a uniform manner by different persons, following rules laid down in regulations for use. Furthermore, in some countries, guarantee marks are a type of collective mark.[26] However, unlike certification marks, collective marks are usually the private property of a group or, in case of legal persons governed by public law, taking into account the essential function of collective marks (that is to distinguish the goods or services of the members of the association that is the proprietor of the mark from those of other undertakings), have to be either associations in a formal sense or need to have an internal structure of an associative nature.[27]

Moreover, collective marks are signs whose essential function is to inform the consumer of the commercial origin, even if they additionally inform consumers about a common quality or characteristic. The owner of the collective mark has the freedom to define the rules of use, without any legal obligation to guarantee the existence of special qualities or characteristics. The relevant information required by law is that the consumer knows that the product comes from an undertaking that is also a member of an association. In addition, the association can normally also use the trade mark, because there is no conflict of interest, unlike with certification marks. With certification marks, the owner cannot use the sign as a trade mark to avoid conflict of interest. This is because with certification marks it is the trade mark owner who is responsible for the control of the certified products and it cannot control its own products. In addition, with collective marks, the association is free to determine who can become a member of the association, and this is different from the legal regime for guarantee or certification marks, where there is no association, and where those who respect the regulations of use cannot be excluded from using the trade mark.

GIs are another type of distinctive sign designed to protect producers from usurpation of the positive reputation acquired by their products, usually derived from a long tradition.[28] They have a function which is to some extent similar to certification marks, as they play a role as an indicator of quality from

---

[26] This was the case before the reform in French and Portuguese law, see Code de la Propriété Intellectuelle, art. L715-1, and Código da Propriedade Industrial, art. 230. This is still the case in some countries such as Morocco : loi no 17-97 relative à la protection de la propriété industrielle.

[27] *Trade Mark and Design Guidelines* (EUIPO 2021), Chapter 15 'European Union collective marks', Chapter 2 'Ownership'.

[28] Pilar Montero García-Noblejas, *Denominaciones de origen e indicaciones geográficas* (Marcial Pons 2016). Regulation (EU) No 1151/2012 (n 11).

both a socio-economic and a legal point of view.[29] They are signs ensuring the existence of constant common characteristics and a certain level of quality.[30] However, they are unique because they require that the common requirements to be certified should be specifically linked to a geographical origin, usually with a tradition and/or reputation.

For instance, Scotch Whisky has been distilled and matured in Scotland for more than 500 years and has been exported from Scotland for around 200 years. There are several factors demonstrating the link between Scotch Whisky and the geographical area and reputation. It is important to highlight as natural factors in the geographical area, the geology and geography of Scotland. The climate of Scotland also has a significant effect on the character of Scotch Whisky. Water is also another important element, as is one of the three natural raw materials of Scotch Whisky. Scotch Whisky distilleries have always been built where there is a good reliable source of water of a particular quality, and distilleries frequently own the source of their water to ensure a continuous supply and that it remains pure and uncontaminated. Peat also still plays an important role in the production of Scotch Whisky and its flavor. Scotch Whisky is made with malted barley, with or without other cereals, yeast, and water. Each malt whisky distillery has its own unique copper stills. It is scientifically established that the different shapes of the stills lead to differences in the flavor of the Scotch Whiskies produced. The distiller is responsible for ensuring that only the best quality spirit is filled into cask for maturation to become Scotch Whisky. The type and quality of casks used to mature Scotch Whisky then have a significant effect on the quality and character of the final product.

Furthermore, with GIs this origin must be decisive for the quality or characteristics distinguishing the product.[31] It is this link with the territory and the existence of a proven tradition that constitute the essential elements for confirming the legal independence of GIs.[32] These distinctive signs are also sometimes used as a special tool to promote the interests of the common agricultural policy, to the extent that they are used to protect unique products that are fundamental to a country's economy. GIs therefore enjoy a higher level

---

[29] Fernández Novoa (n 15), 679.

[30] Paul Godstein, *Copyright, Patent, Trademark and Related State Doctrines* (Foundation Press 1993), 256ff.

[31] Caroline Le Goffic, *La protection des indications géographiques* (LexisNexis 2011).

[32] Ribeiro De Almeida (n 16), 796–7. See extensively on the differences Dev Gangjee , *Relocating the Law of Geographical Indications* (Cambridge University Press 2012), 291ff.

of protection than trade marks.[33] They are, for that reason, the best system for protecting products such as Scotch Whisky, Napa Valley AVA wines, and Coffee Kenya coffees.

CHALLENGES FOR QUALITY SIGNS IN THE DIGITAL MARKET

Interferences between Quality Signs and Domain Names

Quality signs, both trade marks and GIs, may be in conflict with other distinctive signs such as domain names. Such a conflict may arise where a domain name is registered with the words Scotch Whisky, Napa Valley or Coffee Kenya by a person without legitimate authority to do so.

In these cases, registering a trade mark is the best way to protect these unique products against domain name registration or cybersquatting. This is because a trade mark offers the only possibility to protect these products in situations of conflict between GI and domain name registration, under the World Intellectual Property Organization's (WIPO's) Uniform Domain Name Dispute Resolution Policy (UDRP).[34] This policy requires the existence of an earlier trade mark with a legitimate interest and a domain name that is identical or confusingly similar to the trade mark. It requires that the third party that has registered the domain name has no legitimate rights in the domain name, and in addition that the domain name has been registered and used in bad faith.

It would be desirable for GIs to have the same protection as trade marks vis-à-vis domain names. This is because they are distinctive signs that protect collective interests and are of great benefit to regions. A practical example of this situation was the Gorgonzola case dealt with by the WIPO Arbitration and Mediation Center.[35] The consortium for the protection of Gorgonzola cheese, protected as a GI (in this case a protected designation of origin), obtained the transfer of the domain name 'gorgonzola.best'. However, this result was not achieved on the basis of the GI registered in the EU: 'GORGONZOLA', but on the basis of a previously registered word trade mark 'GORGONZOLA'.

---

[33] See the text below at 'Interferences between Quality Signs and Domain Names'.

[34] Michael Blakeney, *The Protection of Geographical Indications* (Edward Elgar 2019), 418, which highlights that this possibility of extending the UDRP to GIs was considered premature because of the lack of global harmonization of international GI norms.

[35] *Consorzio per la Tutela del Formaggio Gorgonzola v WhoisGuard, Inc. / John Tattersall* [2019] WIPO Case No D2019-2848.

In Spanish national jurisprudence the Madrid Court of Appeal issued a favorable decision in the 'La Champanera' case. In this case an enterprise used the term 'Champanera' to designate wedding services on a website with the domain name <lachampanera.es>. The Madrid Court of Appeal considered that the use of the expression 'La Champanera' used by the defendant to identify itself on the market, both in e-commerce, its professional blog and in its activity as a communications, public relations and corporate events management agency, triggered in the mind of an average European consumer a sufficiently strong link with the protected GI 'Champagne' (in this case a protected designation of origin).[36] The reason was the phonetic and visual similarity between the protected name of the plaintiff and the name used by the defendant in its commercial activities. The use included the partial incorporation of the translation of the protected name into Spanish, not very different from the original protected name. For a consumer, the evocation of the designation of origin 'Champagne' is, in such circumstances, practically unavoidable, even if the defendant does not use it for the same kind of product. Following the court decision, the fact that it was a domain name referring to different goods did not prevent the existence of unfair advantage. In this case, the domain name takes advantage of the reputational aura surrounding the Champagne appellation of origin that is evoked, even if not by means of unfair competition.[37] Moreover, the court recalled that competitive disloyalty was not necessary for a successful action for infringement of the GI.

A similar problem occurred with the domain name <dutchtequila.nl> used to sell a Dutch spirit drink without using real tequila. In this case the domain name was modified to the current <dutchgenquila.nl/> taking into account that the GI 'Tequila' is registered as a protected GI at EU level.[38]

In order to avoid these problems, the regulations on GIs have been amended to try to achieve more effective protection in the digital market.[39] In the Regulation on EU GIs for wine, spirit drinks and agricultural products, and

---

[36] *Audiencia Provincial de Madrid*, Case: 62/2022, 4 February 2022.

[37] See Regulation (EU) No 1308/2013 of the European Parliament and of the Council of 17 December 2013 establishing a common organisation of the markets in agricultural products and repealing Council Regulations (EEC) No 922/72, (EEC) No 234/79, (EC) No 1037/2001 and (EC) No 1234/2007 [2013] OJ L347/671, art. 103(2)(b).

[38] 'eAmbrosia: The EU Geographical Indications Register' (European Commission) <https:// ec .europa .eu/ agriculture/ eambrosia/ geographical -indications-register/> accessed 3 May 2024. Registered name: Tequila.

[39] See about this reform Pilar Montero García-Noblejas, "Análisis crítico de las reformas del sistema de indicaciones geográficas de la Unión Europea", (2023), 104 LA LEY mercantil; Alberto Ribeiro de Almeida, "Reforma euro-

quality schemes for agricultural products, there is a specific article on the protection of GIs against domain names.[40] Regulations provide also that EU TLD registries shall ensure that any alternative dispute resolution procedure established to solve disputes relating to the registration of domain names shall recognize GIs as rights that may prevent a domain name from being registered or used in bad faith. The EUIPO could establish and manage a domain name information and alert system that would provide the applicant with information about the availability of the GI as a domain name and, on an optional basis, the registration of a domain name identical to their GI.

In Regulation 2023/2411 of 18 October 2023 on the protection of GIs for artisanal and industrial products, an article has been introduced to approach GIs in a similar way to trade marks as regards their protection against domain names in alternative dispute resolution procedures. As explained earlier, in the WIPO UDRP it is possible to reclaim a domain name that unfairly targets a trade mark, but only a trade mark. In this regard, the new regulation provides that Registries of TLDs established in the EU shall ensure that any alternative dispute resolution procedures concerning domain names recognize registered GIs as a right that may be invoked in such procedures.[41]

Protecting Quality Signs in the Digital Platform Economy

An additional important area where there is a significant risk for the protection of quality signs in the digital market is their unlawful use in digital marketplaces, characterized by platform intermediation. In this context, it is appropriate to refer to recent EU laws: the Digital Markets Act and the Digital

---

peia do regime jurídico das indicaçaoes geográficas", (2024) 1 Revista de Direito Intelectual.

[40] Regulation (EU) 2024/1143 of 11 April 2024 on geographical indications for wine, spirit drinks and agricultural products, as well as traditional specialities guaranteed and optional quality terms for agricultural products, art. 35.

[41] Regulation (EU) 2023/2411 of the European Parliament and of the Council of 18 October 2023 on the protection of geographical indications for craft and industrial products and amending Regulations (EU) 2017/1001 and (EU) 2019/1753 [2023] OJ L, art. 46 (Protection of the rights of geographical indications in domain names). See about this reform Pilar Montero García-Noblejas, "Protección de las denominaciones de origen y las indicaciones geográficas: referencia especial a los productos agroalimentarios", (2020), Problemas actuales de Derecho de la Propiedad Industrial, Tecnos, Madrid. and Pilar Montero García-Noblejas "Estudio sobre la regulación de las denominaciones de origen no agrícolas en España y en contexto comparado" (2023) https://cepi.eoi.es/publicaciones/la-regulacion-de-las-denominaciones-de-origen-no-agricolas-en-espana-en-contexto.

Services Act.[42] These form an EU package that aims to ensure that whatever is illegal offline is also illegal online. To this end, it establishes specific rules that will impact on IP right holders, such as owners of collective or certification marks and GIs.

The Digital Markets Act is a law that targets the large platforms referred to as 'gatekeepers'. These players can significantly affect trade mark right holders, as well as holders of rights in GIs, as they can manifest behavior that may obstruct access to digital markets. They may also be determinant in regulating the behavior of those who will be allowed to enter these markets. This regulation aims to put all companies on an equal playing field in the digital market, regardless of their size. It complements existing competition law. But unlike competition law, it establishes *ex-ante* controls to prevent abuses by large platforms. This digital markets law sets clear rules on what large online platforms can and cannot do in the EU. All of this will benefit the protection of IP rights by allowing a level playing field between market operators.

The Digital Services Act aims to create a safer digital environment for users and companies operating in the digital marketplace. One of the biggest problems that this legislation aims to prevent is the sale of illegal products, such as fake Scotch Whisky or Napa Valley wine, or Coffee Kenya coffee. The manipulation of recommender systems and abuse of advertising systems can fuel dangerous disinformation and propagation of illegal content. The law intends to provide more information to users, so that they can control the recommendations and, therefore, their purchases. The law includes, among many other provisions, effective safeguards for users, including the possibility of challenging platforms' content moderation decisions, as well as transparency measures for online platforms that are wide-ranging, including regarding the algorithms used for recommendation.

Until now, it was necessary to take into account Directive 2000/31, which established the so-called 'safe harbour'.[43] This Directive foresaw when service providers had a responsibility to act to prevent or stop illegal activities.[44] It also foresaw exemptions from liability, although these should only apply in cases where the activity of the information society service provider was limited

---

[42] Pilar Montero García-Noblejas, 'El reto regulatorio de una economía basada en plataformas digitales' (2023) 99 La Ley mercantil.

[43] Fernandos Carbajo Cascón, 'Las plataformas digitales ante la distribución de mercancías y el suministro de contenidos digitales ilícitos' (2022) 30 Revista de Derecho de la Competencia y la Distribución 2.

[44] Directive 2000/31/EC of 8 June 2000 on certain legal aspects of information society services, in particular electronic commerce, in the Internal Market (Directive on electronic commerce) [2000] OJ L178/1, art 2(b): '"service provider": any natural or legal person providing an information society service'.

to the technical process of operating and providing access to a communication network to make the transmission more efficient. The exemption is based on the fact that the activity is purely technical in nature, automatic and passive, and that the service provider has no knowledge or control of the information transmitted or stored. In order to benefit from the liability limitation, the provider of a service that involves the storage of data has to act diligently to remove or prevent access to the data as soon as it has actual knowledge of unlawful activities, such as the sale of counterfeit Napa Valley wine.

The Digital Services Act takes this responsibility a step further by providing that the misuse of online platforms by frequently providing manifestly illegal content or by frequently submitting manifestly unfounded notices or complaints undermines trust and harms the rights and legitimate interests of the market. Therefore, the Digital Service Act puts in place appropriate, proportionate and effective safeguards against such misuse. According to this regulation, information should be considered to be manifestly illegal content and notices or complaints should be considered manifestly unfounded where it is evident to a layperson, without any substantive analysis, that the content is illegal or, respectively, that the notices or complaints are unfounded.

In a case of the sale of counterfeit shoes, *Amazon v Louboutin*,[45] the court found that Amazon could be regarded as itself making use of the sign identical to a trade mark appearing in the advertisement of a third-party seller on its online marketplace, where a reasonably well-informed and attentive user of its site takes away the impression that it is that operator who is marketing, in its own name and on its own account, the infringing goods. The court recalled that the use of a sign identical to a trade mark by a third party means that the latter made use of the sign in the context of its own commercial communication, and that the mere fact of creating the technical conditions necessary for the use of a sign and of being remunerated for that service did not mean that the person providing that service was itself making use of the sign, even if it was acting in its own economic interest.

In the case of the operator of an online marketplace such as eBay or Amazon, the court considered that the use of signs identical or similar to trade marks, in offers for sale posted on that marketplace, was solely by the operator's selling customers and not by the operator itself, where the operator did not use that sign in its own commercial communication. But the marketplace operator could be responsible in cases in which the users of the online marketplace could receive the impression that the advertisements for the infringer's goods came from the marketplace.

---

[45] Joined Cases C-148/21 and C-184/21 *Amazon v Louboutin* [2022] ECR I-1016.

Although, formally, the Digital Services Act does not change the 'safe harbour' rule, it increases the oversight obligations of platforms, which makes it possible to predict greater online protection for these unique products in the future, as can be observed in the *Amazon v Louboutin* case, which can be interpreted as a preview of this increased protection.

The application of this case law to guarantee marks or GIs requires an adjustment considering the special characteristics of these distinctive signs. If we are dealing with a guarantee or certification mark, we should take into consideration that the infringement of the mark will only arise if we are dealing with fake products. And the product will be a fake GI product if it does not fulfil the requirements set out in the regulations for use, which might require prior authorization. In the case of collective marks, the approach will be a bit different, since these are marks where there is a collective owner. In this case, the product will be infringing if it is not commercialized by a member of the association or with the authorization of this association. It is not possible to consider that compliance with the regulation of use by itself authorizes the use of this sign.

Infringement of a GI is closer to the infringement of certification marks, since the product will be considered as a counterfeit product, to some extent, if it does not respect the product specification. In this case it should be noted that in the last reform of the EU GIs regulations, the article related to the protection of GIs was modified to provide that the protection should also apply regarding goods sold by means of distance selling, such as electronic commerce.[46]

This is an approach that was also reflected in the new regulation on GIs. Therefore, in the explanation of the objectives of the regulation it is provided that:

> This regulation will ensure that consumers receive reliable information and a guarantee of authenticity of such products and can readily identify them in the marketplace *including in electronic commerce* and an effective enforcement and marketing throughout the Union and in *electronic commerce* ensuring the integrity of the internal market.[47]

Moreover, in an article devoted to control and enforcement of GIs in the marketplace, the Regulation provided that member states should designate one or more enforcement authorities responsible for controls in the marketplace and

---

[46] Regulation 1151/2012 (n 11), art. 13(1)(a), (b).
[47] Regulation (EU) 2024/1143 of 11 April 2024 on geographical indications for wine, spirit drinks and agricultural products, as well as traditional specialities guaranteed and optional quality terms for agricultural products, art. 4 c) and e).

enforcement of GIs – whether in storage, transit, distribution, or offered for sale at wholesale or retail level, including in *electronic commerce*.[48]

An explicit reference to electronic commerce in the Regulation can be seen as a good sign, although in principle this should already be included, even if it is not specified. This is because it is not possible today to consider the physical market and the electronic market as different marketplaces with different requirements.

A different question may be whether the digital market raises new challenges or has special features to which the rules conceived for a physical market may not always be adequate to cover. By specifying that the market also includes the digital market, it could be questioned if the word 'e-commerce' also includes the metaverse or other alternative realities. We consider that this should be the case.

Infringement of the GI can arise whether the name of the indication is used on an infringing product, or whether other graphic elements are used, as happened in the *Manchego* case,[49] in which it was considered that the use of certain images could evoke the protected product, without using the name. Or if the shape of the protected product is used in an infringing product, as happened in the *Morbier* case,[50] in which it was considered that the use of a certain shape of goods was likely to evoke the protected product, thus constituting infringement. Or even if references to words that are associated with the GI are used so as to constitute an unauthorized 'indirect use'. This happened in the *Glen Buchenbach* case,[51] in which the court held that for the purpose of establishing that there is 'indirect commercial use' of a registered GI, the disputed element must be used in a form that is either identical to that indication or phonetically and/or visually similar to it. Accordingly, it is not sufficient that that element is liable to evoke in the relevant public some kind of association with the indication concerned or the geographical area relating thereto. In this case

---

[48] Regulation (EU) 2024/1143 of 11 April 2024 on geographical indications for wine, spirit drinks and agricultural products, as well as traditional specialities guaranteed and optional quality terms for agricultural products, art. 4 c) and e); Regulation (EU) 2024/1143 of 11 April 2024 on geographical indications for wine, spirit drinks and agricultural products, as well as traditional specialities guaranteed and optional quality terms for agricultural products, art. 42.

[49] Case C-614/17 *Fundación Consejo Regulador de la Denominación de Origen Protegida Queso Manchego v Industrial Quesera Cuquerella SL, Juan Ramón Cuquerella Montagud* ECLI:EU:C:2019:344; [2019] ECR I-344.

[50] Case C-490/19 *Syndicat interprofessionnel de défense du fromage Morbier v Société Fromagère du Livradois SAS* [2020] OJ C53/13.

[51] Case C 44/17 *Scotch Whisky Association v Michael Klotz* [2018] OJ C268/10.

the court needed to decide if an average European consumer thinks directly of the protected GI, 'Scotch Whisky', when the consumer is confronted with a comparable product bearing the disputed designation, in this case 'Glen'. The court needs to decide if it is possible to consider the infringement of the GI in the absence of any phonetic and/or visual similarity between the disputed designation and the protected GI or any partial incorporation of that indication in that designation, where there is a conceptual proximity between the protected GI and the disputed designation.

The European Court ruled that an evocation of a GI-protected product could be possible if, when an average European consumer is confronted with the disputed designation, the image triggered directly in their mind is that of the product whose GI is protected. In making that determination, the referring court, in the absence of any phonetic and/or visual similarity between the disputed designation and the protected GI and any partial incorporation of that indication in that designation, must take account of the conceptual proximity, if any, between the designation and the indication. In addition, for the purpose of establishing that there is an 'evocation' of a registered GI, account is not to be taken either of the context surrounding the disputed element, or of the fact that that element is accompanied by an indication of the true origin of the infringing product. In national courts, in 2019, a Hamburg court ruled that the distillery using this denomination must change its whisky's name and remove the term 'glen', considering that consumers would make a direct connection between 'glen' and 'Scotch Whisky'.

It will therefore be different in the digital marketplace whether advertising or use is made on products that will at some point be consumed physically. If the products are not physically consumed, or if the products cannot be similar, it should be considered whether there is improper dilution of the designation.

This situation happened through the use of a word, 'Champanillo', similar to a protected GI for wines, 'Champagne', by a low-cost establishment which did not sell this type of product, and which could potentially harm its reputation. In this case, the Court of Justice considered that EU Regulations protect geographical indications regarding conduct relating to both products and services. In particular, the court considered that the protection against 'evocation' did not require that the protected product and the product or service covered by the sign were identical or similar and, additionally, the 'evocation' was established where the use of a name created a sufficiently clear and direct link between that name and the protected GI in the mind of an average European consumer. The existence of such a link may arise from several factors, in particular the partial incorporation of the protected designation, the phonetic and visual resemblance of the two names and the resulting similarity, and, even in the absence of those factors, the conceptual proximity between the protected GI and the name at issue or the similarity between the products covered by that GI and the products or services covered by that name.

It is also relevant to note that, after the modifications of the GI's regulations,[52] GIs will be protected against uses exploiting, weakening or diluting the reputation of a GI.[53]

Protection of Quality Signs in the Metaverse

An additional challenge that quality signs are facing, and which would affect these signs for products of origin and with a specific quality, concerns the use of these signs in the metaverse. This requires an analysis of the concept of metaverse and whether or not this differs from e-commerce.

The metaverse is a virtual world where humans, as avatars, interact with each other in a three-dimensional space that mimics reality.[54] This is a digital space resulting from the integration of various digital technologies that allow a higher degree of cohabitation and interaction than ever before. This means that the metaverse is presented as complex worlds that, at this point in time, have been developed through different metaverse platforms, platforms that allow users to get closer to this immersive, higher-level experience than what has been known up to now.[55] E-commerce can be defined, following Eurostat, as the sale or purchase of goods or services, whether between businesses, households, individuals, or private organizations, through electronic transactions conducted via the internet or other computer-mediated (online communication) networks. The term covers the ordering of goods and services which are sent over computer networks, but the payment and the ultimate delivery of the goods or service may be conducted either on- or off-line. Orders via man-

---

[52] Regulation (EU) 2021/2117 of the European Parliament and of the Council of 2 December 2021 amending Regulations (EU) No 1308/2013 establishing a common organisation of the markets in agricultural products, (EU) No 1151/2012 on quality schemes for agricultural products and foodstuffs, (EU) No 251/2014 on the definition, description, presentation, labelling and the protection of geographical indications of aromatised wine products and (EU) No 228/2013 laying down specific measures for agriculture in the outermost regions of the Union [2021] OJ L435/262.

[53] Regulation (EU) 2024/1143 of 11 April 2024 on geographical indications for wine, spirit drinks and agricultural products, as well as traditional specialities guaranteed and optional quality terms for agricultural products., art. 26.b).

[54] 'Metaverse' (Cambridge Dictionary) <https:// dictionary .cambridge .org/ dictionary/english/metaverse> accessed 5 October 2024.

[55] See Preliminary injunctions, Alicante Commercial Court 13 July 2023, Decision No: 168/2023, Judge: Gustavo Andres Martin.

ually typed e-mails, however, are excluded. The Digital Market Act considers 'digital sector' as the sector of products and services provided by means of, or through, information society services.[56] And the P2B Regulation considers 'online intermediation services'[57] as services which meet all of the following requirements: they constitute information society services within the meaning of Directive 2015/1535;[58] they allow business users to offer goods or services to consumers, with a view to facilitating the initiating of direct transactions between those business users and consumers, irrespective of where those transactions are ultimately concluded; and they are provided to business users on the basis of contractual relationships between the provider of those services and business users which offer goods or services to consumers.[59]

From these definitions, we understand that e-commerce should include both the metaverse and any other type of digital commerce regardless of the reality in which it is developed. This can be in a terrestrial, maritime, space or other planetary environment. This debate has already been settled a long time ago, in defining the activities and persons to which commercial law or business law should apply. As is well known, what is essential to characterize a transaction or contract is not the environment in which it takes place, but the subject matter of the transaction or contract.

Therefore, we usually face transactions characterized by what is known throughout the world as commercial law, trade law or business law. And the specificity of this discipline takes into consideration the specific risks arising for third parties as a result of the exercise of commercial or business activities. In these cases, the special technical characteristics of the environment in which they are carried out must undoubtedly be taken into account. Today we are talking about an environment that we characterize as digital, then the metaverse, but in the future there may be other new realities. Therefore, in order to determine the law, we must consider the activity carried out and the place where it is carried out, that is whether or not there is a market and a commercial transaction. It will be a different matter whether the technical environ-

---

[56] Regulation (EU) 2022/1925 of the European Parliament and of the Council of 14 September 2022 on contestable and fair markets in the digital sector and amending Directives (EU) 2019/1937 and (EU) 2020/1828 (Digital Markets Act) [2022] OJ L265/1, art. 2(4).

[57] Regulation (EU) 2019/1150 of the European Parliament and of the Council of 20 June 2019 on promoting fairness and transparency for business users of online intermediation services [2019] OJ L186/57.

[58] Directive (EU) 2015/1535 of 9 September 2015 laying down a procedure for the provision of information in the field of technical regulations and of rules on Information Society services [2015] OJ L241/1, art. 1(1)(b).

[59] Regulation 2019/1150 (n 56).

ments require appropriate rules due to the contracting specialities of each of them. For example, specific rules to adapt the application of the territoriality principle, as a basic principle in IP rights. The Digital Markets Act will apply to core platform services provided or offered by gatekeepers to business users established in the EU or end users established or located in the EU, irrespective of the place of establishment or residence of the gatekeepers and irrespective of the law otherwise applicable to the provision of service. The Act will apply to intermediary services offered to recipients of the service that have their place of establishment or are located in the EU, irrespective of where the providers of those intermediary services have their place of establishment.

Regarding products that are distinguished by a geographical origin and a specific quality, appreciated when consuming them, it will be more difficult to assess a traditional impact on the metaverse. This is because wine, whisky and coffee are products that are consumed in the real world and whose qualities cannot be appreciated by their consumption in the metaverse by avatars. Nevertheless, the uniqueness of these products, their reputation and tradition, make them of considerable marketing and advertising value. For this reason, it will be possible that they could also be infringed in the metaverse, even if they are not consumed in physical form.

Therefore, it would be possible, in principle, to wonder what would happen in cases where these unique products do not register their name as a trade mark but only as a GI, in the sense of analyzing whether it would be possible to protect them if such use were only in the metaverse. In these cases, the question could be asked whether it would be possible that the use of the name in the metaverse, registered only as a GI, could lead to a use that could grant a trade mark right over the name. We do not consider the possibility of use as a well-known unregistered GI, since this is a possibility not foreseen in any of the regulations of the EU, and it is not common in other countries' regulations on GIs.

In order to answer this question, and assuming that the metaverse is a form of e-commerce, it is necessary to consider the Joint Recommendation Concerning Provisions on the Protection of Marks, and Other Industrial Property Rights in Signs, on the Internet adopted by the Assembly of the Paris Union for the Protection of Industrial Property and the General Assembly of the WIPO at the Thirty-Sixth Series of Meetings of the Assemblies of the Member States of WIPO.

Following this Recommendation, the use of a sign on the Internet shall constitute use in a member state only if the use has a commercial effect in that member state. In determining this the competent authority shall consider all relevant circumstances. For example, circumstances indicating that the user of the sign is doing, or has undertaken significant plans to do, business in the member state in relation to goods or services which are identical or similar to those for which the sign is used on the Internet; the level and character of commercial activity of the user in relation to the member state, including: whether the user is actually serving customers located in the member state or has entered into other commercially motivated relationships with persons located in the member state; whether the user has stated, in conjunction with the use of the sign on the Internet, that they do not intend to deliver the goods or services offered to customers located in the member state and whether they adhere to their stated intent; whether the user offers post-sales activities in the member state, such as warranty or service; whether the user undertakes further commercial activities in the member state which are related to the use of the sign on the Internet but which are not carried out over the Internet. Also the connection of an offer of goods or services on the Internet with the member state should be considered, including: whether the goods or services offered can be lawfully delivered in the member state and whether the prices are indicated in the official currency of the member state. Another important factor will be the connection between the manner of use of the sign on the Internet and the member state, including: whether the sign is used in conjunction with a means of interactive contact which is accessible to Internet users in the member state; whether the user has indicated, in conjunction with the use of the sign, an address, telephone number or other means of contact in the member state; whether the sign is used in connection with a domain name which is registered under the ISO Standard country code 3166 TLD referring to the member state; whether the text used in conjunction with the use of the sign is in a language predominantly used in the member state; and whether the sign is used in conjunction with an Internet location which has actually been visited by Internet users located in the member state. Also the relationship between the use of the sign on the Internet and a right in that sign in the member state would be important, including: whether the use is supported by that right and whether, where the right belongs to another, the use would take unfair advantage of, or unjustifiably impair, the distinctive character or the reputation of the sign that is the subject of that right.

Those factors are not pre-conditions for reaching a determination, but guidelines to assist the competent authority to determine whether the use of a sign has produced a commercial effect in a member state. The determination in each case will depend upon the particular circumstances of that case. In some cases, all of the factors may be relevant. In other cases, only some of the factors may be relevant. In still other cases none of the factors may be relevant, and the decision may be based on additional factors that are not listed in the Recommendation.[60]

However, given the value of these names in the marketplace, they are usually registered as trade marks, and the challenge will be to determine whether the use of these names registered as trade marks (whether individual, collective or certification marks), in the metaverse constitutes trade mark infringement in the physical world. Several questions arise in relation to this matter. The first and most obvious is to determine whether or not there is a similarity between a Napa Valley wine sold in real life and a Napa Valley wine sold in the metaverse by the avatars. A preliminary clarification to be made is that if the purchase of the bottle of wine is made in the metaverse, but in order to have the product sent in the real world, there will be an infringement. In such cases, the metaverse only facilitates not having to go to the shop, but the product is the same as in real life, that is, a wine, and it could be an infringing wine.

The difficulties arise when the product is purchased in the metaverse for use only in that environment. This is where the problem of the lack of product identity arises. Even if 'visually' it is the same. In order to solve these problems, the IP rights registration offices are issuing recommendations to guide users.

This is why the EUIPO considers that virtual goods belong to Class 9 because they are treated as digital content or images. However, considering that the term 'virtual goods' lacks clarity and precision, it must be further specified by stating the content to which the virtual goods relate (for example, downloadable virtual goods, namely, virtual clothing). The Office considers that the 12th Edition of the Nice Classification will incorporate the term downloadable digital files authenticated by non-fungible tokens(NFTs) in Class 9. NFTs are this way treated as unique digital certificates registered in a blockchain, which authenticate digital items but are distinct from those digital items. For the Office, the term NFTs on its own is not acceptable and for that reason the type of digital item authenticated by the NFT must be specified. In any case, services relating to virtual goods and NFTs will be classified in line with the established principles of classification for services. Considering the first EUIPO decisions it is interesting to note that the Office notes that the consumer's perceptions of real-world goods can be applied to equivalent

---

[60] Joint Recommendation Concerning Provisions on the Protection of Marks, and Other Industrial Property Rights in Signs, on the Internet (World Intellectual Property Organization 2001), art.3.

virtual goods as a key aspect of virtual goods is to emulate core concepts of real-world goods.[61]

In cases where the trade mark has not also been registered for virtual goods, it will be easier to establish infringement in the case of well-known trade marks, since selling a Napa Valley wine in the metaverse will involve taking advantage of the reputation of this trade mark in a digital environment. This has been the solution in the US in the case of the infringement of the Hermés Birkin bag, for the sale of metabirkins in the metaverse.[62] We also consider relevant for interpreting this kind of case the judgments that have been handed down on the possible infringement of a trade mark for real motorbikes or cars, in cases of their use as miniatures for children,[63] or the use of trade marks in video games. In these cases, the Court of Justice has held that the use in a scaled-down replica of an existing model car of the original model manufacturer's trade mark may constitute an infringement if it undermines the trade mark's functions. That is, if the relevant public may think that the miniature car has been manufactured by the car company or by an undertaking collaborating with it. The same applies in the case of video games, with the exceptions which would allow a use of third-party's trade mark if it is done for the sole purpose of reproducing a reality. Or if it is done for the parody purpose, in which case there are limits to freedom of expression or artistic creation.

Greater problems may arise if the trade marks such as Napa Valley or Scotch Whisky or Coffee Kenya are used in the metaverse for products other than those for which they are registered in real life. If it is questionable whether an NFT representing a bottle of wine is the same as an actual bottle of wine for likelihood of confusion purposes, the likelihood of confusion between, say, an NFT representing a chair or a computer, but using the Napa Valley wine mark, and the actual Napa Valley wine marked with this sign will be even more questionable. In such cases, it will be extremely important to demonstrate the reputation of the earlier mark and the type of use, in order to appreciate if unfair advantage of the reputation is being taken. In any case, the assessment should not be the same between an NFT representing the same product and an NFT representing other products, since in the second case the regulation should be applied in the same way as in the physical world. In other words, considering them as different products.

---

[61] EUIPO Decision, Refusal of application for a European Union trade mark, 8 February 2023, Application No: 018647205.

[62] *Hermes International v Rothschild, U.S. District Court for the Southern District of New York*, No. 1:22-cv-00384, 23 June 2023.

[63] Case C-48/05 *Adam Opel AG v Autec AG* [2007] ECR I-01017.

The Protection of Quality Signs in Influencers' Activity on Social Networks

The protection of those unique products should also be ensured in the digital framework regarding the activity pursued by influencers on social media. In this regard, the influencer using a trade mark or a GI on social networks must ensure that they are not infringing any prior rights.[64] The use of a trade mark in advertising and/or on social media may be considered a genuine use of the trade mark or a proof of reputation.[65] In these cases, it will make a difference whether dealing with an individual, collective or certification mark or a protected GI. That is because the limits and requirements of these distinctive signs are different.

In the case of a collective mark, the use of the sign by an influencer on social networks would require the consent of the association. In the event that the influencer is a member of the association, they may use the trade mark, provided that they respect the rules of the association. In this regard, it is desirable that the regulations governing the use of collective marks include rules on advertising on digital media and social networks, in order to avoid future problems.

In the case of a certification or guarantee mark, the importance of establishing rules on advertising in the regulations for use is even more important. This is because a fundamental rule of such marks is that whoever respects the regulation of use will have the right to use the mark. It is true that the trade marks for products such as Scotch Whisky, Napa Valley AVA wines and Coffee Kenya coffee will need to be used as trade marks on the specific prod-

---

[64] Altea Asensi Merás, 'La licitud de la publicidad a través de influencers o líderes de opinión en redes sociales' (2018) 39 Actas de derecho industrial y derecho de autor 321.

[65] EUIPO, *Guidelines,* 6.1.1.1 (Use of individual marks): 'A representation of the mark on packaging, catalogues, advertising material or invoices relating to the goods and services in question constitutes direct evidence that the mark has been put to genuine use'. EUIPO, *Guidelines,* 3.1.4.4 (Means of evidence): 'As a consequence of the growing importance of information technologies and the Internet to personal, social and economic life, parties are increasingly relying on evidence originating from the Internet to show the use and reputation of their marks. If the earlier trade mark has a significant presence on the Internet (evidenced by the number of subscribers to accounts dedicated to this trade mark on social networks, or the number of visitors to blogs mentioning this trade mark), this may help assess the knowledge of the trade mark by the public concerned and may therefore support a finding of reputation' (26/06/2019, T-651/18, HAWKERS (fig.) / HAWKERS (fig.) et al., EU:T:2019:444, § 33).

ucts. But the advertising activity of influencers is a recognized use of the trade mark and, in the absence of any provision in the use regulations, problems may arise regarding the advertising of the goods using the mark. It is therefore very common for guarantee or certification marks to provide, in their regulations of use, requirements to be met with regard to advertising activities. A further possibility is to require users of the trade mark to inform the trade mark owner in advance of the advertising campaigns they are going to carry out.

If the product is registered as a GI, the system of protection may be different, since we are dealing with a collective right. However, unlike collective marks, the right will be granted as a whole to all producers who comply with the product specifications. In the EU, this is absolute, since there is a right to use the sign. This means that it will not be possible to prevent producers who comply with the product specification from using the designation. In other countries, for example in Latin America, it is necessary to obtain prior authorization in order to use the sign, which is not the case in Europe.

In the EU, use of a GI by an influencer will be possible as long as the influencer fulfils the product specification, that is, that the rules laid down for that product are respected. In other cases, if an actor is shown drinking whisky that is branded Scotch Whisky or Kenyan Coffee, it would be desirable for the actor to have previously approached the producers' association. Otherwise, it would be necessary to analyze, as in trade marks, if there is a commercial use or if the use of the sign is merely descriptive. In the case of commercial uses, the unlawful use of the GI occurs when it is used for products that do not comply with the product's specification. This could happen if the influencer uses the indication Scotch Whisky for a spirit drink that does not comply with the Scotch Whisky specification.

Therefore, influencers must be very careful with the use of third-party trade marks, as well as with the use of GIs. They need to understand that the use of products including a GI needs to respect a different set of requirements, intended to protect this collective right in a unique product, designed to preserve its reputation.

PRELIMINARY CONCLUSIONS

It can be seen how the use of distinctive quality signs can be beneficial for the effective protection in the market of unique products such as Scotch Whisky, Napa Valley AVA wines and Coffee Kenya coffee. The digital market offers many advantages and opportunities that can benefit producers of such products, bringing them closer to consumers and allowing for better protection and promotion of their special characteristics.

However, the existence of different quality labels in different countries requires a comprehensive knowledge of each of them, in order to use them in a way that optimizes the benefits at an international level in both the physical and digital markets. Otherwise, inappropriate use of the quality labels will prevent these products from acquiring the protection they deserve, damaging many producers, as well as the specific regions of each country. This is because the distinctive signs of quality and origin protect a genuine product, with a tradition and historical know-how, and their loss will be detrimental to an entire community, undermining the cultural heritage of the countries concerned.

16. Extended Passing Off – Protecting Goodwill in Place Brands and Other Tales

Catherine W. Ng

While extended passing off can protect the goodwill pertaining to place brands such as Scotch Whisky, Napa Valley AVA, and Coffee Kenya, it presents a conundrum for the law of passing off upon which its foundation is built. The term 'pass off' first appeared in an 1842 case.[1] It has since been used to classify, retrospectively and henceforth, cases that stand for the principle that no trader should pass off its goods as those of another trader.[2] The judge-made law of passing off is now well established in common law jurisdictions such as those in Australia, Canada, and the United Kingdom. In England and Wales, without any general law against unfair competition,[3] the law of passing off protects traders from unfair trading and thereby also consumers from deception by misrepresentation. It protects the goodwill that links the branded goods with the branding trader in the consumers' mind. So consumers looking for JOHNNIE WALKER Scotch Whisky can find it by recognizing the name or the famous Striding Man logo in the marketplace.[4] They may also come across the name or the logo and know it refers unequivocally to a specific brand of Scotch Whisky. Either way, this is the connection or goodwill in the consumers' mind that the law of passing off protects.

---

[1] *Perry v Truefitt* (1842) 5 Beav 66; 49 ER 749 (Ch), 66 and 71; 749, 751.

[2] *Reckitt and Colman Products Ltd v Borden Inc* [1990] 1 WLR 491 (HL), 499.

[3] *Diageo North America Inc v Intercontinental Brands Ltd* [2010] EWCA Civ 920; [2010] ETMR 57, [24].

[4] See for example 'The JOHNNIE WALKER Story' (Diageo) <https://www.johnniewalker.com/en-gb/whisky-guide/the-johnnie-walker-story/> accessed 10 October 2024; 'Trade Mark: JOHNNIE WALKER' (Intellectual Property Office) <https:// trademarks .ipo .gov .uk/ ipo -tmcase/ page/ Results/ 1/ UK00000308458> accessed 6 October 2024; and also, 'Trade Mark: Striding Man (Intellectual Property Office)' <https:// trademarks .ipo .gov .uk/ ipo -tmcase/ page/ Results/ 1/ UK00003099444> accessed 6 October 2024.

A conundrum exists between this classic version of passing off and its extended version because, on the one hand, the classic version offers little, if any, protection to the goodwill associated with generic or descriptive names unless those names have acquired a secondary meaning in the consumers' mind to refer unequivocally to a specific trader or traders.[5] So the goodwill pertaining to a brand called 'Italian Pencils' for pencils from Italy attracts little protection, if any at all, against other traders who use the term to sell pencils from Italy. This allows other traders within the sector to use the generic or descriptive terms freely to convey the nature of their goods to the consuming public.[6] On the other hand, extended passing off protects goodwill that is shared within a class of traders. In England and Wales, traders have successfully deployed extended passing off to protect their shared goodwill pertaining to place brands such as 'Scotch Whisky' from being used for admixtures containing spirits that were not distilled in Scotland,[7] 'Champagne' from being used in 'Spanish Champagne' for wines not produced in the Champagne region in France (in the *Spanish Champagne* case),[8] 'Greek Yoghurt' for yoghurt not produced in Greece (in the *Greek Yoghurt* case),[9] as well as terms such as 'advocaat',[10] 'whisky',[11] and 'vodka' that have no place significance to consumers.[12]

Extended passing off received affirmation from the House of Lords almost half a century ago in a decision (the *Advocaat* case) dealing with advo-

---

[5] *Montgomery v Thompson* [1891] AC 217 (HL) 225, 227–8; *Chocosuisse Union des Fabricants Suisses de Chocolat v Cadbury Ltd* [1998] RPC 117 (HC), 129, affirmed *Chocosuisse Union des Fabricants Suisses de Chocolat v Cadbury Ltd* [1999] RPC 826 (CA), 832, 848–9; *Diageo North America* (CA) (n 3), [24], [51], [53], see also [76]; *Fage UK Ltd v Chobani UK Ltd* [2014] EWCA Civ 5; [2014] ETMR 26 (CA), [62].

[6] *Reddaway v Banham* [1896] AC 199 (HL), 208–13; *Bewlay and Co Ld v Hughes* (1898) 15 RPC 290 (HCJ – Ch D), 293; *Office Cleaning Services Ltd v Westminster Window and General Cleaners Ltd* (1946) 63 RPC 39 (HL), 42–3; *Montgomery*, ibid.

[7] *John Walker & Sons Ltd v Henry Ost & Co Ltd* [1970] 1 WLR 917.

[8] *J Bollinger v Costa Brava Wine Co Ltd (No 2)* [1961] 1 WLR 277 (Ch D).

[9] *Fage UK Ltd v Chobani UK Ltd* [2013] EWHC 630 (Ch), affirmed *Fage* (CA) (n 5).

[10] *Erven Warnink Besloten Vennootschap v J Townend & Sons (Hull) Ltd* [1979] AC 731 (HL).

[11] *The Scotch Whisky Association v Glen Kella Distillers Ltd* [1997] ETMR 470 (Ch).

[12] *Diageo North America* (CA) (n 3).

caat.[13] The decision concluded a series of actions spearheaded by traders of place-branded drinks.[14] As the term 'advocaat' had no place significance to consumers, the House of Lords conferred protection under extended passing off because it found:

> no reason in principle or logic why the goodwill in the name of those entitled to make use of it should be protected by the law against deceptive use of the name by competitors, if it denotes a product of which the ingredients come from a particular locality, but should lose that protection if the ingredients of the product, however narrowly identified, are not restricted as to their geographical provenance.[15]

Recent case law has applied extended passing off to cover services as well.[16] (For simplicity, 'goods' used throughout this chapter includes services.)

As the law continues to expand its scope of protection, why and under what circumstances can the goodwill pertaining to Scotch Whisky for whisky distilled and matured in Scotland be protected under extended passing off while that protection is denied under other forms of passing off? At the suggestion that to be protected under extended passing off, the branded goods in question must have 'cachet', the Court of Appeal stated:

> Of course if, by a cachet, one means no more than distinctiveness then there is no difficulty. But I endorse the view of the judge that the argument that the product must be a premium or luxury one is in fact contrary to the principle which underlies all these cases. So-called premium brands are likely (perhaps more likely) in many cases to acquire the distinctiveness required. But goodwill may attach to a product simply because consumers come to like and value it for its inherent qualities rather than its status.[17]

This chapter resolves the apparent inconsistency that exists between extended passing off and classic passing off, and challenges the idea that the English law of passing off protects goodwill that attaches to goods for their inherent qualities. Resolving this conundrum is important because the law offers complementary protection to that offered in the United Kingdom under the

---

[13] *Erven* (n 10).

[14] Champagne: *J Bollinger v Costa Brava Wine Co Ltd (No 3)* [1960] Ch 262; Sherry: *Vine Products Ltd v Mackenzie & Co Ltd (No 3)* [1967] FSR 402 (ChD); Scotch Whisky: *John Walker & Sons* (n 7); Champagne: *H P Bulmer Ltd v J Bollinger SA* [1978] RPC 79 (CA).

[15] *Erven* (n 10), 745.

[16] *The Military Mutual Ltd v Police Mutual Assurance Society Ltd* [2018] EWHC 1575 (IPEC); [2018] ETMR 33, [67].

[17] *Diageo North America* (CA) (n 3), [51].

Trade Marks Act 1994 against third-party use of trade marks,[18] including certification marks and collective marks,[19] under European Union (EU)-inspired geographical indication schemes (with Northern Ireland under EU schemes),[20] and under legislation such as the Trade Descriptions Act 1968 which offers criminal sanctions. The law of passing off also offers a cause of action for traders to protect the goodwill pertaining to marks and identity signs that are unregistered or unregistrable as trade marks under the Trade Marks Act 1994, and an additional cause of action to protect the goodwill pertaining to registered trade marks.

This chapter will focus on the English law of passing off and builds on an earlier book that examines the concept of goodwill protected under classic passing off and its variants but not extended passing off.[21] That book differentiates two conceptions of goodwill: 'substantive goodwill' denoting the substantive value in every advantage in a business that attracts custom, including the inherent quality of the goods it sells – a position traditionally adopted by authorities and case law,[22] and 'structural goodwill' denoting the public recognition of the distinctive branding on the goods, and thus the unique link between the branded goods and the branding trader in the consumers' mind. The earlier book argues that while substantive and structural goodwill are intertwined, the law of passing off primarily protects the latter. Fundamentally, branding helps traders to express their endorsement of the branded goods by selling them and co-branding with them. The law protects the authenticity of that endorsement. These forms of endorsement and branding help structure and position the branded goods in the consumers' mind based on how these goods are associated with other similarly branded goods and with other similar goods in the consumers' mind.[23] They also help consumers to locate and select the branded goods to purchase and to self-brand and identify with them. This

---

[18] Trade Marks Act 1994, ss 1(2), 9–10.

[19] Trade Marks Act 1994, ss 49–50.

[20] See 'Protected Geographical Food and Drink Names: UK GI Schemes' (Department for Environment, Food and Rural Affairs 2024) <https:// www .gov.uk/guidance/protected-geographical-food-and-drink-names-uk-gi-schemes> accessed 6 October 2024.

[21] Catherine W Ng, *Goodwill in Passing Off - a Common Law Perspective* (Edward Elgar 2021).

[22] Ibid, 3–4, 28–31; see also Suman Naresh, 'Passing-Off, Goodwill And False Advertising: New Wine In Old Bottles' (1986) 45(1) Cambridge LJ 97.

[23] Ng (n 21), 3–6.

chapter applies that argument to extended passing off, and posits that the goodwill protected does not reside in the inherent qualities of goods.[24]

The chapter begins with some fundamental principles of the law of passing off before considering extended passing off. From there, it draws on the shared goodwill associated with place-branding in particular to help illustrate how traders have used place-branding to achieve distinctiveness in the mind of consumers and thereby attract protection under extended passing off.

THE LAW OF PASSING OFF IN PRINCIPLE

To succeed under the law of passing off, a claimant must establish three elements:

> First, he must establish a goodwill or reputation attached to the goods or services which he supplies in the mind of the purchasing public by association with the identifying "get-up" ... under which his particular goods or services are offered to the public, such that the get-up is recognised by the public as distinctive specifically of the plaintiff's goods or services. Secondly, he must demonstrate a misrepresentation by the defendant to the public (whether or not intentional) leading or likely to lead the public to believe that goods or services offered by him are the goods or services of the plaintiff. ... Thirdly, he must demonstrate that he suffers or, in a quia timet action that he is likely to suffer, damage by reason of the erroneous belief engendered by the defendant's misrepresentation that the source of the defendant's goods or services is the same as the source of those offered by the plaintiff.[25]

The misrepresentation here lies in misleading consumers to confuse the defendant's goods for the claimant's. Consumers need not know or care about the identity of the claimant trader, they just need to be able to recognize the trader's branding so that they can locate its branded goods in the marketplace.[26]

The law of passing off however does not address the quality of goods. *Spalding v Gamage* offers a potential point for inflection.[27] The defendant was selling footballs which were genuinely manufactured by Spalding as branded. So consumers were not confused about the branding trader for the goods. The defendant, however, was selling goods which Spalding had earlier found to be substandard, withdrawn from the market, and sold to a waste rubber merchant

---

[24] *Chocosuisse Union* (Ch) (n 5), 128; cf *Erven* (n 10), 741, 743–5, 748 (Lord Diplock); *Diageo North America* (CA) (n 3), [51]; Christopher Wadlow, *Wadlow on the Law of Passing-Off* (6th edn, Sweet & Maxwell 2021), [5–11], [8–161].

[25] *Reckitt* (n 2).

[26] *The Birmingham Vinegar Brewery Co Ltd v Powell* [1897] AC 710 (HL), 713–5.

[27] *AG Spalding & Bros v AW Gamage Ltd* (1915) 32 RPC 273 (HL).

even though those goods still bore Spalding's branding. The defendant advertised them for sale with reference to the more recent and improved footballs that Spalding was selling at the time. The House of Lords stated:

> A cannot, without infringing the rights of B, represent goods which are not B's goods or B's goods of a particular class or quality to be B's goods or B's goods of that particular class or quality. The wrong for which relief is sought in a passing-off action consists in every case of a representation of this nature.[28]

As traders are always at liberty to change the quality of their branded goods,[29] the wrong in *Spalding* lies in the defendant misrepresenting goods to be the claimant's goods which the claimant had disclaimed and no longer wished to be associated with or seen to be endorsing. In *Advocaat,* Lord Diplock saw the case as having:

> led the way to recognition by judges of other species of the same genus, as where although the plaintiff and the defendant were not competing traders in the same line of business, a false suggestion by the defendant that their businesses were connected with one another would damage the reputation and thus the goodwill of the plaintiff's business.[30]

The law, however, did not explicitly recognize false endorsement claims where the parties were not rival traders until almost 90 years after *Spalding*. In *Irvine v Talksport Ltd*,[31] Formula 1 driver Eddie Irvine's image was, without Irvine's consent, manipulated and used in an advertisement for the defendant's radio station. Notwithstanding the diversity of trade sectors between the parties such that the defendant's goods could not have been confused with Irvine's in the consumers' mind, the court nevertheless found 'there is nothing which prevents an action for passing off succeeding in a false endorsement case'.[32] Following *Irvine*, English courts have applied the same principle to protect traders from false endorsement claims in merchandising where the image of the pop star Rhianna Fenty was used on a T-shirt and sold by a high street fashion retailer. The court there saw harm to Fenty not only in economic terms, but also in terms of her loss of control over the use of her image where the third-party use would have likely misled the public into thinking that she

---

[28] Ibid, 284.
[29] *Scandecor Developments AB v Scandecor Marketing AB* [2001] UKHL 21, [22].
[30] *Erven* (n 10), 741–2.
[31] *Irvine v Talksport Ltd* [2002] EWHC 367 (Ch); [2002] 1 WLR 2355, affirmed *Irvine v Talksport Ltd* [2003] EWCA Civ 423; [2003] 1 WLR 1576.
[32] *Irvine* (Ch), ibid, [46].

had endorsed the merchandise.[33] In both *Irvine* and *Fenty*, while the claimants enjoyed celebrity status, the law did not purport to protect the substance of their reputation. Instead, the law sought to protect the authenticity in the claimants' endorsement of their selected goods in contradistinction to goods that the defendants sought to pass off as associated with the claimants.

This focus on protecting the distinctive position of commercial brands in the mind of the consuming public makes sense from the traders' perspective. For traders to be recalled accurately in the consumers' mind when making a purchase decision, traders must be able to control what consumers perceive as the traders' authentic representations of themselves in public. Consumers then map these perceptions by association with their related memories. The three primary reasons for branding are 'to stamp the brand's *ownership*, *anchor* desired associations to the brand's part of the memory network for category buyers, and act as a *bridge* between disparate marketing activities'.[34] In the cases of *Irvine* and *Fenty* respectively, the claimants' sporting successes and music icon status helped inform how they were placed in the consumers' memory.[35] Where claimants are falsely implicated in endorsing the defendants' goods, advertising or merchandising, they lose the ability to express themselves by selecting their desired associations and bridging their disparate but authentic activities in the consumers' mind through branding.

For consumers, branding provides a way of orientating their purchases. Branding not only helps direct consumers to purchase goods as advertised or as recommended by word of mouth to fulfil their utilitarian needs, it also allows consumers to self-brand as a way of expressing to themselves as well as to others their association with a trader's brand as a part of their identity. They may seek a sense of self-satisfaction with a purchase that fulfils more than physical needs and that reflects their personal taste and enjoyment.[36] Conspicuously consumed branded goods such as JOHNNIE WALKER whisky as a social drink provide opportunities for consumers to express their

---

[33] *Fenty v Arcadia Group Brands Ltd* [2013] EWHC 2310 (Ch); [2013] WLR(D) 310, [74], affirmed *Fenty v Arcadia Group Brands Ltd* [2015] EWCA Civ 3; [2015] WLR 3291.

[34] Jenni Romaniuk, *Building Distinctive Brand Assets* (OUP 2018), 15 (original emphasis).

[35] Ibid, 9–13; 133–4.

[36] Jean-Noël Kapferer and Vincent Bastien, 'The Specificity of Luxury Management: Turning Marketing Upside Down' in Jean-Noël Kapferer, Joachim Kernstock, Tim Oliver Brexendorf and Shaun M. Powell (eds), *Advances in Luxury Brand Management* (Palgrave Macmillan 2017), 70–71; Karen W Miller and Michael K Mills, 'Probing Brand Luxury: a Multiple Lens Approach' in ibid, 176.

branded identity to others and feel a sense of belonging to their desired brand community, be it live in person or perceived (in advertising and other media).[37] These brand communities become social reference points for consumers. 'To be part of a social group, the person doesn't just need to adhere to the group's attitudes and beliefs, but also to reflect these attitudes and beliefs through displaying the right sorts of brands.'[38] Where a brand becomes associated with a consumer group that holds attitudes and beliefs that are incommensurate with those of the branding trader's target market, that target market may reject the brand.[39] Recently, the law of passing off has explicitly addressed the issue of consumer confusion in a post-sale context, often in a social environment where misleadingly branded goods are in use. So even though purchasers might have recognized the goods as counterfeits when they purchased the goods and thus were not confused themselves, those who see the goods away from the point of sale might not have recognized the goods as counterfeits and were thus confused. The court found 'the owner of goodwill in a product [was] entitled to have this goodwill protected throughout the life of the product, not just at the point of sale'.[40]

The law enables traders to express themselves to the purchasing public without having their voices – whether in the form of branded goods, advertising, merchandising, or endorsement, hijacked by others in their guise. It also enables consumers to rely on branding as a way of orientating their purchases and thereby aligning their own self-expression and associations through the consumption of the branded goods. In endorsing and self-branding with goods, consumers project some of their social values, attitudes, and beliefs onto the brand. Brands thus become imbued with social meanings and values not only from their traders but also from their consumers as a collective. The distinctive position occupied by these social meanings and values associated with branded goods in the consumers' mind that influences consumer purchase decisions

---

[37] Kevin Lane Keller, 'Managing the Growth Tradeoff: Challenges and Opportunities in Luxury Branding' in Jean-Noël Kapferer et al. (n 36), 188.

[38] Leslie de Chernatony and Malcolm McDonald, *Creating Powerful Brands in Consumer, Service and Industrial Markets* (2nd edn, Butterworths Heinemann 1998), 116.

[39] See for example, Claire Bothwell, 'Burberry versus The Chavs' (*BBC*, 28 October 2005) <http://news.bbc.co.uk/1/hi/business/4381140.stm> accessed 7 October 2024; Michel Phan, Ricarda Thomas and Klaus Heine, 'Social Media and Luxury Brand Management: The Case of Burberry' (2011) 2(4) J Global Fashion Marketing 213, 216.

[40] *Freddy SPA v Hugz Clothing Ltd* [2020] EWHC 3032 (IPEC); [2021] RPC 9, [88].

constitutes the structural goodwill that is protected under the law of passing off.

EXTENDED PASSING OFF

Where the consumers' brand selection is centered around their sense of self, identity, and belonging, the same logic for brand selection applies whether the branding is for a single trader or shared among a class of traders. For branding by a single trader, the distinctive position that the brand occupies in the consumers' mind assumes an inherent coherence. Norms and anomalies are all attributed to the one branding trader. For branding that is shared by a class of traders, this coherence must be demonstrably present to constitute extended passing off. Even more challenging for these traders and the courts is that, unlike others who share goodwill such as those in a music group or a band[41] that the public perceives as sharing a brand by consent implicitly or explicitly at some point, membership of the class of traders who share goodwill in extended passing off scenarios is open for others to join without prior consent so long this coherence is maintained from a consumers' perspective.

The initial challenge for the courts was, therefore, in defining a class of traders who would have right of action under extended passing off. This was where the extension of the tort was manifest. Questions such as how wide should the class of goods be for the traders to be afforded a collective right to protect their associated goodwill;[42] how far along the chain of commerce should the class of 'traders' be afforded a right of action because those traders have suffered or would likely suffer harm to goodwill;[43] and how long must

---

[41] See for example *Dent v Turpin* (1861) 2 Johnson and Hemming 139, 70 ER 1003 (KB), 147–9, 1007; *Byford v Oliver* [2003] EWHC 295 (Ch), [19], [25], [26]; *Williams v Canaries Seaschool SLU* [2010] RPC 32 (Appointed Person), [27], [29], [30], [43]; *Ian Thomas v Luv One Luv All Promotions Ltd* [2021] EWCA Civ 732, [58]–[62]; *Ian Thomas v Luv One Luv All Promotions Ltd* [2022] EWHC 964 (IPEC), [16]–[18].

[42] *Erven* (n 10), 744, 747–8; *Consorzio Del Prosciutto di Parma v Marks & Spencer* [1991] RPC 351 (CA), 381–3.

[43] *J Bollinger v Costa Brava Wine Co Ltd (No 2)* (n 8), 281; *John Walker & Sons* (n 7), 930; *H P Bulmer* (n 14), 96–9; *Erven* (n 10), 747 (Lord Diplock), 754 (Lord Fraser); *Consorzio Del Prosciutto di Parma* (n 42), 357, 368; *Scotch Whisky Association v JD Vintners Ltd* [1997] ELR 446 (Ch), 452; *Chocosuisse Union* (CA) (n 5), 842–4; *The Military Mutual Ltd* (n 16), [15].

a trader be dealing within the relevant class of goods to enjoy standing in an extended passing off action[44] all needed to be addressed.

However, as the action matures, this chapter urges the focus of analysis to include the point of convergence between classic passing off and extended passing off: in ensuring what consumers perceive as a brand with coherent social meanings and values is accurately attributed to the branding traders. The assertion here is that while it is claimed that the law of passing off can, in some cases, protect the accuracy with which defendants use generic or descriptive terms to refer to their goods,[45] the fundamental purpose of the law is however to protect the link that consumers perceive as lying between these terms or signs (such as JOHNNIE WALKER or the Striding Man) expressed as part of the branding that represents their traders with their social meanings and values projected thereby and their branded goods (whisky). Extended passing off offers protection where a shared branding (for example Scotch Whisky shared between JOHNNIE WALKER and KILCHOMAN[46]) signifies that the underlying goods meet qualifications that are important to consumers to fulfil needs that often lie beyond the physical qualities inherent in the goods. The law would protect the goodwill pertaining to the example of 'Italian Pencils'[47] where the pencils from Italy have acquired a collective and common consumer perception or a distinctiveness that is beyond the physical qualities that they are pencils which originate from Italy.[48] Otherwise, the goodwill in 'Italian Pencils' for pencils from Italy as a descriptive term attracts little, if any, protection against traders who use the term to sell pencils from Italy. This interpretation of the law of passing off gives it a coherence in meaning and value.[49]

---

[44] *Erven* (n 10), 744 (Lord Diplock), 754 (Lord Fraser); cf *Chocosuisse Union* (Ch) (n 5), 126–7, a position not commented on by at the Court of Appeal for *Chocosuisse Union* but adopted in *The Military Mutual Ltd* (n 16), [41].

[45] Wadlow (n 24), [7-310], [8-159], [8-161], [8-203]; *Diageo North America, Inc v Intercontinental Brands Ltd* [2010] EWHC 17 (Ch); [2010] ETMR 17 (Ch), [29], [34]; see also *Diageo North America* (CA) (n 3), [51].

[46] 'Kilchoman Distillery' <https://www.kilchomandistillery.com> accessed 7 October 2024; see also Anthony Wills, 'Scotch Whisky- A Perspective from Islay', Ch 18.

[47] *Chocosuisse Union* (Ch) (n 5), 129.

[48] See also *Fage* (Ch) (n 9), [114], [122], affirmed *Fage* (CA) (n 5), [70]; *The Military Mutual Ltd* (n 16), [36].

[49] Cf *Erven* (n 10), 740; Wadlow (n 24), [5-33], [8-165].

In *Advocaat*, Lord Diplock expressed some of the initial concerns about the extended action at the House of Lords:

> Of course it is necessary to be able to identify with reasonable precision the members of the class of traders of whose products a particular word or name has become so distinctive as to make their right to use it truthfully as descriptive of their product a valuable part of the goodwill of each of them; but it is the reputation that that type of product itself has gained in the market by reason of its recognisable and distinctive qualities that has generated the relevant goodwill.[50]

In the same decision, Lord Fraser went further:

> I do not think that the terms "descriptive" and "distinctive," as applied to names of products, are mutually exclusive. Names which begin by being descriptive, such as Carrara marble and Vichy water and, of course, Champagne, may in the course of time become distinctive as well as descriptive.[51]

Almost 20 years later, in 1997, Laddie J in the High Court for *Chocosuisse Union de Fabricants Suisses de Chocolat* ('*Chocosuisse*') steered the focus of analysis toward one based on consumer perception:

> It should be possible to protect by the extended form of passing off a descriptive term if it is used in relation to a reasonably identifiable group of products which have a *perceived* distinctive quality. If there is no difference or discernible difference in quality and ingredients between goods sold under or by reference to the term and competing goods, that should not prevent a successful passing off action from being brought. ...
> When Lord Diplock referred ... to the reputation that the type of product has gained "by reason of its recognisable and distinctive qualities", I do not understand him to be saying that those qualities have to exist in fact and be distinctive in fact. If the relevant public believe or perceive there to be special qualities, that should be enough. If it were otherwise, this would be a significant difference between classic and extended passing off actions.[52]

He found 'many who thought ['Swiss' for chocolate] meant more than just a geographical origin. It appeared to have a reputation for quality, expense and exclusivity.'[53] 'The fact that public have no clear idea of the characteristics

---

[50] *Erven* (n 10), 747.
[51] Ibid, 755.
[52] *Chocosuisse Union* (Ch) (n 5), 128 (original emphasis), affirmed *Chocosuisse Union* (CA) (n 5).
[53] *Chocosuisse Union* (Ch) (n 5), 130.

of the goods which have the reputation is of little consequence.'[54] In the end, he found a substantial number of members of the public would be confused into thinking that Cadbury's 'Swiss Chalet' chocolate was Swiss chocolate or chocolate made in Switzerland.[55]

Inherent Qualities of Branded Goods

However, the goodwill protected under extended passing off does not lie in the inherent quality of the branded goods. First, the Court of Appeal for *Chocosuisse*, affirming the substantive findings of Laddie J, also found that there was no material difference in quality between Swiss chocolate compared with the chocolate made by Swiss manufacturers outside Switzerland.[56] Likewise, in a later case involving 'Greek Yoghurt', its characteristic 'thick and creamy' texture could be achieved by the use of thickening agents rather than by the traditional Greek process of straining.[57] Nevertheless, the courts extended protection under passing off. As Laddie J stated 'the ability of the Champagne houses to sue successfully for passing off would not be destroyed if, in fact, other manufacturers in other areas of the world produced a sparkling wine equal in quality and indistinguishable in taste from any one of the numerous wines accurately sold as Champagne'.[58] The law is indifferent to the perceptible quality of these goods.[59]

This extension of the law is thus consistent with the principle in passing off cases that no trader should have any claim to the goodwill associated with the descriptive terms in relation to the particular qualities of the underlying goods.[60] So while Kenyan coffee is claimed to have a unique set of flavor profiles,[61] if the Coffee Kenya mark were to refer descriptively to coffees that fell within those flavor profiles, other coffees that claim to achieve the same flavor profiles should be permitted to use that description, unless the descrip-

---

[54] Ibid, 136, affirmed *Chocosuisse Union* (CA) (n 5), 849; *Fage* (CA) (n 5), [74].
[55] *Chocosuisse Union* (Ch) (n 5), 143.
[56] *Chocosuisse Union* (CA) (n 5), 832, 836.
[57] *Fage* (CA) (n 5), [75], [120].
[58] *Chocosuisse Union* (Ch) (n 5), 128; *Fage* (CA) (n 5), [128].
[59] *Diageo North America* (CA) (n 3), [49].
[60] *Chocosuisse Union* (Ch) (n 5), 124.
[61] Joseph Kieyah and Richard Leresian Lesiyampe, *Report of the National Task Force on Coffee Sub-Sector Reforms* (2016), 26.

tion refers unequivocally to goods of one or more specific traders in the mind of a substantial number of relevant consumers.[62]

Indeed, whether or not a defendant's coffee achieves the same flavor profiles is not a matter within the law of passing off. Courts ought not be arbiters of quality or aesthetics in goods.[63] 'The law does not concern itself with subjective quality, and it has long been recognized that the courts cannot be invited to provide what would in effect be a form of quality control when determining disputes between rival traders.'[64]

Finally, among the food and drinks cases which dominate the case law for extended passing off so far, many of the goods in question are regulated in the processes and composition in their manufacture.[65] Even with such regulation, the end products do not present a consistent quality. Indeed, the quality and tastes in these goods can vary widely within a class that shares the goodwill from the use of a common brand.[66] For example, the same batch of Scotch Whisky produced using identical ingredients, processing, and even casks, would produce a very different taste in three years compared with that in 25 years. Indeed, some distillers extend their product portfolio by offering whiskies with different 'finishes' by using a variety of casks. Regional differences in the taste of the whisky have also been exploited to highlight distilleries for consumers to visit.[67] Yet, these variants may all have legitimate claims to be branded 'Scotch Whisky'.

However, while the protection offered under the law of passing off does not depend on any institutionalized standards,[68] these standards – whether or not enforced or enforceable within the jurisdiction,[69] help create a sense of coherence within a class of goods that links the goods to a common branding term. Extended passing off can be invoked to protect this link. These standards help inform the public about the processes and composition in the manufacture of

---

[62] *Wotherspoon v Currie* (1871-2) LR 5 HL 508, 521; *Montgomery* (n 5), 225, 227–8; *Diageo North America* (CA) (n 3), [26]–[28].

[63] *White v Mellin* [1896] AC 154 (HL), 165; *Consorzio Del Prosciutto di Parma* (n 42), 372–3 (Nourse LJ), 375–8 (Balcome LJ), 379–82 (Leggatt LJ).

[64] *Consorzio Del Prosciutto di Parma* (n 42), 379.

[65] For example, *Chocosuisse Union* (Ch) (n 5), 135.

[66] See for example, ibid, 135; *The Scotch Whisky Association* (n 11) 474–5.

[67] Charles MacLean, *Scotch Whisky – a Liquid History* (Cassell Illustrated 2003), 265–7.

[68] *Fage* (CA) (n 5), [68].

[69] See for example, *The Scotch Whisky Association* (n 11), 491; *Chocosuisse Union* (n 5), 829, 839–40; *Diageo North America* (Ch) (n 45), [64]–[75], [136]–[138], [145]–[146]; *Fage* (Ch) (n 9), [6], [51]; cf *Consorzio Del Prosciutto di Parma* (n 42), 379.

the goods and create a public perception of the qualifications that underpin the branding.[70] Practically, these perceived qualifications can be useful in setting clear and objective boundaries for the law to guard the goodwill engendered in association with qualifying goods from being confused with non-qualifying goods.[71] If a requirement for passing off is that 'what is done represents the defendant's goods to be connected with the plaintiff's in such a way as would lead people to accept them on the faith of the plaintiff's reputation',[72] then consumers looking to the shared marks or identifiers to guide their purchases in extended passing off cases are making their purchase decisions on the faith of what the shared mark or identifier means to them. To merit protection under the law, this goodwill must be distinctive and material to consumers in their purchase decision making.[73]

Meaning to Consumers

Adherence to production standards creates a quirkiness and a relative scarcity in the relevant goods and thus a distinctiveness that is beyond the quality inherent in the goods themselves. This quirkiness can enable consumers to connect with their brand communities and distinguish themselves from those outside this community. This is particularly so for premium or luxury branded goods. The more elaborate the narrative embodied in the goodwill or the consumers' recognition of the branding, the more intimately consumers can relate to the brand, the more distinctive it becomes in the mind of those consumers. An elaborate, lifestyle-oriented narrative also creates occasions for consumers to interact with the brand in their social surroundings, rendering the brand more mentally available to them.

For example, knowledge about the processes and composition prescribed in the qualification for branded goods such as Scotch Whisky can become a form of brand narrative that consumers engage with. The connoisseurs and afficionados among them thrive not only on the value in the usefulness of the goods in question, but, moreover, on an understanding regarding the authenticity of the goods and the craftsmanship behind them,[74] which inform

---

[70] *Fage* (Ch) (n 9), [112], *Fage* (CA) (n 5), [17]; *The Military Mutual Ltd* (n 16), [29].

[71] *Siegert v Findlater* (1878) 7 Ch D 801, 813; *Fage* (CA) (n 5), [68], [123]; see also *Diageo North America* (Ch) (n 45), [149].

[72] *H P Bulmer* (n 14), 117.

[73] *The Military Mutual Ltd* (n 16), [35]–[38].

[74] Manfredi Ricca and Rebecca Robins, *Meta-Luxury - brands and the culture of excellence* (Palgrave Macmillan 2012), 10, 46.

the collective product biographies, culture, and ongoing heritage. Thus, the particular processes and composition in the manufacture of the goods provide a narrative which engages public imagination and may become currency for interactions with like minds. They may confer among themselves about the quality inherent in a particular three-year-old Scotch Whisky as compared with that in a particular 25-year-old version. Furthermore, some may collect vintage whiskies, visit whisky distilleries in Scotland, or sample life on a vineyard in Napa Valley to witness first-hand the authenticity of the goods and partake in the heritage surrounding the creation of those goods.[75] These stories become personal reminders of, as well as testimonials for, the brands in question, making the brands more accessible to retrieve from memory both for those recounting the narrative and those receiving it when purchase decisions are made.[76] In consuming the goods, consumers have their psychological and emotional needs met by being perceived as part of a community of consumers who share, to varying degrees, knowledge about the processes and compositions in the manufacture of these goods, or at least the knowledge that these goods are distinctive over their functional equivalents (such as other whiskies or wines).[77] These consumers distinguish themselves from those who do not have this knowledge.

Place-branded goods and goods meeting specific qualifications may also be scarcer in supply than their generic counterparts. For example, Napa Valley wines are limited in production quantities because of the finite geographical area within Napa Valley allocated for vineyards and for wine production.[78] This scarcity may put a premium on the price and on the perception of exclusivity of the goods in a mass market.[79] It renders knowledge about those

---

[75] Glyn Atwal and Alistair Williams, 'Luxury Brand Marketing - the experience is everything!' in Jean-Noël Kapferer et al. (n 36), 47–9.

[76] Jenni Romaniuk and Byron Sharp, *How Brands Grow - part 2* (revised edn, OUP 2021), 126–38.

[77] Olga Louisa Kastner, *When Luxury Meets Art - forms of collaboration between luxury brands and the arts* (Springer Gabler 2014), 13–4.

[78] See also Elena Casprini, Jacopo Cammeo, and Lorenzo Zanni, 'Sustainable Luxury Trajectories for "Made in Italy" Wine Businesses - the Cantine Ferrari case' in Manuela De Carlo Serena Rovai (ed), *Made in Italy and the Luxury Market - Heritage, Sustainability and Innovation* (Routledge 2023), 195.

[79] Jean-Noël Kapferer, 'The End of Luxury as We Knew It?' in Jean-Noël Kapferer et al. (n 36), 31–2; Kapferer and Bastien (n 36), 79; Franck Vigneron and Lester W Johnson, 'Measuring Perceptions of Brand Luxury' in Jean-Noël Kapferer et al. (n 36), 207–8; Jean-Noël Kapferer, *Kapferer on Luxury - how luxury brands can grown yet remain rare* (KoganPage 2015), 131–44.

goods all the more valuable.[80] Additionally, for place-branded goods, the distinctiveness or structural goodwill of the place in the brand helps inform the distinctiveness or structural goodwill of the place brand of the goods in question. Geo-identities may play a role in how consumers perceive these place-branded goods and classify them for recall in purchase decisions. For example, the meanings and values in Scottishness may transfer onto goods such as Scotch Whisky.[81] Scotch Whisky and other Scottish-branded goods in turn inform the Scottishness of their claimed place of origin.[82] Consumers may also use these narratives for their own 'self'-construction[83] as a member of the brand community, blending their own biographies with those of the goods they consume. Prospective consumers may see them as peer references who endorse the branded goods.

From the point of view of the traders, the vast majority of their prospective consumers, and thus the more significant part of their product community consists not of connoisseurs and afficionados but of purchasers who recognize the qualifying product as something distinct from other functionally equivalent goods.[84] These consumers would look to their peer references in real life, in the media, or in advertisements to purchase goods which meet their needs for specific occasions. For example, when novice consumers see Champagne served, given as gifts, or advertised for celebratory occasions, these occasions form cues for consumption in their mind.[85] These cues evoke a specific class of drinks perceived as appropriate and distinct from other classes of drinks (such as other sparkling wines) for the occasions.

Extended passing off helps traders and consumers ensure that goods that do fall within the class that meets the perceived qualification are distinct from those that do not fall within the class in the consumers' purchase decision making. So while 'Spanish Champagne' and 'Elderflower Champagne' appear oxymoronic to those who know that 'Champagne' means sparkling wines produced in accordance with the required specifications in the defined Champagne

---

[80] Johan Bruwer and Ray Johnson, 'Place-Based Marketing and Regional Branding Strategy Perspectives' (2010) 27(1) J Consumer Marketing 5, 12; Johan Bruwer, Emily McCutcheon and Elton Li, 'Region of Origin and its Importance among Choice Factors in the Wine-Buying Decision Making of Consumers' (2009) 21(3) International J Wine Business Research 212, 230.

[81] Kapferer, 'The End of Luxury as We Knew It?' (n 79), 33; Miller and Mills (n 36), 161–2.

[82] Kapferer, *Kapferer on Luxury - how luxury brands can grown yet remain rare* (n 79), 102–3, 109.

[83] Atwal and Williams (n 75), 45–6; see also Ng (n 21), 52–65.

[84] Kastner (n 77), 7 – 9; Romaniuk and Sharp (n 76), 227.

[85] Romaniuk and Sharp (n 76), 68, 182–3.

region of France,[86] extended passing off cases have also considered sections of society who have heard of 'Champagne' or similar shared branding but do not know any more about it.[87] 'Less knowledgeable consumers were not to be disregarded, however. Indeed, they were perhaps the most likely to be deceived and it was precisely against such deception that the original producers were entitled to be protected.'[88] Furthermore, misrepresentation can also occur where consumers are inclined 'to read the overall representation as being not that the contents were Champagne but that the product was in some way associated with or connected with or derived from Champagne'.[89] By protecting 'the reputation that that type of product itself has gained in the market by reason of its recognisable and distinctive qualities that has generated the relevant goodwill',[90] extended passing off cases have addressed the interests of the brand and the brand community as a whole as well as those who may join it if even occasionally.[91] They have protected the interests of the brand traders so that they can expand their trade in the qualifying goods through market penetration by broadening their consumer base.[92] From the perspective of most traders, it is these light or occasional purchasers who can generate the most volume of sale.[93] Furthermore, as the law of passing off also protects against post-sale confusion, traders can help maintain a coherence within the brand community and thereby also protect their consumers' and prospective consumers' social capital in their associations with the class of goods.[94]

As mentioned at the start, these points of distinction need not concern only luxury goods. The Intellectual Property Enterprise Court in 2018, addressing the claimant MML which arranged the provision of insurance services, stated:

> Even if MML were able to show that financial mutuals were invariably owned by some or all of their customers, that would not have been enough to establish their case on the meaning of "mutual". It would be still have been consistent with there having been only a single broad meaning together with a further understanding on

---

[86] *J Bollinger v Costa Brava Wine Co Ltd (No 2)* (n 8), 282; *H P Bulmer* (n 14), 96; *Taittinger SA v Allbev Ltd* [1993] FSR 641 (CA), 665.

[87] *J Bollinger v Costa Brava Wine Co Ltd (No 2)* (n 8), 289–91; *Vine Products* (n 14), 427; *H P Bulmer* (n 14), 96, 102, 148, 150; *Taittinger SA* (n 86), 666–7; *Fage* (CA) (n 5), [66].

[88] *Fage* (CA) (n 5), [45].

[89] *Taittinger SA* (n 86); see also *H P Bulmer* (n 14), 99, 117, 120, 142.

[90] *Erven* (n 10), 747.

[91] For example, *Vine Products* (n 14), 422–3; *Taittinger SA* (n 86), 666–7.

[92] Romaniuk and Sharp (n 76), 15, 27–39.

[93] Byron Sharp, *How Brands Grow - what marketers don't know* (OUP 2010), 110–11; Romaniuk and Sharp (n 76), 112.

[94] Keller (n 37), 188–9.

the part of the relevant section of the public that to date financial mutuals had always been owned by their customers. MML had to show *something more*: the existence of the second narrower meaning. MML bore the evidential burden of showing that Forces Mutual would not merely have been recognised as an exception to the usual pattern that financial mutuals tend to be customer-owned.[95]

Here, '[t]he evidence does not support MML's claim to collective goodwill held by that class because the public did not in April 2016 recognise any such class as being distinct. The term "mutual" had not acquired a narrow meaning used to define the ownership structure of that class'.[96] Moreover, taking a consumers' perspective:

> if extended passing off were really made possible by an objective misrepresentation, it would follow that the relevant public need not be misled about anything. I do not believe that this is what either the House of Lords [in *Advocaat*] or Danckwerts J [in *Spanish Champagne*] can have had in mind.[97]

'Something More'

The most challenging issue in extended passing off cases is what constitutes this 'something more'[98] that distinguishes the goodwill susceptible to protection in relation to a class of goods from the goodwill in relation to the broader class of generic goods which share the same inherent and objective qualities. For place-branded goods, the issue is often less acute for three reasons. First, place brands often implicate an element of *terroir* to the goods which, even without production standards being applied to the goods, nevertheless lends a narrative to the goods which may attract custom.[99] Furthermore, as discussed earlier, place-branding can link the brand in the mind of consumers not only to the branded goods but also to the consumers' impression of the place in the brand. This evocation of place as well as the evocation of *terroir*, however, do not always materialize in a place-brand. For example, in a case concerning 'Glenfield Starch', the House of Lords found 'nothing whatever to give particular celebrity to the name of *Glenfield* so connected with a starch manufactory, beyond the fact that the Appellants had manufactured an article

---

[95] *The Military Mutual Ltd* (n 16), [93] (emphasis added).
[96] Ibid, [118].
[97] Ibid, [51].
[98] See also *Fage* (Ch) (n 9), [114], affirmed *Fage* (CA) (n 5), [70], [73], [139]–[140].
[99] For example, *Montgomery* (n 5), 221; *Barnsley Brewery v RBNB* [1997] FSR 462 (Ch) ,468.

known by that name, and having a very large sale under that name'.[100] The term had acquired a secondary meaning to refer unequivocally to the appellants in that case. However, where the evocation of place does materialize, the triangulation helps distinguish place-branded goods in the mind of consumers from generic equivalents of those goods. Finally, place-branded goods are often a subset of a broader class of equivalent goods. Thus, Champagne is but one type of sparkling wine; Scotch Whisky, a type of whisky. These reasons may explain the prominence of place-branded goods among extended passing off cases.

Nevertheless, '[i]f [the term conveys] nothing more than [its] descriptive meaning, the action must fail'.[101] In classic passing off, the protected goodwill allows consumers to recognize the goods of their desired branding traders, even without knowledge of who those traders are.[102] In extended passing off, the protected goodwill allows consumers to recognize goods that belong to a distinctive class of traders sharing a brand, even without knowing specifically the qualification that makes the brand distinctive.[103] For example, the traditional way of producing yoghurt in Greece has made Greek Yoghurt 'special' in England beyond being a product description with geographical origin significance.[104] This understanding of Greek Yoghurt offers a coherence in the mind of the relevant public,[105] for the class of goods to signify something extraordinary and specific within the broader product category of yoghurts.[106]

Where the brand in question refers to a class of goods for which there is no generic substitute, the issue of what constitutes 'something more' is more challenging. For example, in a case dealing with 'Glen Kella Manx Whiskey' which did not taste like whisky and, unlike whisky, was white in colour as a result of an additional redistillation of the blended Scotch Whisky in the Isle of Man, the court determined it was not 'whisky'. The court found it 'irrefutable that whisky has gained a public reputation that distinguishes it from

---

[100] *Wotherspoon* (n 62), 512.
[101] *Chocosuisse Union* (Ch) (n 5), 129, affirmed *Chocosuisse Union* (CA) (n 5), 848–9.
[102] *The Birmingham Vinegar Brewery* (n 26), 713–5.
[103] *Chocosuisse Union* (Ch) (n 5), 133, 136.
[104] *Fage* (CA) (n 5), [70], [73], [75].
[105] *Chocosuisse Union* (Ch) (n 5), 135; *Fage* (Ch) (n 9), [114].
[106] *Fage* (CA) (n 5), [70], [73].

competing products of different composition' in 'an aura around whisky that attracts publicity and knowledge, because people know what whisky is'.[107]

> [T]he real risk of damage to the goodwill of the first and second plaintiffs from the defendant's being allowed to continue calling its product "whiskey" when it is not is the commencement of an insidious process of erosion of the integrity of the reputation of "aura" of true whisky, which the defendant rightly accepted that it has in the minds of potential consumers.[108]

The court granted injunction to protect from erosion this 'aura', which existed beyond the ingredients and processes required to produce whisky. It did not elaborate on what constituted this 'aura' and how it was engendered.

The case dealing with 'vodka' takes this chapter back to its starting point: the Court of Appeal in the case determined that 'cachet' was not a requirement the claimant had to show for extended passing off unless 'by a cachet, one means no more than distinctiveness'.[109] Following *Advocaat*, the High Court found that vodka had acquired a 'reputation as a "party spirit" [that] (rightly or wrongly) [caused] fewer hangovers than other spirits'[110] and as 'a drink with recognisable qualities of appearance, taste, strength and satisfaction'.[111] The analysis appears closer to that for protecting a certification mark with reputation from infringement under Trade Marks Act 1994,[112] than that for protecting the goodwill that distinguishes the branded goods in the mind of consumers when it stated:

> Even if there was no evidence of lost sales, I consider that it is clear that ICB's marketing of VODKAT is likely to erode the distinctiveness of the term "vodka". It will cease to be a term reserved for 37.5 per cent ABV spirits ... The advent of the me-too products like VODKOVA is likely to accelerate this trend if it is not checked.[113]

While the law of passing off here appears deployed to determine the accuracy of vodka as a generic term, the Court of Appeal noted that '[t]he law of passing-off is there to protect the unlawful appropriation of goodwill through misrepresentation. It is not there to guarantee to the general consumer the

---

[107] *The Scotch Whisky Association* (n 11), 491.
[108] Ibid, 493.
[109] *Diageo North America* (CA) (n 3), [51].
[110] *Diageo North America* (Ch) (n 45), [79].
[111] Ibid, [155]–[156].
[112] Trade Marks Act 1994, ss 1(2), 10(2), (3), 50.
[113] *Diageo North America* (Ch) (n 45), [235].

quality of what he buys. For that he must look elsewhere'.[114] Nevertheless, the Court also commented that 'goodwill may attach to a product simply because consumers come to like and value it for its inherent qualities rather than its status'.[115] By focussing on the analysis of 'goodwill' as engendered by 'the product' alone and not as a social construct that exists in the mind of consumers informed only in part by the quality of the product, it becomes difficult to differentiate the generic term that stood for a particular quality in the drink and the term that had 'something more' to help organize purchase decisions in consumers' mind. Rix LJ cautioned: 'the extended form of passing off should not by dint of extensions upon extensions trespass beyond the legitimate area of protection of goodwill into an illegitimate area of anti-competitiveness'.[116]

> There ought ... to be room for its manufacturer to market what might be called a vodka-type product in such a way that the consumer (barring the ignorant or foolish) knows what he or she is and is not getting, and yet the association with vodka is legitimately and not deceptively made.[117]

This 'something more' is therefore not something new that is required of extended passing off actions alone. As discussed earlier, the law of passing off has come to terms with the idea that consumers' purchase decisions are informed by more than the physical functioning or the inherent quality of the relevant goods. In *Irvine*, Laddie J noted: 'no matter how irrational it may seem to a lawyer, those in business have reason to believe that the lustre of a famous personality, if attached to their goods or services, will enhance the attractiveness of those goods or services to their target market'.[118] This 'something more' adds to and yet coheres with the social meanings and values embodied in a brand as perceived by consumers. It need not refer to a luxury or premium product or brand. For example, the place-branded Aberdeen Football Club ('AFC') offers 'entertainment; sporting services'.[119] Arguably, Aberdonians attend AFC games because they can enjoy the live entertainment locally. Fans who travel to away games however have options of seeing other live football games which may be of higher quality than those involving the

---

[114] *Diageo North America* (CA) (n 3), [29].
[115] Ibid, [51], [53]; see also [76].
[116] Ibid, [76].
[117] Ibid, [77].
[118] *Irvine* (Ch) (n 31), [39].
[119] Under Class 41, UK00003039448 for design mark <https://trademarks.ipo.gov.uk/ipo-tmcase/page/Results/1/UK00003039448> accessed 9 October 2024; see also UK00003854821 for word mark <https://trademarks.ipo.gov.uk/ipo-tmcase/page/Results/1/UK00003854821> accessed 9 October 2024.

AFC. Yet, many choose to follow the AFC even when they travel because this 'something more' – such as the communal brand associations of shared fan experience and the rituals of team identification – [120] attracts them to watch the AFC notwithstanding its successes and losses in matches throughout the season. '[T]he loyalty for "Lovemarks" brand is "loyalty beyond reason"'.[121] Non-place-branded teams such as the Arsenal Football Club similarly command loyalty from fans. As illustrated in *Irvine,* successful stars such as Irvine in professional sports such as Formula 1 racing can thus leverage this loyalty or 'something more' among a relevant audience for lucrative commercial sponsorship arrangements.[122]

> When a [Formula 1] driver comes in one of the first three places in a race [as Irvine did for half the races in the 1999 season], he stands on the winner's podium at the end of the race and usually indulges in a tradition of spraying champagne over his co-drivers and anyone within striking distance.[123]

This high profile and extravagant ritual endorsed by podium place winners through their participation reinforces a celebratory social meaning and value in 'Champagne' that is beyond its inherent quality as a sparkling wine. Celebratory occasions need not implicate sparkling wines, much less Champagne specifically. '[A] reference to champagne imports nuances of quality and celebration, a sense of something privileged and special. But this is the reputation which the Champagne houses have built up over the years, and in which they have a property right.'[124] As discussed earlier, consumers, as peer references, con-

---

[120] Henry Wear, Stephen Hills, Bob Heere and Matthew Walker, 'Communal Brand Associations as Drivers of Team Identity and Consumer Behavior' (2018) 3(3) J Global Sport Management 302, 314 in respect of rugby; see also Dimitrios Kolyperas, Georgios Maglaras and Leigh Sparks, 'Sport Fans' Roles in Value Co-Creation' (2019) 19(2) European Sport Management Quarterly 201.

[121] Kevin Roberts, *Lovemarks: The Future beyond Brands* (2nd edn, NY Powerhouse Book 2005), 66 as cited in Avichai Shuv-Ami, Demetris Vrontis and Alkis Thrassou, 'Brand Lovemarks Scale of Sport Fans' (2018) 24(2) J Promotion Management 215, 222; see also 228–9 in the same article; Kevin Roberts, 'The Lovemarks Effect' (2006) British Brands Group Lecture (<www .britishbrandsgroup .org .uk/ the -brands -lectures/ #: ~: text = The %20Lovemarks %20effect & text = These %20are %20the %20products %20that ,creation %20of %20enduring%20emotional%20connections> accessed 9 October 2024); Rajeev Batra, Aaron Ahuvia and Richard P Bagozzi, 'Brand Love' (2012) 76(2) J of Marketing 1.

[122] *Irvine* (Ch) (n 31), [40].

[123] Ibid, [51].

[124] *Taittinger SA* (n 86), 678.

noisseurs, and afficionados, also contribute to the social meanings and values in Champagne and thereby help position it in the mind of the relevant public and render the term mentally available at purchase decisions when celebratory occasions arise.

Following its predecessors of Mumm, Moët & Chandon, and Carbon Champagnes, Italian luxury wine Ferrari Trento was named the Official Sparkling Wine of Formula 1 in 2021 'to create and enhance [its] fan experience on and off the podium'.[125] Irvine's and others' Formula 1 successes thus inform the shared goodwill pertaining to Champagne as a class of drinks for celebrations and similarly later the goodwill pertaining to Ferrari Trento as a brand of sparkling wine in the consumers' mind. Ferrari Trento is not related to the Ferrari Formula 1 team or the car manufacturer. Its CEO noted 'We never want to create confusion between us and Ferrari cars ... But in a sense, every time we go abroad if we say Ferrari, everybody will think about the red car'.[126] Place-branding creates a similar effect. With the Formula 1 sponsorship, 'Ferrari [Trento] achieved over 50 percent sales growth in the USA in 2021 despite the pandemic's disastrous impact on restaurant wine sales. In Texas, where the only USA Grand Prix took place in 2021, sales grew 500 percent'.[127] Although this is due in part to the increased exposure through the prestigious event, the celebratory exposure on the Formula 1 winning podiums arguably also played a role as the 'something more' that helped position its goodwill in the consumers' mind alongside Champagne. There is no suggestion of any change in the quality of the goods to account for this increase in the sale of Ferrari Trento. The goods were 'made in the same traditional method and with the same grape varieties as sparkling wines from Champagne'[128] but with the distinctiveness of mountain viticulture from a 120-year-old winery in Trentino, Italy. The 'Made in Italy' brand also brings with it 'social values of the territory and, before that, of the [Ferrari and later Lunelli] family owner'.[129]

---

[125] Ferrari Trento, 'Ferrari Trento Named Official Toast of Formula 1®' (2 March 2021) <https://www.ferraritrento.com/en/ferrari-trento-named-official-toast-of-formula-1/> accessed 10 October 2024.

[126] Matteo Lunelli as cited by Jessica Broadbent, 'Italy's Ferrari Trento sees US Sales Uptick on Back of Formula One Deal' (*Just Drinks,* 19 June 2023) <www.just-drinks.com/news/italys-ferrari-trento-sees-us-sales-uptick-on-back-of-formula-one-deal/#catfish> accessed 9 October 2024.

[127] Matteo Lunelli as cited by Jessica Dupuy, 'Ferrari Trento Shares the Podium in Austin for Another Celebration of F1 Racing' (*Forbes,* 27 October 2022) <www.forbes.com/sites/jessicadupuy/2022/10/27/ferrari-trento-shares-the-podium-in-austin-for-another-celebration-of-f1-racing/> accessed 9 October 2024.

[128] Ibid.

[129] Casprini and Cammeo (n 78), 200.

As a sparkling wine, it is nevertheless distinctive from Champagne which offers further 'something more' in its place-brand significance to a broad swathe of consumers.

CONCLUSION

As Laddie J admitted above, this 'something more' is not easy to rationalize in physical utilitarian terms and even harder to quantify. In classic passing off where the branded goods are attributable to specific branding traders, the physical goods and this 'something more' are attributed in tandem to those traders in the eyes of the consumers. In false endorsement cases such as *Irvine*, the physical goods of the claimant are not directly implicated, hence the need to identify this 'something more' at stake. In extended passing off cases, this 'something more' must likewise add to and yet cohere with the social meanings and values embodied in a brand as a collective as perceived by consumers. In cases such as those dealing with Greek Yoghurt and Swiss chocolate, courts[130] drew on consumers' perspective to substantiate claims of this coherent perception of the place brands that distinguished the qualified goods from those which shared identical inherent qualities but were not qualified goods. The cases of Scotch Whisky, Napa Valley wines, and Coffee Kenya branded coffees like the place-branded drinks cases that led up to *Advocaat*, offer opportunities for consumers to engage with the brands beyond their underlying goods. This engagement can render the brands more mentally available by structuring consumers' recollection according to the classes of goods, the places of the brands, and the consumers' experiences with either or both. Where there are social meanings and values in each of these brands and its goods that resonate in unison from a consumers' perspective, these brands have achieved a shared goodwill that is protected under extended passing off.

Thus, what is at stake in classic passing off is the authenticity of the branding trader's identity and its social narrative as perceived by consumers that is material to their purchase decision. What is at stake in extended passing off is the authenticity of the social narrative as perceived by consumers to be underpinning the claimant traders' collective identity in their shared brand. As in classic passing off, this narrative must be material to the consumers' purchase decision.[131] In both classic and extended passing off, the law seeks to protect the authenticity of the branding traders' voice in the tales they tell consumers about themselves through the goods they sell and endorse and the

---

[130] *Chocosuisse Union* (CA) (n 5), 848–9; *Fage* (Ch) (n 9), [113], [114], [116].

[131] See for example, *Chocosuisse Union* (Ch) (n 5), 136; *Chocosuisse Union* (CA) (n 5), 841.

narratives and experiences they share with consumers in order to become part of the consumers' own 'self' narratives. In this light, extended passing off does not pose a conundrum to the law of passing off; it is merely a 'species of the same genus'[132] as Lord Diplock said of *Spalding* in *Advocaat* almost half a century ago.

---

[132] *Erven* (n 10), 741–2.

PART VI

The Producers' Experiences of Place-Branding

17. Place-Branding – Scotch Whisky
Graham G. Stewart and Anne Anstruther[1]

When Scotland emerged from the last ice age, some 10,000 years ago, it was a land of clear mountain streams, verdant valleys and islands. Settlers grew grain (mainly barley) in order to provide a year's sustenance for themselves and their cattle. In a good year, after the year's payments and the store barns were filled, each farm used their own still to distil the remaining grain to make whisky (in Gaelic, *uisge beatha*), which musically translates into 'water of life'. This was a valuable currency in order to pay the rent and barter for goods and was, in its own right, essential for important ceremonies, such as weddings, funerals, and so on.[2] In any year of inclement arable farming weather they struggled!

'Place-branding' is not new. These early settlers 'branded' their surroundings with their soft Gaelic accents – *Meall na h-Iolaire* (the round hill of the eagles), *Gleann Seileach* (the willow glen), *Àird nam Murchan* (the headland of the sea-hounds (seal or otter)). Whisky stills and early distilleries were consequently named by their location or their family name. For example, amongst our oldest surviving distilleries are: Glenturret (1775), 'in the Glen of the Little Dry stream'; Bowmore Distillery (1779) 'The big reef' on the Isle of Islay; and Strathisla Distillery (1786) 'Wide valley of the River Isla', in Keith. Scottish Gaelic is largely integral to the branding of Scotch Whisky, particularly single malts, and it has come to epitomize a Scotch Whisky's identity at the higher end of the market.

Scotland and whisky evolved together, but not always amicably. The first Excise Duty raised by the Scottish Government in 1644 was to fund a war and found whisky a very lucrative source of taxation and, consequently, *poit dhubh* (illicit stills) moved into remote glens to make *peatreek* (the making of whisky over a peat fire) where the excisemen (of which the famous poet Robert Burns was one) would struggle to find them (unless they spoke Gaelic and if they

---

[1] We would like to thank Olga Stewart for her patience and advice during the production of this chapter.
[2] Edward Burns, *Bad Whisky: The Scandal That Created the World's Most Successful Spirit* (3rd edn, Angel's Share 2009), 59–61.

lived that long!). Smugglers (of whisky and other contraband goods) were the heroes of the people and many often met an early death hanging from a rope! A well-known example is the hanging of the smuggler Andrew Wilson in 1736 in the Grassmarket of Edinburgh which resulted in the Porteous Riots.[3]

CONSTRAINTS AND CONSEQUENCES

Along with the 'joys' of successful production, the pressures of taxation and regulation continuously increased. Early regulation decreased the legal capacity of a legal still. Increasing taxation forced distillers into greater production volumes, albeit with poorer spirit quality. In 1823, The Wash Act demanded a distiller's license for each still, outlawing any private still. As a result of these constraints, many Irish and Scots distillers emigrated to North America where there was less regulation – their skills were welcomed and they flourished.

When Aeneas Coffey in 1831 had perfected the continuous still (continuous consistent distillation and blending), whisky became an industry. Lowland distilleries, in particular, began producing very pure, very high strength, perhaps somewhat bland, spirit from grain whisky and this created competition both for customers and within the whisky markets. At this time, food and drink (including whisky – the 'poor man's strong drink') adulteration was rife with dilution, 'flavor enhancers' and colorants which were often poisonous to the consumer! Indeed, one reported sample in September 1872 taken from a public house states that it 'probably contains no pure whisky'.[4]

RISING PRESTIGE

Scotch Whisky was not particularly popular outside Scotland until the *Phylloxera vastatrix* beetle was brought to Europe through inter-breeding with grapes from America. Over 40% of all French vineyards were devastated between 1860 and 1875 and, as the popular French brandy became scarce, the increasingly palatable, quality, and diverse characteristics of Scottish whiskies steadily became the drink of choice, diverting the focus of attention from Europe and North America.[5] This can also be regarded as active Scottish place-branding. However, this attracted product adulteration and counterfeiting in order to make money.

---

[3] Charles Maclean, *Scotch Whisky a Liquid History* (Cassell Illustrated Octopus Publishing Group Ltd, 2005), 32.
[4] Burns (n 2).
[5] Allen Andrews, *The Whisky Barons* (Angels' Share 2002).

SCOTCH WHISKY'S EVOLVING WORLDWIDE IDENTITY

In 1908, the Royal Commission defined whisky as 'a product obtained by the distillation from a mash of cereal grains saccharified by the diastase of malt'[6] and Scotch Whisky as 'whisky so defined distilled in Scotland'. The increasingly complex maze of regulations and restrictions required clarification and control and, by 1912, the Wine and Spirit Brand Association had been founded which, in 1917, became the industry's governing body, then the Scotch Whisky Association (SWA) in 1942. The SWA tenaciously acts as the regulatory body that ensures that Scotch Whisky is produced in accordance with traditional practices, as well as ensuring a sustainable future for the Scotch Whisky industry by promoting sustainable production, global trade, and responsible consumption.

Since its inception, the SWA has persistently pursued the legal definition of Scotch Whisky until it has become the most rigidly defined spirit worldwide. However, it also legally pursues and defends against counterfeiters and so on with approximately 60–70 live legal cases being pursued at any one time.[7]

The SWA has identified five traditional whisky regions in Scotland – Highland, Speyside (with the largest number of distilleries), Islay, Campbeltown and Lowland each with its unique whisky characteristics (tastes, appearance and aroma) due to its topology and climate. By delineating these areas, the SWA categorized these characteristics, making it easier for the whisky tourist (amongst others) to visualize and focus on their appeal and benefits, effectively place-branding these Scotch Whisky regions.

Large companies continually search for 'the best' in their competitive world in order to be ahead of the market. This includes the world of whisk(e)y. The purity and drinkability of Scotch Whisky has been sought after as many smaller distilleries have been annexed in order to incorporate their products and create top market blends (Diageo – Johnnie Walker, Talisker; The Edrington Group – Famous Grouse, Macallan)[8] and thus increase their company's world position.

---

[6] 'The Royal Commission on Whiskey and Other Potable Spirits' (1909) 2 BMJ 399; Graham Moore 'Decoding Labels' (*Whisky Magazine,* 2000), 8.

[7] 'Legal Protection in the UK' (Scotch Whisky Association) <https:// www .scotch -whisky .org .uk/ industry -insights/ protecting -scotch -whisky/ legal -protection-in-the-uk/> accessed 10 October 2024.

[8] JOHNNIE WALKER (Diageo) <https:// www .diageo .com/ en/ our -brands/ brand-explorer/johnnie-walker> accessed 6 December 2023; 'Talisker Distillery' (*Difford's Guide*) <https:// www .diffordsguide .com/ producers/ 72/ talisker -distillery/history> accessed 10 October 2024; 'The Famous Grouse' (Erdington)

Nevertheless, at ground level, the distiller understands that it is essential that the integrity of the distillery's sources (air, water, crops, and thus its product purity) and also its environment must be maintained and protected against pollution of any kind. Should the product lose its physical integrity, the local community which has built up to support the distillery could be negatively affected.

POTENTIAL PITFALLS

'Scotch Whisky is the UK's biggest drink export, with turnover of £4.1 billion in 2019.'[9] In that year 'our whisky accounted for a fifth of all UK food and drink exports'.[10] However, success brings its own problems, responsibilities and potential pitfalls!

War is largely unpredictable but must be handled with care. Due to the stringencies of the last two World Wars and during Prohibition, the distilling industries have endured catastrophic bans and some companies produced distilled products such as glycerol and butanol-acetone to enhance the war efforts.[11]

Plague is a constant threat. During the Covid-19 pandemic, Scotch Whisky exports from the United Kingdom declined, distilleries were required to close for some time and the sector experienced £1.1 billion in lost sales. Due to the whisky tariff that was imposed in the US on Scotch Whisky, exports to the United States 'fell by 23% in value to £3.8bn' during 2020 from the previous year. Thankfully, this tariff has now been lifted.[12]

<https:// uk .edrington .com/ en/ our -brands/ scotch -whisky/ the -famous -grouse> accessed 6 December 2023; 'The Macallan' (Erdington) <https:// uk .edrington .com/en/our-brands/scotch-whisky/the-macallan> accessed 6 December 2023; and 'The Macallan' (The Macallan) <https:// www .themacallan .com/ en> accessed 6 December 2023.

[9] Scottish Government, *Building New Scotland: A stronger economy with independence – summary* (Scottish Government 2022).

[10] *Building New Scotland: A stronger economy with independence – summary* (n 8).

[11] See '1885 to Present Day' (The North British Distillery Company) <https:// thenorthbritish .co .uk/ our -story/> accessed 6 December 2023 and 'Grangestone Distillery' (*Railscot*) <https:// www .railscot .co .uk/ locations/ G/ Grangestone _Distillery/> accessed 10 October 2024.

[12] Kenny Smith, 'COVID costs Scotch Whisky Exports £1.1.billion in lost sales' (*Scottish Field,* 12 February 2021) <https://www.scottishfield.co.uk/scotland-travel/covid-costs-scotch-whisky-exports-1-1-billion-in-lost-sales/> accessed 10 October 2024.

Changes in the consumption culture affect Scotch Whisky sales. In the first half of 2023, exports fell by 3.6% compared to 2022 (which had been a record year for Scotch Whisky sales globally), reflecting consumers 'trading up' to more premium brands but drinking less alcohol overall.[13]

Considering 'climate change' and current weather excesses, the vagaries of weather requires no introduction. A poor crop will wreak havoc, particularly to the smaller distilleries, which would be a reflection on the whole industry!

PLACE-BRANDING SCOTCH WHISKY

Currently, a brand is seen as one of the most powerful forces in the human environment and leads to a stronger world image (JOHNNIE WALKER, Coca Cola).[14] It is expensive, but it is essential to keep the industry 'in the public eye'. It is the identity that the potential consumer reaches out to, and feels the better for 'the feel good factor' and also forms an emotional connection with, whether for their mood, their idealized standing in society or, in some cases, one's own 'company' (relaxation and satisfaction).

Scotland's unique identity, due to its geographic position, its history, its heritage, and modern perception (and the efforts of the SWA) is a precious factor. Scotland benefits from the prestige and appeal of Scotch Whisky, and Scotch Whisky benefits from Scotland's history and the heritage of Scotland. Both are 'living icons'. Popular films, such as: *Whisky Galore*, *Braveheart*, and *Harry Potter*, and so on, as well as American author, Diana Gabaldon's books and subsequent TV series, boost worldwide interest for both. Tourist attractions evolve – The Glenfinnan Viaduct, famous for the Raising of the Standard in 1745 with 'The Young Pretender', Bonnie Prince Charlie, has now become 'the Harry Potter Bridge' with tourists from all over the world, filling car parks and packing train carriages for their 'unique' photographs, consequently increasing local employment.

The famous explorations of Ernest Shackleton (an Irishman) to Antarctica during the 19th century carried only the essentials for life and survival: it is no coincidence that his rations included cases of 'Scotch Whisky'![15]

---

[13] Greig Cameron 'Scotch Whisky Exports to America and India on the Slide' (*The Times*, London, 18 August 2023), 35.

[14] See generally Stephen Brown, *Brands and Branding* (SAGE Publications 2016).

[15] See 'Shackleton Whisky' (*Whisky Shop*) <https://www.whiskyshop.com/blended-scotch-whisky/brand/shackleton> accessed 10 October 2024.

REPUTATION

Through time, the whisky industry has supported local employment, tourism and all its supporting commerce, within a pristine environment. This reputation must be protected. As of 2022, 'Scotland is home to over 140 malt and grain, making it the greatest concentration of whisky production in the world'.[16] Scotch Whisky tourism alone has developed around this industry, with distilleries being the third most visited attractions in Scotland with approximately two million visits being recorded in 2018.[17] In this, now global, market the distiller's dedication to preserving the purity and drinkability of the product which depends on the integrity of the environment, such as pure river water (avoiding effluent – Thames Water and sewage)[18] and air purity (compare Chernobyl;[19] and Nine Mile Island – radiation[20]) and also avoiding or minimizing agricultural pesticides (no British cases to date),[21] rubbish tipping (Walmart – hazardous waste)[22]; and local sea pollution (Exxon and oil spills).[23]

Today's distiller continues to strive for the 'perfect' whisky (pure single malt with the right attributes for the consumers with the greatest influence) which will seal the company name in history (and in effective advertising). Loyalty remains with the local economy around which the distillery evolved, and which possibly depends on its existence. The distiller must ensure increas-

---

[16] 'Map of Scotch Whisky Distilleries' (Scotch Whisky Association) <https://www.scotch-whisky.org.uk/media/2114/052023-whisky-map-high-quality-export.pdf> accessed 10 October 2024.

[17] See 'Scotch Whisky Distillery Visits Reach 2 Million' (Scotch Whisky Association 2019) <https://www.scotch-whisky.org.uk/newsroom/scotch-whisky-distillery-visits-reach-2-million> accessed 10 October 2024.

[18] Sandra Laville and Helena Horton, 'Water firms discharged raw sewage 300,000 time last year court hears' (*The Guardian,* London, 4 July 2023).

[19] 'Chernobyl Accident 1984' (World Nuclear Association) <https://world-nuclear.org/information-library/safety-and-security/safety-of-plants/chernobyl-accident.aspx> accessed 6 December 2023.

[20] 'Three Mile Island Accident' (World Nuclear Association) <https://world-nuclear.org/information-library/safety-and-security/safety-of-plants/three-mile-island-accident.aspx> accessed 6 December 2023.

[21] Samira Mosalaei Rad, Ajay K Ray and Shahzad Barghi, 'Water Pollution and Agriculture Pesticide' (2022) 4(4) Clean Technologies 1088.

[22] 'Walmart illegally dumps 1m toxic items in landfills yearly, law suit claims' (*The Guardian,* London, 20 December 2021).

[23] 'Exxon Valdez' and 'Damage Assessment: Remediation and Restoration Program' (DARRP NOAA) <https://darrp.noaa.gov/oil-spills/exxon-valdez> accessed 30 April 2024.

ing demand for the core products, ensuring their integrity while protecting the environment and constantly reducing usage/wastage through cyclical and economic processes. Even more, considering 'the global market' the distiller must defend against the threats of modern technology, scammers, imitators, theft, and so on.

However, one incorrect move involving corporate identity or public perception could be disastrous! For example: Marks & Spencer and sweat shops; Pepsi and 'Black Lives Matter'; Boohoo and working conditions, are stories that have detracted from these brands and their reputations and economic viability.[24]

SCOTCH WHISKY

In a continuously changing world Scotch Whisky has evolved from a product providing income which allowed a family to survive annually, to a world-class product which must itself survive the rigors of the world market while maintaining the integrity of its source (both product and country). Scotch Whisky must continue to represent the 'rock' of its past; proudly maintaining, protecting, and promoting its promises of the present and, like all others, attempting to predict, pre-empt and prepare for the future.

---

[24] Gethin Chamberlain, 'Gap, Next and M&S in new sweatshop scandal' (*The Observer,* India, 8 August 2010) <www.theguardian.com/world/2010/aug/08/gap-next-marks-spencer-sweatshops> accessed 10 October 2024; Daniel Victor, 'Pepsi Pulls Ad Accused of Trivialising Black Lives Matter' (*The New York Times,* New York, 5 April 2017) <https://www.nytimes.com/2017/04/05/business/kendall-jenner-pepsi-ad.html> accessed 10 October 2024; 'Boohoo says reports of poor warehouse working conditions not reflective of site' (*Reuters*, 2022) <https://www.reuters.com/business/retail-consumer/boohoo-says-report-poor-warehouse-working-conditions-not-reflective-site-2022-11-23/> accessed 10 October 2024.

18. Scotch Whisky – A Perspective From Islay

Anthony Wills

Islay has a long and successful history of whisky distilling over the centuries and its inherently pleasing that Clan MacBeatha, physicians to the Lord of the Isles, lived in the Kilchoman Parish of Islay and may well have been responsible for bringing the art of distilling to Scotland.

In the 17th and 18th centuries Islay had over 35 licensed distilleries, the oldest one being Bowmore, which is still in operation today. Currently there are nine distilleries in operation with a further four in the planning or building stage.

Islay was chosen as the perfect location for malt whisky distilleries due to the fertile land used to grow barley, a supply of good quality water and, most importantly, a plentiful supply of peat to impart the salty, briny, peaty characteristics to the whisky at the malting stage.

Islay malt whisky has always played an important part in the structure and character of the brands of blended whisky on the market. It was only in the 1960s that Single Malt Whisky was first marketed and sold and only in the last 20 years that it has had such worldwide success.

I have worked in the drinks industry for over 45 years and the last 30 of them in the whisky industry. I initially started an independent bottling business, buying single malt casks and bottling them as individual cask bottlings and selling and marketing them to whisky specialist shops in the United Kingdom and worldwide. From this experience I saw the growing demand for premium single malt whisky and in 2002 decided to build a distillery. I could have bought a closed or mothballed one, but I wanted to stamp my own style on the whisky I was going to produce, market, and sell.

It was then a question of location. My wife's family had connections to Islay going back to the 1930s, but more importantly Islay was, in my view, the perfect place to locate a new distillery. Seven distilleries were in operation on Islay at the start of the 2000s. A small island off the west coast of Scotland with a population of 3,000 people, building a worldwide reputation for its single malts with a distinctive style. The decision was made and we moved to Islay in 2004 and the project was started.

I wanted to build a distillery with a unique proposition and point of difference. In my mind, building one like all the others on Islay and around Scotland wouldn't have helped us stand out from the crowd. I decided to locate it on a working farm in the parish of Kilchoman: Rockside Farm. The farm has some of the most fertile fields for growing malting barley and the idea was to grow, malt, distil, mature, and bottle our single malt on site. Today, 20% of our product is produced from barley we grow on the farm.

Timing is everything and when the project got underway there were a growing number of single malt whisky enthusiasts around the world. The malt whisky industry was on the march and, Kilchoman, the first new distillery on Islay for 124 years, created a great deal of interest.

The Islay Whisky brand is massive around the world, due to the tremendous job the other distilleries have done in promotional and marketing activities. Kilchoman has benefited from this tremendous work the other distilleries have done for brand 'Islay'. The nine distilleries currently in operation on Islay produce their own unique style of peated whiskies which have become hugely popular with a worldwide following.

As the other distilleries on Islay, apart from Ardnahoe, are owned by multinational companies, being independent and family run has been a big advantage. People are now more interested in provenance, tradition and traceability and Kilchoman can offer all these facets. We are a small team that can make quick decisions and react positively as things change in the marketplace.

Right at the start of the project the aim was to produce a style of single malt that could be bottled at a relatively young age. I employed Dr Jim Swan as my consultant. He had vast experience in whisky production and cask maturation. I asked him to design a distillery that could produce a light, fruity, clean style of spirit that, if aged in good quality wood, could possibly be released at a relatively young age. When the stills ran for the first time in November 2005 Jim turned to me and said 'if we look after this spirit you will be able to release a 3 year old single malt'.

Production quantities were relatively small in the initial years. My plan was to use all the maturing stock to bottle as Kilchoman single malt. The majority of malt whisky distilleries sell a percentage of their annual production to blenders and bottlers. I wanted to test the market before having the confidence to increase production.

In 2006 and 2007 I decided to visit the ten key markets around the world I had targeted for distribution, attend whisky shows and visit key retailers to let people try our new make spirit. The majority of people were impressed with the character and quality of the spirit and were excited about our first single malt release. In September 2009 we released 8,000 bottles of single malt, at three years of age, as a non-aged single malt. The excitement and anticipation from whisky enthusiasts from around the world to try our single malt was

Figure 18.1 Photograph of Kilchoman

unbelievable. Fortunately, the reaction was very positive. Price positioning was important and was researched thoroughly before our launch. The bottling strength of 46% abv without chill filtration and natural colour was a decisive decision. It allowed consumers to try our single malt at its most natural with just a bit of filtration prior to bottling.

It was important to price our single malt at an affordable level but at a premium to the standard ten-year-old single malts. We settled on £45 per bottle for a limited release of 8,000 bottles. The bottles sold out in two days and were very well received. The feedback was very positive with people telling us that it tasted a number of years older than it was. It was the reaction we were hoping for.

Over the next two years we launched a number of limited releases with different cask maturations, targeting the growing number of whisky enthusiasts and connoisseurs around the world. In 2011, we launched a limited-edition annual release called '100% Islay'. This was produced from barley grown in fields surrounding the distillery, malted on a traditional malt floor, distilled, matured and bottled at the distillery. This is now our flagship annual release and, at the time, was the only single malt Scotch Whisky produced entirely at one distillery. This gave us the point of difference we were looking for and it resonated with whisky enthusiasts.

I was aware that to build on our initial success we would need to release core expressions which would be constantly available, so in 2012 we launched Machir Bay, a non-aged single malt matured mainly in ex-bourbon barrels and in 2014, a second matured in mainly sherry casks, called Sanaig. Pricing was again at a slight premium to the standard ten-year-old single malts, £45 for Machir Bay and £55 for Sanaig. The reaction was very positive, and sales outstripped our expectations.

We have now settled on two core expressions and four limited edition releases annually. The core expressions build brand awareness and the limited releases, at higher prices, target the whisky enthusiasts and connoisseurs around the world.

The single malt whisky industry has tended to use ex-bourbon and sherry casks for maturation and, on occasion, finish a release in experimental casks to give the whisky a different layer of characteristics. For 10% of our maturing stock, we have experimented with full maturation in all sorts of different cask types from rum, Port, Cognac, Armagnac, Tequila, mezcal, and Calvados. The fortunate thing for us is our spirit character lends itself to be matured in a variety of different cask types and these limited edition releases have gone down exceptionally well with whisky enthusiasts.

I took a big risk when I built Kilchoman in 2005. Plenty of people in the industry thought of doing it but backed away due to the high risks attached to starting from scratch. It allowed Kilchoman to get a head start before a raft of new distilleries were built from 2013 onwards.

Kilchoman is now an established brand, and the intention is to build on the success to date. In 2009 we launched in ten export markets and Kilchoman is now available in 65 markets worldwide. Our core expressions, at competitive prices, drive awareness and the limited and single cask releases are targeted at the whisky enthusiast end of the market.

19. The Large Producers' Experiences of Place-Branding

Ian Swanson

The strength of the Napa Valley brand is well known, both within the industry and by consumers. Due to Napa Valley's ideal climate, diverse soils, and concentration of winemaking expertise, the wines produced in this area are among the best in the world. It is this unique terroir, the sense of place and climate, that allows for the cultivation of high-quality grapes. At the same time, skilled winemakers have honed their craft over generations, producing exceptional wines that have won many international awards, including the famous Judgment of Paris in 1976,[1] which put Napa Valley firmly at the top of the global wine rankings.

From this, Napa Valley wineries command premium prices for their wines. Indeed, when the world hears the name California wine, they invariably think of Napa Valley, and there are certainly some wine drinkers out there who think all California wine is from Napa – remarkable, given that Napa Valley represents less than four percent of the grapes grown in California.[2] The Napa Valley brand has also benefited from strategic marketing efforts from all involved, not just the wineries and winemakers and various industry associations, but also tourist information organizations, such as 'Visit Napa Valley'.

It is no surprise, then, that for large wine producers, having Napa Valley wines in your portfolio is highly desirable, although not a necessity. A large winery can successfully make and sell California wines from somewhere other than Napa Valley. After all, 96 percent of California wines are not from Napa Valley. But representing such great wines does bring prestige to any winery.

---

[1] 'The Judgement of Paris 1976' (Christopher Stewart Wines & Spirits) <https:// www .christopherstewart .com/ Articles/ history/ the -judgement -of -paris -1976/> accessed 20 October 2024.

[2] *California Grape Crush: Final Report* (California Department of Food and Agriculture, USDA Department – National Agricultural Statistics Service 2022) <https://www.nass.usda.gov/Statistics_by_State/California/Publications/Specialty _and _Other _Releases/ Grapes/ Crush/ Reports/ index .php> accessed 20 October 2024.

I have always said that for comparison purposes, wineries in Napa Valley are like the Mercedes Benz of the automobile industry – a great wine but at a higher price, whereas the largest wineries, making most of the California wines, are more like General Motors – high volume and more affordable. But even so, for a large winery, the ability to represent or own Napa Valley wines as part of your portfolio brings a lot of prestige.

However, in addition to the more apparent benefits of being a desirable portfolio item, there is another reason that the largest wineries look to represent or own Napa Valley wines (and by large, I am talking about wineries making and selling over 100,000 cases of wine per year). And this reason is based on the history of alcohol production and distribution in the United States (US). It all boils down to distribution and gaining access to distribution. To understand this, you must go back to Prohibition.

Following the repeal of Prohibition in 1933,[3] control of the taxation and distribution of alcohol was handed over to the states, and the three-tier system was introduced. Under the three-tier system, the distribution of alcohol was separated among three tiers: production, distribution, and retail. Within the three-tier system, all sales within the state had to flow through a distributor. Producers were required to sell to state distributors, who would then sell to retailers, and producers were not allowed to sell directly to retailers.

Within each state, now responsible for oversight and taxation of alcohol distribution within its borders, independent distributors were established to manage the distribution and collection of taxes on behalf of the state. Distributors certainly play many vital roles, including ensuring compliance with state regulations, consumer protection, and logistics and inventory management. But they also control market access and competition. They can affect the competitive landscape by choosing which products to prioritize, potentially giving certain brands an advantage over others.

With the distributors now planted firmly in the middle and exercising influence over the market with producers unable to work directly with retailers, the distributor effectively became the gatekeeper. This unintended consequence of the three-tier system became apparent as the years rolled by. As in many industries, there was consolidation amongst distributors as they all sought to grow and increase the scale of operations within the state.

Of course, the wineries were also trying to grow. To do this, they needed support and access to the resources of the state distributors. As the state distrib-

---

[3] 'The Repeal of Prohibition' (The Mob Museum) <https:// prohibition .themobmuseum .org/ the -history/ the -end -of -prohibition/ repeal -of -prohibition/ #: ~: text = Control %20of %20licensing %20and %20regulating ,personal %20and %20family%20use%20only> accessed 20 October 2024.

utors consolidated and increased control of distribution, wineries found getting the time and attention of distributors became harder. Wineries quickly discovered that they needed to own or represent wines that the trade and consumers wanted. And when two wines (1973 Stags Leap Cabernet Sauvignon and 1973 Chateau Montelena Chardonnay) from Napa Valley won at the Judgment of Paris in 1976, Napa Valley suddenly became a brand the consumer wanted.

In the years that followed the end of Prohibition, and with the three-tier system firmly in place, distributors, in the search for growth and increased profits, drove consolidation within the distribution sector, and today, only several hundred distributors remain in the US,[4] with over 11,000 wineries competing for attention.[5] And even across the remaining distributors, many are owned by larger holding companies that distribute across multiple states and act as one company. Today, the top five distributors control approximately 80 percent of wine distribution in the US[6] and they also represent spirits alongside wine, making it even more competitive.

So, the competition is fierce. For the largest wineries, their scale in this battle has always been an advantage compared to smaller wineries, and they have always had access to large distributors as a result. But still, even in the most prominent wineries, there was always a need to have wine brands in demand that other wineries did not. In response, the largest wineries began to acquire Napa wineries and vineyards to further strengthen their portfolios and have acquired many family wineries over the years; indeed, the Robert Mondavi Winery was acquired along with other assets by Constellation Brands in 2004. Since then, many more wineries have followed the same route and have been acquired by larger wineries: Silverado Vineyards, Joseph Phelps, Schafer Vineyards, and Frank Family Vineyards, just to name a few.

Additionally, the large wineries have continued to invest in Napa Valley wineries, building extensive visitor experiences, developing wine clubs, and working with top winemakers to achieve the highest competitive scores for their wine quality. For these wineries, it was about creating consumer demand, brand awareness, and highly rated wines, as together, these would lead to

---

[4] 'Wine Distributor Statistics' (Wine Business Analytics) <https://winebusinesanalytics.com/statistics/distributor/> accessed 20 October 2024.

[5] 'Review of the Industry - 11,691 Wineries: US Winery Growth Remains Positive' (Wine Business) <https://www.winebusiness.com/news/article/266918#:~:text=Feb%208%2C%202023&text=According%20to%20the%20Wines%20Vines,the%20growth%20rate%20since%202010> accessed 20 October 2024.

[6] 'Top 14 Wine Distributors in the USA' (USA Wine Ratings – Beverage Trade Network) <https:// usawineratings .com/ en/ blog/ insights -1/ top -14 -wine -distributors-in-the-usa-49.htm> accessed 20 October 2024.

increased support from the distributors and retail trade, all essential to continued growth and success.

Napa Valley also serves as a hub of innovation and expertise in the wine industry. Large wineries can tap into the region's knowledge base, learn from experienced winemakers, and adopt best practices in viticulture and winemaking by having Napa Valley wines in their portfolios. This can elevate the overall quality of their wines and enhance their winemaking capabilities across all their wine portfolios. It also adds to their winemaking credentials.

So, while large producers have diverse portfolios and may source grapes and produce wines from various regions worldwide, Napa Valley wines can be a valuable addition as wineries often aim to offer a range of styles, varietals, and price points to cater to different consumer preferences. Ultimately, including Napa Valley wines within the portfolio depends on a winery's strategy, target market, and overall brand positioning.

20. What's in a Name? Thoughts on 50 Years of Winemaking in the Napa Valley

Dawnine Dyer

If you had told me, back in 1974 when I first moved to the Napa Valley, with stars in my eyes about making great wines, that it could possibly look the way it does today, I would have laughed. I was a recent graduate from the University of California with a degree in biology and aspirations of making my mark in the exciting field of winemaking. In 1970 the California census[1] reported a total population of 79,140 in Napa County and not much had changed by 1974. There were five towns on roughly 30 miles of California State Highway 29. I recall a single stop sign between Calistoga and the town of Napa and a dining scene that consisted of diners, steak houses and drive-ins – not one of the Michelin-starred restaurants or Relais Chateau hotels that now dot the landscape in Napa Valley. My husband and I had traveled in Europe and visited California's wine countries during college and had become interested in wine and winemaking. What that rural Napa Valley did have, and what drew us to it, was over 100 years of grape-growing and winemaking history and a promise for the future.

Wine grapes were first planted in Napa Valley in the 1830s by European immigrants and by 1875 more than 24,664 acres were planted to vines. In 1889, at the Paris World's Fair, Napa Valley first gained international attention when ten Napa Valley wineries took awards, including some that remain prominent today – Inglenook Winery, Beringer, Larkmead, and Krug.[2] However after the initial successes and promise, the wine industry in Napa Valley and all of California was dealt serious blows by both the phylloxera epidemic that first arrived in Napa in the 1870s and America's decade long Prohibition against alcohol brought on by the passing of the Volstead Act in 1919. After each of

---

[1] 'Napa Country' (Bay Area Census) <www.bayareacensus.ca.gov/counties/NapaCounty70.htm> accessed 10 October 2024.
[2] 'World's Largest Wine Press at Krug' (*St Helena Star,* St Helena, 23 August 1989).

these episodes Napa's wine industry rebounded. Yet in 1974, with 14,070 acres planted to grapes,[3] it had not returned to the levels of vineyard planting that it had first reached 100 years earlier. There were 40+ wineries and a small but growing group of idealistic individuals who felt strongly about the potential for high quality grapes and wines and who were committed to the prospect and the lifestyle that went with it.

Was I lucky? Yes, I was! I was fortunate to first work for Robert Mondavi at his eponymous winery in 1974 and then for Moët & Chandon, the French Champagne house, at their start-up California sparkling winery, Domaine Chandon, in Napa Valley from 1976–99, and, ultimately, to be able to plant my own vineyard (1993) and make a wine under my own name.

In 1974 the Robert Mondavi Winery was the hub of modern winemaking in California and Robert Mondavi himself was an incredible force and charismatic leader in Napa Valley. During those heady days, newly minted winemakers and grape-growers worked together to focus on making the best wines possible – with lots of room for growth and not much to lose. In the wineries we experimented with barrels, new equipment to minimize extracting bitter tannins, temperature control during fermentation, pump overs and punch downs were all under the microscope. At first it was more about wine*making* but as wineries got their acts together and finances allowed for the employment of better equipment, they began to look to the vineyards and their management to make the incremental improvements to quality. It was, after all, ultimately about the quality of the grapes and efforts to ensure even ripeness, balanced crops, developed tannins, concentrated flavors and varietal correctness reinforced the importance of 'terroir' to Napa Valley winemakers.

The Paris Tasting of 1976 again brought international recognition to Napa Valley wines and the rush was on. Those 40+ wineries would grow to 540 by 2023.[4]

That same year I was hired by the start-up Domaine Chandon, founded by the French wine company Moët & Chandon to make sparkling wine. From my new colleagues, I became familiar with *Le Comité Interprofessionnel du vin de Champagne* (CIVC), founded in 1941 to organize and protect winemakers in Champagne during the German occupation. This government-sponsored body continues to organize and control the production, distribution, and

---

[3] Bob Thompson, *Wine Atlas of California* (Simon and Schuster 1993); LT Wallace and Napa County Board of Supervisors, *Annual Crop Report Gross Values 1974* <https://www.countyofnapa.org/ArchiveCenter/ViewFile/Item/110> accessed 10 October 2024.

[4] 'History of the Napa Valley Vintners' (Napa Valley Vintners) <https://napavintners.com/about/history.asp> accessed 10 October 2024.

promotion of the wines of Champagne. One primary role taken on by the CIVC is safeguarding the name Champagne. While Champagne is a protected designation of origin, the CIVC is aggressive at going after unauthorized use of the Champagne name. They understood the value of their brand and had experienced its dilution and were serious about protecting it.

As early as 1891 the Madrid Agreement (Madrid Agreement Concerning the International Registration of Marks)[5] established the rule that only wine produced in the Champagne appellation could bear the name. This was later reiterated in the Treaty of Versailles after World War I. While the United States (US) was a signatory to the treaty, the US Senate never formally ratified it and, as the US was headed into Prohibition, it seemed unimportant. However, this created the loophole for US producers of sparkling wine to continue to label their products 'champagne'. Ironically, in 1976 most of the sparkling wine produced in California was still labeled as champagne. From my vantage point at Domaine Chandon (where we made sparkling wine using the traditional method, but *not* champagne!) I watched this play out. In 1983, the US finally entered into comprehensive trade talks on wine labeling with the European Commission. The CIVC was an active participant. It took two decades of negotiations, but finally, on 10 March 2006, the US and the European Union reached an agreement. In exchange for easing trade restrictions on wine, the US Government agreed that Champagne and a half-dozen other 'semi-generic' names, including Burgundy, Chablis, Chianti, Moselle, Sauterne, and Port[6] would no longer appear on domestic wine labels unless a producer was already using one of those names.[7] This was a first step for the Champenoise but left a cadre of large producers in the US still using the names California (or New York or American) Champagne on their labels. The years of legal misuse of the name created the situation where these brands were grandfathered into the regulations. Here was a cautionary tale.

The US adopted its own version of an appellation system for wine grapes in 1980. Overseen by the Alcohol and Tobacco Tax and Trade Bureau (TTB), the US version identifies American Viticultural Areas (AVAs) as delimited

---

[5] 'Senate Rejects the Treaty of Versailles' (US Senate 19 November 1919) <https://www.senate.gov/about/powers-procedures/treaties/senate-rejects-treaty-of-versailles.htm> accessed 10 October 2024.

[6] TTB 27 CFR 4.24 <https://www.ecfr.gov/current/title-27/chapter-I/subchapter-A/part-4/subpart-C/section-4.24#> accessed 10 October 2024.

[7] 'Industry Circular: 06-01 Impact of the US/EU Wine Agreement on Certificates of Label Approval for Wine Labels With a Semi-Generic Name or Retsina' (Department of the Treasury Alcohol and Tobacco Tax and Trade Bureau 2006) <https://www.ttb.gov/public-information/industry-circulars/archives/2006/06-01> accessed 10 October 2024.

grape-growing regions with specific geographic or climatic features that distinguish them from the surrounding regions and affect how grapes are grown. Using an AVA designation on a wine label allows vintners to describe more accurately the origin of their wines to consumers and helps consumers identify wines they purchase.[8]

The first AVA was Augusta, Missouri, followed a year later by Napa Valley, California.[9] It was the Napa Valley Vintners (NVV), the trade group that represents the majority of wineries in Napa Valley along with the Napa Valley Grape Growers who filed the petition. The NVV ultimately came to play a major role in promoting the quality of wines from Napa Valley over promoting individual brands. By 2000, there were 12 sub or nested AVAs (there are now a total of 16)[10] within the Napa Valley and the first really egregious effort to hijack the Napa name. At the time, I was on the board of the NVV and, knowing the experience of Champagne, it was a relief to see the NVV respond proactively to the misuse of its name. Armed with original research conducted by the Field Research Corp on behalf of NVV on perception of quality in the marketplace, the NVV went toe to toe with Bronco Wine Co which was bottling wine under the Napa Ridge label. The finding of that research that 'if it says Napa on the label, the consumer expects the contents to be wine grown and made in Napa Valley' made the case in the California Superior Court where, in 2004, the NVV ultimately prevailed. Bronco appealed the case to the US Supreme Court which declined to hear it in 2006.[11]

When my winemaker husband and I decided to plant a small vineyard in 1993, we had 20 years of experience with grapes from different vineyards and nested AVAs in Napa Valley. We had worked with young vineyards and old vineyards, seen many vineyards replanted to different varieties and seen ownership and names change frequently. We were most interested in participating

---

[8] 'American Viticultural Area (AVV)' (Department of the Treasury Alcohol and Tobacco Tax and Trade Bureau) <www.ttb.gov/wine/american-viticultural-area-ava> accessed 10 October 2024.

[9] 'American Viticultural Areas' (Missouri Wines 23 April 2019) <https://missouriwine.org/news/american-viticultural-areas#:~:text=Augusta%20AVA,square%20mile%20area%20surrounding%20Augusta> accessed 10 October 2024.

[10] 'Napa Valley Nested AVAs' (Napa Valley Vintners) <https://napavintners.com/napa_valley/appellations.asp#:~:text=Napa%20Valley%20AVA,-To%20navigate%2C%20press%20the> accessed 10 October 2024;'List of AVAs by Establishment Date' (US Department of the Treasury Alcohol and Tobacco Tax and Trade Bureau 2023) <www.ttb.gov/wine/ava-establishment-dates> accessed 10 October 2024.

[11] *Bronco v Jolly* 33 Cal 4th 943 (California SC 2004).

in the exploration of an individual vineyard planted and farmed by us, the winemakers who would make the wine for over two decades. Napa Valley was increasingly recognized as the premium region for winegrowing in California and the sub or nested AVAs were defining specific characteristics associated with different parts of the Valley. Individual vineyards were also being recognized and sought out by winemakers.

A century before, some of the most famous vineyard sites in Napa Valley were already recognized. Vineyards like To-Kalon, Dr Crane, Larkmead, and Haynes were highly regarded then and retain their names and reputations to this day. As planting increased and new vineyards crept up the hillsides into previously unplanted areas, new names, like Eisele, Mayacamas and Diamond Creek were added to the list. Our conviction was, and continues to be, that winemaking is an overlay on the essential characteristics of the grapes and should not be imposed carte blanche on all wines. In 1992 we found a place to test that conviction in the form of a 12-acre parcel on Diamond Mountain Road near Calistoga. In 1993, it was already clear that Cabernet would thrive in the rocky volcanic soils and we planted the vineyard to Cabernet Sauvignon and other Bordeaux red varieties. Not long after, the growers and winemakers on Diamond Mountain banded together to petition to form the Diamond Mountain District AVA. The Diamond Mountain District AVA was approved in 2001.[12]

Diamond Mountain is a steep mountainous region with only 15% of the land being suitable for planting vineyards. Diamond Mountain is one of Napa Valley's 'hillside' AVAs with all vineyards at between 400 to 2,200 ft elevation. The soils are volcanic in origin; well drained and porous. The wines are known to be concentrated in flavor and tannin, with distinctive, dark fruit, savory flavors and minerality.[13] While there are flavor characteristics that are imparted by winemaking practices and others that are attributable to the grape varieties, specifics of soil, aspect, and climate are important factors to how a wine tastes and support the concept of terroir and geographic indications.

Grape and bottled wine prices are perhaps the most concrete representation of how consumers and wineries value vineyard locations in the world of wine. In 2021 the average price of a ton of Cabernet Sauvignon in Napa County was $8,082 – roughly three times the $2,728 price in neighboring Sonoma County. And according to a recent report from Silicon Valley Bank,[14] in 2022 the

---

[12] 'List of AVAs by Establishment Date' (n 10).

[13] 'Diamond Mountain District AVA' (Napa Valley Vintners) <https://napavintners.com/napa_valley/diamond-mountain-district-ava/#history> accessed 10 October 2024.

[14] *Direct-to-Consumer Wine Survey: Report, Results and Benchmarks* (Silicon Valley Bank 2023), 28, <https://www.svb.com/globalassets/library/uploadedfiles/wine/2023-direct-to-consumer-wine-report.pdf> accessed 10 October 2024.

average price for a bottle of Napa Valley Cabernet Sauvignon rose to $108 (in comparison, Sonoma County average bottle price was reported at $57).

While we are firmly committed to our own vineyard and wines, it would not be possible to promote and sell our wine widely without the layered place names of Diamond Mountain District and Napa Valley. When I travel far from home and am asked where I am from, I frequently say California and, if they ask for more detail, I elaborate with 'north of San Francisco' or Napa – and if people are still with me, I say Calistoga. The same is true when talking about our wines – we start by saying the vineyard is in Napa Valley, everyone recognizes that. Then we drill down to Diamond Mountain District, our nested AVA and, ultimately, to our vineyard and brand name. We make a very small quantity, roughly 350 cases of vineyard designated Cabernet Sauvignon from 2.5 acres of vines. Our own brand name and logo, Dyer, which we have trademarked, is the most granular identification. But with such a miniscule quantity there is little chance to amplify that in a crowded market. Diamond Mountain District, on the other hand, informs a consumer that the wine shares the volcanic soils and climates with a group of super premium wines that have typicity in the rarified world of wine connoisseurs. Finally, we are in the Napa Valley and Napa Valley is known throughout the wine world and the world. In the Napa Valley, as in many wine regions, there are trade organizations with marketing programs and promotional opportunities for their members. Wine critics and journalists frequently review wines by region and educate their readers on the characteristics and lifestyles of each region. In Napa Valley many of the nested AVAs also work cooperatively on telling their stories. For a small producer in the Napa Valley these channels make up the bulk of our marketing.

Because of its storied history, the laser focus of its growers and winemakers on maintaining a level of excellence in the wines, and the coordinated effort to create and maintain awareness of its reputation – Napa Valley is the name that has the most impact. Fifty years after I arrived in Napa Valley, winemakers are still refining their skills and today's challenges – climate change, water, direct-to-consumer sales, proliferation of labels in a crowded marketplace – are different from those of the 1970s. But the integrity of the place name is a solid base from which to continue to make progress and Napa Valley is once and for all on the world stage.

21. Place Brand and Coffee: Perspectives from the Gichangi Coffee Estate

Owen Gichangi

THE GICHANGI COFFEE ESTATE

The main coffee variety grown in Kenya is Arabica because it is suitable for the high altitudes in the central region near the slopes of Mount Kenya. There, we have Gichangi's Estate Coffee Farm which grows and markets high quality clean coffee, some of which we roast and package under the Stephen's Coffee brand. Arabica has a sweet taste profile compared to Robusta from Uganda, for example, which has a bitter and harsh taste.

My family owns a farm where we are licensed as a Coffee Estate called Gichangi Coffee Estate. This is located in Kamuiru – Mutira, Kirinyaga County on the slopes of Mount Kenya. The estate was established in late 1955 by my late grandparents, patriarch and matriarch Stephen and Jane Gichangi, and then run by my parents. My family took over after their demise and have been building it since. The estate is professionally run with input from a qualified agronomist who guides the entire farming process, including aspects such as pruning, manure and fertilizer application, disease control and berry picking. We have planted a few new varieties on the farm and harvested the same coffee bushes that we started with in 1955. Coffee processing undertaken at the farm includes cherry pulping, fermentation, washing, soaking, and drying. Part of this processed coffee is sold in the international market while the rest is roasted and ground for sale in the Kenyan local market as Stephen's Coffee.

I decided to get into the family coffee business as soon as I completed my secondary education and then joined a college to start studying Automotive Engineering. The bond with and passion for coffee overwhelmed me as I have always been interested in the coffee business. It is a way of living that my family has passed on.

COFFEE ESTATES IN KENYA

Not everyone can be an estate farmer. Estate farmers need over two hectares of land and about 1,500 coffee bushes. Gichangi Estate is licensed by the Coffee Directorate as an estate farm and also as a pulping station. The cost of running an estate farm is higher but the outcome is better because we can command a higher income than other farmers. As we do not have a license to mill coffee currently, we outsource to licensed millers, just like other farmers, at the beginning of secondary processing. For us, the milling process is transparent; we are invited to observe it. In particular, we can be present throughout the preparatory process, including when the coffee is moved from the warehouse to the milling machine. Outturn numbers are issued by the millers for traceability. Each estate farmer has a unique but constant code number, for example Gichangi Estate AJ0115. The millers then sift the coffee to sort the beans by size. Based on size, shape and density, there are seven main coffee bean grades in Kenya: E, AA (Kenya's highest grade of coffee), AB, C, PB, TT, and T. Other grades are MH and ML and so on which have a different processing method. The millers weigh and pack the coffee into jute bags, usually 60kg bags.

For other farmers, once their coffee is taken to the millers, they will have their coffee mixed, depending on similarities of the cup profiles, before their coffee is milled and given a different outturn number compared to that of the estate farmers. Coffee jute bags bearing the African map with the writing 'produce of Kenya' can be a mix of coffee beans from different regions as long as they are of the same grade and a similar cup profile. These bags of coffee can also change hands several times before reaching the consumers. Subsequent buyers may be unable to tell the exact source of the coffee sold, since intermediaries often mix the coffee purchased from different regions with those that seem to have similar characteristics. For the buyers, they are issued with samples of the coffee upon which they conduct analysis and purchase the coffee that meets their demands. Also, if there are issues, the buyers can trace the coffee if they have lot numbers and outturn numbers. If buyers buy directly from farmers, they know where their coffee is coming from and if the sample from the farmer does not match the coffee, they can get the farmer to remedy. If they cannot do that, they have less quality assurance. Farmers too try to make sure their coffee is analyzed and graded accurately and what their customers get matches the samples they send to customers.

OUR PRACTICE

We, as Gichangi Estate Coffee Farm, produce premium coffee: grades AA, AB and a bit of C. We export green coffee from the Gichangi Estate – it is cherries that are just picked, sorted, pulped, washed, dried, hulled, and milled but not yet roasted. After milling, as estate farmers, we get our own coffee back in 60kg jute bags with the Kenyan map inside the African map printed on the bags and a tag that says 'Produce of Kenya'. Other tags contain information that includes: outturn number, lot number, estate code number, and the name of the estate. Much of this green coffee will then be sold through the Nairobi Coffee Exchange. We also directly sell green coffee abroad to markets such as Nigeria and China.

OUR BRANDING

We sell green coffee under the tag Gichangi Coffee Estate AJ0115. Separately, we also market roasted coffee under the 'Stephen's Coffee' brand which started two years ago. We roast the grade of coffee that is demanded by particular customers. We sell roasted coffee through Stephen's Coffee's social media platforms. We are licensed as grower-marketers. This means that we can market and sell our coffee directly to both domestic and foreign buyers. The advantage of selling directly to buyers is that we determine the price at which the coffee is sold, and the revenue generated from the sale comes directly to us. Over time, we get to know our customers. We can tailor our packaging to our customers' needs. Exported roasted coffee beans are supposed to bear the Coffee Kenya logo on their packages and, regardless, the packaging should bear country of origin even if it does not have the Coffee Kenya logo which is normally paid for in licensing fees. The Coffee Kenya logo is mainly for promotion, value addition and traceability of exported coffee. We are just now building up our brand domestically; once Stephen's Coffee is better established, we will definitely license the Coffee Kenya logo for use, especially, but not only, for the export market. With the Coffee Kenya logo, our coffee will gain visibility. It can help market our coffee and help us charge a premium price for it. But, as it is another expense, for now, while we are still establishing the market, we are just branding our packaging with the Stephen's Coffee logo with the taglines:

> Rich in Aroma
> From the slopes of Mount Kenya
> Producers of No 1 AA Coffee Since 1998[1]

Currently it is mostly big companies that are using the Coffee Kenya logo. Very few estate farmers are using the logo because they lack the resources required to roast and market at retail in sufficient volume which would justify the expense of licensing the logo.

REFLECTIONS AND FUTURE

Since not all coffee farmers in Kenya can sell their produce directly, selling through marketing agents remains the only answer for most farmers. One of the primary disadvantages of selling through marketing agents is the low price paid to sellers. Some agents may strike a hard bargain with the farmer. Coffee growers also have to pay other associated costs for the sale. Thus, the price that eventually gets to the growers is often lower than the price they would have received if they had sold the coffee to the market directly.

Nonetheless, there are risks associated with direct marketing. It is expensive to be certified as a direct seller. Also, as part of the pre-sale negotiations, sellers may dispatch samples, but they may fail to reach the prospective buyer, leading to potential delays. And, of course, what we ship later must match those samples. Direct sellers also have to look for their own markets. It is not easy in the direct sale market. Our hope is to be able to develop a long-term relationship between farmers and buyers but now there are so many agents in the market for coffee sales that will change the market. There will also be changes in coffee prices too. As a producer of good coffees, Kenyan coffee prices should be better.

---

[1] 'Stephen's Coffee, Since 1998' <https://www.facebook.com/p/Stephens-Coffee-Since-1998-100051748736315/> accessed 10 October 2024.

22. Perspective From a Kenyan Coffee Grower: Selling to Market Through a Co-operative

James Ireri John

MARKETING KENYAN COFFEE

Over 85% of Kenyan coffee is marketed through a centralized auction managed by the Nairobi Coffee Exchange (NCE)[1] and 15% through direct sales. Up to 1989, coffee marketing system pricing was based on a quota system allocated by the International Coffee Agreement (ICA) to stabilize prices through regulation of supplies. The collapse of the quota system in 1989 allowed free trading in the world market where price was left to market forces.[2]

The current challenges in coffee marketing in Kenya include:

1. global price volatility;
2. lack of modern infrastructure at the NCE;
3. insecurity of coffee during transportation;
4. limited business management skills for growers;
5. high deductions along the value chain resulting in low returns for growers.

In the international coffee markets, Kenyan coffee offers quality coffee grades, making it a key component for blending with other coffees from other producing countries. This comparative advantage for quality should be jealously guarded through mandatory standards in order for Kenya to continue playing its lead role in global coffee markets, which is currently under threat. Coffee growing in Kenya has been reducing because of other competing and

---

[1] See the Home page for the Nairobi Coffee Exchange <https:// www .nairobicoffeeexchange.co.ke/> accessed 10 October 2024.

[2] Edward Quill, 'The Failure of International Commodity Agreements: Forms, Functions, and Implications'(1994) 22(2) Denver Journal of International Law & Policy 503 <https://digitalcommons.du.edu/cgi/viewcontent.cgi?article=1752&context=djilp>.

more profitable enterprises in the main coffee growing areas. Kenya needs to position itself for the emerging and lucrative specialty coffee. Specialty coffee is high quality Arabica coffee that scores over 80/100 points on the specialty Coffee Association of America quality scale. Just like wine, these coffees are further differentiated by taste profiles that are unique to geographical conditions of origin (soils, altitude) and workmanship.

Coffee growers in Kenya comprise of 700,000 smallholder growers who are organized into 500 grower co-operative societies and 3,000 small, medium and large estates. Out of the 3,000 estates, 2,400 are small estates with an acreage of 5–20 acres which are spread across the coffee growing areas. The small estates produce good quality coffee but have challenges in accessing finances and processing facilities.

HOW I SELL AND MARKET MY COFFEE TO THE PUBLIC

I am one of the smallholder growers. I sell my coffee through a grower co-operative known as the New Kirimiri Farmers' Co-operative Society Ltd. It is situated in Embu County, on the slopes of Mount Kenya in the republic of Kenya. The Co-operative has around 2,000 members. The coffee milling process entails pulping, hulling, sorting and grading of parchment to clean coffee. After milling, the Co-operative, which now owns the coffee, sources a marketing agent. The functions of marketing agents include facilitating warehousing of clean coffee, preparing a sale catalogue, selling coffee at NCE, offering finances and distributing coffee proceeds to various stakeholders.

Most of our coffee is sold and marketed through the NCE auction. The ownership of NCE is vested in the Agricultural Food and Fisheries Authority. It is managed by a Management Committee which consists of various stakeholders in the coffee industry. Trading in the NCE is conducted by registered marketing agents and dealers representing farmers and buyers respectively.

THE REASONS WHY I AM NOT SELLING COFFEE DIRECTLY TO THE MARKET

Direct trade in coffee is when a roaster buys coffee straight from a producer/ coffee grower. This means the establishment of a direct channel of trade between two parties. It refers to the relationship fostered and nurtured between producers and roasters. Direct sales, commonly referred to as the 'second window', were introduced through the Finance Act 2005. The objective of creating this window was to give the growers a direct link with the international buyers of Kenya's coffee in the hope of getting better prices. Since its inception, the volume sold through this window has been low.

I choose not to sell my coffee directly to the market because co-operatives in the coffee sector promote collaborative entrepreneurship and economic growth unlike selling coffee through direct sales. Co-operatives also reduce individual growers' risk in the business venture and create a culture of shared productivity and decision-making and market awareness amongst their members, unlike selling of coffee directly to the market. Most of the growers in the co-operatives, such as myself, are not able to supply the required volume consistently. We have limited overseas market intelligence and capacity to handle export logistics and lack the capacity to market our coffee, negotiate and handle a contract. The transactions under direct sales are time consuming and as a result do not always meet our cash flow needs. Finally, there is poor promotion of Kenya as an origin of premium coffee.

The New Kirimiri Farmers' Co-operative Society Ltd is not a licensee for Coffee Kenya.

THE RISKS AND OPPORTUNITIES OF BEING ASSOCIATED WITH THE COFFEE KENYA BRAND

Some of the opportunities associated with the Coffee Kenya brand include:

1. Creating awareness among consumers for Kenyan coffee to be recognized on the world market.
2. Helping the Kenyan coffee industry to generate large revenue. Through branding of Kenyan coffee, the business would develop a good position in the market. Kenya's coffee, through branding, would be able to sell at a good margin since customers would be willing to pay higher prices for our coffee, which is of a reputed brand. We can charge what the coffee is worth.
3. Helping Kenyan coffee to stand out in a saturated market.
4. Lending Kenyan coffee credibility amongst the consumers, building customers' loyalty to our coffee and giving consumers confidence when consuming Kenyan coffee so that growers like us will have returning customers and referrals, saving us money and time in the long run.
5. Providing the producers of Kenyan coffee with a clear strategy for moving forward.

Brand risk is the potential for a valuable brand like 'Coffee Kenya' to lose value in the market. Brand reputation risk is the possible damage to the Coffee Kenya brand in overall standing that derives from negative signals regarding the brand. Kenya is known for producing quality coffee which is used to blend other inferior coffees worldwide. Kenyan coffee is known to fetch premium prices worldwide. If all the players in the coffee value chain are not well remunerated, they can sabotage the brand. This is why the Kenyan Government should prevent risk to reputation – they should ensure that Coffee Kenya branded coffee is produced to a consistent and reliable quality. (Allow me to give an example, you have heard of some vehicle brands being recalled due to defects, for example, defective braking systems. Such vehicles lose their reputation.) In other words, if the Kenyan Government sorts the issue of coffee branding, all the players in the coffee value chain, starting from the growers, will get better returns. As things stands in Kenya, coffee growers are not benefitting from the sweat of their labor. Coffee branding to ensure a consistent and reliable quality of coffee is the silver bullet that can cure the poor payment which we coffee farmers currently get.

However branding Kenyan coffee involves a huge cost because brands are not created overnight and entities have to spend huge sums on advertising and publicity. Often the brand marketers must calculate the return to brand investment as they tend to predict and justify the brand development process. I see this as one of the risks associated with the Coffee Kenya brand. Changing the perception of a brand is hard. However, the 'Coffee Kenya' branding is important despite the enormous resources it requires. It not only creates a memorable impression on customers but also allows consumers of Kenyan coffee and clients know what to expect from the coffee. It is a way of distinguishing Kenyan coffee from competitors and clarifying what it is that we put in our coffee that makes it a better choice.

WHAT AN ASSOCIATION WITH THE 'COFFEE KENYA' BRAND COULD ACHIEVE FOR A COFFEE GROWER

An association with the 'Coffee Kenya' brand could achieve a lot for me individually and directly as a coffee grower. Since the branding allows users and consumers to form an opinion and a preference for the product, our Kenyan coffee would fetch me more money in the international market after it is sold. Our Kenyan coffee would stand out among the rest of world's coffee. Buyers would prefer our coffee and pay higher prices in our international markets. The branding of our coffee as Kenyan coffee would create real value in the eyes of industry partners and perceived value in the eyes of product users. This would be an achievement on my part as a coffee grower because the demand for our Kenyan coffee would increase in the international market. This could mean that as a supplier (grower) of Kenyan coffee, I would be assured of a ready market for my coffee. At no time would I have to worry that there were no buyers for my coffee. The moment the coffee then increases its value, more clients and buyers would want to be associated with Kenyan coffee. This creates more demand. Every consumer would want to be associated with Kenyan coffee.

This would mean that our Kenyan coffee is placed on the international map, resulting in better returns.

WHAT AN ASSOCIATION WITH THE 'COFFEE KENYA' BRAND COULD ACHIEVE FOR MY CO-OPERATIVE

An association with the 'Coffee Kenya' brand could achieve a lot for my co-operative. It could enable it to sell its coffee abroad and hence acquire better prices with excellent marginal profits as well as a premium for social and community development. This would contribute a lot to social developments such as school renovations, dispensaries, and provision of clean and safe water to my village. This would be an added advantage to the co-operative of which I am a member. The association with the 'Coffee Kenya' brand can be a barrier to entrance for new coffee competitors outside Kenya. On the other hand, the 'Coffee Kenya' branding would open up the market for Kenyan coffee. The Coffee Kenya branding lets buyers and consumers know that the branded coffee has been tested for performance and quality and could assist co-operatives in opening up new markets for our coffee. As a farmer this could assist me because coffee farming could become more sustainable.

PART VII

Conclusions

23. Place-Branding Experiences – Perspectives From Three Case Studies

Catherine W. Ng, Titilayo Adebola and Abbe E. L. Brown

This chapter takes an interdisciplinary approach to focus on the three case studies examined in this volume: Scotch Whisky, the Napa Valley AVA, and the Coffee Kenya figurative mark, to draw lessons for academics and stakeholders such as traders, marketers, law practitioners, and policy makers as well as other practitioners. These three case studies offer a wide range of experiences: 'Scotch Whisky' is the most mature as a place brand having been in use in the United Kingdom (UK) in reference to drinks for some time before its formal, albeit non-binding, definition in 1908[1] and statutory definition in 1933.[2] In both the UK and the European Union (EU),[3] the term is now guarded under two of the most protective regimes in the world, as discussed later. 'Napa Valley' was established as an American Viticultural Area (AVA) in 1981,[4] a newly created status for protection in the United States (US). Finally, the 'Coffee Kenya' figurative mark was registered by the Coffee Board of Kenya (later the Coffee Directorate) as a certification mark there and also at the World Intellectual Property Organization (under the Madrid System)

---

[1] 'The Royal Commission on Whisky and Other Potable Spirits' (1909) 2:2537 British Medical J 399 <http://www.jstor.org/stable/25283150> accessed 19 April 2024.

[2] Finance Act 1933, s 24.

[3] In Great Britain, EU-inspired protection continues to apply; in Northern Ireland, EU protection continues to apply. Department for Environment, Food and Rural Affairs, 'Guidance Protected Geographical Food and Drink Names: UK GI Schemes' (2024) <https://www.gov.uk/guidance/protected-geographical-food-and-drink-names-uk-gi-schemes> accessed 10 October 2024; see also Gareth Jenkins, Kirsten Gilbert, Claire Keating, Elise Cant and Ann Lee, Ch 12.

[4] 'List of AVAs by Establishment Date' (Alcohol and Tobacco Tax and Trade Bureau, US Dept of the Treasury 2023) <https://www.ttb.gov/regulated-commodities/beverage-alcohol/wine/ava-establishment-dates> accessed 10 October 2024.

in 2015.[5] This volume illustrates how Scotch Whisky and the Napa Valley AVA have travelled different paths to become successful brands which have conferred enormous social and economic impacts on their eponymous regions. It discusses the developments in legal protection that ensued, and how Coffee Kenya is making its start as a brand in the marketplace and a certification mark in law in view of its potential role in the local economy.[6]

These diverse realities among the three case studies reflect not only differences among legal regimes at the time, but also shifts in the primary raison d'être for place brands and thus the rationales for their protection in law under the umbrella term of Geographical Indications (GIs). Reflections on the three case studies in this chapter therefore help address some of the questions raised in Dutfield's thought-provoking Foreword 'Geographical Indications: What are They Good for?'. The points raised are important because GIs are used both in physical and digital marketplaces;[7] and their protection in law continues to expand in jurisdictions such as the EU.[8] The EU also actively promotes the introduction and expansion of GI systems globally. Meanwhile, international efforts regarding GIs appear increasingly fragmented.[9] This chapter examines the rationales for GI protection in its various forms.

BASIC LEVELS OF PROTECTION

As discussed in this volume, at its most basic level, GIs are signs used on products that have a specific geographical connection or possess qualities, reputation, or characteristics that are essentially attributable to that connection. GI protection refers to legal mechanisms put in place to safeguard GIs. Due to the latitude offered in the Agreement on Trade-Related Aspects of Intellectual Property Rights (TRIPS), countries are free to introduce different legal mechanisms to protect GIs, including *sui generis* (special) regimes, collective and certification marks, unfair competition laws and the law against passing off.[10] With GIs, the geographical connection between the underlying goods and their eponymous places informs us of something about the specific qualifications that appeal to consumers. GI protection therefore safeguards consumers who,

---

[5] See figurative mark (Number: WO500000001250302) by accessing the World Intellectual Property Organization, 'Global Brand Database' <https://www.wipo.int/reference/en/branddb/> accessed 17 April 2024.
[6] Tom Kabau, Ch 9.
[7] Pilar Montero, Ch 15.
[8] Catherine W Ng, Titilayo Adebola and Abbe EL Brown, Ch 1.
[9] Titilayo Adebola, Ch 14.
[10] Titilayo Adebola, Ch 14; Catherine W Ng, Ch 16.

by requesting the place-branded goods, are assured they are receiving goods that have the geographical connection that is salient to their purchase decisions. At the same time, GI protection safeguards traders by preventing unauthorized parties from using the geographical name to market goods that do not meet the requisite specifications for GIs. This protection ensures that those who invest in meeting the specifications are not unfairly disadvantaged by those who may attempt to exploit the reputation associated with the GIs without complying with the specifications. The protection conferred upon GIs can thus be rationalized from both the consumers' and traders' perspectives. A form of this type of protection is available in all of the jurisdictions considered in the volume.[11]

WHAT IS *TERROIR*?

The geographical connection in a GI is often attributed to the concept of *terroir*. *Terroir* is the composite of human as well as geographical factors such as soil, climatic and topographical conditions, which contribute or are believed to contribute to the desirable qualities in agricultural products such as whiskies, wines, and coffees. For example, the nesting of AVAs for Napa Valley wines further highlights regional differences that are attributed to *terroir*.[12]

By contrast, while the Scotch Whisky Regulations 2009 stipulate the use of malted barley and that the distillation and maturation processes must take place in Scotland, they do not require any other raw ingredients used in the production of Scotch Whisky to be sourced from Scotland.[13] Notably, companies such as United Distillers (now part of Diageo[14]) in 1988 emphasized regional differences in the taste of whiskies.

> "Regional differences" in flavor had been noted by writers since the 1930s. They had historical precedents in the ancient division between "Highland" and "Lowland", and the later identification of "Islay" and "Campbelltown". For modern consumers,

---

[11] J Scott Gerien, Ch 10; Katharina H Reuer and Wiebke Baars, Ch 11; Gareth Jenkins, Kirsten Gilbert, Claire Keating, Elise Cant and Ann Lee, Ch 12; Chebet Koros and Melissa Omino, Ch 13; Catherine W Ng, Ch 16.
[12] Dawnine Dyer, Ch 20; see also in respect of Scotch Whisky, Atsuko Ichijo, Ch 6.
[13] The Scotch Whisky Regulations 2009 (SI 2009/2890), Section 3.
[14] Charles MacLean, 'The Guiness/Distillers Saga: the aftermath' (*Scotchwhisky.com*, 19 April 2016) <https://scotchwhisky.com/magazine/features/8991/the-guinness-distillers-saga-the-aftermath/> accessed 4 April 2024.

familiar with wine regions, regional differences in malt whisky were comprehensible, made malts more accessible, and most important, encouraged exploration.
... The company had in mind the fact that consumers would want to visit the distilleries...[15]

Relatedly, the GI itself must be used exclusively for goods that enjoy a connection with the prescribed factors within the geographical boundaries. Retro-imposing this exclusivity in the use of GIs is difficult in a marketplace where the terms are already in general usage. To their frustration, Scotch Whisky distillers experienced this when they sought a legal definition[16] to unify the fragmented landscape of Scotch Whisky production and labelling. While a non-binding definition appeared in the 1908 Royal Commission report,[17] a binding statutory definition finally came in 1933.[18] Likewise, while Napa Valley branded wines must contain at least 85% grapes grown within the AVA and finished within California,[19] the Napa Valley Vintners, as guardians of the Napa Valley AVA, also had to deal with those who had acquired prior right to use 'Napa' on their bottles when the Napa Valley AVA came into play.[20]

Similarly, at the launch of the certification mark 'Coffee Kenya', the word 'Kenya' was already used in association with coffee at Starbucks under its single origin program,[21] for example, and registered by diverse parties in association with coffees.[22] This has meant that 'Coffee Kenya' as a brand for coffees that are 100% produced in Kenya, was launched in a market that was already populated with similar names for coffees[23] which do not necessarily

---

[15] Charles MacLean, *Scotch Whisky – a Liquid History* (Cassell Illustrated 2003), 264.

[16] Ibid, 152.

[17] 'The Royal Commission on Whisky and Other Potable Spirits' (n 1); see also ibid, 402; Julie Bower and David M Higgins, Ch 5; Graham G Stewart and Anne Anstruther, Ch 17.

[18] Finance Act 1933, s 24; see also Atsuko Ichijo, Ch 6.

[19] J Scott Gerien, Ch 10.

[20] Ibid.

[21] Dominique Barjolle, Xiomara F. Quiñones-Ruiz, Monique Bagal and Hermann Comoé, 'The Role of the State for Geographical Indications of Coffee: Case Studies from Colombia and Kenya' (2016) 98 World Development 105, 106.

[22] Tom Kabau, Ch 9; Dawnine Dyer, Ch 20.

[23] See for example, Monique Bagal, Giovanni Belletti, Andrea Marescotti and Giulia Onori, *Study on the Potential of Marketing of Kenyan Coffee as Geographical Indication* (European Commission, December 2013) <https://agriculture.ec.europa.eu/system/files/2019-12/ext-study-gic-acp-countries-case-study-coffee-kenya_2013_en_0.pdf> accessed 23 February 2024; see figura-

meet the 100% requirement. The uncontrolled use of the word 'Kenya' for coffees makes it difficult to educate consumers about the trustworthiness of Coffee Kenya branded coffees and to create a specific demand for them.[24] Commitment of marketing as well as legal resources will be needed to enforce the exclusive use of 'Coffee Kenya' in the marketplace and impress the distinctiveness of its relationship with the underlying goods upon the minds of the consuming public there.

BEYOND THE BASIC: COMMERCIAL AND SOCIAL IMPACT OF PLACE-BRANDING

From the experiences of Scotch Whisky and Napa Valley AVA illustrated in this volume, however, it is clear that place-branding is about more than the accuracy of trade connections. Place-branding can confer enormous economic advantages to the eponymous regions. These advantages often exceed what may be the inherent qualities of the goods attributable to *terroir*. While both Scotch Whisky and Napa Valley wines secure premium pricing for their underlying drinks[25] and place-branded goods tend to secure a higher level of consumer loyalty,[26] these tendencies may also be attributable, at least in part, to consumer perception of 1. authenticity, 2. premium quality, 3. preservation of traditional methods and 4. culture and something to be proud of associated with the place-branded goods.[27]

In the first three of these four factors, place-branded goods can have a symbiotic relationship with place due to the esteem the place holds in the minds of the consumers for the goods. Where place-branding is successful, as in the case of Scotch Whisky, the imagery and memories of pristine landscape associated with Scotland can be evoked to help sell the drink.[28] Further, attracted by Scotch Whisky, tourists visit Scotland for the distilleries[29] and witness for themselves Scotland and its culture and traditional methods. This is so even

---

tive mark (Number: WO500000001250302) by accessing the World Intellectual Property Organization, 'Global Brand Database' <https://www.wipo.int/en/web/global-brand-database> accessed 10 October 2024.

[24] Tom Kabau, Ch 9.

[25] Dawnine Dyer, Ch 20; Rex Stults, Ch 3; Henry Farr, Rosie Mallory and Penny Erricker, Ch 8; Catherine W Ng, Ch 16.

[26] Henry Farr, Rosie Mallory and Penny Erricker, Ch 8.

[27] Ibid.

[28] Atsuko Ichijo, Ch 6.

[29] Ibid.

though some may raise questions of how authentic[30] and how 'Scottish'[31] this imagery is in fact because it is not a complete reflection of Scottishness. Likewise, the reputation of Napa Valley is now inextricably tied to its wine industry,[32] which brings in tourists and wine afficionados alike to witness the method of production in its eponymous home, the third factor above. In both cases, these place-branded industries now account for a significant part of their regional economies. This is achieved directly through the sales of these drinks; and indirectly, through drinks-inspired tourism and other place-branded industries in the region caused by the rise in their profiles in consumer consciousness and by the positive imagery associated with those profiles.[33]

As noted above, unlike the Scotch Whisky and Napa Valley wine industries, where their interests in developing the sector and marketing as a collective were initially coordinated organically by grassroot producers in the region,[34] the Coffee Directorate in Kenya has taken an active role in the operation of its coffee industry since 1933. Having a public body manage the image of its coffee production can help shape and coordinate the industry in a way that aligns with broader governmental policies such as for environmental protection. Where governmental agencies such as the Coffee Directorate are the licensors of place brands such as Coffee Kenya, they can ensure that such developments are made sustainably, at least for their constituents, and that the fruits of developments are shared equitably among those who contribute to the sector. Indeed, place brands can be used to project a positive image onto the place of the brand, and thereby onto other brands associated with the place and also other industry sectors in the region. A coordinated approach to place-branding can therefore play a role in regional development. When the Coffee Directorate launched Coffee Kenya as a certification mark of origin, it too used Kenya's reputation for athletic talents and wildlife to associate with its coffees.[35]

However, associating a place brand with imagery and narratives of origin alone may not sustain the sale of place-branded goods, especially drinks that consumers would be proud of being associated with – the fourth factor

---

[30] Julie Bower and David M Higgins, Ch 5; cf Anthony Wills, Ch 16.
[31] Atsuko Ichijo, Ch 6.
[32] Ian Malcolm Taplin, Ch 7.
[33] Ibid; Julie Bower and David M Higgins, Ch 5.
[34] Ian Swanson and Michael Mondavi, Ch 2; Rex Stults, Ch 3; Dawnine Dyer, Ch 20; Jule Bower and David M Higgins, Ch 5; Graham G Stewart and Anne Anstruther, Ch 17.
[35] Grenville K Melli, 'Coffee Kenya Mark of Origin' (Coffee Directorate 2015) <www.ico.org/documents/cy2014-15/Presentations/115-pmdc-coffee-kenya-mark-of-origin.pdf> accessed 23 February 2024.

above. The leapfrog by the, then relatively unknown, Napa Valley wines into prominence as a surprise result of a blind tasting comparison with their well-regarded and well-established French counterparts is one example that taste ultimately matters to consumers.[36] For Scotch Whisky and Napa Valley wines, Kilchoman Distillery[37] and Dyer Wine[38] respectively are examples where farmers sell directly to consumers and are therefore alert to consumer tastes and demands to cater to them. They can determine which of their outputs they want to use under place brands to contribute to the pride of the place, and which might be sold under broader branding such as 'whisky' or 'California wine' or sold to non-retail markets. Their more recent successes are at least in part attributable to the success of Scotch Whisky and Napa Valley as place brands which represent to consumers a sense of authenticity, attention to quality, and perhaps also a lifestyle. This representation benefits even the more mass produced Scotch Whiskies and Napa Valley wines by enrobing the place-branded goods with the imagery in the consumers' mind. The benefit can also be less direct. Some mass producers carry prominent place-branded drinks as leverage to secure a better bargaining position within their value chain to promote less prominently branded goods in their stable.[39]

Building such a connection is more difficult for Coffee Kenya which is still to establish itself in the consciousness of global consumers. The Coffee (General) Regulations 2018 stipulate:

> A person shall not pulp, mill, warehouse, export, trade, transport, possess or otherwise deal in or transact any business in coffee unless the person holds a valid licence or movement permit issued by the Authority or the County Government for that purpose.[40]

For most coffee farmers in Kenya, once processing of their coffees is completed, their coffees are sold through the Nairobi Coffee Exchange or, in a minority of the cases, through a 'second window' via marketing agents. Few farmers, like the Gichangi Estate,[41] have any direct contact with consumers and thus control over the pricing of their coffee. They also do not have any control over how their coffee will be destined: for higher end or specialty consumption, or for processing as instant coffee and other low- to medium-end

---

[36] Ian Swanson and Michael Mondavi, Ch 2; Ian Malcolm Taplin, Ch 7; Rex Stults, Ch 3.
[37] Anthony Wills, Ch 18.
[38] Dawnine Dyer, Ch 20.
[39] Ian Swanson, Ch 19.
[40] The Coffee (General) Regulations 2018 (Kenya), s 9.
[41] Owen Gichangi, Ch 21.

use. Further, without consumer feedback, the vast majority of the coffee farmers in Kenya have little input to gauge the popularity of their output, little incentive to maintain or achieve higher quality, and little to gain from place-branding, if they are aware of it at all.[42] For those who are, such as John,[43] place-branding may help bring consumer awareness and loyalty to their goods to lift their sales.

The Coffee Directorate currently has four licensees for the Coffee Kenya mark. They work with local farmers to purchase their crop and market the final product.[44] However, some smallholder farmers may lack the resources needed to comply with licensing requirements and be thereby excluded from the opportunity of using the mark.[45] Scholars have also expressed concern that the requirement for farmers to ensure their produce meets certain qualifications may be particularly costly for smallholders.[46] Others have argued that with demand driven by flavour profiles of choice in lucrative markets, the farmers' interests might be overlooked in favour of the blenders' who can produce that flavour, irrespective of the coffee's origin.[47]

BEYOND THE BASIC: FURTHER PROTECTION

Under EU law which protects 'Scotch Whisky' within the EU as well as in Northern Ireland and which has its parallel in UK law for Great Britain, the protection extends beyond traders' and consumers' interests against false or misleading use of GI. It also protects against:

> [Art. 21(2)(b)] any misuse, imitation or evocation, even if the true origin of the products or services is indicated or if the protected name is translated or accompanied by an expression such as "style", "type", "method", "as produced in", "imitation", "flavour", "like" or similar, including when those products are used as an ingredient;[48]

---

[42] Yvonne Wamuca Kimani, 'Is Kenya's Coffee Certification Mark Destined to Fail? A Legal Discussion' (2023) 9 Commonwealth L Rev J 50, 53.
[43] James Ireri John, Ch 22.
[44] C Dormans, Kenya Nut Company, Kimathi University of Technology and Super Gibs Ltd – see Tom Kabau, Ch 9; Kimani (n 42), 52, 55.
[45] Kimani (n 42), 56.
[46] Chebet Koros and Melissa Omino, Ch 13.
[47] Philip Magowan, Ch 4.
[48] Regulation (EU) 2019/787 of the European Parliament and of the Council of 17 April 2019 on the definition, description, presentation and labelling of spirit drinks, the use of the names of spirit drinks in the presentation and labelling of other foodstuffs, the protection of geographical indications for spirit drinks, the

This protection of GIs builds on long established recognition in the EU of a further rationale for the protection of GIs.[49] From as early as Council Regulation (EEC) No 2081/92 of 14 July 1992 on the protection of geographical indications and designations of origin for agricultural products and foodstuffs (no longer in force), the European Economic Community (predecessor to the EU) recognized that 'the promotion of products having certain characteristics could be of considerable benefit to the rural economy, in particular to less-favoured or remote areas, by improving the incomes of farmers and by retaining the rural population in these areas'.

As noted, the Kenyan Government has so far opted for the use of certification marks which guarantee that goods bearing the marks meet the certification standards. The idea of installing an EU-GI style of broader protection is however not uncontroversial for countries such as Kenya which have different considerations.[50] First, as mentioned for all standard-setting and certification schemes, there are the costs required for the installation and operation of the schemes imposed upon some stakeholders.[51] As a result, some smaller farmers might be excluded from the system. Second, the success of the EU model is hinged on strong government support across the production and supply value chains.[52] Accordingly, a transplantation of the EU model without the attendant government support will fail to deliver the full socio-economic benefits of GIs.

Finally, if one of the initial drivers for GI protection is to ensure competition is fair among traders, and also that consumers are protected from confusion and deception,[53] then, ironically, the EU style of protection raises questions of possible anti-competitiveness[54] and of disadvantages for consumers. Such protection prevents traders from telling consumers that they are able to offer similar or even identical goods as the GI-branded versions by reference to GI branded goods, albeit that their goods may be cheaper, but may not meet some

---

use of ethyl alcohol and distillates of agricultural origin in alcoholic beverages, and repealing Regulation (EC) No 110/2008 [2019] OJ L130/1.

[49] Daniele Curzi and Martijn Huysmans, 'The Impact of Protecting EU Geographical Indications in Trade Agreements' (2022)104 (1) American J of Agricultural Economics 364, 366–9.

[50] Chebet Koros and Melissa Omino, Ch 13.

[51] Ibid.

[52] Susy Frankel, 'Geographical Indications and Mega-Regional Trade Agreements and Negotiations' in Irene Calboli and Wee Loon Ng-Loy, *Geographical Indications at the Crossroads of Trade, Development, and Culture: Focus on Asia Pacific* (Cambridge University Press 2017), 147–9.

[53] Dwijen Rangnekar, *The Socio-Economics of Geographical Indications: A Review of Empirical Evidence from Europe* (ICTSD and UNCTAD 2004), 13–4.

[54] Graham Dutfield, Foreword.

of the specifications required for GI-branding that are otherwise imperceptible to consumers. This is so even if the trader is truthful and forthright that its goods do not meet those specifications. As a result, consumers lose choices in the marketplace. Traders lose freedom of expression and also the freedom to trade honestly and competitively if they are prohibited from using GIs as terms of reference, such as 'Scotch Whisky-style spirit distilled in USA' however prominently branded on bottles.

CONCLUSIONS

This leads back to Dutfield's question: 'Geographical Indications: What Are They Good for?' From the perspective of legal policy, they can protect consumers from confusion and deception about certain qualities they want in goods and thereby protect traders from losing custom as a result any such confusion or deception. They help inform traders of consumer tastes and preferences so that traders are incentivized to cater to consumer demands. GI protection safeguards the reputation and distinctiveness of the place with which place-branded goods are connected and discourages unfair competition from those who exploit this reputation and distinctiveness without meeting the required standards consumers seek in place-branded goods.

From the perspective of socio-economic development, because place brands are geographically based, with relevant support and structures, they allow for the collective promotion of a class of goods that would benefit the branding region. As demonstrated in the cases of Scotch Whisky and Napa Valley wines, these benefits reach well beyond the regional whisky and wine industries respectively to contribute to tourism, and other Scottish- and Napa Valley-branded industries and their eponymous regions. In turn, the reputation of the eponymous regions informs that of the place-branded industries in them. The role of the law, especially in the EU, has shifted to include this broader implication as a rationale for its expansive GI protection.[55]

The Coffee Directorate in Kenya is looking to position its coffee sector to reap these socio-economic benefits.[56] In doing so, it must look inward to ensure that its Coffee Kenya brand can perform its role in informing the rele-

---

[55] Irene Calboli, 'Geographical Indications between Trade, Development, Culture, and Marketing: Framing a Fair(er) System of Protection in the Global Economy?' in Irene Calboli and Wee Lon Ng-Loy (eds), *Geographical Indications at the Crossroads of Trade, Development and Culture: Focus on Asia-Pacific* (Cambridge University Press 2017), 18.

[56] Joseph Kieyah, *Report of the National Task Force on Coffee Sub-Sector Reforms* (Republic of Kenya, May 2016), xx, xxi, xxv–xxvii.

vant traders about consumer tastes and preferences and in incentivising them to cater to consumer demand. It must also look outward to create consumer demand by educating consumers about the distinctiveness of the coffees bearing the place brand. The Coffee Directorate can then use the Coffee Kenya brand as a way to shape the development of the coffee industry and also to seek alignment with broader governmental policies and goals for the region, such as sustainability and environmental protection.[57]

We live, however, in a world of mobile labor markets with expertise and free flow in raw materials, with technologies that can mimic consumer-desired tastes in GI-branded goods regardless of the origin of the raw materials. This is combined with ever-expanding GI protection which is increasingly negotiated on bilateral terms[58] between countries rather than openly in international arenas, as well as issues of restrictions on freedom of expression and to trade for competitors. So the question may well also be asked: 'whom are GIs and GI protection, in each of its forms, good for?' Ultimately, the perspectives of these intended beneficiaries hold the answer to what GIs are good for and to what extent each form of GI protection is effective and necessary. It is hoped that this volume has shed some light on how these perspectives can help inform the structure of industries at their eponymous homes and the dynamics of international negotiations where place brands are valued.

---

[57] The Crops Act 2013 (No. 16 of 2013), s 31, The Coffee (General) Regulations 2016.
[58] Titilayo Adebola, Ch 14.

Index

4C Association 123–4
2023 Direct to Consumer Wine Shipping Report 26

Aberdeen Football Club (AFC) 271–2
Advocaat case 252, 256, 261, 270
Africa Continental Free Trade Area 131
Africa, nascent geographical indication framework in 219–23
African Coffee Roasters (ACR) 124
African Continent Free Trade Area(AfCFTA) 223
African Intellectual Property Organisation (OAPI) 220
African Regional Intellectual Property Organisation (ARIPO) 220
   Banjul Protocol on Marks 220–21
African Union 222
Agreement on Trade Related Aspects of Intellectual Property Rights (TRIPS Agreement) 9, 143, 181, 197, 202, 310
   Article 22(1) of 114, 196, 199
   Article 23(4) of 207
   Article 24 of 206
   Article 24(5) of 205
   consequences of non-compliance with 206
   definition of GIs 146
   protection of GIs under 115
Agricultural Food and Fisheries Authority 304
Alcohol and Tobacco Tax and Trade Bureau (TTB) 295
alcohol, consumption of 16
   social movements to limit 82
alcohol distribution, taxation of 290
Alta California 76
Amazon 238
Amazon v Louboutin 238–9

Ambition 2030: A Growth Strategy for Farming, Fishing, Food and Drink 70, 72
American Origin Products (AOPs) 27
American Viticultural Area (AVA) 6, 20–22, 137–8, 170, 295–6, 309
   Diamond Mountain District AVA 297–8
   Napa Valley AVA 140
   process for recognition of 138–9
ancillary hospitality industries, development of 75
Anholt-Ipsos Nation Brands Index 69
Anti-Counterfeit Agency (ACA) 121
Appellation d'Origine Controlée (AOC) 21
Appellations of Origin (AOs) 198, 200, 208
arabica coffees 33–4, 110–11, 230, 304
   cultivation of 33
   historical origin of 34
   wet processing of 33
Arguello, Luis, Lieutenant 14
Argyll Group 52–3
Arthur Bell (company) 53
Assembly of the Paris Union for the Protection of Industrial Property 244
Auction Napa Valley 23–4

Bangui Agreement 220
Banjul Protocol 220–21
Ben Nevis Distilleries 45
Berringer and Christian Brothers 15
Bett, Willy 112
biodiversity protection 124
Bordeaux red varieties 297
Bordeaux wine 80–81, 84, 89
   classification of 82
   Left Bank Bordeaux 81
brand awareness 103

brand building, benefits of 80–81, 88
brand communities 258, 267
Brand Dialogue 100
branded goods, inherent qualities of 262–4
brand familiarity and recognition 101, 103
Brand Finance Plc group 93, 95
brand names 92, 141
    goodwill associated with 4
    Napa Ridge 141
brand positioning 292
brand recognition, of the logo 103
brand's identity
    protection of 57
    sense of belonging 258
brand's value 166
brandy 83
Brexit 66–7
British consumer market 34
British Empire 63
British Imperial product 32
Bronco Wine Company 27, 141
Bruce, Malcolm 53
Bryant Family wine 87
Burns, Robert 63, 71, 277

Cabernet Sauvignon 17, 19, 23, 26, 80–81, 88–90, 297, 298
Cabernet wine 89
Cairngorms National Park (UK) 73
Cakebread, Jack 18
Californian wines 7, 82, 89, 289
California State Agricultural Society 77, 79
California State Legislature 89
California Wine Association (CWA) 82
    marketing power of 81
Cambozola 68
Canary Islands, wines from 230
Canar Y Wine 230
Carpe Diem Coffee and Tea Company 119
Central Valley of California 27–8
certification marks 198, 202
    Cognac case 146
    crossover with Geographical Indications 170
    geographical 144–6
    infringement of 239
    in United Kingdom (UK) 168–9
Champagne 28, 235, 295
    Elderflower Champagne 266
    Spanish Champagne 252, 266
chaptalisation, use of 78
Chardonnay wine 88
Charles Krug winery 17
Chateau Montelena Chardonnay 291
Class of 1972 18
Coca Cola 281
Code of Federal Regulations, Title 27 of 27
Coffee and Farmer Equity (CAFÉ) Practices 123
Coffee Association of America 304
coffee diseases 38
coffee estates, in Kenya 300
coffee farmers, in Kenya 302, 315
coffee farming 38, 307
coffee industry
    in Costa Rica 35
    in Kenya 33
    in Sri Lanka 35
    threats to place-branding 39
Coffee Kenya 7, 32, 248, 251, 301, 312
    advantage to the co-operatives 307
    benefits for coffee grower 306–7
    certification mark of origin 110, 113
    custody of 122
    enduring sectoral problems despite 125–32
    limitations of 125–30
    as mechanism of place-branding 114–22
    as necessitated by realities of generic exploitation of 'Kenya' brand 118–22
    registered at KIPI and WTO 121
    use of 114
    at WIPO 117
    institutional shift from CBK to Directorate 122
    marketing strategy 113
    place-branding of 125
    protection in Germany 162
    registration and the scope of protection 116–18
    risks and opportunities of being associated with 305–6

slogan of 114
Coffee Leaf Rust (coffee disease) 38
coffee marketing, in Kenya 303
Coffee Planters' Conference in Nairobi (1932) 38
coffee processing 299
Coffee (General) Regulations 2018 315
Coffee Research Institute (CRI), Kenya 117, 124
Coffey, Aeneas 278
Colgin wine 87
collective identity 3, 84, 274
Collective Napa Valley 24
collective trademark 147, 151, 198, 220
  'Taita Basket' collective mark 183
Colombian Mild coffee 35
colorants 278
Common Code for the Coffee Community (4C Association) *see* 4C Association
Common Market for Eastern and Southern Africa (COMESA) 131
community knowledge-building 6
Conchita 129
consumer decision making 92, 99, 106
consumer loyalty 108, 110, 166, 313
consumer perceptions, of GI brand 94–5
Continental Strategy on Geographical Indications in Africa 2018 – 2023 (Continental Strategy) 222
Coombs, Nathan 15
Corison, Cathy 83
Cornish economy 99
Cornish pasty (GI product in the UK) 99
corporate ownership 6
Costa Rica, coffee cultivation in 35
country of origin 126, 138, 204, 301
Court of Justice of the European Union (CJEU) 67–8, 159
  'Chiemsee' ruling of 155
  Glen Buchenbach decisions of 161, 163
  on interpretation of EU regulations 163
COVID-19 pandemic 24
Cowie, Alexander 45
crop-related GI products, characteristics of 210
culinary heritage 95–6
cult wines 75, 87

Daniel, John, Jr 83
da Pombol, Marquis 21
Davidson, Carolyn 103
Davies, Jack 18
decision-making 99, 210
Deere, Carolyn 222
de Latour, George 81–2
Department of Food, Environment and Rural Affairs (DEFRA) 66
de Rothschild, Baron Philippe 19
Description of Scotch Whisky 61–2
DeSoucey, Michaela 216
Dewar, Donald 69
Diamond Creek Lake Vineyard Cabernet Sauvignon 26
Digital Markets Act 236–7, 244
digital platform economy, protecting quality signs in 236–42
Digital Services Act 236–9
distilled spirit, production of 59
Distillers Company Limited (DCL) 52, 42
distinctive signs, that identify traditional and unique products 227–34
Dodo Ikire case 221
Dolmio's Dolmio Family 92
Domaine Chandon 294–5
Dyer Vineyard 9
Dyer Wine 315

East African Community (EAC) 131
eBay 238
economic growth and cultural preservation 102
electronic commerce (e-commerce) 239–40
environmentally friendly farming 215–16
Ethiopia 34
Ethiopian Intellectual Property Office (EIPO) 148
EU laws 214, 236
EU membership referendum of 2016 66
European Commission 151, 218–19, 295
  GI schemes 173
European Communities - Protection of Trademarks and Geographical Indications for Agricultural Products and Foodstuffs 205
European Court of Justice 167
European Economic Community 317

European missionaries 34
European Union (EU) 196
    bilateral agreement with the US 219
    Common Agricultural Policy (CAP) 215
    expansionist agenda and protectionism 206
    geographical indication framework in 213–18
    GI Regulations 4, 57, 206
    Register of Protected Designations of Origin and Protected Geographical Indications 156
    Regulation No 1151/2012 191
    Spirits Regulation 67
    Trade Mark registers 171
    TRIPS Plus agreements 216
European Union (Withdrawal Agreement) Act (2020) 66
European Union Intellectual Property Office (EUIPO) 122, 126, 225, 246
European wine regulatory systems 21
Eurostat 242
EU Trade Mark Regulation (EUTMR) 152
evocation, concept of 159
extended passing off 251–5, 259–62, 266–71, 274–5

Fair Trade Labelling Organisation (FLO) 123
family coffee business 299
Famous Grouse, The 50
famous whisky companies, foreign acquisition of 48
farm distillery 9
farm management 123
Federal Administrative Procedure Act (US) 139
Federal Alcohol Administration Act (FAA Act, 1933), US 136–42
Federal Alcohol and Tobacco Tax 20
Fenty v Arcadia Group Brands Ltd 256–7
Feta Cheese 216
Finance Act 1933 (Britain) 60
Finance Act 2005 (Kenya) 304
fine wine, demand for 89
flavor enhancers 278

Food and Agriculture Organization of the United Nations (FAO) 210
food production 216
food security 223
Food Tourism Scotland (2019) 70
fortified drinks 83
Francophone Africa 222
Frank Family Vineyards 291
Frank, Robert 88
Franzia, Fred 89
French wines 18–19, 23, 85–6, 294
French wine trade 23
Frost, David 65–6

Gachagua, Rigathi 131
Gangjee, Dev 202
Geneva Act 207–8
    Article 13(1) of 208
    protection and registration of trans-border AOs and GIs 209
geographical indications (GIs) 3, 55, 57, 60, 66, 92–3, 188, 226, 254, 266, 310
    and appellations of origin 114
    as a barrier to entry 102–3
    Bill (2009) 114–15, 179
    British GI brands 93
    challenges in practice of the enforcement of 163
    defined 146, 179–80, 196, 199–201
    enforcement of 240
    environmental, social and governance (ESG)-related claims 99
    exceptions and unresolved issues reserved for future negotiations 204–6
    impact on climate change 198
    infringement of 239–40
    international standards for 197–210
    for Italian brands 96
    in Kenya 179–80
    legal independence of 233
    legal protection systems for 202–3
Manchego case 240
misuse of 93
Morbier case 240
Napa Valley GI status 96–7

politics of introducing and
    maintaining 211–23
proliferation of 197
Protected Geographical Indication
    (PGI) 99
protection of
    basic levels of 310–11
    Council Regulation (EEC) No
        2081/92 of 14 July 1992
        on 317
    in EU law 316–17
    under German law 153
    under trade mark system of the
        US 143–8
    under TRIPS Agreement 115
    provisions for wines and spirits
        203–4
    at regional and national levels
        211–23
    registration systems 127, 197
    for Scotch Whisky 55, 66, 95, 200
    of Spirit Drinks system 213–15
    sui generis mechanism for
        protecting 115
    of Tequila 235
    as tool for socio-economic
        development 223
    trade agreements relating to 197
    in United Kingdom (UK) 66,
        169–70
    WIPO norm setting for 207–10
    WTO standards for 198–9
geographical origin of products 3–4, 146,
    166–7, 225
George, Lloyd 64
George Williamson & Co Ltd. 186–7,
    189–90
German Coffee Association 124
German Federal Court of Justice
    (Bundesgerichtshof (BGH)) 154
German Federal Patent Court
    (Bundespatentgericht (BPatG))
    156
German Government's international
    development agency (GTZ) 124
German Trademark Act 151
German Wine Act ('WeinG') 161
Germany, protection of place brands in
    according to product-specific EU
        Regulations

agricultural products and
    foodstuffs 156–8
Napa Valley and Coffee Kenya
    GIs 162
spirits drinks 158–61
wines 161–2
challenges in practice of the
    enforcement of GIs and DOs
    163
creation of protection 153
under German law 151–2, 155–6
Law against Unfair Competition
    (UWG) 151
loss of 154–5
overview of 150–5
product-specific EU Regulations for
    GIs and DOs 152–3
as registered trademarks 155–6
scope of 154
GI brands and products
    commercialization of 101
    market dominance by 102
Gichangi's Estate Coffee Farm (Kenya)
    299, 315
    branding of 301–2
    export of green coffee from 301
    'Stephen's Coffee' brand 301–2
Glen Buchenbach (whisky produced by
    a German distiller) 67–8, 160–61,
    163
Glen Buchenbach case 240
'Glenfield Starch' case 268
'Glen Highland' trade mark 204
Glen Kella Manx Whiskey 269
Global Brand Equity Monitor Research
    of Brand Finance 103
Global Environment Facility 124
Global North 5, 211
Global South 5, 110, 211, 212
global wine rankings 289
global wine trade fairs 24
gold rush, in California 76
good governance 72
goodwill
    concept of 254
    protection of 271
grape
    grape juice production 1
    high-quality grapes, cultivation of
        289

Greek Yoghurt case 252, 262
greenhouse gas emissions 210
Grgich, Mike 17, 83
gross domestic product (GDP) 113
Guinness (Anglo-Irish brewer) 52
Guinness affair 53

Handler, Michael 206
Hansard 42
Harlan Estate wine 87
Harris Tweed 48
Harris Tweed Association 48
Heumilch ('hay milk') 157
highland culture and tradition, concept of 43
highland Distilleries 50, 52
Hilgard, Eugene 79
Hiram Walker (Canadian firm) 50, 52
home distilling 48
home-made wines
  demand for 83
  quality of 83

imitation, concept of 159
Improvement and Growth of the Grape-vine in California 77
Indian whiskeys 107
  controversy related to Strotts brand 107–8
indication of geographical origin (IGO) 198
indications of source 198, 200
influencers' activity on social networks, protection of quality signs in 248–9
Inglenook Winery (Niebaum-Coppola Estate Winery) 15, 80, 82
intellectual property (IP) 120, 196
  infringements of 226
  laws 2, 4, 58
  rights 93, 180
  risk of misuse 231
  use of the trademarks 104
Intellectual Property Enterprise Court 267
International Coffee Agreement (ICA) 303
International Coffee Organization (ICO) 110

international law-making, politics of 209
Irish Whiskey 44
Irvine v Talksport Ltd 256–7
Islay malt whisky 284–5
'Islington cases' of 1905 44
'Italian Pencils' brand 252, 260

Jacobite rebellion (1746) 63
Jerez 28
Joaquim Jose Estves Lopes Granja v European Union Intellectual Property Office (EUIPO) 213
John Gillon & Co 45
Johnnie Walker Scotch Whisky 251, 257
  Black Label 50, 279, 281
  Striding Man logo 251, 260
John Walker & Sons 2, 45
Joint Declaration to Protect Wine Place & Origin (2005) 28
joint ventures 19, 50
Joseph Phelps (winery) 291
Judgment of Paris (1976) 18–20, 23, 289, 291

Kahawa Company 119
Kenya
  adoption of GI law in 115
  approach to authentic and credible place-branding 110
  under British colonial rule (1895–1963) 33
  challenges in the current legal GI framework in 186–8
  Coffee Board of 33, 36, 113, 230
  coffee cultivation in 34
  Coffee Directorate (CD) 98, 122, 132, 314, 318–19
  coffee farmers in 315
  coffee industry of 33
    British Empire and 34–6
  coffee-producing regions of 12
  colonial legacy of regulation of the coffee sector 130
  contemporary practices relating to other certifications in coffee sector 123–5
  Department of Agriculture (US) 38
  Draft Geographical Indications Bill (2007) 179, 180

Empire Marketing Board 36
gross domestic product (GDP) 113
implications of implementing an
    EU-style GI protection in
    190–93
Intellectual Property Bill (2020)
    180, 185–6
Industrial Property Institute (KIPI)
    115, 183
    Trademarks Registry 184
legal framework of place-branding
    in
    definition of geographical
        indications 179–80
    examples of protected GIs
        183–5
    Intellectual Property Bill (2020)
        185–6
    protection of geographical
        indications 180–81
    registration by individuals of
        trade marks 185
    trade marks protection for GIs
        181–3
Maasai Community Trust 183
protection of geographical
    indications in 180–81
reasons for not selling coffee
    directly to the market 304–5
*Report of the National Task Force
    on Coffee Sub-Sector
    Reforms* (2016) 111, 121,
    126–7
reputation for athletic talents and
    wildlife 314
settler-monopolized coffee culture
    39
as third largest producer of arabica
    coffee in Africa 110
trade marks protection for GIs in
    181–3
UK-Kenya Economic Partnership
    Agreement (EPA) 173
varied perspectives regarding GI
    protection in 189–90
Kenya AA (coffee brand) 112–13,
    119–21
    generic use of 120
Kenya Bean 118
Kenya Coffee & Sweet Dessert 118

Kenya Espresso 118
Kenya Export Promotion and Branding
    Agency 131
Kenya Industrial Property Institute
    (KIPI) 115, 183
Kenyan coffee 192
    advertising of 36
    Britain's consumption of 35
    classification of 112
    first-harvest benefits of 36
    flavors associated with 128–9
    government-regulated sale of 130
    history of 229
    marketing of 303–4
    national trade mark registration 118
    popularity of 114
    public knowledge of 36
    quality and exclusion 37–40
    quality brand 37
    quality of 36, 39
    reputation possessed by 38
    Screen 18 (brand name) 119
Kenya Tea 192
Kenya Tea Development Agency
    (KTDA) 187
Kilchoman Distillery 260, 288, 315
Kimemiah, George 118
KIPI Trademarks Registry 184
Klotz, Michael 67
Kramer, Matt 87
Krug, Charles 15, 78–9
Krug's winery 15

'La Champanera' case 235
Lanham Act (US) 143, 146
law of passing off 255–9, 260
    in United Kingdom (UK) 167
*Le Comité Interprofessionnel du vin de
    Champagne* (CIVC) 294–5
legal protection, of Scotch Whisky
    preliminary considerations for
    225–7
*Lessons Learned from 15 Years of
    FAO Work on Geographical
    Indications* 210
Lisbon Agreement for the Protection of
    Appellations of Origin and their
    International Registration (1958)
    128, 200–201, 208
    Geneva Act of 207

tripartite advantages of 209
"Lovemarks" brand 272
lowland distilleries (Scotland) 278
loyalty beyond reason 272

Maasai Community Trust (Kenya) 183
Macpherson, James 63
Madrid Agreement for the Repression of False or Deceptive Indications of Source on Goods (1891) 119, 128, 200, 295, 309
malt distillers 50
malted barley, use of 311
MarkenG 152–4
market research 100, 107
McCook, Stuart 35
merchants, power of 81–2
metaverse
 concept of 242
 protection of quality signs in 242–7
micro-brewing 48
Ministry of Foreign Affairs of Denmark (DANIDA) 124
Mirugi, Timothy 131
Mondavi, Cesare 16
Mondavi, Michael 18
Mondavi, Robert 6, 16–17, 19, 22–3, 83
Monopolies and Mergers Commission (MMC) 42, 50
Moët & Chandon (French wine company) 294

Nairobi Coffee Exchange (NCE) 130, 303
Napa Name Law 28
Napa Name Protection Committee 29
Napa Valley (California) 30, 229, 309
 American Viticultural Area (AVA) 90
 GI status 96–7
 journey abroad 143
 Krug's winery 15
 Prohibition era (1920–33) 15–16
 Spanish military expedition 14
 'Visit Napa Valley' 289
 Wappo people of 14
 wheat farming 15
 wine industry of 15–16
 winemakers in 22, 78

Napa Valley American Viticultural Area and Nested AVAs 25
Napa Valley Conjunctive Labeling Law 27
Napa Valley Grape Growers Association (NVG) 84, 140, 296
 see also grape
Napa Valley Technical Group 83
Napa Valley Vintners Association (NVV) 6, 22, 84, 89, 140, 142, 296, 312
 Board of Directors 24
 Certification Mark for Napa Valley 29
 Collective Napa Valley 24
 objective to obtain the Certification Mark 29
Napa Valley wine 6–7, 78, 292, 313, 315
 AVA wines 248
 Cabernet Sauvignon 17, 19, 23, 26, 80–81, 88–90, 297–8
 characteristics of 19
 CK Mondavi label 17
 Class of 1972 18
 as luxury product 75
 marketing strategies on 23
 Napa Ridge mark 142
 protection in Germany 162
 protection of brand 27–30
 quality control 96–7
 quality of 23, 82, 85
 reputation of 19, 82, 86
 Stag's Leap Wine Cellars 23
 wine quality and brand awareness of 22
 wine-tasting event 18
Napa Valley Wine Auction *see* Auction Napa Valley
Napa wine community 24
Napa wineries and vineyards, acquisition of 291
New Kirimiri Farmers' Co-operative Society Ltd. (Kenya) 304–5
New World countries 211–12
New York Bakery Co 92
Nichols, Connie 127
Niebaum, Gustave 15, 80
Nike's 'Swoosh' logo 103
non-fungible tokens (NFTs) 246–7
non-GI brands, barriers for entry for 101

non-governmental organisations (NGOs) 123
non-profit organizations 23
Nordmilch eG v OHIM 167
Northern Ireland Protocol 218
North of Scotland Malt Distillers' Association 45
Notice of Proposed Rulemaking (NPRM) (US) 139
Nyeri Coffee Exposition (2023) 130

Oakville American Viticultural Area (AVA) 19
Ontarian fine-wine industry 46
Opus One winery (Oakville) 19
Orb trade mark 48
organic farming 124
Organization for an International Geographical Indications Network (oriGIn) 27, 209
Otieno-Odek, James 115

P2B Regulation 243
Panama-Pacific International Exhibition (PPIE) 82
Paris Convention for the Protection of Industrial Property (1883) 200
   Article 6(3) of 126
Paris Tasting of 1976 294
Parker, Robert 85–6
Parmigiano Reggiano (Italian hard cheese) 95–6, 100
PDO (Product of Origin) Status 95–6
peatreek (the making of whisky over a peat fire) 277
Philadelphia (brand of cream cheese) 146–7
Philippines Law 226
phylloxera epidemic 15, 81, 293
Phylloxera vastatrix beetle 278
Pittock, Murray 63
place-branded industries 314, 318
place-branding 199, 255, 277
   and appellations of origin 128
   best practice for exploiting commercial benefit from 103–8
      by challenging the pretenders and by expanding barriers to entry 107–8
      by explaining to customers 106–7
      by making it prominent in marketing 105–6
      by understanding the perceptions surrounding their place brand 107
   of coffee 114
   of Coffee Kenya 125
   commercial and social impact of 313–16
   definition of 93–4
   with direct sales and diversified markets 130–32
   Kenya's approach to 110
      legal framework 179–86
      see also Kenya
   legal instruments relating to 128
   location branding 93
   market assessment 93–103
      of authenticity 99
      consumer perceptions 94–5
      of consumer understanding 100–102
      of GI status 102–3
      Parmigiano and PDO 95–6
      place-name protections 93–4
      of sustainability credentials 99–100
   as marketing tool 74
   mutual benefits of 96–8
   for protection of goodwill 271
   rights and obligations 128
   of Scotch Whisky 281
   stakeholder perceptions of GI brands 94
   threats to 39
place brands 57
   challenges in obtaining trade mark registration for
      deceptiveness 175–6
      descriptiveness and non-distinctiveness 175
      prohibition under 'any enactment or rule of law' 176
   competition from new entrants 107

consumer perceptions of 94–5
impact on marketplace 2
IP laws for protection of 4
meaning to consumers 264–8
phrases associated with protected status 94
protection of
   according to product-specific EU Regulations 156–62
   agricultural products and foodstuffs 156–8
   in Germany *see* Germany, protection of place brands in
   as registered trademarks 155–6
   spirits drinks 158–61
   wines 161–2
   traders' perspective of 3
place-name protections, understanding of 93–4
poit dhubh (illicit stills) 277
'Porto' PDO 28, 213–14
Portugal 21, 213, 216
Port wine 21
Premiere Napa Valley 24
   see also Napa Valley
product adulteration and counterfeiting 278
production-scale economies 78
Prohibition (1919–33) 82–3, 290
Protected Designations of Origin (PDO) 92, 180, 191, 198, 213
   products registered as 213
Protected Geographical Indication (PGI) 99, 180, 191, 198, 204, 213
Protocol Relating to the Madrid Agreement Concerning the International Registration of Marks (1989) 119
ProWein 24

quality assurance 100, 300
quality control 17, 81, 96–7, 169, 263
Quality Schemes Regulation (QSR) 152
quality signs, in the digital market
   challenges for 234–49
      interferences between quality signs and domain names 234–6
      protecting quality signs in the digital platform economy 236–42
      protection of quality signs in influencers' activity on social networks 248–9
      metaverse 242–7
quality wine, demand for 78
quasi-property rights 159

Rainforest Alliance 123–4
Reckitt & Colman Ltd v Borden 171
registered trademarks, protection for 150
Reiff, Linda 22
resource partitioning, theory of 41, 47
Ricard, Pernod 50
Robert Brown & Co (Scotland) 44–5
Robert Mondavi Winery (US) 17, 291, 294
Roland, Michel 86
'Roquefort Delicacies' trade mark 205
Roquefort GI 205
Royal Commission 42, 44, 312
   definition of whisky 279

sacramental and medicinal wines 16
'safe harbour' rule 237, 239
Sale of Food and Drugs Act (1875), Scotland 44
San Joaquin Valley 16–17
Sayof Foods (cheese producing company) 205
Schafer Vineyards 291
Schram, Jacob 78
Scotch Whisky 44, 265, 315
   attributes of 'Scottishness' and 'heritage' 43
   authenticity and ownership issues 47–54
   brand name and reputation 53
   certification mark 46
   competition from Indian whiskeys 107
   consumer perceptions of 43
   controversy on the use of 'Glen' 68
   distilleries 95
   evolving worldwide identity of 279–80
   GI status of 55, 66, 95, 200
   heritage and traditional status of 54
   historical context 43–7

impact of Covid-19 pandemic on export of 280
importance in the UK economy 60
integrity and reputation of 58
method of production for 61
origin of 6, 61–2
place-branding of 281
political campaign to protect 42
potential pitfalls 280–81
prestige value of 45
production of 54–5
and the projection of Scotland 69–73
protection from counterfeiting/imitation 97
purity and drinkability of 279
recognition as a GI 55
registered owner of 46
reputation of 282–3
rising prestige of 278
role in the promotion of inbound tourism 70
role of geography in making 61
Scottishness of 59–64, 71, 314
  protection of 64–9
  SWA's work to protect 68
status as 'Scotland's national drink' 57
Striding Man figurative mark for 2
tax on 59
Scotch Whisky Act (1988), UK 42, 54, 60
Scotch Whisky Association (SWA) 6, 42, 48, 58, 60, 64, 68, 107–8, 168, 214, 279
  as defender of Scotch Whisky 66
  influence on UK legislation on taxation on alcohol 65
  Scotch Whisky Industry Sustainability Strategy 62
  work to protect the Scottishness of Scotch Whisky 68
Scotch Whisky Association v Unibev Ltd 107–8
Scotch Whisky distilleries 95, 233, 312
Scotch Whisky industry 46, 48, 53
  leadership of 52
  as major industry in Scotland 59
  proposal for the ban on the use of peat with the SNP 62
Scotch Whisky Order (1990) 41, 54

Scotch Whisky Regulations (2009) 41, 60, 158, 174, 311
Scotland
  GIS and place-branding in 74
  national branding of 72
  Romantic view of 63, 69–70, 72–3
  system of land ownership 73
  whisky-producing areas in 11
Scotland Food & Drink Partnership 70
Scottish Greens 62
Scottish independence referendum of 2014 66
Scottish National Party (SNP) 65
Scottish protected food names, future of 66
Scottish Romantics 63
  view of Scotland 63, 69–70, 72
Scottish Tourism Alliance 70
Scott, Walter 63
Screaming Eagle wine 87
Screen 18 (brand name) 119
self-satisfaction, sense of 257
sense of belonging 258
sense of self 257, 259
Shackleton, Ernest 281
Shafer, John 83
'Sideways' phenomenon 89
Silicon Valley Bank 297
Silverado Vineyards 291
single malt whiskies 48, 50, 284, 287
Smith Commission on Devolution 65
socio-economic development 3
soft power, perception of 95
Solidaridad 124
Soter, Tony 83
Sovos ShipCompliant 26
Spalding v Gamage 255–6
Spanish Champagne case 252
specialty 'estate' wines 47
spirit drinks 151, 213
  protection of GIs for
  scope of 158–9
  Scotch Whisky 159–61
Spirit Drinks Regulation (SDR) 152
  scope of protection of GIs for spirit drinks under 158–9
Spurrier, Steven 18, 23, 85
Stags Leap Cabernet Sauvignon 291
Stag's Leap Wine Cellars 17
Starbucks 312

State Viticultural Convention in San Franscisco (1888) 80
Strategy for the Enforcement of Intellectual Property Rights in Third Countries 218
Strathisla Distillery 277
Striding Man figurative mark, for a brand of Scotch Whisky 2
structural goodwill 254, 259, 266
substantive goodwill 254
sui generis geographical indications 191, 198, 213, 220–21
    see also GIs
Sunny St. Helena Winery 16–17
sustainable development 197, 217
sustainable rural development 223
Swan, Jim 285

Taita Basket collective mark 183
Taita Baskets Association (Kenya) 183
tax, on Scotch Whisky 59
Tchelistcheff, Andre 83
Technical File for Scotch Whisky 61–2
Tequila 201, 235
territoriality, principles of 127
territory of origin 95
terroir, idea of 60, 201, 268, 297, 311–13
Tinderet case 186, 188–9, 194
Tinderet Tea Farm 186, 189
To Kalon (experimental vineyard), near Oakville 81
Traceable Organic Coffee from Kenya (TRACE Kenya) 124
TRACE Kenya project 124–5, 130
Trade Descriptions Act (1968) (UK) 254
    see also United Kingdom
trade marks
    applications for alcohol beverage products 29
    benefits of 171
    certification 43
    challenges in obtaining registration for place brands
        descriptiveness 175–6
        descriptiveness and non-distinctiveness 176
        prohibition under 'any enactment or rule of law' 176
    collective 151
    for corporate brands 4
    German Trademark Act 151
        see also Germany
    'Glen Highland' trade mark 204
    grounds for refusal 230
    infringement of 246
    Lanham Act (US) 143, 147
    monopolization of a geographic term as 148
    Orb trade mark 48
    protection of 127
    protection of geographical indications in
        Kenya 181–3
        US 143–8
    registered for virtual goods 247
    'Roquefort Delicacies' trade mark 205
    territoriality principle of 127
    in United Kingdom (UK) 165–7
        see also United Kingdom
    use of 104
Trade Marks Act (1905) (UK) 46
    see also United Kingdom
Trade Marks Act (1938) (UK) 46
    see also United Kingdom
Trade Marks Act (1994) (UK) 254
    see also United Kingdom
    section 40(1) of 115
Traditional Speciality Guaranteed (TSG) 157, 180, 191, 215
Transatlantic Trade and Investment Partnership (TTIP) 217
Treaty of Versailles (1919) 295
Treaty on the Functioning of the European Union (TFEU) 151
Trench, Le Poer 35, 38
TRIPS Council
    negotiations on enhanced GI protection in 207
    Review of Proposals at the TRIPS Council 206
Turkana Bio Aloe Organization (Tubae) 184
Tuscan wine 203

Ugandan railway 34
UK-Kenya Economic Partnership Agreement (EPA) 173
Unibev Ltd (UK) 107

United Distillers (Scotland) 311
United Kingdom (UK)
    benefits of trade mark registration in 170–75
    challenges in obtaining trade mark registration for place brands in 175–6
    crossover between certification trade marks and geographical indicators 170
    emerging geographical indication framework in 218–19
    HM Revenue & Customs (HMRC) 169
    Intellectual Property Office (UKIPO) 164, 167
    Manual of Trade Marks Practice 174
    law of passing off 167–8
        enforcement action on the basis of 176–7
    protection of place brands in
        certification marks 168–9
        impact of Brexit on 164–5
        law of passing off 167–8
        trade marks for 165–7
        specific considerations for place brands like Scotch Whisky, Napa Valley and Coffee Kenya in 172–5
    Trade Marks Act 1994 (UKTMA) 164–5
    withdrawal from the EU 164
United Nations Development Program 124
United States (US)
    Department of Agriculture 81
    Department of Treasury
        Alcohol and Tobacco Tax and Trade Bureau (TTB) 21–2, 138–9
    Lanham Act 143, 147
    legal protection of geographical indications in 135–49
        creation of the US Appellation System for wine 137–8
        Napa Ridge and the AVA brand name loophole 141–2
        Napa Valley AVA 140
        Notice of Proposed Rulemaking (NPRM) 139
        process for recognition of an AVA 138–9
        pursuant to FAA Act 136–42
    Patent and Trademark Office (USPTO) 29–30, 143
    re-establishment of the wine industry after Prohibition 136
    trademark system of
        geographical certification marks 144–6
        protection of geographical indications under 143–8
Utz certified 123

Valdez, Juan 129
Vallejo, Salvador 15
VinExpo 24
vineyard management 19, 77, 86
virtual goods 246
    trade mark registered for 247
VisitScotland 71
viticultural and winemaking practices 21
vodka 252, 270
Volstead Act (1919) 293

Waldhorn Distillery 67
Walker, Alexander 45
Walker, Bill 53
Wappo people, of Napa Valley 14
Wash Act, The (1823) 278
Watson, William C. 15
Wetmore, Charles 79
Whisky Association 65
whisky, definition of 279
whisky-producing areas, in Scotland 11
whisky production 53
Willoughbys Coffee 119
Wine Advocate magazine 85
Wine and Spirit Brand Association 279
wine appellation
    history of 43
    use of 54
wine consumption 75, 83
wine cultivation 7
wine industry 77, 201
winemaking 77, 83, 90, 289
    American vision of 87

    importance of location to 29
    professionalism in 79
    techniques 19
winemaking industry 7
    collective identity 84
    of Napa Valley 15–16
Wine Origins Alliance 29
wine production 21
Wine & Spirit Brand Association 64
wine-tasting events 18
wine tourism 19
wine trade 23
wine trade associations 28
Winiarski, Warren 17, 83
World Intellectual Property Organization
    (WIPO) 9, 104, 116, 117, 128,
    186, 197, 309
    Arbitration and Mediation Center
        234
    General Assembly of 244

Gorgonzola case 234
'La Champanera' case 235
norm setting for geographical
    indications 207–10
Thirty-Sixth Series of Meetings
    of the Assemblies of the
    Member States of 244
Uniform Domain Name Dispute
    Resolution Policy (UDRP)
    234
World Trade Organization (WTO) 65,
    121, 131, 196
    minimum standards for geographical
        indications 198–9
Wright & Greig Co (Scotland) 45

Yount, George 30, 76
Yousaf, Humza 72